Practical Finance for Operations and Supply Chain Management

Practical Finance for Operations and Supply Chain Management

Alejandro Serrano and Spyros D. Lekkakos

Foreword by James B. Rice, Jr.

The MIT Press
Cambridge, Massachusetts
London, England

This book was set in Times New Roman by Westchester Publishing Services.

Printed and bound in the United States of America

Library of Congress Cataloging-in-Publication Data

Names: Serrano, Alejandro, author. | Lekkakos, Spyros D., author.
Title: Practical finance for operations and supply chain management / Alejandro Serrano and Spyros D. Lekkakos; foreword by James B. Rice, Jr.
Description: Cambridge, MA : MIT Press, [2019] | Includes bibliographical references and index.
Identifiers: LCCN 2019019585 | ISBN 9780262043595 (hardcover : alk. paper)
Subjects: LCSH: Business logistics. | Production management. | Business enterprises--Finance. | Managerial accounting.
Classification: LCC HD38.5 .S47 2019 | DDC 658.15--dc23 LC record available at https://lccn.loc.gov/2019019585

Contents

Foreword

This book, simply entitled *Practical Finance for Operations and Supply Chain Management*, is a gem among many finance books, and it packs a lot more than this humble title suggests. Not only does this book serve the reader as an invaluable resource for understanding the financial aspects of managing operations and supply chains, it provides a grounds-up reference for the financial foundation that will serve the reader well in subsequent application. The title is apropos given the breadth of what it covers—encompassing the decisions made in procurement and sourcing, in design and production, in downstream distribution to the customer, and in the return process. This range of operational activities we know as the supply chain, and these activities and functions comprise the majority of the personnel and assets deployed in the product/service creation and delivery for the business. It is indeed practical as the title suggests, but it also provides the financial underpinnings for the practitioner to understand the big picture in application.

Business leaders have come to appreciate the supply chain and business operations as the core elements and critical enablers for the growth of the franchise. This was not always the case—traditionally those managing operations and supply chains were relegated to focusing on minimizing cost and meeting production quotas. While this is still important, managing supply chains and operations involves making critical business decisions that will enable the firm to compete, to grow, and to evolve to serve the increasingly demanding customer requirements in order to satisfy the firm's fiduciary obligation to its shareholders. One can see this critical role in action in the current dynamics playing out in the competition among incumbent brick-and-mortar retailers and emerging direct-to-consumer players, as well as all the organizations attempting to leverage technology to dramatically change their business and its performance. These operational decisions are affecting the current and future success of the business—and these decisions must be made with a thorough understanding of the implications of those decisions. This book capably guides the reader through the foundations necessary to understand how to identify the financial impact of those decision for ongoing business operation and capital investment in operations as well.

Providing such a foundation is a tall order, but thankfully, both Professor Serrano and Professor Lekkakos each have more than a decade of experience working in operations in product/service businesses, prior to their highly accomplished academic and teaching careers. This practitioner-academic combination has served each author well, as they each are accomplished instructors serving both inside and outside of the MIT Global SCALE Network. In this book, they have used their unique deep experience in operations and supply chain management to craft the concepts and write in such a way that speaks directly to practitioners in the most effective ways.

The authors' deep experience as practitioners benefits the reader in other ways as well. They recognize that companies are successful when the firm integrates and aligns the business functions to support the business strategy and serve that strategy both effectively and efficiently. (Serrano and Lekkakos start the book with a wonderful example of this—Zara, which has very effectively aligned their operations to support their business go-to-market approach.) Alignment can only occur when all the parties speak a common language—the lingua franca of business, finance. Serrano and Lekkakos effectively lay out a road map for operations and supply chain personnel to not only understand finance but to communicate with senior executives in financial terms. As such, this book can help bridge the gap between functions by serving as the foundation for instructors to help students and practitioners learn a common language, help engineers learn about how their actions enable the firm to better utilize assets, and to improve financial performance.

Circling back to the title—*Practical Finance for Operations and Supply Chain Management*—it surely does seem a humble title for this wonderful manual that provides such a rich resource for those managers and leaders in operations, supply chain management, and/or logistics that are intent on building the business to success. Enjoy this book, as I'm confident you will.

James B. Rice, Jr.
Deputy Director—MIT Center for Transportation and Logistics
May, 2019

Preface

There are literally hundreds of finance books on the market. So, why write another one? Anything you might need to know about finance has most likely already been written elsewhere. However, finance books are usually written by finance people for finance people. While this is expected, there is a relatively large audience outside the finance zone—for example, managers working in the operations and supply chain areas. They also need to understand financial tools but have a different mindset due to their different academic backgrounds. In our experience, both undergrad and post-graduate students from engineering or related areas often complain about the dryness of finance as a discipline. Inevitably, this has the knock-on effect of being boring, which often leads to a lack of interest in the topic. Later in their careers, as managers in operations-related departments, they realize how important having a solid understanding of the basics of finance is in order to become able, proficient professionals. In fact, from our conversations with senior managers in operations-related areas, it was surprising that, more often than not, operations practitioners' knowledge about finance is very unsophisticated and actually embarrassingly minimalistic. This reality illustrates the gulf that exists between operations and finance. These two functions often operate independent silos in a corporation. We believe that there are two major reasons for this disconnect: First, each function lacks a basic knowledge of the theoretical foundations of the other function. Second, the unaligned performance indicators chosen by senior management make each function focus on their own domain, ignoring—if not actually harming—the other function. This creates win–lose situations, vicious circles that could potentially cause bitter confrontation within a firm.

Coming back to why this gap exists, we believe that, among other reasons, finance is not properly taught to students of engineering disciplines. It is our belief that finance can and should be taught, taking into consideration that engineering students have engineering minds. Engineers' minds live in a world of stocks and flows, of cause and effect, where simple is beautiful, where there is a reason for everything, where identical concepts have identical names. This appears to be in contrast to finance, where complexity *seems* to abound—try to understand the annual report of a corporation, where the number of accounts seems to grow exponentially, buzzwords and acronyms are the rule, and a panoply of different names are used to refer to the same concept.

The main goal of this book is to help operations and supply chain management students and practitioners develop the necessary skills for a solid understanding of the financial tools that are necessary to (a) interact with finance people at a practical level and (b) make sound decisions when addressing the usual cross-functional trade-offs between operations and finance. This includes, but is not limited to, understanding and inferring the financial performance of an organization from the three main financial statements: balance sheet, income statement, and statement of cash flows. Operations and supply chain management practitioners should also understand the various project valuations tools, such as net present value, and should become familiar with the basic concepts of managerial accounting. As a result, they will be able to understand the impact of their decisions on the financial statements, financial ratios, risk, and ultimately, the firm's value.

This book assumes no previous knowledge of finance or accounting and is written to serve as a textbook for BS and MS financial systems courses in operations-related programs, as well as a reference for teachers and practitioners involved in any one of the processes within operations and supply chain management. This includes various functions, such as product design, purchasing, procurement, manufacturing, maintenance, distribution, logistics, transportation, and retailing.

There are two principal parts in the book. After the introduction, the first part (chapters 2 to 9) presents the topic of financial accounting, starting from scratch: it explains the accounting mechanics and how to create and interpret the three main financial statements: balance sheet, income statement, and statement of cash flows. It also introduces the idea of operating working capital (OWC), a key concept that links operations management and finance and is used extensively in the second part. The first part ends with a chapter dealing with inventory in production environments and another devoted to interpreting financial statements, including a description of the most important financial ratios, emphasizing those related to operations management.

The second part of the book (chapters 10 to 15) opens with a chapter on financial forecasting, addressing important topics such as sustainable growth and the trade-off liquidity/profitability. The impact of operating working capital on these topics is pointed out. Chapter 11 presents an introduction to managerial accounting, for readers to understand concepts such as variable versus fixed costs, direct versus indirect costs, and the idea of contribution margin. Special emphasis is made on how decisions dramatically change when production facilities are at capacity versus under capacity. Two chapters on investment analysis follow. They present the two most common tools for valuing investments, net present value (NPV) and internal rate of return (IRR). Again, the focus is on how to use these tools in the operations sphere and how changes in OWC impact the value of a project. Additional topics, such as real options or the link of NPV with operational models, are also addressed. Chapter 14 deals with operating working capital, addressing the crucial question of how to create value in a firm through operating working capital, managing inventory, payables, receivables, and cash. Finally, the last chapter presents a good number of strategic and tactic trade-offs that operations and supply chain managers typically face, such as offshoring versus local sourcing or centralizing versus not. The recurrent question in this chapter when addressing these trade-offs is possibly the most important question in this book: What is the impact of operational decisions on the financial side of the firm?

Alejandro Serrano and Spyros D. Lekkakos

Acknowledgments

We want to acknowledge and thank our students in the two master programs at the Zaragoza Logistics Center, who helped improve this book by contributing many comments and suggestions on various drafts, as well as asking challenging questions in class that forced us to hone our thoughts in and create the path to communicate them. A special thanks to Issac Mccracken (and Lianna!), who helped us find the title of the book.

We are also eager to thank our professor, mentor, and friend, Santiago Kraiselburd, who bet on us against all odds and helped us discover the captivating interface of operations/finance; our colleague at MIT Jim Rice, for embracing the book enthusiastically; and the members of the editorial team, including but not limited to, our production editor Deborah Grahame-Smith, Laura Keeler, the copyeditor Karen Oemler, and especially our acquisitions editor Emily Taber, who believed in the project from the beginning and guided and supported us throughout the process. Finally, Alejandra Oliva deserves immense credit for her great work reviewing preliminary versions of this book.

1 Introduction: Finance Is Important, Even to You

Finance is not merely about making money. It's about achieving our deep goals and protecting the fruits of our labor. It's about stewardship and, therefore, about achieving the good society.
—Robert J. Shiller, Nobel Laureate economist

1.1 The Archetypal Case of Zara

The first Zara store opened in La Coruña, Spain, in 1975. Since then, Inditex, the firm that owns the brand Zara as well as Bershka, Pull & Bear, and Massimo Dutti, among others, has grown exponentially. By 2018, Inditex had become one of the world's largest fashion retailers, selling roughly $25 billion, with nearly 8,000 stores in roughly 100 countries. The founder and main shareholder, Amancio Ortega, was ranked second in Forbes World's Billionaires list in 2015, sharing the podium with Bill Gates and Carlos Slim. Gates and Slim's main sources of wealth, Microsoft and Telmex respectively, have enjoyed long periods of market dominance with market shares around 80 percent in both cases; in contrast, Inditex's market share in Spain, its largest market, is a mere 10 percent. How is it possible for Inditex, competing in an unforgivingly fierce competitive market, to achieve a net profit of 15 percent? How can such outstanding success be explained? This question forms the focus of this book.

Thirty years ago, the typical firm in the fashion industry offered two collections a year. Most of the big players in the United States and Europe (such as, respectively, Gap and H&M) started buying in Asia, mainly in China, given the attractive labor costs for a labor-intensive industry, the cheap transportation costs—by ship—and the relatively low quality standards required for garments. Sourcing from a low-cost distant country was satisfactory, as production costs were low. However, lead-times grew tremendously, so that the companies had to estimate demand for their products six or more months in advance of the selling season. Add the recent trend of SKU[1] proliferation and you have all the ingredients for a perfect storm: Inevitably, forecasting errors would increase dramatically, customers would

---

1. SKU stands for stock keeping unit, that is, each of the distinct items a firm sells.

be frustrated by not being able to find their preferred hot designs, and leftover inventory would be deeply discounted before piling up at the end of the season in back rooms and distribution centers to be written off.

The focus of the average firm was the income statement—that is, saving costs through purchasing and producing efficiently. In contrast, Inditex took a different approach by focusing on the balance sheet. By doing so, it completely changed the paradigm of the fashion industry. While competitors were going to China, Inditex relied on national suppliers, mainly in Galicia—close to Inditex headquarters—and neighboring Portugal and Morocco. Of course labor was significantly more expensive, but the clear advantage was speed of distribution from warehouse to store. As *The Economist* put it in an article about Zara in 2012, "by the time a boat has sailed halfway round the world, hemlines may have risen an inch and its cargo will be as popular as geriatric haddock" (*The Economist* 2012). Inditex does not have to forecast demand for the most part, they have just to wait and see what customers like and buy. There is no need to offer deep discounts or write off large amounts of inventory. As a result, Inditex can offer as many as eight collections a year, increasing customer traffic at the stores and sales per visit tremendously. The focus of Inditex is not the income statement but the balance sheet—that is, saving costs through fast production and distribution processes and reduced inventories.

As an aside, note that Inditex's model resembles that of Toyota, the Japanese vehicle manufacturer. Neither of the two firms focuses directly on profitability. In the 1950s, Toyota decided to focus not on making money but on removing waste—by improving product quality, eliminating over-production, reducing process variability, and so on (Womack, Jones, and Roos 1990). Sometimes, firms have to zigzag, rather than going straight, to achieve their desired goal (Kay 2010).

Zara's secret

Unlike competitors who focus on boosting profits in the income statement, Zara mainly focuses on reducing inventory in the balance sheet. That does the trick.

Some business gurus may tell you that the key driver of Inditex's success is the way it manages its supply chain, which is certainly true. But it is the orchestrated integration of the two functions—the alignment of operations best practices with a focus on the balance sheet (rather than the income statement)—that makes Inditex's value proposition truly unique.

1.2   The Imperative Need to Understand Finance

Zara's archetypal case exemplifies the two ideas that make up the leitmotif of this book, namely (a) firms' strategies and decision assessments should be holistic and (b) understanding that the operations-finance interaction is essential to do business in today's

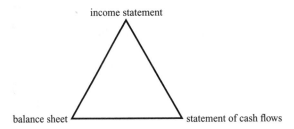

Figure 1.1
The triangle, as drawn by Roger Bloemen. To be a supply chain professional, you have to understand the impacts of the decisions on the triangle.

competitive world. In contrast to the classic divide-and-conquer strategy, there is a need to unify and align these two key functions of the corporate world. In particular, operations and supply chain managers and practitioners should be able to understand the impact of their decisions on the financial domain of the firm—that is to say, on the financial statements, the financial key process indicators (KPIs), risk, and ultimately, the value created for shareholders.

The ultimate goal of this book is to help operations and supply chain managers make better operations decisions. Having a holistic perspective of the firm and understanding the operations-finance link are key essential conditions for achieving such a goal.

To absolutely hammer this message home, we would like to share a quote with you. In a talk aimed at supply chain professionals given by Roger Bloemen, former supply chain vice president of Solutia, a manufacturer in the chemical industry, now part of the Eastman group, he said: "We supply chain people are accountants. We have to understand finance." Stating that supply chain people are accountants may sound shocking, but moving inventories from one place to the other in a long supply chain is not all that different, mutatis mutandis, from moving money from one account to the other. Both worlds, physical and financial, are parallel, and each physical movement has its counterpart in the financial world. Plus, inventories have to be quantified, adjusted, taken care of, justified, and audited, exactly like everything else in a firm's financial records. Following this theme, Bloemen was even more convincing: "If you do not understand the impact of your decisions on the triangle, you cannot be a supply chain professional." What triangle was he talking about? Let us plot it as we saw it on the chalkboard of the lecture room (figure 1.1). Income statement, balance sheet, and statement of cash flows are the three main financial statements, as we will learn in subsequent chapters.

This unambiguous statement may shed some light for those operations and supply chain professionals whose careers are stuck because they are unaware of (a) the triangle and its meaning and (b) its intrinsic link to their success in their operations management area.

Roger Bloemen, former supply chain VP of Solutia, on the interactions between operations and finance

- "We supply chain people are accountants. We have to understand finance."
- "If you do not understand the impact of your decisions on the triangle, you cannot be an operations professional."

Let's face it: due to globalization, the supply chains of many companies have become too complex to be managed only with operational tools. At the end of the day, an operations manager has to show a great command of financial tools if he or she wants to convince the board of the appropriateness of new projects, whether it is centralizing inventory, renewing the fleet, reducing the firm's assortment, outsourcing a noncore production phase, or building a new distribution center. If the operations manager cannot discuss finance with the chief financial officer (CFO), assess the impact of a decision on the firm's liquidity or risk, challenge the use of a particular cost of capital, and so on, the odds are high that they will not be able to pull it off.

1.3   Impact of Operational Events on Firms' Value

You could argue that the Zara example addressed earlier in the chapter is just anecdotal evidence of how a company was able to create astounding value through operational excellence. To reinforce the message through more objective arguments, consider table 1.1. It shows the average change in public firms' stock price two days after a piece of relevant news hit the major newspapers. For instance, if a firm announces new investments in information technology (IT), the market price of that firm's stock will go up by 1 percent on average. As the table reveals, operational events may have a major impact on the firm's value.

More specifically, table 1.2 presents the reaction of the market to operational problems. As shown, relevant problems in operations, from parts shortages to quality problems, may reduce the value of the entire company by roughly 10 percent on average, not at all a negligible figure. Reversing the argument, mastering the operational side of a firm may be a formidable source of value and competitive advantage alike.

1.4   The State of the Practice

Having addressed the importance of finance to the operations profession, a valid question is to ask: How much finance do operations practitioners know? To answer this question, we refer to Oliver Scutt, cofounder and chief strategy officer of Jonova, one of the consulting

Table 1.1
Stock market reaction to corporate events (mean return after the event is given, in percentage).

Operational	%	Marketing	%
Increase in R&D expenditure	1.4	Affirmative action awards	1.6
Increase in capital expenditure	1.0	Change in firm name	0.7
TQM implementation	0.6	New product introduction	0.7
Automotive recalls (US)	−0.4	Brand leveraging	0.3
Plant closing	−0.7	Celebrity endorsement	0.2
Decrease in capital expenditure	−1.8		
Information technology	**%**	**Financial**	**%**
IT investments	1.0	Increasing financial leverage	7.6
IT problems	−1.7	Proxy contest	4.2
		Open market share repurchase	3.5
		Stock splits	3.3
		Seasoned equity offering	−3.0
		Decreasing financial leverage	−5.4

Source: Hendricks and Singhal (2003).
Notes: R&D = research and development; TQM = total quality management.

Table 1.2
Stock market reaction to operations glitches.

Reason for supply chain glitches	Mean return (%)
Parts shortages	−8.2
Order changes by customer	−13.4
Production problems	−12.4
Ramp-up and roll-out problems	−12.7
Quality and testing problems	−8.1
Development and engineering changes	−11.1

Source: Hendricks and Singhal (2003).

firms that best understands and addresses firms' cross-functional challenges. Its software helps clients, usually leading multinationals, to solve fundamental trade-offs on a worldwide scale, focusing on the operations-finance interface. Scutt's opinion on the state of the practice does not cast much hope: "In real life though, we find that companies do not do cross functional trade-offs very well, have very little financial driver insight and very rarely understand or have any analytical understanding of real options.... Bottom line, the state of the practice is very unsophisticated." This comes as both bad and good news. Bad, because firms usually leave a lot of money on the table because of not addressing these trade-offs well; good, because something can be done about it. There is a huge opportunity to improve if the above-mentioned gaps are closed. Furthermore, those operations and supply chain practitioners who understand the fundamental trade-offs well also have a great opportunity to significantly advance in their careers, as they may have the edge over their peers who lack such financial knowledge.

> ⓘ **Oliver Scutt, cofounder and chief strategy officer of Jonova, on the state of the practice in the operations-finance interface**
> "In real life though, we find that companies do not do cross functional trade-offs very well, have very little financial driver insight and very rarely understand or have any analytical understanding of real options.... Bottom line, the state of the practice is very unsophisticated."

1.5   A Final Caveat: Try to Look Past the Jargon

Before you start walking the path to becoming a finance-oriented operations or supply chain professional, you should be aware of an important fact, frustrating to many engineers, who usually come with black-or-white, yes/no mindsets, a fact which makes many nonfinancial people give up before they have started: the jargon. A little secret is that finance people love using many fancy names and acronyms for the same simple thing and enjoy unnecessary complexity. Of course, this is a caricature of the financial function. But consider the following two examples:

(1) The following eight names all refer to the very same financial piece of information: *income statement, profit and loss account, statement of profit and loss, revenue statement, statement of financial performance, earnings statement, operating statement, and statement of operations.*

(2) The definition of *liabilities*, an important financial concept, according to the Financial Accounting Standards Board (the FASB is the organization that develops the Generally Accepted Accounting Principles—GAAP—in the United States) Concepts Statement Number 6, is as follows: "Liabilities are probable future sacrifices of economic benefits arising from present obligations of a particular entity to transfer assets or provide services to other entities in the future as a result of past transactions or events" (FASB Accounting Standards Codification).

If you read and understood the last definition without blinking, maybe this book is not the right one for you. If you had some trouble understanding it, then this book may suit your needs. Finance people use a large number of buzzwords and jargon that only they understand. Do you really need to learn those buzzwords? Only to some extent. Since one of the goals of this book is for you to be able to talk to finance people on their terms, we will walk you through some of these buzzwords along the way, but we will try to avoid them for the most part.

Exercises

1. Read a bit about Zara's manufacturing and distribution model (Wikipedia will do). Why was Zara's business model so successful?

2. What are the main costs types associated with *holding* inventory at firms—manufacturers and retailers alike?

3. Why does sourcing lead-time have a major impact on a manufacturing firm's inventory level?

4. Name a couple of industries that could potentially benefit from shifting focus the way Zara did.

5. Browse the internet to find examples of companies whose stock price changed by more than 5 percent right after a relevant announcement was made to the media.

     a. Which area of the firm is mostly accountable for the announced facts?

     b. Why is the impact of these events on the value of a firm so large?

References

"Fashion Forward." *The Economist*, March 24, 2012.

Hendricks, Kevin B., and Vinod R. Singhal. 2003. "The effects of supply chain glitches on shareholder wealth." *Journal of Operations Management* 21: 501–522.

Kay, John. 2010. *Obliquity: Why our goals are best achieved indirectly.* London: Profile Books.

Womack, James P., Daniel T. Jones, and Daniel Roos. 1990. *The machine that changed the world.* New York: Free Press.

2 Financial Accounting

You have to know accounting. It's the language of practical business life. It was a very useful thing to deliver to civilization. I've heard it came to civilization through Venice which of course was once the great commercial power in the Mediterranean. However, double entry bookkeeping was a hell of an invention.
—Charles T. Munger, investment manager

Financial accounting, or just accounting or accountancy, can be defined as the set of rules and practices that dictate how to elaborate and present the financial information of a firm during a certain period of time. It concerns itself with collecting, elaborating, and summarizing financial data to create reports of financial information. These financial reports are commonly called financial statements. Financial accounting is at the core of any firm's information system. In fact, an enterprise resource planning (ERP) system is simply an extension of an original system that dealt only with financial information. Data from other domains, such as operations or human resources, was incorporated later on. Broadly speaking, the goal is that data, financial and nonfinancial, be converted into relevant information, such that managers can make more informed, better decisions.

This chapter introduces the concept of financial accounting. It gives a succinct historical perspective and explains the goals of an accounting system. It points out some limitations of accounting as a discipline and describes the elements of the framework within which it is embedded.

2.1 Origins

Accounting, in a broad sense, is a relatively old science. For centuries, merchants and business people have needed to keep track of the evolution of their businesses. Modern accounting as we understand it today originated in Italy in the fifteenth century. During the medieval period in Europe, specifically in the late Middle Ages, merchants faced the question of knowing how well their business were doing. In order to figure that out, they would record all relevant facts of the business. For instance, they had to know from whom, when, and for how much they had acquired materials as well as to whom, when, and for how much they had sold the goods made from those materials. Furthermore, they had to keep track of pending payments, both from customers and to suppliers, and have a good sense of how much inventory of each type they had stored in their warehouses. Taking into consideration the limited resources available at the time, one can imagine the tremendous difficulties merchants, some of them illiterate, faced to come up with accurate financial asessments of their businesses. When they had more than, say, a few dozen customers, merchants were likely to be only able to make a rough estimate of how well things had done during the previous period. Today's relatively easy question, How well did the business do last year? was a very tricky one for them to answer. That, in turn, posed a major problem: that of deciding how much money was actually available to undertake a potential investment or invest in other business activities, for example.

 Origins of (financial) accounting

Accounting, as we know it, is more than five hundred years old.

All this significantly changed at the end of the fifteenth century. Luca Pacioli, an Italian mathematician who lived in Venice (pictured in figure 2.1), spread the use of a new accounting method that soon became fashionable, the precursor of today's double-entry accounting system, or simply double-entry accounting.[1] Pacioli did not devise the new method himself, but he did enrich and systematize it. It is remarkable that his method has not changed substantially in over five hundred years. Pacioli wrote his new method of bookkeeping as part of his first book, *Summa de arithmetica, geometria, proportioni et proportionalità*, published in 1494, a summary of the mathematical knowledge of his time.

His book found a propitious environment, as literacy amongst the middle class had seen a sharp rise in Europe during the first half of the fifteenth century, and Venice—a major

Figure 2.1
Portrait of Luca Pacioli, attributed to Guidobaldo da Montefeltro.
Source: Wikimedia Commons.

1. See Gleeson-White (2011) for a great description of the origins of double-entry accounting.

center of international commerce at the time—had been an early adopter of the new printing press techniques devised by the German Johannes Gutemberg in 1452. In the decades and centuries that followed, Pacioli's method was adopted by an increasing number of countries. Its popularity spread and has survived into the twenty-first century. Pacioli's tools are used not only by corporations but also by nonprofit organizations, governments, and other institutions all over the world. A remarkable system in fact, that bears out the old adage: If it's not broken, why fix it?

2.2 Goals

From this anecdote, it should be apparent that the main goal of an accounting system is to answer that very same question that merchants asked themselves five hundred years ago: How well has the firm done during the last period? As you will realize along the way, the answer to this important question is never categorical, as it is subject to opinions, perceptions, and even pressures.

The key business question answered by Pacioli

How well has the firm done during the last period?

In addition, accounting aims to answer a number of other questions, usually considered very relevant within a business context, such as the following:

- Where does the firm currently stand in terms of financial health?
- What does the firm own and owe?
- How did the firm end up where it is now?
- How did the firm end up with the current amount of cash?

These are indeed important, related questions, with plenty of interesting subtleties. We will disentangle all of them along the way.

2.3 Limitations

Accounting is useful in a number of ways, and it can help investors understand the reality of firms and help managers make informed decisions. However, it also has various limitations and drawbacks that prevent it from being the panacea that some managers pretend it is. Some major drawbacks include:

- Accounting deals with the past and the present, not the future. If you reread the four questions posed in the previous section you will realize that none of them have to do with the future. Accounting cannot shed much light on future sales, costs, or profits unless these are very stable over time.

• Accounting cannot capture changes in market value accurately, as it has relatively strict rules to assign value to the various elements of firms. For instance, plastic components purchased by a firm should be valued at acquisition cost. If the price of oil increases afterwards, the value of the plastic components in the market may go up, but no adjustments are usually made in a firm's books to allow for such changes.

• Accounting is a soft science. It is not mathematics, as it is partially based on opinions. For instance, consider the question: At what point should a product sale be recognized in the books? A straightforward answer might be: when the product is sent to the customer. But there are more options, such as: when the product is received by the customer, when the customer pays for the product, one week after the customer has received the product, and so on. If you consider online sales, things can be even trickier: for instance, in the United States, more than 30 percent of online sales are returned by customers. That forces online retailers to use percentage estimates about when a sale should be recognized in the accounting books. For instance, Amazon's company Zappos.com, a US online retailer selling mainly shoes, has a lax return policy, as customers have 365 days to return a pair of shoes free of charge (figure 2.2). (Or four whole years if the shoes have been bought on Feb. 29 in a leap year!)

When should Zappos recognize that a pair of shoes has actually been sold? It depends on managers' opinions or estimates about what percentage of returns will eventually materialize.

This dependency on managers' opinions is what sometimes makes the subject of accounting controversial, as bad management practices may result in significant distortions of the business reality. Some of the largest financial scandals in history, such as those of

Figure 2.2
Zappos.com has a 365-day return policy. When should it recognize sales?

Enron in 2001 or Lehman Brothers in 2008, illustrate how vulnerable firms can be if the appropriate control mechanisms are not in place.

2.4   Audience

Accounting is meant to serve various external audiences, as many as types of stakeholders (i.e., people or institutions with an interest in the business) a firm has. These include at least investors, banks, customers, suppliers, and even the government.

 Stakeholders

Stakeholders are the people or entities with an interest in the business, such as banks, customers, suppliers, and employees.

Investors and banks alike allow firms to hold their money to conduct business. The concerns of these agents include if the money taken by the firm will ever come back or if the company will make good use of the money in terms of profitability. Accounting provides some of the clues to answer such important questions.

Customers and suppliers make agreements with firms to, respectively, buy and sell products or services. Customers may want to know if the firm will be reliable in delivering the products, on time and with the right quality. A supplier facing financing problems may be unable to buy and hire as much as needed, keep machines in good condition, perform appropriate quality controls, and so on. Likewise, suppliers' main concern may be if the firm will pay on time (or at all!) the products delivered or the services rendered.

Finally, governments—state, local, federal, or national—will, among other things, be interested in collecting taxes from the firm. Since the firm's accounting results determine a large portion of the taxes to pay, governments usually have a vested interest in controlling the accuracy of firms' financials.

Accounting also helps internal audience, such as managers, to have a general understanding of the overall financial situation of the firm. However, C-level managers (such as the chief operations officer [COO]) usually have much more internal information about the financials of the firm that the one disclosed in periodic reports to all stakeholders. Using additional financial information, they can more closely and more frequently control key indicators, such as levels of inventory, budget deviations, or days of payments to suppliers.

2.5   Elements

In this section we will switch gears to introduce some of the elements that will be used later in the book. Having these elements in mind will be useful to better understand the various concepts introduced in the chapters that follow.

2.5.1 The Firm

The first element is the firm. It will be our main element of analysis and usually the subject of our decisions. We will refer to the firm—and not to the entity or the organization—because our main focus is the for-profit, business world. However, most of the contents of this book can also be extrapolated, mutatis mutandis, to other institutions, such as nonprofit organizations.

This book will treat the firm by regarding it as a separate entity, separately from its shareholders. In fact, for accounting purposes, as soon as a firm is created, it becomes an independent entity. This treatment will help guide our discussion. In particular, it will allow us to reduce the number of elements of the balance sheet from three (assets, liabilities, and shareholders' equity—all three to be defined later) to two (assets and equities), for instance, making it easier to understand what the balance sheet is really about.

 The firm as a separate entity

It is useful to think about the firm as a independent entity, set apart from its shareholders.

2.5.2 Trade Partners

In a business to business (B2B) relationship, a firm trades with its trade partners, suppliers, and customers, buying from the former and selling to the latter. We will assume that the firm will trade goods, as is the case of manufacturers or retailers. As such, suppliers will provide the firm with parts, either components or products, and the firm will fulfill customers' demand for products. In a business to consumer (B2C) relationship, a firm sells to final users. For instance, for a firm such as Walmart, Procter & Gamble is a supplier, and the final user that buys at a Walmart store is a customer. We can see a pictorial representation of these relationships in figure 2.3. This simple representation of a supply chain will serve our purpose for most of our discussions.

2.5.3 Value

Everything a firm owes, from a piece of land to a pallet of raw material, has some value to it, and can be valued according to at least two different criteria: book value and market value.

Figure 2.3
A simple supply chain: connection to suppliers and customers.

Book value The book value of an item, also known as *nominal* or *face* value, is its original acquisition cost, which may be adjusted over time in the case of some items following accounting rules. For instance, the initial book value of a machine goes down over time due to ageing and possible obsolescence. The initial book value of fashion goods will go down if it becomes out of fashion. The book value of items is recorded in the firm's accounting books.

Market value The market value of an item is the price at which the item can be sold, irrespective of its book value.

The market value is definitely more subjective than the book value, as it normally depends on the decision being considered. For instance, a second-hand truck that changes hands in the secondary market has different values for the buyer (higher value) and the seller (lower value); otherwise, markets for second-hand trucks (or anything else) would not exist. In some cases, however, it makes sense to talk about market value in general: for instance, assuming no transaction costs, the price of one share of Google in the secondary market is the same irrespective of who sells or buys it.

 Book value

> **Book value**, or nominal or face value, is the monetary value that an item has in the firm's (accounting) books.

 Market value

> **Market value** is the transaction price an item has in an actual market, for instance, the price at which an item is actually sold.

Given these definitions, it should be apparent that both book and market values are, in general, different. This distinction turns out to be an important one. Financial accounting deals only with book values, while investment and disinvestment decisions have mainly to do with market values.

2.5.4 Risk

The risk of a firm concerns itself with the fluctuations of cash flows it faces: the more they fluctuate, the higher the risk, and vice versa. For instance, if a company has steady sales over time and the payment it has to make to suppliers and others are fairly stable, then the firm faces low risk. Main risk sources are the industry risk (external to the firm) and operational and financial risks (internal to the firm).

• **Industry risk** depends on how overall demand (in dollars) changes over time. Smooth changes result in low industry risk, while abrupt changes—due to volatile prices, fluctuations of exchange rates, or changes in demand patterns—lead to high industry risk.

• As for internal sources of risk, **operational risk** mainly depends on the amount of fixed costs in the operational structure of the firm. The higher the percentage of fixed costs, the higher the risk (exercise 6 invites you to argue why).

• Similarly, **financial risk** depends on the amount of fixed costs in the financial structure of the firm, a function of how much debt it has and how much each dollar of debt costs.

Section 9.2.2.4 provides more details and addresses the impact of operating decisions on risk.

2.5.5 Standards

The fact that accounting is partially based on opinions raises the question of whether it is possible to have a single set of standards that unifies the way accounting is used across firms and countries. Most countries have their own set of rules, or generally accepted accounting principles (GAAP), but differences among countries persist. It makes sense, for instance, to talk about the Canadian GAAP or the French GAAP. Efforts have been made to reach international agreements. For example the European Union devised the so called International Financial Reporting Standards (IFRS), which have been adopted by more than one hundred countries already.

Comparing US GAAP and IFRS, the former are mainly based on rules, the latter in principles. As such, IFRS leave more room for interpretation. In the operations realm, a key difference between GAAP and IFRS involves the way they treat inventory. IFRS ban the use of last-in first-out (LIFO) method, whereas GAAP rules allow for LIFO. (Both allow for FIFO and weighted average cost methods though, see chapter 8 for details.) Also, GAAP does not allow for inventory reversals, while IFRS accepts them under certain circumstances. We will not stick to any particular set of rules, although we will keep IFRS as our main reference. That said, we will sometimes deviate from IFRS: for instance, IFRS calls the balance sheet financial position; we will still prefer and use the more prevalent term *balance sheet* in this book.

 International Financial Reporting Standards

> **International Financial Reporting Standards**, or IFRS for short, are a set of accounting standards developed by the International Accounting Standards Board that is becoming the global standard for the preparation of financial statements.

Accounting rules are not written in stone but change over time to refine existing rules and adapt to dynamic business reality. For instance, large firms increasingly tend not to own but to lease fixed assets, such as buildings or trucks. This improves some performance ratios, but less information is given to investors, as lease contracts figures do not appear in the balance sheet (owned assets figures do). Possibly as an answer to this trend, from

2019, IFRS require firms to bring most long-term leases onto the balance sheet.[2] This is a major (and controversial) change that may significantly impact some firms' performance ratios.

2.5.6 Basic Accounting Principles

Among the principles and industry practices included in any accounting standards, there are a number of basic accounting rules or principles that are widely accepted. We describe the most notable next.

Ongoing concern This underlying assumption states that, when preparing the financial statements, a firm will continue to exist for a sufficiently long period of time and will not be liquidated in a foreseeable future.

Consistency Accountants have to apply accounting procedures uniformly over time. For instance, the criteria to determine when to recognize sales should be fixed over the periods; they cannot be changed for convenience.

Conservatism This determines that if a situation arises where there are two acceptable alternatives for reporting an event, the more conservative alternative should be chosen— that is, the one that leads to lower profits or assets. Sometimes this is referred to as prudence concept.

Materiality A convention that allows accounting to be inaccurate when reporting an event if the relative importance of the inaccuracy is not expected to have an impact on the decisions made by any stakeholders. For instance, an expenditure of ten cents on paper is immaterial.

Matching Matching of costs with revenues determines that revenues and the corresponding costs (i.e., those needed to obtain the revenue, such as the cost of the item or its distribution cost) should be recognized in the same period.

Accrual basis This states that revenues should be recorded when earned and expenses when incurred, irrelevant of when collection of payment occurs. For instance, sales are recorded when the products are sent to the customer, not when the customer actually pays for the products. (Section 4.1.1 gives more detailed information.)

 Accounting principles

The **accounting principles**, also known as *accounting standards* or *accounting policies*, are the set of rules, conventions, and guidelines that govern the way financial statements are prepared.

---

2. IFRS Foundation 2018.

2.5.7 Stocks and Flows

Stocks and flows are common elements in both the engineering and financial worlds. Understanding the differences and the relationship between them will also make it easier to
understand a number of concepts, from the financial statements to the role of certain stocks
on investment assessment.

A stock is the quantity of something accumulated, as in a repository. For instance, the
amount of water in a container or the amount of inventory in a balance sheet are examples
of stocks. Stocks give a static picture of a system at a specific point in time; for example,
they give information about the current state of the system but are not concerned with how
the system ended up being where it is and how it will evolve in the future.

 Stock

> A **stock** is the quantity of something accumulated, as in a repository. For instance,
> the amount of water in a container or the amount of inventory in a balance sheet.

A flow is the amount of something that circulates through a passage during a period of
time. For instance, the amount of water that leaves a container per minute or a firm's annual
sales are examples of flows. In contrast to stocks, flows give a dynamic view of a system
during a specific lapse of time; they explain what actually occurred during a particular
period.

 Flow

> A **flow** is the amount of something that circulates through a passage during a period
> of time. For instance, the amount of water that leaves a container per minute or a
> firm's annual sales.

Identifying stocks and flows may sometimes be tricky. To distinguish flows from stocks,
consider if the units of measure include time in the denominator. For instance, annual sales
is a flow because it is measured in dollars per year. However, inventory is a stock because
it is measured in dollars or pieces.

The basic equation that links stocks and flows is as follows:

stock level = initial stock level + input flow − output flow

For instance, in the accounting domain, the amount of cash that a firm holds after a period
of time has to satisfy

cash level = initial cash level + cash in − cash out

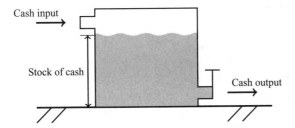

Figure 2.4
Cash stocks and flows are intimately related.

In layman terms, the latter equation just says that money does not disappear or appear out of the blue (see figure 2.4 for a pictorial representation).

We can think of stock as the level of water in a container. We can think of the flow as the water that enters or leaves the container during a specific period of time. This simile will come in handy when dealing with the financial statements. In particular, we will learn that the balance sheet is made up solely of stocks and that the income statement and the statement of cash flows are made up exclusively of flows. The relationship among all three financial statements is intimately related to the relationship between financial stocks and flows, a characteristic that we will explore later in the book.

2.5.8   Financial Statements

The core elements of financial accounting are the financial statements. These are reports that show financial information in a structured manner, such as the current financial position of the firm or the changes that occurred during a period regarding cash or shareholders' wealth. The three financial statements we will be dealing with are as follows:

Balance sheet   The balance sheet shows the financial status of a firm at a specific point in time. It is also called the financial position.

Income statement   An income statement explains how the wealth of the firm's owners has changed in a given period. It is also called the profit and loss account.

Statement of cash flows   This financial statement shows a firm's sources and uses of funds during a given period. It explains why the cash of the firm has changed.

Additional financial statements exist, such as the statement of changes in equity, or the state of comprehensive income, but a complete explanation of them goes beyond the scope of this book.

As these three financial statements are of paramount importance in business, the next chapters will be devoted to explaining them in detail.

2.6   Moral Hazard and Adverse Selection Motives

Some of the accounting principles—mainly ongoing concern, consistency, and conservatism—are devised so that accounting protects investors (and stakeholders in general) from managers taking more risks than they should, knowing that their risk-taking is borne by others—for example, shareholders, suppliers, insurance companies. For instance, the managing director of a retail firm very close to bankruptcy may decide to make a crazy bet on future sales by purchasing large amounts of inventory, even if the probability of sales rising is very small. If sales boost as planned, he would have saved the firm; but most likely, sales will not increase and the firm will go bankrupt. The manager will not be worse off (the firm was going bankrupt anyways), but shareholders will be (as cash decreased, while obsolete inventory increased). This negative behavior is usually referred to as moral hazard in economics.

Similarly, accounting principles are meant to protect stakeholders from managers hiding negative relevant information related to their management practices. For instance, an operations manager may decide not to write off obsolete inventory from the balance sheet so that his or her bonus—which depends on the firm's profit—is not reduced. An investor may buy shares of the firm thinking that profits are larger than they actually are. Having different information than managers, investors will make a bad choice. This negative behavior is usually referred to as adverse selection in economics.

Admittedly, accounting principles are just guidelines; therefore they cannot prevent managers from not adhering to the accounting principles following personal interests. That's why additional control tools, such as supervision of the board or external auditing processes, are necessary. In coming chapters, we will provide some examples of opportunities that managers have to cook the books.

Exercises

1. What is the main goal of accounting?

2. What is the main difference between book value and market value?

3. Name four types of stakeholders who may be interested in knowing a firm's financial information.

4. What is the main difference between a stock and a flow?

5. Are these stocks or flows?

   a. The amount of water stored in a container

   b. The amount of monthly rain fallen in Mawsynram, India

   c. An employee's annual salary

   d. The money you keep in your wallet

   e. How much you know about music

   f. How much a student learn in an academic year

6. A firm faces fluctuating sales (in thousands of dollars) following the monthly pattern: 100, 80, 100, 80, ..., 100, 80. Compare the risk the firm faces in the following two scenarios:

a. Costs vary proportionally to sales

b. Costs are fixed at $70k per month

7. Is a major disruption of components supply an example of industry risk or operational risk?

8. What accounting principles does allow for the surveillance services bill not to be divided among the three months to which it applies?

9. A manufacturer of catalytic converters holds large amounts of palladium as raw material. If the price of palladium suddenly surges by 15 percent, what accounting principle prevents the manufacturer from increasing the value of palladium inventory in its books?

References

Gleeson-White, Jane. 2011. *Double entry: How the merchants of Venice created modern finance.* New York: W. W. Norton.

IFRS Foundation. 2018. *IFRS Standards 2018.* Part a (IFRS 16).

3   Accounting Mechanics and the Balance Sheet: The Basics

It sounds extraordinary, but it's a fact that balance sheets can make fascinating reading.
—Mary Archer, British scientist

This chapter introduces the rudiments of accounting mechanics as well as the balance sheet, possibly the most important piece of financial information in a firm. We firmly believe that understanding the mechanics of accounting is essential to comprehend the impact of managers' operational decisions on a firm's financials. For instance, it is simply impossible to calculate the value of an investment without understanding the mechanics of financial accounting. Therefore, we will devote this and chapter 4 to learning the essentials of accounting mechanics.

The usual way to introduce the balance sheet is to present its constituents and explain how each one works. That approach may leave some readers puzzled, as it may not be clear to them where each element of the balance sheet comes from. To overcome this difficulty, we will take a different approach by working out two simple examples during which we will identify the main elements of the balance sheet.

Our goal is not to get a comprehensive description of the balance sheet but to identify its main elements. These will make up the seven-item balance sheet, an abridged version of the standard balance sheet that we will present in section 4.2.

3.1   Sharon the Shareholder

Today's financial accounting aims to answer the very same question as the merchants in Pacioli's Venice: How well has the business done? As such, the goal of this first exercise is to obtain relevant information from the facts shown below to assess the performance of the business at the end of a three-month period; meaning, to answer the above question exactly.

Exercise

Sharon the Shareholder (abridged version)

While on campus in May, you discovered that a bookstore in the neighborhood was selling a very popular book at a deep discount. You realized that it made sense to buy some of those books and sell them online to students at regular price later in the summer. You did not have much money, so you asked your rich friend Sharon to contribute some money and start a new business with you. Sharon agreed to invest $10,000 from her savings.

1. On June 1, you created the firm and made a $10,000 deposit (from Sharon's savings) into a bank account.
2. Using that money, you bought a laptop. You paid $2,000 for it.
3. The rest of the money was used to buy one hundred books at $80 each.
4. You aim to sell the books at $100 each. *Three months go by. ...*
5. On August 31, you have $11,000 in cash: $9,500 from selling ninety-five books at $100 each, and an extra $1,500 from selling your laptop to your neighbor. You were glad to see that unexpected additional $1,500.
6. The difference between the one hundred books bought and the ninety-five books sold was due to the fact that five books were damaged stock in your apartment.

In the pages that follow, we will make use of three different methods to address the questions asked. The first approach is simple and intuitive; subsequent approaches introduce additional refinements, so they are more useful but less intuitive.

3.1.1 Brute-Force Approach

A straightforward, brute-force method of addressing Pacioli's question posed is to calculate some measure of profit or utility for the business during the quarter; in this particular case, the difference between final and initial cash.

$$\$11,000 - \$10,000 = \$1,000$$

We can even explain where that $1,000 comes from: Selling ninety-five books gives a profit of $20 each, or $1,900. But we have to deduct $400 due to the five spoiled books ($80 each) and $500 for the difference between the selling price and the acquisition cost of the laptop:

$$\$1,900 - \$400 - \$500 = \$1,000$$

Left column	Right column
What the firm owns	What the firm owes

Figure 3.1
Double-entry refers to the two columns that make up the main report of a double-entry accounting system.

Naturally, Sharon is happy with a $1,000 profit over a three-month period. Furthermore, if it were possible, she could quantify her happiness in dollars. Loosely speaking, we could say that she is $1,000 happier.

We can imagine a Venetian merchant prior to Pacioli's book feeling exactly the same: he would also feel $1,000 happier. So why go ahead with more intricate methods if we are satisfied with the current conclusion?

Well, the method is both appropriate and valid within a simple setting. However, within the context of some of our modern-day, more complex settings, sheer logic and common sense is simply not enough. Pacioli's method has withstood the test of time—more than five hundred years in fact—which cannot and should not be ignored. Therefore, it makes a lot of sense to bear with Pacioli and use his method to address the same example again.

3.1.2 Pacioli's Basic Approach

Pacioli's method is called double-entry accounting: the main report of the accounting system consists of two columns (left and right) and financial events are recorded twice. The left column contains what the firm owns, while the right column contains what the firm owes. A simple pictorial representation is given in figure 3.1.

Given this scheme, let's record the six events described above in the two-column report in figure 3.1.

? Event 1

On June 1st, you created the firm and made a $10,000 deposit (from Sharon's savings) in a bank account.

We have to record what you did with the money. To decide in which column we should annotate that it may be helpful to answer the following two questions.

Left column	Right column
What the firm owns	Sharon's pocket 10,000

Figure 3.2
Right column includes the firm's sources of funds, such as Sharon's pocket.

Left column	Right column
Money box 10,000	Sharon's pocket 10,000

Figure 3.3
Left column includes everything a firm owns, such as a box with money.

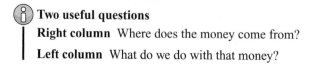 **Two useful questions**

Right column Where does the money come from?

Left column What do we do with that money?

The first question can be reformulated for event 1 as:

Where does the $10,000 come from? The answer is from Sharon's pocket. Therefore, we will put $10,000 in the right column as Sharon's pocket, as in figure 3.2. We will see that it makes sense to ask these two questions whenever the amount in the right column increases.

The second question becomes:

What do we do with this $10,000? We put it into a money box. Admittedly, it may not be a physical box, but a bank account. But a mental image of a physical cardboard box placed somewhere on the firm premises may be a useful one. Figure 3.3 shows the event recorded once the left column has been duly updated.

Let's verify that both columns contain the appropriate pieces of information. After event 1, the firm owns a box with $10,000 inside (left column) and owes $10,000 to Sharon (right column). To better understand the fact that the firm owes the money to Sharon, it is helpful again to consider the firm as a separate entity. Sharon is smart, therefore she expects some money back; hopefully, the $10,000 that she has just put down, plus some additional money that makes her happiness grow. She also understands that things may go badly, so she may not even get the initial $10,000 three months down the road. This is a risk that Sharon is bearing. But in any case, that $10,000, or whatever amount it will end up being, belongs to Sharon. These are the business rules, as she was the one who put down the initial amount of money to start the business.

An interesting observation in this regard is that both quantities in both columns are coincident. This is *always* the case, as what the firm owns and what the firm owes can never be different, given that any change in Sharon's pocket, either positive or negative, is automatically assigned to Sharon. We can generalize this observation and state that:

sum of left column = sum of right column   (3.1)

This expression turns out to be a simple but important one.

 Event 2

Using that money, you bought a laptop. You paid $2,000 for it.

Next, we have to buy a laptop worth $2,000.

Where do we get the money to pay for it?   Well, we can assume that it comes from the money box.

What do we do with the money?   We acquire the laptop. Therefore, we have to (1) deduct $2,000 from the money box, since the amount of cash in the box has been reduced, and (2) recognize that the firm has a laptop in the left column. (Remember, the left column contains what the firm owns.)

Figure 3.4 shows the status of the firm right after event 2.

How is this event different from the previous one?   In event 1, the answer to the question—Where does the money come from?—has to do with an increase in the right column, as additional cash flows into the firm from the outside (Sharon's pocket). However,

Left column	Right column
Money box 8,000	
	Sharon's pocket 10,000
Laptop 2,000	

Figure 3.4
Money to acquire the laptop comes directly from the money box.

in event 2, no additional money flows into the firm, but money that was already in the firm has been used to buy some equipment. Having said that, we can ask the following question:

Is Sharon happier or sadder due to event 2? You could argue that Sharon is sadder due to event 2, given that cash has diminished by $2,000. However, note that the firm has now a laptop worth $2,000; thus, Sharon is neither happier nor sadder, but even. You could also argue that cash is more versatile than a laptop, thus $2,000 cash is worth more than a laptop for the firm. This may be true, but accounting cannot take these subtleties into consideration. This is what we will call the accounting criterion.

 The accounting criterion

In accordance with the **accounting criterion**, everything the firm owns and owes is worth exactly its book value.

Note that, in accordance with an accounting criterion, Sharon's happiness, measured in dollars, depends only on the Sharon's-pocket level in the right column.

Finally, you may argue that the laptop enable future sales, therefore Sharon is happier after event 2. Again, this might be the case, but again we face a limitation of accounting. Unfortunately, accounting cannot cope with the future, it only deals with the present and the past. And as far as event 2 is concerned, future sales have not been realized yet, thus we cannot argue that Sharon is happier right after event 2. In conclusion, Sharon is neither happier nor sadder, but even as a result of event 2 *in accordance with the accounting criterion.*

? **Event 3**

The rest of the money was used to buy one hundred books at $80 each.

Assuming we pay cash, we will have to pay the supplier of books on delivery from the cash box. As shown in figure 3.5, the money box has been emptied in return for eighty brand-new books in our warehouse.

Left column	Right column
Books 8,000	
	Sharon's pocket 10,000
Laptop 2,000	

Figure 3.5
All items in the financial reports have to be measured in dollars (or other currency).

Left column	Right column
Money box 9,500	
Books 400	Sharon's pocket 10,000
Laptop 2,000	

Figure 3.6
Note that something is wrong with this report, as the sums in the right and left columns do not coincide.

Note that we do not write "80 books" in the left column, but $80 \cdot 100$ books = $8,000. Everything has to be converted into hard cash before assigning it to either column.

In accordance with the accounting criterion, is Sharon happier or sadder as a result of event 3?   Using the same reasoning as in event 1, it should be clear that she is even, as the value of the books makes up exactly for the loss of $8,000 cash.

? Event 4

> You aim to sell the books at $100 each. On August 31, you have $11,000 in cash: $9,500 from selling ninety-five books at $100 each, . . .

Once we have the books, we are ready to sell them. As event 4 describes, we are able to sell ninety-five books. Selling is good because the firm gets cash; the bad news is that, in return, the firm has to give the books to its customers. The money collected from customers is $100 \cdot 95$ books = $9,500. The wealth that goes away through books is $80 \cdot 95$ books = $7,600. We value the books at $80 because that was the acquisition cost, the usual practice in accounting. The assumption is that the value of books does not change (neither increase nor decrease) while in the firm. The firm's financial status after event 4 is shown in figure 3.6.

What is odd with the data in figure 3.6? The sums of the columns do not match. We know that this cannot be the case, which possibly means that we made a mistake. In fact, we forgot to do something. Let's ask ourselves:

Is Sharon happier or sadder after selling ninety-five books?   Sharon is happier, because we bought cheap and sold expensive, which means that we obtained some profit or utility:

$$(\$100 - \$80) \cdot 95 \text{ books} = \$1,900$$

Sharon's happiness increased by $1,900, therefore *we have to acknowledge this fact in the right column as additional money in Sharon's pocket* at the time of recognizing the sale (figure 3.7).

Left column	Right column
Money box 9,500	
Books 400	Sharon's pocket 11,900
Laptop 2,000	

Figure 3.7
After selling ninety-five books, Sharon's happiness has increased by $1,900, and the sum of the figures in the two columns matches.

Left column	Right column
Money box 11,000	
	Sharon's pocket 11,400
Books 400	

Figure 3.8
After selling the laptop, Sharon's happiness has decreased by $500.

Note than now, it holds that: $9,500 + $400 + $2,000 = $11,900, as it should be.

? Event 5

... and an extra $1,500 from selling your laptop to your neighbor. You were glad to see that unexpected additional $1,500.

We have sold most of the books, so it makes sense to get rid of the laptop, as we do not need it any longer. Our neighbor is willing to pay us $1,500 for it which is great. Is that the whole story? Well, not really. Let's return to the proverbial question:

Is Sharon happier or sadder due to selling the laptop?   She is happier because of the additional cash ($1,500) but sadder because the laptop went away ($2,000). Overall, she is sadder by $500. Again, we have to acknowledge this fact by lowering Sharon's pocket in the right column, as this $500 is money that the firm does not owe Sharon anymore (figure 3.8).

You could argue at this point that three months down the road the value of the laptop was not as high as $2,000. You would have been right; but for convenience, we have (wrongly) assumed thus far that the value of the hardware did not decrease over time. We will take care of these subtleties in the next chapter.

Left column	Right column
Money box 11,000	Sharon's pocket 11,000

Figure 3.9
After spoiling five books, Sharon's happiness has decreased by $400.

？ Event 6

The difference between the one hundred books bought and the ninety-five books sold was due to the fact that five books were damaged stock at your apartment.

We close this first exercise with some bad news: five books were spoiled and could not be sold. Therefore, we have to get rid of them as well in the firm's books: we just remove them from the left column (five books at $80 each = $400) and acknowledge that Sharon is sadder by $400 because the books are gone (right column).

By how much did Sharon's happiness increase? Or, more formally, how did the three-month period do overall? Sharon puts $10,000 from her pocket, and there is now $11,000 in the box; thus, her happiness increased by $1,000. The quarter went well for Sharon the shareholder.

Not surprisingly, the solution given by this method is identical to the one obtained by the brute-force approach. This second method is correct because it gives the right solution; and although not as efficient as the first method, it lays the groundwork to tackle more complex situations. Finally, we will solve a full version of this exercise, this time as accountants.

3.1.3 Pacioli's Refined Approach (June)

We will go through Sharon the shareholder's example once more, but this time we will make use of additional information that explains what occurred during each of the three months. This time we are interested in assessing how well the business did *at the end of each month*.

Exercise

Sharon the Shareholder (full version, June)

1. On June 1, you and Sharon made a $10,000 deposit (from Sharon's savings) into a bank account.

2. You bought a laptop worth $2,000.

3. You bought thirty books at $80 each from Susan, the bookstore manager. At the end of June, you had paid $2,000 for books.

4. You sold twenty-four books. It is worth mentioning that ten of your friends bought one book each, but they did not pay for them (you expected all of them to pay up later on).

5. On June 30, you accidentally spilled a cup of coffee over five books on your desk, completely ruining them.

As we are only interested in assessing the firm's situation at the end of each month, it is convenient to keep track of the changes that occur in each account within the month. This can be done using T-accounts, where *changes* (increases or decreases) are recorded, as shown in figure 3.10. Even if T-accounts are not used in practice (computers do not need them), they come in handy when learning the mechanics of financial accounting.

Also, we will start giving proper names to the various financial items that appear along the way. Accountants like to use fancy names for things. For instance, the names left column and right column that we used in the previous section would be totally unacceptable for accountants. In fact, the two columns deserve colorful labels, such as assets (left column) and equities (right column).

Asset comes from Old French *asez* (*assez* in modern French, meaning enough. It has the same Latin root—*satis*—as *satisfy*). It refers to the fact that the amount in the left column has to be enough to repay all the money owed by the firm, as shown in the right column.

 Assets

| **Assets** are the items that a firm owns to conduct business, such as stores or inventory.

		Cash		
	8,000		5,000	
Increases	6,000		2,000	Decreases
	1,000			

Figure 3.10
T-account example. (Can you guess why it is called a T-account?)

Equities comes from Old French *equité*, a word whose Latin root means even, just, and equal. Equities are rights held by or claims made by external parties to the firm, such as suppliers, banks, or shareholders.[1]

 Equities

> **Equities** are the items owed by the firm to external parties, such as suppliers, banks, or the owners of the firm.

Finally, the general ledger is the book (today, the computer) where changes in assets and equities are summarized and organized by accounts. From the general ledger, all financial statements can be derived.

 General ledger

> The **general ledger** is the book (computer) where changes in assets and equities are summarized and organized.

As we are using T-accounts, we can simply define the general ledger as the collection of T-accounts. It will allow us to go over all the movements that occurred from the beginning of the period (such as a month or a quarter) at a glance. Examples will be shown later in this section.

Equipped with these definitions, we are ready to go through the detailed version of the exercise.

? **Event 1**

> On June 1, you and Sharon made a $10,000 deposit (from Sharon's savings) into a bank account.

Sharon contributed $10,000 to the firm with money from her pocket. The name given by financiers to someone like Sharon is a shareholder.

 Shareholders

> **Shareholders** are people who invest money in a firm from their pocket. They expect to get some money in return in the future (called dividends).

---

1. In this book, we will adopt the convention of William Bruns of Harvard Business School and call the right column equities (Bruns 2004). A more common name for equities is liabilities plus shareholder's equity, which we find too long. Another used name is liabilities. We will use *equity* in singular to refer to shareholders' equity.

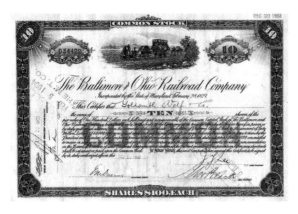

Figure 3.11
Ten-share certificate at $100 per share issued in 1902 by the Baltimore and Ohio Railroad Company.
Source: Wikimedia Commons.

 Dividends

Dividends are the money that firms pay its shareholders.

They call Sharon a shareholder because she holds shares. Shares used to be represented by paper certificates to prove that shareholders had invested money in the business (figure 3.11). Today, computers may be used instead.

 Shares

Shares are certificates that prove that their owners, the shareholders, have invested money in the business. Shares are issued by firms.

The money coming from Sharon's pocket is called owners' equity, or simply equity. To be more precise, equity does not only capture the money coming from Sharon's pocket but also the wealth generated by the business (mainly through sales after deducting expenses) which also belongs to Sharon. Every time Sharon's happiness increases, the additional profit or utility created can be claimed by Sharon. Likewise, every time Sharon's happiness decreases, the additional profit or utility destroyed cannot be claimed by Sharon any longer. In other words, Sharon can claim the wealth of the firm that is not bound to other creditors, such as suppliers or banks.

The money invested by Sharon ends up in a money box as far as event 1 is concerned. The name used to label the money box is simply cash" (figure 3.12). In fact, *cash* comes from Middle French *caisse* (box, usually for keeping money). Figure 3.12 shows both T-accounts.

Figure 3.12
Cash shows the available money that a firm has in a bank account. The alternative image of a money box may be a useful one.

 Equity

Equity, or shareholders' equity, is the money that shareholders would get if a firm sold all its assets at book value and repaid all the money owed to everyone else without transaction costs. In this book, equity is a category within equities.

Observe the cash account in figure 3.12. The $10,000 on the left indicates that this account has increased as a result of event 1. Now look at the equity account. The $10,000 in the *right* indicates that this account has *increased* as a result of event 1. Note that the convention is reversed depending on the column: the assets account increases are annotated on the left, while the equities account increases are annotated on the right. Likewise, assets account decreases are annotated on the right, while equities account decreases are annotated on the left. If this convention seems rather intricate to you, just bear in mind that finance people thrive on complexity.[2]

? Event 2

You bought a laptop worth $2,000.

To record the acquisition of the laptop, we deduct $2,000 from cash and add a new account to the assets side. The laptop falls into the fixed assets category (figure 3.13). Fixed assets are called fixed because they are normally bought to stay in the company for a long period of time. Examples include land, buildings, factories, distribution centers, furniture, or equipment. This is in contrast to merchandise, such as books, which are bought from suppliers in order to be sold to customers later on. Of course, fixed assets can eventually be sold as well.

2. The convention stems from the existence of the concepts credit and debit used by accountants. Going through these concepts in this book seems unnecessary to us.

Assets				Equities

Cash		Fixed assets		Equity
10,000	2,000	2,000		10,000

Figure 3.13
According to the convention on the assets side, cash reductions are annotated on the right, fixed assets increases are annotated on the left.

 Fixed assets

> **Fixed assets** or noncurrent assets are the firm's assets that are not usually acquired to be sold. This account typically includes items such as land, buildings, furniture, or equipment.

Within fixed assets, several categories may be identified, but we don't need to go into them, as we will mainly deal with nonfixed or current assets.

 Current assets

> **Current assets** are the firm's assets that are not in the category of fixed assets. (See the definition of *fixed assets* above.)

 Event 3

> You bought thirty books at $80 each from Susan, the bookstore manager. At the end of June you had paid $2,000 for books.

To buy the first thirty books, in principle we need to pay the supplier $30 \cdot \$80 = \$2,400$. However, note that only $2,000 is paid to the supplier by the end of June. The rest of the money will be paid later. A postponed payment is called a payment on account, as opposed to a cash payment. Therefore, cash will be reduced by only $2,000 and a new account will be needed to annotate the acquisition cost of the thirty books ($2,400). The name of such an account is inventory. The name comes from Latin *inventarium*, literally "a list of what is found," from Latin *invenire* ("to come upon"). With those origins, you can infer the caliber of merchants' warehousing practice in Pacioli's times.

Inventory is placed on the assets side, because it is something that the firm owns. We will devote substantial portions of several chapters to discussing the role of inventory.

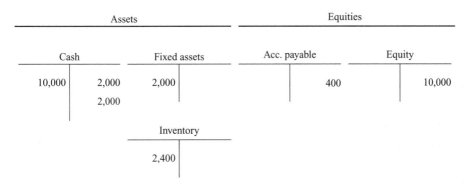

Assets				Equities	
Cash		Fixed assets		Acc. payable	Equity
10,000	2,000	2,000		400	10,000
	2,000				
		Inventory			
		2,400			

Figure 3.14
After event 3, the firm owes the supplier $400, as shown in accounts payable.

 Inventory

> **Inventory** is the collection of products and components/supplies to make products that a firm acquires or produces in order to satisfy customer demand. Inventory is a category of assets.

The difference between the acquisition cost and the money paid to the supplier is $2,400 - \$2,000 = \$400$. What should we do with this amount? Remember that this is money that the firm owes; thus, it should be placed in equities. The name given to the money owed to suppliers is accounts payable for obvious reasons (figure 3.14).

 Accounts payable

> **Accounts payable**, payables, or A/P, is the money owed by the firm to its suppliers. It may be extended to other creditors, such as employees or the government. Accounts payable is a category of liabilities.

Is Sharon happier or sadder as a result of the firm buying the books?

The firm now has books worth $2,400 and has only paid $2,000 for them. One may be tempted to think that Sharon is happier because of the positive $400 gap. However, the firm now has a piece of paper that says that it has the obligation to pay the supplier $400. This makes Sharon sadder. Overall, she is neither happier nor sadder, but even.

All things being equal, when buyers pay suppliers on account (in thirty days, for instance), suppliers are effectively lending money to buyers for free. If this is not clear to you, consider the following example: Say that you go to a store to buy a widget, and you pay $100 cash for it. When you are about to leave the store, Susan, the store manager, tells you, "I am in a good mood today, so I have decided to lend you $100 for free. You can give me the money back in thirty days." This situation is equivalent to the previous one, when buyer and supplier agree that the buyer will pay on account. This mechanism is called trade credit and is extremely important in business, since a major portion of firms' funds come from suppliers.

 Trade credit

> **Trade credit** is the credit obtained by a firm from its supplier, such that the former does not have to pay immediately (with cash) upon the reception of the goods or the execution of the service.

? Event 4

> You sold twenty-four books. It is worth mentioning that ten of your friends bought one book each, but they did not pay for them (you expected all of them to pay up later on).

We are ready to sell our first batch of twenty-four books, which is great. The good news is that you obtain some cash, $(24 - 10) \cdot \$100 = \$1,400$. The bad news is that a number of books will disappear from the warehouse, worth $24 \cdot \$80 = \$1,920$ (remember that inventory is valued at acquisition cost).

What should we do regarding the ten books sold to our friends? Much like what we did with the money owed to suppliers, we have to acknowledge the fact that ten customers owe the firm a total amount of $10 \cdot \$100 = \$1,000$.

Where should we put this amount, assets or equities? Is this something that the firm owns or the firm owes? Well, the firm does not owe anything as far as this event is concerned; on the contrary, some customers do owe some money to the firm. Therefore it cannot be equities and thus it must be assets, as there are no other options. But the firm does not have the money yet.

If it is assets, what is it that the firm has then? The firm has a piece of paper (or a number of them) saying that some customers have the obligation to pay some money to the firm.

What is this piece of paper worth? Exactly $1,000. Therefore, we should add $1,000 to the firm's assets, under a new account called accounts receivable. Accounts receivable is the counterpart of accounts payable. A firm's receivables should be in its customers' payables, and a firm's payables should be in its suppliers' receivables.

Are we done with event 4 yet? Not yet. We still have to take care of Sharon's happiness. We sent away $1,920 in books and got in return $2,400, either as green (cash) or

Assets				Equities			
Cash		**Fixed assets**		**Acc. payable**		**Equity**	
10,000	2,000	2,000			400		10,000
1,400	2,000						
Acc. receivable		**Inventory**		**Revenue and expenses** **(Sharon's happiness)**			
1,000		2,400	1,920			Increasing equity	480

Figure 3.15
The revenue and expense account shows the changes in Sharon's happiness.

white (accounts receivable) pieces of paper, thus Sharon's happiness has increased by the difference, $480. A straightforward way to acknowledge it would be to increase equity by that amount on the equities side. But remember that accountants like complexity. They want to keep track of all changes in equity; thus they have a special account for that—the revenue and expense account. This account turns out to be extremely important, as we will see in chapter 4. It has two distinctive features:

(1) It is a temporary account, which means that it will disappear (i.e., it will be emptied or zeroed out) at the end of the month.

(2) All annotations made on it have special names.

With that in mind, our first attempt to record the change in equity is shown in figure 3.15.

Although conceptually correct, accountants like to have more detail about that change in Sharon's happiness: they want to know why it increased or decreased. The net change shown in figure 3.15 is not enough, according to the noncompensation principle.

 Noncompensation principle

The **noncompensation principle** states that the details of the financial accounts should be reflected in the financial statements. For instance, assets and debt or revenue and expenses of the same amount do not cancel out.

Remember that, on the one hand, happiness increased because of selling the books; that is to say, it is wealth coming from customers, as either green or white pieces of paper. We will call this simply "sales." On the other hand, happiness decreased because of thirty books leaving the warehouse of the firm. The accounting name is cost of goods sold, or just COGS. These details are shown in figure 3.16.

Assets			Equities	

Cash		Fixed assets	Acc. payable	Equity
10,000	2,000	2,000	400	10,000
1,400	2,000			

Acc. receivable		Inventory	☹	Revenue and expenses (Sharon's happiness)	☺
1,000		2,400	1,920 COGS	1,920 Sales	2,400

Figure 3.16
The revenue and expense account keeps track of increases and decreases in Sharon's happiness. The good news, which makes Sharon happier, is annotated under the smiley face. The bad news, which makes Sharon sadder, is annotated under the frownie face.

 Cost of goods sold

The **cost of goods sold (COGS)** is the sum of acquisition and production costs of the products or services sold by a firm. It typically includes raw materials, direct product costs, and some indirect production costs.

 Revenue and expense account

The **revenue and expense account** records all changes in Sharon's happiness, both positive and negative. It is a special account, as it is temporary and all figures on it are given special names.

Finally, is Sharon happier or sadder as a result of event 4?   She is clearly happier, as the good news is larger than the bad news—that is, equity increased by $480 (net).

? Event 5

 On June 30, you accidentally spilled a cup of coffee over five books on your desk, completely ruining them.

Spoiling five books is bad news indeed for Sharon. We have to remove the value of the books from the firm's records ("write inventory off" in accounting jargon), and acknowledge Sharon's increasing sadness in the revenue and expense account. Spoiling inventory is usually considered additional COGS (figure 3.17).

Assets				Equities			
Cash		Fixed assets		Acc. payable		Equity	
10,000	2,000	2,000			400		10,000
1,400	2,000						
Acc. receivable		Inventory		☹	Revenue and expenses (Sharon's happiness)		☺
1,000		2,400	1,920	COGS	1,920	Sales	2,400
			400	COGS (5 books)	400		

Figure 3.17
Spoiling inventory makes Sharon sadder.

3.1.3.1 Preparing the Balance Sheet as of June 30

We have reached the end of June. Since we want to know how well June went, we can summarize the content of each account in a report. Such a report is called the balance sheet. The balance sheet is also called the statement of financial position, although balance sheet is a much more popular name.

The name of the balance sheet comes from the fact that it is always balanced; that is to say, the total amount of its two elements, assets and equities, are always identical to each other (recall expression 3.1). Formally:

total assets = total equities   (3.2)

which is the fundamental accounting identity.

The fundamental accounting identity

total assets = total equities

 Balance sheet

The **balance sheet**, or statement of financial position, is possibly the most important financial report. It is made up of two parts, assets and equities, where assets show what the firm has and equities what the firm owes at a given point in time. It gives a static view of the firm, as all its elements are stocks.

Table 3.1
Balance sheet as of June 30.

Cash	7,400	Accounts payable	400
Accounts receivable	1,000	Equity[a]	10,080
Inventory	80		
Fixed assets	2,000		
Total assets	**10,480**	**Total equities**	**10,480**

[a]Equity includes $80 worth of retained earnings.

In order to prepare the balance sheet, we will calculate the current stock of each account knowing the initial amount at the beginning of the month (zero in this first example) and the inputs and outputs that occurred during the month. For instance, the stock of cash at the end of June is:

Cash at the end of June $= \$0 + \$10,000 + \$1,400 - \$2,000 - \$2,000 = \$7,400$

As for the revenue and expense account, remember that it is a temporary one, and we have to close it. To do that, we calculate how much equity increased by:

Additional equity $= \$2,400 - \$1,920 - \$400 = \$80$

and we move that amount from the revenue and expense account to the equity account.

New stock of equity $= \$10,000 + \$80 = \$10,080$

Accountants like to name the increasing equity ($80 in this case) as retained earnings. The name suggests that these earnings are not paid out to shareholders as dividends. By doing this, accountants can keep track of where equity originated from, whether from shareholders' pockets (sometimes called common stock, issued capital, or funds contributed by shareholders) or from conducting business through buying and selling (as said, usually called retained earnings).

 Retained earnings

Retained earnings is the portion of profit not paid to shareholders but kept within the firm at the end of a given period.

Table 3.1 shows the balance sheet as of June 30.
The balance sheet shows:

What the firm owns Some green papers worth $7,400, some white papers worth $1,000, one book worth $80, and a laptop worth $2,000.

What the firm owes $400 to the book supplier and $10,080 to Sharon.

Note that equation 3.2 holds, that is, total assets = total equities.

An important observation is that the balance sheet is a collection of stocks. As such, it gives a static view of the financial situation of a firm at a given point in time. The balance sheet is not concerned with how the firm ended up being where it is today. The other two main financial statements will take care of that, as we will see in future chapters.

 The two sides of the balance sheet

The balance sheet shows what a firm owns—assets on the left side—and what a firm owes—equities on the right side.

Another observation is that the sequence of presentation of items in the assets side is determined according to what is called liquidity. The first item is cash, which is the most liquid item. Well, admittedly, banknotes are solid, not liquid. The word *liquidity* comes from centuries ago, when (liquid) oil was used as a means of payment. The name has survived since then to refer to how close an asset category is to cash. Therefore, in the balance sheet, after cash comes accounts receivable, as they will be (hopefully) converted into cash at the time of collection. Then comes inventory, which will be converted into accounts receivable, then into cash. Finally, fixed assets are the least liquid assets. Similarly, equities are sorted according to payment due date (shorter due dates come first).

 Liquidity

Liquidity measures the degree of similarity of a balance sheet item to cash. In the case of assets, cash is the most liquid item, with fixed assets being the least. As for equities, most liquid items are the ones with the shortest due date.

In some countries, the convention is reversed; that is, fixed assets and equity come first, and cash and accounts payable come last.

3.1.4 Pacioli's Refined Approach (July and August)

Having presented the balance sheet, we resume our work on the Sharon the Shareholder example so as to assess the performance of the firm in July and August.

 Exercise

Sharon the Shareholder (full version cont'd, July and August)

6. Six out of ten of your friends eventually paid for their books. By the end of July, you still had four pending payments.
7. You sold forty books for cash.

8. On July 31, there were twenty books in stock in your apartment.

9. On July 31, you owed nothing to Susan, the book store manager.

10. You bought the remaining books with cash, bringing your total up to one hundred.

11. The four pending payments were made by your four friends.

12. On August 31, you had neither books in stock nor pending payments from customers.

13. On August 31, you sold the laptop to your neighbor for $1,500.

We start by considering the status of the firm at the end of June (figure 3.18). The revenue and expense account does not appear, as it was closed at that time. It will be opened again as needed.

? Event 6

Six out of ten of your friends eventually paid for their books. By the end of July, you still had four pending payments.

As six friends paid what they owed for the books, we deduct $600 from accounts receivable and increase the cash account by the same amount.

Is Sharon happier or sadder as a result of this transaction? One might think that Sharon is happier, because it is better to have cash than promises of cash in the future. The latter is true, but that fact does not make Sharon happier *in according with the accounting criterion*. In fact, Sharon is indifferent regarding cash and accounts receivable. As far as

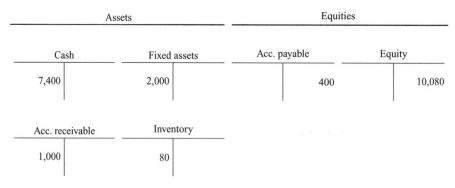

Figure 3.18
General ledger of the firm at the end of June.

she is concerned, the only thing that has changed as a result of this transaction is the color of the papers, which turned from white into green (US dollars). Therefore she is even, not happier.

? Events 7 and 8

You sold forty books for cash. On July 31, there were twenty books in stock in your apartment.

Selling (and delivering) forty books implies that the warehouse has enough inventory to satisfy the demand. As there was only one book at the end of June, we first need to buy a number of books in July to sell forty of them. How many books did we buy in July? Well, event 8 tells us that ending inventory on July 31 is twenty books. Therefore, as far as July is concerned:

$$\text{Inventory}_{\text{end of July}} = \text{Inventory}_{\text{beginning of July}} + \text{Purchases} - \text{Sales} \Rightarrow$$

$$20 = 1 + \text{Purchases} - 40 \Rightarrow$$

$$\text{Purchases} = 59 \text{ books}$$

Therefore we will record the purchase of fifty-nine books first and the sale of forty of them later in July.

To record the former, we annotate their acquisition value in the inventory account ($59 \cdot \$80 = \$4,720$) and acknowledge that we will pay the supplier later under accounts payable.

To acknowledge the sale of forty books, we follow four steps:

(1) Inventory is depleted at acquisition cost: $40 \cdot \$80 = \$3,200$.

(2) Cash increases by $40 \cdot \$100 = \$4,000$.

(3) Revenue increases through sales by $4,000.

(4) Expenses increase by $3,200.

Figure 3.19 shows the referred changes.

? Event 9

On July 31, you owed nothing to Susan, the book vendor.

This piece of information tells us that accounts payable should be zero at the end of August. The current stock is $\$400 + \$4,720 = \$5,120$, thus we have to deduct this amount from accounts payable. Likewise, we deduct $5,120 from cash to pay the supplier. Again:

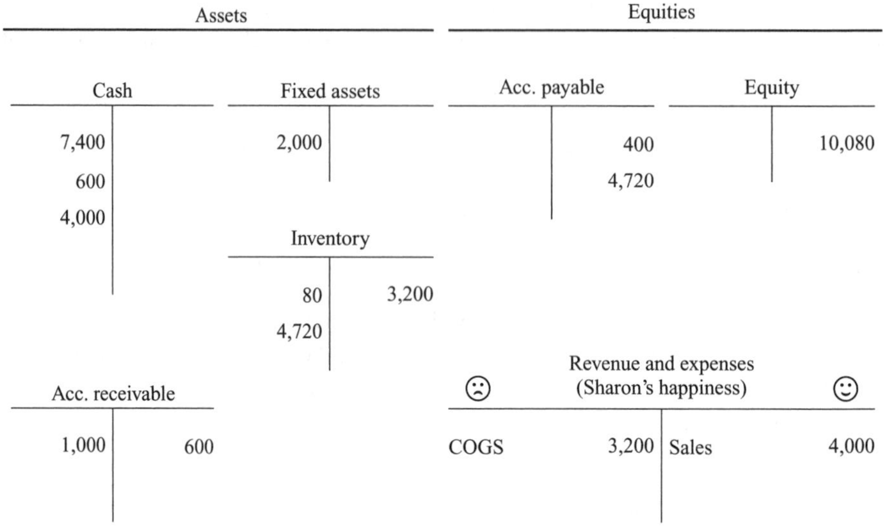

	Assets			Equities	

Cash		Fixed assets		Acc. payable		Equity	
7,400		2,000			400		10,080
600					4,720		
4,000							

Inventory

80	3,200
4,720	

Revenue and expenses
(Sharon's happiness)

☹   ☺

Acc. receivable	
1,000	600

COGS	3,200	Sales	4,000

Figure 3.19
General ledger of the firm after event 8.

Is Sharon happier or sadder?   She is even, despite the fact that cash decreased, because the obligation to pay the supplier (which made Sharon sad) disappears after paying the supplier.

? Event 10

You bought the remaining books with cash, bringing your total up to one hundred.

How many additional books do we have to buy? So far we bought thirty in June and fifty-nine in July, hence we have to buy eleven more books ($100 - 30 - 59 = 11$). As payables should be zero at the end of the month, we can assume that we pay cash this time, so we can deduct \$880 from cash ($11 \cdot \$80$) and increase inventory by the same amount.

? Event 11

The four pending payments were made by your four friends.

It is good news that the remaining four friends showed up to pay for their books, so that we still can call them friends! As we did before, we convert "white papers" into "green papers" by decreasing accounts receivable by \$400 ($4 \cdot \$100$) and increasing cash by the same amount (figure 3.20).

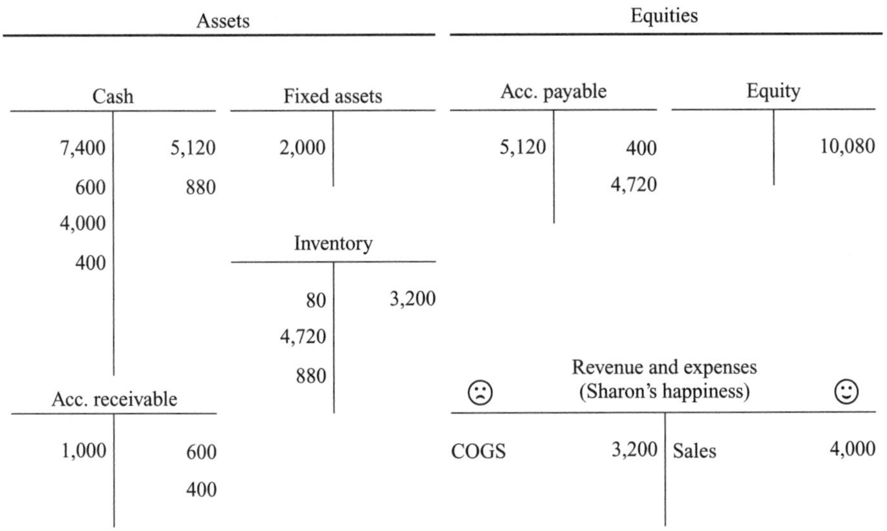

Assets				Equities			
Cash		**Fixed assets**		**Acc. payable**		**Equity**	
7,400	5,120	2,000		5,120	400		10,080
600	880				4,720		
4,000							
400		**Inventory**					
		80	3,200				
		4,720					
		880		☹	**Revenue and expenses** **(Sharon's happiness)**		☺
Acc. receivable							
1,000	600			COGS	3,200	Sales	4,000
	400						

Figure 3.20
General ledger of the firm after event 11.

? Event 12

On August 31, you had neither books in stock nor pending payments from customers.

This item entails that in August we sold all remaining books in the warehouse, namely:

$$\frac{\$80 + \$4,720 + \$880 - \$3,200}{\$80 \text{ per book}} = 31 \text{ books}$$

To acknowledge the sale we decrease inventory by $2,480 (emptying the warehouse), increase cash by $3,100 (31 · $100), and note the corresponding changes in Sharon's happiness in the revenue and expenses account.

? Event 13

On August 31, you sold the laptop to your neighbor for $1,500.

Although we had not planned selling the laptop, it was great to find someone who wanted to pay $1,500 for it. To annotate this event, we remove $2,000 from fixed assets (since the equipment has gone) and increase cash by $1,500.

What should we do with the difference? Is Sharon happier or sadder after selling the laptop? The answer may seem contrived, but she is actually sadder, because she

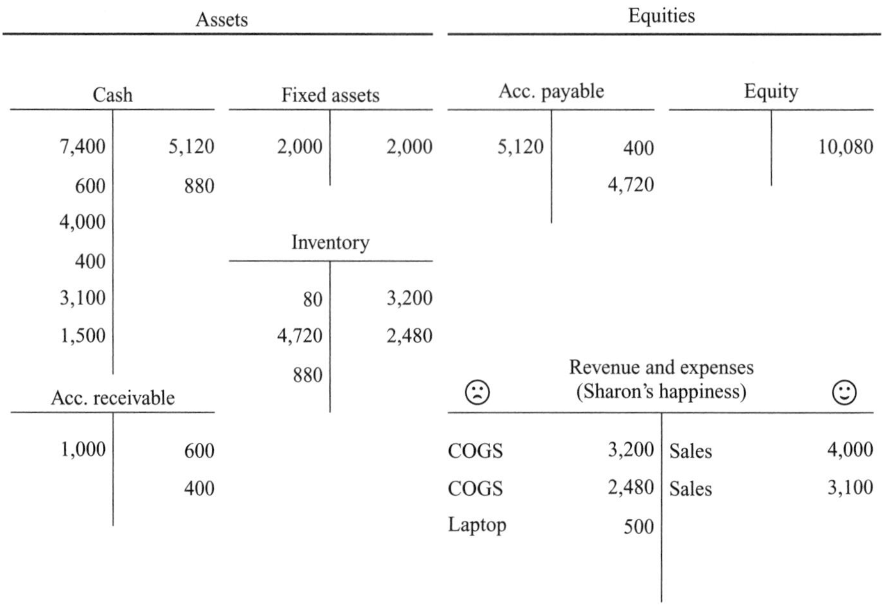

Assets				Equities			
Cash		**Fixed assets**		**Acc. payable**		**Equity**	
7,400	5,120	2,000	2,000	5,120	400		10,080
600	880				4,720		
4,000							
400		**Inventory**					
3,100		80	3,200				
1,500		4,720	2,480				
		880					
Acc. receivable				☹	**Revenue and expenses (Sharon's happiness)**		☺
1,000	600			COGS	3,200	Sales	4,000
	400			COGS	2,480	Sales	3,100
				Laptop	500		

Figure 3.21
General ledger of the firm after event 14.

had assets worth $2,000 and obtained less cash than that for them. Therefore she is sadder by $500. We acknowledge this fact in the sadness column of the revenue and expense account (the one with a frowny face on it, as shown in figure 3.21).

Note that this time, we did not outline the two components of the net change in Sharon's happiness due to selling the laptop. This is the case when a fixed asset is sold and turns out to be a bit inconsistent according to the noncompensation principle. Whether further details are given in practice depends on each country's set of accounting rules.

Also, you may argue that the value of the laptop is not that high after three months of use. You are right. We did not take that into consideration here for simplicity, but we will show how to do that in a future example.

3.1.4.1   Preparing the Balance Sheet as of August 31

Let's take a look at the balance sheet at the end of August. To close the revenue and expenses account we move the current stock:

$$\$920 = \$4,000 + \$3,100 - \$3,200 - \$2,480 - \$500$$

from that account to the equity account (remember that accountants would use a complementary account called retained earnings). Having done that, note that all accounts are empty, except for cash and equity, thus the balance sheet is fairly simple (table 3.2).

Table 3.2
Balance sheet as of August 31.

Cash	11,000	Equity	11,000
Total assets	**11,000**	**Total equities**	**11,000**

This balance sheet, when compared to the initial situation at the beginning of June, answers the question:

How well has the business done? Sharon initially invested $10,000; now, she has $11,000 of available cash. That means that Sharon's wealth has increased by $1,000 during the quarter, which is great for her.

This approach gives the same answer as approaches 1 and 2. This was expected, as the course of action in all three cases was the same. Only the methods used and the detail of events were different. As this particular example was relatively straightforward, we may not appreciate in full the advantages of the third approach over the other two. However, as we address more complex examples, the advantages of approach 3 over the other two will become apparent.

3.2   Summary

This chapter has introduced the basic mechanics of financial accounting and presents a key piece of financial information, the balance sheet. The balance sheet shows what a particular firm has at a given point in time (assets) and where the money used to acquired such assets comes from (equities). The balance sheet is a static picture or a snapshot, as it gives the state at a given point in time. It is concerned with the current situation of the firm; it is not concerned with how the firm got to where it is now. As such, the balance sheet is a collection of stock. The balance sheet always balances—that is, total assets and total equities always coincide.

Exercises

1. State the accounting identity.

2. On October 2, a book retailer decides to place an order for five hundred books at $100 each from a supplier for the purpose of resale to its customers. On October 5, the retailer actually orders the books. The order is still fully cancelable. On October 20, the retailer receives the five hundred books from the supplier. Although the contract requires the payment be made thirty days after delivery, ownership of the books passes to the retailer when she takes delivery of the books. The retailer pays the supplier $50,000 on November 20. When should the retailer recognize a $50,000 liability to her supplier?

a. On October 2   b. On October 5

c. On October 20   d. On November 20

3. Why is inventory less liquid than accounts receivable?

4. Explain the accounts that are modified by the following transactions.
   a. The purchase of office equipment for the sales team

   b. The payment of a supplier invoice at due date

   c. The reception of raw materials in the firm's warehouse

   d. The sale of merchandise on account at a margin

5. Can you think of one example where total assets is larger than total equities (that is, the sum of liabilities plus equity)?

6. If a company buys and sells construction land plots on a regular basis, in which account of the balance sheet should the value of these appear?

7. Does equity in the balance sheet coincide with the market value of a firm (that is, the price of each share times the number of shares)?

8. Indicate which accounts in the balance sheet usually change when the following events are recorded:
   a. A batch of raw material from the supplier is received

   b. A contract to build a new warehouse is signed with a construction company

   c. A brand-new machine is received and installed in the firm facilities

   d. Two hundred pallets of bricks are sold on account to a distributor

   e. Money is received from an internet customer to pay for a gadget that will be sent to the customer in two weeks

   f. Nine thousand dollars are collected form a customer at due date

9. Do the Sharon the Shareholder exercise on your own (items 1 to 13).

10. Explain how Sharon feels (happy, sad, even) and by how much as far as these transactions are concerned:
    a. Inventory worth $8,000 is bought for cash

    b. A car that costs $10,000 is sold on account

    c. A machine to improve productivity is bought and installed in the factory

    d. Twenty thousand dollars are collected from customers on due date

    e. Salaries worth $100,000 are paid at the end of the month

Reference

Bruns, William J. 2004. "The accounting framework, financial statements, and some accounting concepts." *HBS* 9-193-028.

4 Accounting Mechanics and the Balance Sheet: Additional Topics

Equity isn't this pile of money sitting somewhere; it's an accounting construct.
—Bethany McLean, journalist (known for her writing on the Enron scandal)

Having addressed the basics of financial accounting mechanics, we can now pay attention to some additional topics, such as the accrual principle or depreciation.

4.1 Ethan and Ryan's New Firm

We will make use of a new, slightly more involved, example.

> **Exercise**
> **Ethan and Ryan's New Firm, part 1 of 2** (facts from January 2 to January 8)
>
> On January 2, Ethan and his friend Ryan started their own business importing widgets from Germany to sell in the United States. The widgets had been successfully launched in Germany the previous year, which made Ethan and Ryan think theirs was a sound business concept.
>
> 1. On January 2, Ethan and Ryan made a deposit in a bank account to start the business, $20,000 each.
> 2. On January 3, they rented a store for the following three months. They paid the rent upfront, $12,000 for three months.
> 3. On the same day, a $24,000 loan was taken out from a local bank, with a 10 percent annual interest rate. It was a short-term loan agreement of only six months.
> 4. On January 4, they bought equipment necessary to run the business. They paid $20,000 cash. Ryan estimated the life of the equipment to be approximately three years.

5. On January 6, the first batch of widgets was bought. The cost was $70,000; only $22,000 was paid in cash.

6. On January 7, $10,000 worth of defective units were returned to the supplier, who agreed to take the parts back.

7. On January 8, the store opened for business.

4.1.1 Recording the Firm's Events until January 8

We will go through all seven events paying special attention to those that introduce new concepts.

? Event 1

On January 2, Ethan and Ryan made a deposit in a bank account to start the business, $20,000 each.

To start with, $40,000 simply go from Ethan and Ryan's pockets to the firm's cash box.

? Event 2

On January 3, they rented a store for the following three months. They paid the rent upfront, $12,000 for three months.

In this case, money comes clearly from cash ($12,000); but:

What do we do with the money? What should be the counterpart of the cash account decrease? Ethan and Ryan have just signed an agreement with the owner of the store, thus they have a white paper (a contract) with a value of $12,000 to the firm. The firm has bought *the right* to use the store. This right is something valuable ($12,000) that the firm owns. Therefore, we need a new account on the assets side to acknowledge this fact. We will name this account prepaid expenses.

Are shareholders happier or sadder? Some money has gone, which makes them sadder; but the contract, worth $12,000, gives the firm the right to use the store for three months, which makes them happier. Overall, shareholders are even *as of today*—that is, right after signing the contract. However, *as time goes by*, they will become sadder, due to the expiration date of the contract getting closer and closer. But note that what makes them sadder is not the fact that the money has been outlaid but the fact that the value of the contract decreases as time goes by. This is the basis of the so called accrual principle. *Accrual* comes from Latin *accrescere*, which means "grow progressively, increase, become greater." In this case, the expired portion of the right to use the store increases continuously as time goes by.

 Accrual principle

The **accrual principle** is a generalized accounting practice that records events as they occur over time, not when cash is paid.

Therefore, strictly speaking, the contract should be losing value to the firm *at a constant rate*, and it should be acknowledged in the books as such. Admittedly, this would be a nightmare for accountants, who would have to update the books every single minute! As this is not feasible, accountants resort to discretizing time in buckets, typically of one-month length. At the end of the month, they look at everything that should have happened during the month at a continuous rate and update the firm records accordingly at once. For instance, figure 4.1 shows the actual and book values of the renting contract as time goes by.

 Accrual principle is *not* about changing cash

In accordance with the accrual principle, what makes shareholders sadder is *not* the fact that the money has been outlaid but the fact that the value of an asset decreases—or the value of a liability increases—as time goes by.

Actual value [$k]   Book value [$k]

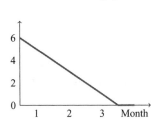 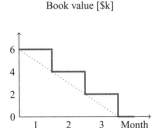

Figure 4.1
In accordance with the accounting criterion, the value of the renting contract would theoretically decrease at a constant rate over time (left). However, monthly buckets used by accountants convert the straight line into a staircase function (right).

❓ Event 3

On the same day, a $24,000 loan was taken out from a local bank, with a 10 percent annual interest rate. It was a short-term loan agreement of only six months.

We are dealing with banks for the first time. Getting money (a loan) from a bank is an advantage, because funds may not be available to run the business otherwise. But the process is not automatic. In fact, Debbie, the branch manager, will ask Ethan and Ryan a good number of questions, will analyze several financial ratios (e.g., see section 9.2), and will perform some cash projections before the loan gets eventually approved. Also, as one would expect, getting money from a bank (or, in general, a debt holder) comes at a cost, as not only the money borrowed, called the principal, has to be returned to the bank sooner or later but also some additional money, called the interest, is charged by the bank for the firm having the right to enjoy the loan for a specific period of time.

For instance, if an annual 10 percent interest is charged on a $24,000 loan signed at the beginning of the year, $2,400 will have to be paid to the bank as interest at the end of year, assuming that the principal ($24,000) has not been returned yet.

 Principal

The **principal** of a loan is the money borrowed by a firm from a bank (or, in general, a debt holder). As such, the principal is owned by the bank, not by the firm. The firm enjoys using the bank's money for a period of time.

 Interest

The **interest** of a loan is the money that a firm has to pay a bank (or, in general, a debt holder) for enjoying using the bank's money (the principal) for a period of time.

In our example, as far as event 3 is concerned:

Where does the money come from?   It comes from a bank. Therefore we need an account on the equities side, which we will call debt, to acknowledge the fact that the firm owes $24,000 to the bank. (Remember, it is the bank's money!)

What do we do with that money?   As of today, we just put it in the money box (figure 4.2).

Are Ethan and Ryan happier or sadder?   Right after obtaining the loan, they are even. They are not happier, despite the fact that the firm has more money in the money box, because they have an obligation to repay that money to the bank, which makes up for it. They are not sadder as a result of having to pay interest to the bank, because that obligation has not been born yet. It will be born over time. And given the time buckets that accountants

Assets				Equities			
Cash		Prepaid expenses		Equity		Debt	
40,000	12,000	12,000			40,000		24,000
24,000							

Figure 4.2
The general ledger of the firm after event 3.

use, it will be acknowledged in the books after one month. (We have to remember to take note of interest at the end of January.) Finally:

Is it relevant that the loan is expected to be returned in six months?   Accounting is not concerned with that, as this is a potential future event and accounting is only concerned with the past and the present, not the future.

? Event 4

On January 4, they bought equipment necessary to run the business. They paid $20,000 cash. Ryan estimated the life of the equipment to be approximately three years.

When equipment is bought (remember the laptop from the last example) money is deducted from cash, and fixed assets increase by the same amount.

What about Ryan's estimate about life expectancy of the equipment? What do we have to do about it?   We can assume that after three years the value of the equipment will be zero. Therefore, the equipment value will decrease over time, but, as of today, we do not have to care about it. Again, at the end of the month, we have to remember to do something about it.

? Event 5

On January 6, The first batch of widgets was bought. The cost was $70,000; only $22,000 was paid in cash.

Ethan and Ryan buy widgets to sell them in the market, thus widgets become inventory in the firm's books. We deduct $22,000 from cash, increase the value of inventory by $70,000, and acknowledge that the firm owes the unpaid portion to the supplier in accounts payable—$48,000.

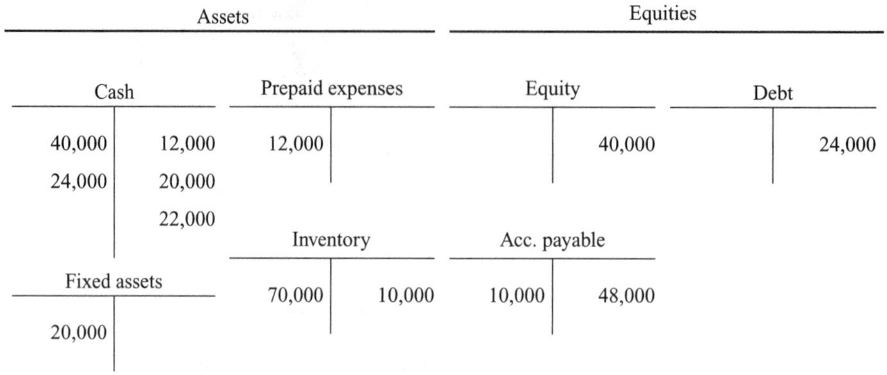

Chapter 4

Assets				Equities			
Cash		**Prepaid expenses**		**Equity**		**Debt**	
40,000	12,000	12,000			40,000		24,000
24,000	20,000						
	22,000						
		Inventory		**Acc. payable**			
Fixed assets		70,000	10,000	10,000	48,000		
20,000							

Figure 4.3
The general ledger of the firm after event 7.

? Event 6

On January 7, $10,000 worth of defective units were returned to the supplier, who agreed to take the parts back.

In this case, we deduct $10,000 from inventory and cancel a portion of accounts payable (figure 4.3).

? Event 7

On January 8, the store opened for business.

Well, this piece of information does not contain any monetary values, therefore accounting is not concerned about it.

4.1.2 Preparing the Balance Sheet as of January 8

At this intermediary point, as we are done with preparations, we can ask again:

How well has the business done so far? Despite everything that happened during the first week of January, and following the accounting criterion, Ethan and Ryan's happiness did not change at all. In fact, the revenue and expense account remains untouched. Therefore, in order to prepare the balance sheet, we don't even have to consider it. Table 4.1 shows the balance sheet of the firm as of January 8.

Table 4.1
Balance sheet as of January 8.

Cash	10,000	Accounts payable	38,000
Prepaid expenses	12,000	Debt	24,000
Inventory	60,000	Equity	40,000
Fixed assets	20,000		
Total assets	**102,000**	**Total equities**	**102,000**

As of now, the firm owns a stock of green notes (cash), a stock of white notes (prepaid expenses), a stock of inventory, and some fixed assets. Also, it owes money to suppliers (accounts payable), banks (debt), and shareholders (equity).

On the equities side, there is a key difference between the first two accounts, payables and debt, and the third one, equity: Payables and debt have to be paid to suppliers and banks respectively on the due date. However, equity doesn't have to be paid to shareholders on any specific date; there is not even the concept of equity due date. To reinforce this point, the first two accounts are encompassed within the concept of liabilities, so that we can write the accounting identity as follows:

$$\text{assets} = \text{liabilites} + \text{equity}$$

The word *liability* comes from French *lier*, to bind, ultimately from Latin *ligare*, as in *ligament*. Liability is the ability to be bound or obliged (by law) to pay the money owed to outside creditors—such as suppliers, employees, governments, or banks—on the due date.

 Liabilities

> **Liabilities** is the total amount of money that the firm has to pay creditors—such as suppliers, employees, governments, or banks—on any given due date. It does not include equity.

Once preparations are done, the second part of the exercise describes the firm's relevant events to the end of the month.

> **Exercise**
> **Ethan and Ryan's New Firm, part 2 of 2** (facts from January 9 to January 31)
>
> 8. On January 9 a student was hired to be in charge of the store. She started working on January 10; her salary was $3,200 per month.
> 9. Sales during the month amounted to $100,000; 80 percent of that amount was cash from customers. The acquisition cost of the sold units was $60,000.

10. A payment of $28,000 was made to the supplier.

11. The firm collected $12,000 from customers (out of $20,000). The remaining amount was expected to be collected the following month.

12. On January 31, the student worker received $2,000. The firm still owed her $200.

13. On January 30, a second batch of widgets was bought on account. The cost was $40,000.

14. On January 31, Ethan received a call from an important retailer, who showed interest in buying a large number of widgets on a regular basis.

15. January utilities totaled $700, paid for in cash within the month.

16. Due to a glitch in the bank system, the firm couldn't pay the loan interest on January 31.

17. On January 31, the firm acknowledged the expense of the rent for January in the books.

18. The same day, half of the loan principal was repaid.

4.1.3   Recording the Firm's Events until January 31

? Event 8

On January 9, a student was hired to be in charge of the store. She started working on January 10; her salary was $3,200 per month.

No action is needed at this time. The fact that the student starts working does not impact the accounting records yet. No money has been paid to her yet and her salary has not been accrued yet. Only as time goes by, Ethan and Ryan will be sadder because the obligation to pay her will steadily increase. Once again, we will deal with the student's salary at the end of the month.

? Event 9

Sales during the month amounted to $100,000; 80 percent of that amount was cash from customers. The acquisition cost of the sold units was $60,000.

This time, selling has an impact on four accounts as follows:

(1) Inventory decreases by $60,000.

(2) Cash increases by $80,000 (80 percent of $100,000).

(3) Accounts receivable go up $20,000 (the difference between $100,000 and $80,000).

(4) Ethan and Ryan's happiness go up due to sales ($100,000) and down due to COGS ($60,000).

? Event 10

A payment of $28,000 was made to the supplier.

Cash decreases by $28,000 and payables decrease by the same amount.

? Event 11

The firm collected $12,000 from customers (out of $20,000). The remaining amount was expected to be collected the following month.

Accounts receivable go down by $12,000 and cash increases by the same amount (figure 4.4).

? Event 12

On January 31st, the student received $2,000. The firm still owed her $200.

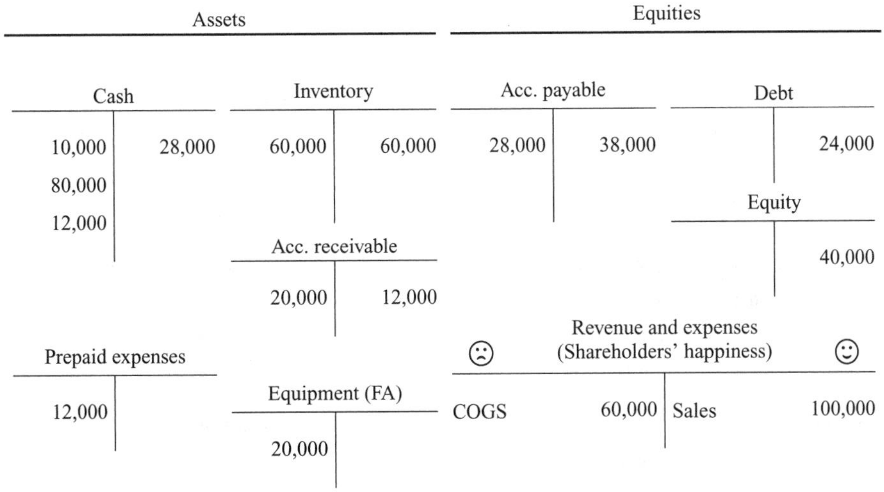

Assets				Equities			

Cash		Inventory		Acc. payable		Debt	
10,000	28,000	60,000	60,000	28,000	38,000		24,000
80,000							
12,000						Equity	
		Acc. receivable					40,000
		20,000	12,000				

Prepaid expenses				Revenue and expenses (Shareholders' happiness)			
12,000		Equipment (FA)		☹ COGS	60,000	Sales ☺	100,000
		20,000					

Figure 4.4
General ledger of the firm after event 11.

This one may be tricky. First, note that the student has worked for twenty-two days, so she roughly deserves $\frac{2}{3}$ of the month's salary, or approximately $2,200. We know cash decreases by $2,000, as that is the money that the student has actually received.

What to do with the unpaid portion ($200)?   This situation is equivalent to the one we had in our first example (Sharon the Shareholder) the first time we bought books from the supplier. In this case, the student is lending the firm some money for free, exactly as the book store manager in Sharon the Shareholder. Therefore, a conceptually correct answer would be to put that $200 into additional accounts payable. But accountants like to have separate accounts—not a big surprise anymore, thus an additional account is opened on the equities side: Accrued, not paid. Why this name? Time passed, so the firm has already the obligation to pay the student, but it has not paid her yet.

How much sadder are Ethan and Ryan? $2,000 or $2,200?   The answer is $2,200, because all that amount has been accrued due to time going by. As a result, we have to increase Ethan and Ryan's sadness by $2,200 in the revenue and expense account.

? Event 13

On January 30, a second batch of widgets was bought on account. The cost was $40,000.

Accounts payable increase by $40,000 and inventory increases by the same amount.

? Event 14

On January 31, Ethan received a call from an important retailer, who showed interest in buying a large number of widgets on a regular basis.

There is nothing to record at this point. So:

Why is event 14 relevant? Are Ethan and Ryan happier or sadder after the customer's call?   Following the accounting criterion, they are even, as no additional sales (hence profits) have been realized yet. However, if Ethan and Ryan sold their shares after event 14, they would most likely get a much higher price for them than before event 14.

Why is that?   The market value of the shares has significantly increased given the promise of future cash flows. However, note that accounting cannot tell us anything about the future; it can only deal with the past and the present. Therefore, the book value of shares has not changed as far as event 14 is concerned.

? Event 15

January utilities totaled $700, paid for in cash within the month.

Having spent money on utilities during the month has a cost, which makes Ethan and Ryan sadder. Consequently, we deduct $700 from cash and increase expenses (same amount) in the revenue and expense account. This cost is not part of the cost of goods sold but a general expense. Accountants put these costs together under the SGA category. SGA stands for selling, general, and administrative expenses.

 SGA expenses

SGA expenses is the short name given to selling, general, and administrative expenses. It includes items such as rent, utilities, telephone, insurance, advertising, travel expenses, and some of the firm's salaries.

? Event 16

Due to a glitch in the bank system, the firm couldn't pay the loan interest on January 31.

Given that the firm did not pay any interests to the bank:

Are Ethan and Ryan happier or sadder?   They are actually sadder. Again, it does not matter whether the payment actually occurred or not. What is relevant is that time went by while the firm was using the bank's money. Therefore, we have to acknowledge the obligation to pay that already exists (interest expenses) in the revenue and expense account, even if the firm has not paid for them yet. Now:

How do we acknowledge the fact that the firm has not paid yet?   Like the case of the money owed to the student, this is a case of accrued, not-paid expenses, which we will put in the equities.[1] Finally:

How much money is involved?   Since twenty-eight days went by since the day the loan was taken, interest expenses can be approximately calculated as:

$$\$24,000 \cdot 10\% \cdot \frac{31-3}{365} \approx \$184$$

---

1. We are assuming here that the interest expenses were not paid because the bank was not able to receive the money (a glitch in the bank information system that prevented customers from paying). Therefore, there is no obligation to pay additional interests on the interests already accrued.

Assets

Cash

10,000	28,000
80,000	2,000
12,000	700

Inventory

60,000	60,000
40,000	

Acc. receivable

20,000	12,000

Prepaid expenses

12,000	

Equipment (FA)

20,000	

Equities

Acc. payable

28,000	38,000
	40,000

Accrued not paid

	200
	184

Debt

	24,000

Equity

	40,000

Revenue and expenses
(Shareholders' happiness)   ☹   ☺

COGS	60,000	Sales	100,000
SGA-Salary	2,200		
SGA-Utilities	700		
Interest	184		

Figure 4.5
General ledger of the firm after event 16.

The actual calculations may vary a bit (sometimes banks assume that a year has 360 days!) but the logic is correct in either case (figure 4.5).

 Event 17

On January 31, the firm acknowledged the expense of the rent for January in the books.

Remember that the firm paid $12,000 in advance to rent the store. Now after one month, and given the fact that accountants work with monthly buckets, it is time to acknowledge that Ethan and Ryan are sadder because the firm has enjoyed the use of the store in January. Hence, we deduct $4,000 from prepaid expenses and acknowledge a $4,000 expense (part of SGA) in the revenue and expense account.

Event 18

The same day, half of the loan principal was repaid.

Finally, to repay half of the outstanding debt, we deduct $12,000 from cash and reduce the debt account by the same amount. Are Ethan and Ryan happier or sadder as a result of event 18? They are even, because the money repaid has always belonged to the bank.

Are we done yet?   Almost there: we still have to adjust the value of the equipment that Ethan and Ryan bought. The rationale is that equipment, and in general, fixed assets—except for land, lose part of their value as time goes by.

This process is called depreciation by accountants, from Latin *de* (down) and *pretium* (price). Sometimes you will see the word *amortization* to refer to the depreciation of intangible assets, such as software. *Amortization* comes from Latin *ad* (toward) and *mors* (death), as fixed assets move "toward their death" as time goes by. We will use the term *depreciation* to refer to both depreciation and amortization.

 Depreciation

Depreciation is the loss of (book) value of a fixed asset over time. Depreciation makes shareholders sadder, although it does not involve any cash disbursements.

Remember that in our example the price paid for the equipment was $20,000. We can assume that the value of the equipment in thirty-six months (three years) will be zero. This gives us two points (P and Q) in panel A of figure 4.6.

How do we go from point P to point Q in figure 4.6?   A natural way to do it is through a straight line; that is to say, diminishing the value of the equipment at a constant rate, as in Panel B.[2] This method is called, logically, straight-line depreciation. However, the straight line in panel B of figure 4.6 is in practice distorted by accountants due to the monthly time buckets. Once time is discretized, the straight line ends up being a staircase (panel C).

What should be the equipment value deducted per month?   We can use the following expression for straight-line depreciation:

$$\downarrow \text{value per month} = \frac{\text{acquisition cost} - \text{residual value}}{\text{number of months}}$$

where the residual value is the management estimate for the value of the asset at the end of its life or at the end of a project where the asset will not be needed any more. Residual value can be positive—if we plan to sell it in the secondary market, for instance; zero—in most of the cases; and even negative—when getting rid of the asset costs money, for instance because of environmental issues.

---

2. Other methods exist, such as accelerated depreciation, in which equipment—depreciates more during the first periods.

A. Initial and ending points

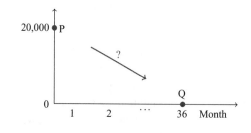

B. Market value [$]

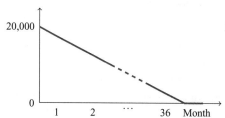

C. Book value [$]

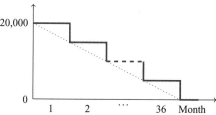

Figure 4.6
Building the logic of straight-line depreciation.

Assets	Equities

Equipment (FA)

| 20,000 | 556 |

Figure 4.7
A too-simple solution for accountants regarding depreciation.

 Residual value

The **residual value**, or salvage value, is the remaining market value of an asset at the
end of its useful life.

In our case, we assumed equipment residual value to be zero, hence:

$$\downarrow \text{equipment value} = \frac{\$20,000 - 0}{36} \approx \$556 \text{ per month}$$

As this is the loss of value of equipment during January, we could possibly deduct this
amount from the fixed assets account (see detail in figure 4.7) and increase shareholders'
sadness in the revenue and expenses account.

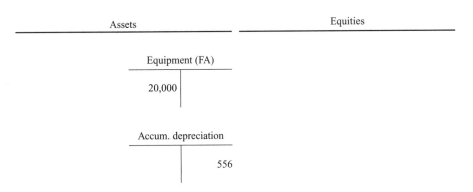

Figure 4.8
The accountants' approach regarding depreciation.

However, guess what? Intricate accountants would never do that. They split this information into two accounts—the second of which is called accumulated depreciation (figure 4.8). By doing this, it is possible to keep track of the original cost of fixed assets (figure 4.9).

Note that the account accumulated depreciation should not be considered in isolation—it wouldn't make sense to deduct value from an empty account—but together with equipment. These accounts (e.g., accumulated depreciation) are usually called contra accounts. Accountants distinguish gross fixed assets (fixed assets if depreciation did not exist) and net fixed assets (deducting accumulated depreciation from gross fixed assets). Fixed assets and net fixed assets can be used interchangeably. Mathematically,

gross fixed assets = (net) fixed assets + depreciation

 Gross fixed assets

  Gross fixed assets is the original value of fixed assets at the time of acquisition. In other words, the book value they would have if they never depreciated.

4.1.4 Preparing the Balance Sheet as of January 31

Having recorded all relevant events, we proceed to prepare the balance sheet at the end of January. Remember that the first step should be to close the revenue and expense account. We have $32,360 on that account:

$100,000 − $60,000 − $2,200 − $700 − $184 − $4,000 − $556 = $32,360

So we close it by adding $32,360 to the left (Income summary) and move that amount to retained earnings. Table 4.2 shows the balance sheet at the end of January after calculating the value of current stock of the remaining accounts.

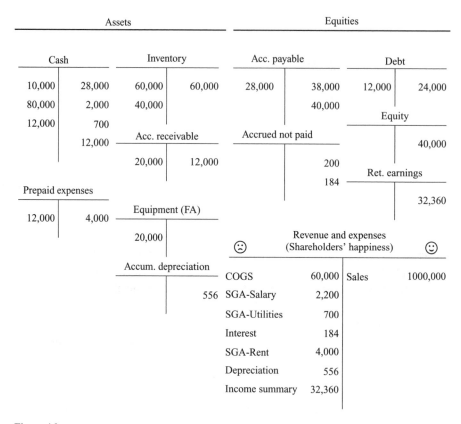

Figure 4.9
General ledger of the firm at the end of January.

Something comforting about financial accounting is that you can always verify if you did the annotations and calculations correctly through checking whether or not the identity assets = equities holds.

4.2   The Seven-Item Balance Sheet

A good characteristic of the last balance sheet in the previous section is that it only has ten accounts. That makes it easy to read and understand.

In real life, balance sheets and, in general, financial statements of large corporations may have dozens, if not hundreds of accounts. These corporations, especially if they are public (i.e., if you can buy a portion of its shares and become a shareholder), release an annual document, usually called the annual report, where relevant information—financial for the most part—of the corporation during the previous period is given. As table 4.3 shows, these documents are usually long, which might make them a bit tedious or difficult to read.

Table 4.2
Balance sheet as of June 30.

Cash	59,300	Accounts payable	50,000
Accounts receivable	8,000	Accrued not paid	384
Prepaid expenses	8,000	Debt	12,000
Inventory	40,000	Equity (common stock)	40,000
Fixed assets	19,444	Retained earnings	32,360
Total assets	**134,744**	**Total equities**	**134,744**

Table 4.3
Annual report statistics for selected corporations.

	Annual report #pages	Balance sheet #accounts
Apple	94	21
Ford	162	22
Inditex	321	25
Siemens	372	34
Walmart	62	28
Average	**202**	**26**

Source: Last published annual report in the corresponding firm website as of March 2018.

Aware of this fact, corporations usually offer abridged versions of their financial statements, typically called consolidated financial statements. An abridged balance sheet may well have twenty-five accounts or so (table 4.3). Twenty-five accounts is indeed a huge improvement in comparison to hundreds, but they can be further reduced for an operations management audience as they needn't understand every single detail.

One of the problems faced by many operations professionals is that they do not know how to interpret intricate balance sheets correctly. Hence the need arises for a much simpler version of the balance sheet containing the information essentials, the bigger picture, which is usually enough.

In 2014, we gave a talk to the supply chain team of a major multinational European retailer, including some C-level participants. As part of our presentation, we showed them their firm's financial statements, not in their original form as they appeared in the annual report but condensed as much as possible. Some of them were thrilled to be able to (finally!) understand the bigger picture of the financial situation of their company. That is how the seven-item balance sheet concept (and later the triple-seven-item financial statements concept—see appendix A) came to us. Therefore, from now on, and as far as possible, we will deal with the seven-item balance sheet, an abridged version of the balance sheet with four assets accounts—cash[+], accounts receivable[+], inventory, and fixed assets—and three equities accounts—accounts payable[+], debt, and equity (figure 4.10).

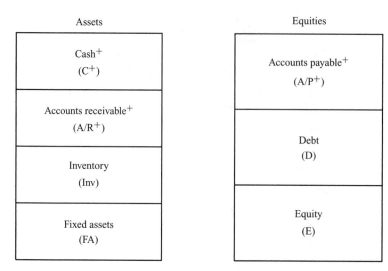

Figure 4.10
The seven-item balance sheet.

The four accounts in the assets side are as follows:

(1) Cash$^+$ (note the plus superscript) is the money available in the firm's cash box, but it also includes investments with very short maturity dates (typically days, weeks, or months) that firms use to improve the yield rate on deposits. These investments appear in the balance sheet as cash equivalent or short-term investments. Both accounts can be merged into just one extended cash account—denoted cash$^+$—as follows:

$$\text{cash}^+ = \text{cash} + \text{cash equivalents} + \text{short-term investment}$$

(2) Accounts receivable$^+$ is a stock of documents that represent the money owed to the firm by customers, but this notion can be extended to other white papers, such as prepaid expenses. We will define:

$$\text{accounts receivable}^+ = \text{accounts receivable} + \text{other white papers}$$

A point in case is that of provisions. Provisions are amounts set aside out of profits for a potential liability—whose specific amount is not know—or for the reduction in value of an asset. For instance, in the case of asset provisions, allowance for doubtful accounts (or provisions for doubtful debts) is an asset account that holds debts from customers that won't be paid with high probability. This account is the contra-asset of accounts receivable (see exercise below). Therefore, as far as allowance for doubtful accounts is concerned, we can write:

$$\text{accounts receivable}^+ = \text{accounts receivable} - \text{allowance for doubtful accounts}$$

Provision

A **provision** is an amount set aside out of profits for a potential liability—whose specific amount is not know—or for the reduction in value of an asset. Provisions may appear on the assets side (e.g., allowance for doubtful accounts) or on the equities side.

(3) Inventory is the value of merchandise in the firm, valued at acquisition cost.

(4) Fixed assets are assets necessary to conduct the business, such as buildings or machines; they typically last several years and are not acquired to be sold to customers.

The three accounts on the equities side are as follows:

(1) Accounts payable$^+$ is a stock of documents that represent the money owed to suppliers by the firm but also other non-bearing-interest items, such as taxes or salaries accrued but not paid. We will define:

accounts payable$^+$ = accounts payable + other nonbearing-interest liabilities

(2) Debt is the money lent to the firm by debt holders, such as banks. It *always* entails paying interest to the lenders. That is the key difference with accounts payable$^+$.

(3) Equity is total equities less accounts payable$^+$ less debt. It can also be thought as the money shareholders would get if the firm's assets were sold at their current book value after repaying suppliers and debt holders. Equity also includes the retained earnings that a firm accumulates over time. To distinguish the equity that comes from shareholders' pockets from the equity that generates through the business' profits (retained earnings), the former is usually referred to as common stock. We will avoid these names for the most part, as we are not concerned with the various categories within shareholders' equity.

Although these definitions may sound strange or artificial to financiers, it enhances enormously the ability of nonfinancial managers to grasp the firm's bigger picture at a glance. Furthermore, for retailers or industrial firms, odds are high that the total amount in these seven accounts make up at least 90 percent of the total amount of all accounts of the complete balance sheet.

 The seven-item balance sheet

The **seven-item balance sheet** is an abridged version of the balance sheet composed of only seven accounts, four on the assets side—cash$^+$, receivables$^+$, inventory, and fixed assets—and three on the equities side—payables$^+$, debt, and equity.

For instance, Ethan and Ryan's new firm's extended seven-item balance sheet is shown in table 4.4.

Table 4.4
The seven-item balance sheet as of June 30.

Cash	59,300	Accounts payable+	50,384
Accounts receivable+	16,000	Debt	12,000
Inventory	40,000	Equity	72,360
Fixed assets	19,444		
Total assets	**134,744**	**Total equities**	**134,744**

Assets	Equities
Green papers	Money owed to Susan the supplier
White papers	Money owed to Debbie the debt holder
Stuff that the firm usually sells	Money owed to Sharon the shareholder
Stuff that the firm doesn't usually sell	

Figure 4.11
The informal seven-item balance sheet.

Finally, we can leverage on the previous examples to obtain a less formal, more intuitive pictorial representation of the seven-item balance sheet, which may be useful to gain intuition on the elements of the balance sheet (figure 4.11).

 Exercise

Asset Provisions at Sell&Forget

Sell&Forget is a retailer that sells its cheap products on account to thousands of customers every month. Its collection policy is quite lax, which leads to a relatively large percentage of customers defaulting on their payments. Record the following facts in the firm's books:

1. Sales in May totaled $800,000. Based on historical records from the firm, 5 percent of that amount is expected not be paid by customers.
2. Some customers defaulted on their payments at $24,000.
3. Later on, a collection agency was able to collect $10,000 (out of $24,000).

? Event 1

Sales in May totaled $800,000. Based on historical records from the firm, 5 percent of that amount is expected not be paid by customers.

We first record sales on account as usual: $800,000 as sales in the revenue and expenses account and $800,000 in accounts receivable. Now, 5 percent of $800,000 is $40,000. Even if we don't know which customers will later default, we already know (with high probability) that some of customers will never pay, which make shareholders sad. Therefore, we increase expenses by $40,000 as bad debt expense and increase allowance for doubtful accounts by the same amount. Exactly as with depreciation or any other contra account, increasing allowance for doubtful accounts is annotated on the right side of the account (figure 4.12).

? Event 2

Some customers defaulted on their payments at $24,000.

At some point, we will find out that some customers are not planning to pay, then we remove $24,000 from receivables and adjust allowance for doubtful accounts accordingly.

? Event 3

Later on, a collection agency was able to collect $10,000 (out of $24,000).

Assets				Equities			
Acc. receivable		Allowance for doubtful accounts		☹	Revenue and expenses (Shareholders' happiness)		☺
800	24	24	40	Bad debt expense	40	Sales	800
10			10				

Figure 4.12
Annotations in the general ledger at Sell&Collect (in thousands).

Table 4.5
Consolidated balance sheet of Amazon.com, Inc. (US$ millions).

	2016	2017
Assets		
Cash and cash equivalents	19,334	20,522
Marketable securities	6,647	10,464
Inventories	11,461	16,047
Accounts receivable, net and other	8,339	13,164
Total current assets	45,781	60,197
Property and equipment, net	29,114	48,866
Goodwill	3,784	13,350
Other assets	4,723	8,897
Total assets	83,402	131,310
Liabilities and stockholders' equity (i.e., equities)		
Accounts payable	25,309	34,616
Accrued expenses and other	3,739	18,170
Unearned revenue	4,768	5,097
Total current liabilities	43,816	57,883
Long-term debt	7,694	24,743
Other long-term liabilities	12,607	20,975
Total stockholders' equity	19,285	27,709
Total liabilities and stockholders' equity	83,402	131,310

We just revert what we did in the previous item by increasing receivables by $10,000 and adjusting allowance for doubtful accounts. Figure 4.12 shows all annotations made.

4.3   Understanding Amazon's Balance Sheet

Having presented the seven-item balance sheet, in this section we will convert the consolidated balance sheet of a well-known e-retailer, Amazon.com, Inc., into a seven-item balance sheet. The consolidated balance sheet of Amazon.com, Inc. is shown in table 4.5.[3]

We will associate each account in Amazon's report to each of the seven accounts. Let's go through the list of accounts on the assets side:

Cash and cash equivalents These both belong to cash$^+$.

Marketable securities This is a new term to us. To know under which category it is, we read the accompanying notes in the annual report: "We generally invest our excess cash in investment grade short-to intermediate-term fixed income securities and AAA-rated money market funds. Such investments are included in Cash and cash equivalents or Marketable

---

3. Amazon 2017, p. 48.

securities on the accompanying consolidated balance sheets, classified as available for sale, and reported at fair value with unrealized gains and losses included in Accumulated other comprehensive loss" (Amazon 2017, 48).

Therefore, marketable securities are also short-term investment, so it should be part of $cash^+$ as well.

Then we have for 2017 (in US$ millions):

$cash^+ = $ cash and cash equivalents $+$ marketable securities $=$

$$= 20,522 + 10,464 = 30,986, \text{ certainly a huge pile of cash!}$$

Inventories The inventories total 16,047. It is interesting to observe that the natural sequence of accounts in the balance sheet, which is based on liquidity—cash—accounts receivable—inventory—fixed assets, has been altered in this case.

Accounts receivable, net and other These make up accounts receivable$^+$.

After going through the accounts in current assets, we take care of the fixed assets.

Property and equipment, net This includes tangible fixed assets such as buildings, land, distribution centers, machinery, vehicles, and furniture.

Goodwill Goodwill usually arises when a firm (say firm A) buys another firm (B) for a price higher than firm B's equity. That creates a contradiction in the accounting world: the value of the asset bought (firm B) is its book value (i.e., its equity); however, the acquisition cost is the actual price paid by firm A. Accounting solves this contradiction by resorting to goodwill, an artificial account that appears in firm A's fixed assets and takes care of the difference between firm B's equity and the actual price paid.

Other assets The other assets must be fixed assets as well, as they are not included in the current assets category.

Therefore (in US$ millions),

fixed assets $=$ property and equipment, net$+$

$$+ \text{ goodwill} + \text{other assets}$$

$$= 48,866 + 13,350 + 8,897 = 71,113$$

As for equities:

Accounts payable Accounts payable are part of accounts payable$^+$.

Accrued expenses and other These can potentially be part of accounts payable$^+$ or debt. The key question is if these accrued expenses imply paying a financial burden, such as interest. To find out, we look at the annual report (Amazon 2017, p. 48): "Included in, Accrued expenses and other, on our consolidated balance sheets are liabilities primarily related to unredeemed gift cards, leases and asset retirement obligations, current debt, acquired digital media content, and other operating expenses."

These items entail no financial burden (with the exception of current debt, which we will ignore, given that no information is provided and we will assume it is small) and will be considered in accounts payable$^+$.

Unearned revenue This is "recorded when payments are received in advance of performing our service obligations and is recognized over the service period. Unearned revenue primarily relates to prepayments of Amazon Prime memberships and AWS services" (Amazon 2017, 48). Therefore, no interest to be paid on this, as this is money lended by customers for free.

Current liabilities total:

$$\text{accounts payable}^+ = \text{accounts payable} + \text{accrued expenses and other}$$
$$+ \text{ unearned revenues}$$
$$= 34,616 + 18,170 + 5,097 = 57,883$$

As for long-term liabilities:

Long-term debt This is financial debt due in more than one year.

Other long-term liabilities These include some costly accounts that bear interest, mainly leasing contracts, and some free accounts that do not, mainly deferred taxes.

Then:

$$\text{debt} = \text{ long-term debt} + \text{other long-term liabilities (costly)}$$
$$= 24,743 + 20,975 = 45,718$$

Stockholders' equity A synonym for shareholders' equity, it includes six accounts whose detail may not be of interest to us.

Therefore, we can simply state that

$$\text{equity} = \text{total stockholders' equity} = 27,709$$

Having calculated the value of all relevant accounts, building the seven-item balance sheet is straightforward (figure 4.13).

Although we lose some information, the seven-item balance sheet shows the big picture of the firm, which will suffice for our purposes.

Furthermore, we can go one step beyond and (1) make the height of each account in figure 4.13 proportional to the amount it contains and (2) convert the figure into percentages (figure 4.14). By doing this, we do not even have to read the figures in the boxes to have a rough idea of the status of the firm. For instance, in the case of Amazon, we can see that two accounts, fixed assets and accounts payable, stand out from the rest. We can look at relative sizes of specific accounts, such as debt and equity, or cash and debt, or accounts payable and receivable, to obtain some preliminary conclusions about the firm.

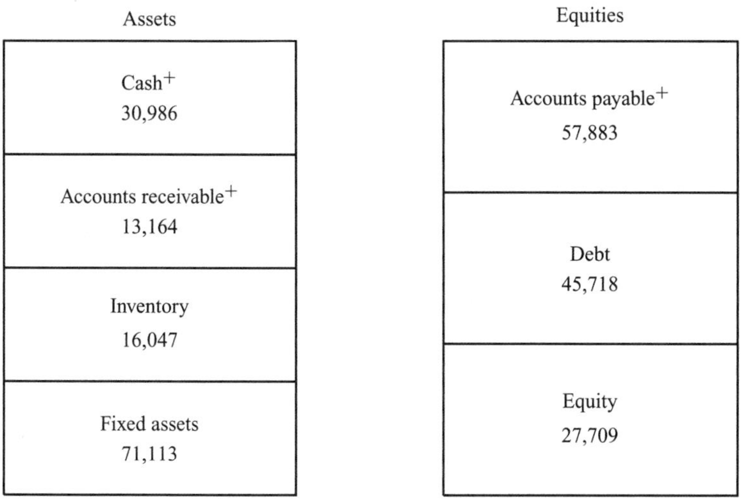

Figure 4.13
Amazon.com's 2017 seven-item balance sheet (US$ millions).

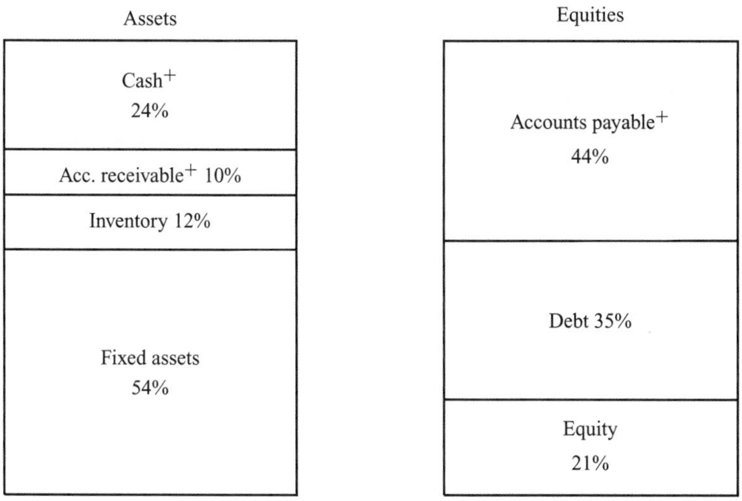

Figure 4.14
A more intuitive version of the balance sheet, where the account's height is proportional to the amount in it.

Of course, this rough-cut view can never substitute the thorough study of the financial analyst, but together with some financial ratios that we will cover in chapter 9 it may give enough information to understand where the firm stands and what its financial position is.

4.4 Summary

This chapter has presented further concepts regarding accounting mechanics, such as the accrual principle and depreciation. Also, in order for operations and supply chain managers to understand the sometimes involved balance sheets presented by firms in their annual reports, we propose the use of the seven-item balance sheet, an abridged version of the balance sheet that contains a summary of the most important accounts: cash$^+$, receivables$^+$, inventory and fixed assets on the assets side; and payables$^+$, debt, and equity on the equities side. This version of the balance sheet should facilitate the interpretation of the financial position of a firm to those managers not directly involved in the financial department of a firm.

Exercises

1. What are the elements of a seven-item balance sheet on the assets side? What about the equities side?

2. Which accounts of a seven-item balance sheet, if any, may be negative?

3. Calculate annual straight-line depreciation expense for a machine having a $135,000 acquisition cost, $15,000 estimated scrap value, and a six-year estimated life.

4. Some people claim that by increasing depreciation, firms may save corporate taxes. Do you agree? Why, or why not?

5. If the very same asset is depreciated by firm A in four years and by firm B in five years, either firm A or B are not following accounting best practices. Do you agree? Why, or why not?

6. What do liabilities and equity have in common? What is the key difference between them?

7. A machine has been depreciated on a straight-line basis for four years, assuming a six-year life and a 10 percent salvage value. Last year's depreciation adds up to $80,000. If the machine is sold at $100,000, how much more/less taxes will the firm have to pay this year compared to the case that the machine is not sold?

8. On September 1, Adolfo Banderas was working as an accountant for Life Is Wine Co. The firm had just received a new machine for labeling wine bottles that was supposed to start working in a couple of days.

    Please read the facts described below and help Adolfo to record the described events on the general ledger.

    1. On September, 1 Adolfo receives the invoice from the manufacturer of the machine. Information on the invoice includes:

- Price: $30,000
- Payments: 60 percent at delivery, 40 percent on October 30

2. The same day, Adolfo receives an e-mail from the production manager, Mr. Dislexis, with his best estimate for some of the parameters of the machine. The parameters are as follows:
   - Expected life of the machine: six years.
   - Scrap value: $5,000.
   - The machine is expected to start operating in a couple of days.

3. On Nov, 1 Adolfo receives another e-mail from Mr. Dislexis. The e-mail reads as follows:

   ```
   Hi Adolfo,
    I regret to inform you that the information I sent to you about the
   labeling machine was wrong. The right values are as follows.
   • Expected life of the machine: five years
   • Scrap value: $6,000
   Sorry about the inconvenience,
    Mr. Dislexis
   ```

4. During November, Mr. Dislexis happened to visit the packaging fair in Paris, where he found a faster and cheaper machine for labeling. He got so excited that he decided to buy it. Lead-time for delivery was one month, the price being $15,000. He was lucky to find someone willing to buy the old machine at $20,000. The agreement included that the old machine would be sent to the new owner on November 30 and he would be paid cash. Adolfo received this information the following day.

   a. Given facts 1 and 2, record all necessary transactions on the general ledger (use T-accounts) for September and October.

   b. Given fact 3, modify the general ledger taking into account the new information provided.

   c. Given fact 4, record all the transactions regarding the machines in the general ledger until November 30.

   d. For the three questions above, what accounting principles did you use when recording the transactions?

9. Do the Ethan and Ryan's new firm exercise on your own.

10. Calculate the level of interests accrued in a year if a loan of $200,000 is taken at the beginning of the year and $\frac{1}{4}$ of it is repaid on September 1. The cost of the debt is 12 percent per year.

11. What is the equivalent monthly rate to an annual rate of 24 percent?

   a. Using a simple interest approximation   b. Using exact compound interest

12. Explain how shareholders feel (happy, sad, even) as far as these transactions are concerned:

   a. A brand-new machine is bought for cash and installed in the factory.

   b. That machine is depreciated at the end of its first month of life.

   c. Interest is paid at due date.

   d. Corporate tax for the year that has just ended is not paid; it will be paid in three months.

   e. A loan is taken from a bank today.

13. In which of the items in the previous exercise does cash change? Do shareholders' happiness and cash move simultaneously (that is, shareholders are happy if cash increases and vice versa)?

14. How is accrual accounting different from cash accounting?

15. Which firm does better meet the prudence principle in each of the following situations?

   a. Firm A assumes fixed assets will last longer than firm B.

   b. Firm A assumes lower salvage values for fixed assets than firm B

   c. Firm A uses straight-line depreciation in contrast to firm B, which uses accelerated depreciation.

16. A machine was acquired three years ago at $850,000. Its life was estimated at five years, and its residual value after five years at $50,000.

   a. What is its current book value?

   b. If the machine is sold today at $250,000, what is the extraordinary profit/loss to be recorded in the revenue and expenses account?

Reference

Amazon. 2017. "Annual report 2017," p. 48. Accessed May 2019. https://ir.aboutamazon.com/annual-reports?c= 97664&p=irol-reportsannual.

5 Operating Working Capital

Beware of little expenses. A small leak will sink a great ship.
—Benjamin Franklin, American president

In this chapter, we will briefly digress from the main theme—the presentation of the three main financial statements—to present one of the essential elements of this book, namely the concept of operating working capital (OWC). OWC management is the core of task of any manager in the operations and supply chain realms. As we will see in various examples in chapter 15, most of the decisions made in the operations management sphere will have an impact on OWC. Therefore, grasping the meaning of and establishing an intuition for OWC will enormously facilitate the comprehension of important topics in subsequent chapters. In particular, it will be very useful when introducing the statement of cash flows in chapter 7.

5.1 Minimum Cash and Excess Cash

Before we present the definition and the idea behind OWC, we need to introduce two new concepts, minimum cash and excess cash.

Minimum cash Every firm needs a minimum level of cash to conduct business. This minimum cash level ensures that the firm can pay its suppliers and its workers' payroll on time. This level of cash is required, in the sense that going below that level would generate harmful cash tensions in the firm. The level of required cash mainly depends on the industry uncertainty and the firm's business model. The firm's treasurer is the person who forecasts how the actual level of cash will evolve over time and will take action to anticipate those changes whenever possible so that the firm can meet its payment commitments on time. Firms operating in uncertain environments will need more cash (safety cash). Uncertainty may come from customers' demand, evolving technology, patent resolution, customers' willingness to pay, macroeconomic circumstances, political instability, and so on. Also, the cash kept to anticipate possible unpredictable disruptions (strategic or risk mitigation cash) is also part of required cash (section 14.5 elaborates on this).

Excess cash The rest of cash in the cash and cash-like accounts is considered excess cash, which is the portion of cash not required to conduct business. Still, firms may want to keep cash because their owners are very conservative, for tax-saving purposes, or to keep the option of acquiring another firm in the future as part of the firm's long-term strategy.

It should be apparent that:

$$\text{cash}^+ = \text{minimum cash} + \text{excess cash}$$

Recall that the plus sign represents those accounts in the balance sheet that are not strictly cash, but are very liquid, such as short-term bank deposits.

 Minimum cash

> **Minimum cash** is the minimum amount of money required to run a firm's daily operations without liquidity tensions.

 Excess cash

> **Excess cash** is the extra cash or cash-like accounts a firm has in addition to minimum cash.

Assessing which portion of cash is minimum cash may be tricky. As a rule of thumb, a firm holding a significant amount of debt has no excess cash: it wouldn't make much sense to pay interest on a loan when you have idle cash generating lower yields than the cost of the loan. This is especially true in firms operating in developed countries with ample access to technology, which makes it possible to work with a minimum cash level close to zero. Assessing the portion of strategic cash is trickier, as it depends both on the industry risk and the firm's strategy. As a rule of thumb, strategic cash should grow, *ceteris paribus*, with the risk of the industry. If you want to find out the amount of strategic cash in your firm, you can ask your CFO. For other companies, you will probably need an educated guess. Why is it that Apple Computer keeps $75 billion in cash$^+$ (as of September 2017)? Not many firms in the world *sell* that much annually!

5.2   Operating Working Capital and the Financial Balance Sheet

Having defined minimum and excess cash, we are ready to define OWC. Simply speaking, operating working capital is defined as

$$\text{OWC} = \text{minimum cash} + \text{accounts receivable}^+ + \text{inventory} - \text{accounts payable}^+$$

At first glance, this may seem like a somewhat artificial definition. In order to understand why OWC is defined the way it is, consider its pictorial representation, together with other elements of the balance sheet in the case that the firm holds debt—and then excess cash is zero—in figure 5.1.

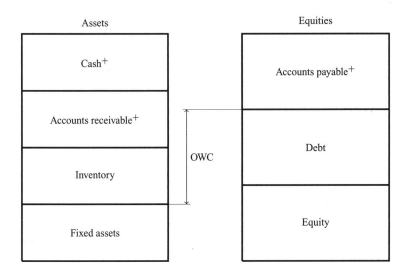

Figure 5.1
OWC and the seven-item balance sheet (excess cash is assumed to be zero).

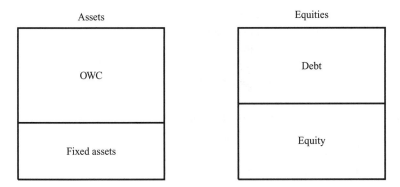

Figure 5.2
Financial balance sheet when excess cash is zero.

If we chop the balance sheet, removing accounts payable$^+$ and the corresponding portion of the assets from the standard balance sheet, we obtain a modified representation of the balance sheet, sometimes referred to as the financial balance sheet (figure 5.2).

What do both accounts in the equities side of the financial balance sheet have in common? It turns out that both come at a cost. Indeed, banks lend firms money because they expect future returns, namely interest. Likewise, shareholders invest money in firms because they expect future returns, namely dividends. Therefore both debt and equity come at a cost. In contrast, suppliers lend money to the firm for free, as no interest has to be paid to suppliers for paying them late. This may not be exact, as some suppliers offer customers early-payment discounts, de facto charging interest if customers do not benefit from those discounts. Also, suppliers may want to increase their prices to make up for the delay in the payments received from customers. Whether this occurs in reality or not is an open debate. We will hereby assume that suppliers lend money to customers for free, but we will discuss the case of costly trade credit in sections 14.3 and 14.4.

 Debt and equity are not free lunch

Holding debt and equity in the balance sheet comes at a cost, respectively, interest expenses and dividends.

 Operating working capital

Operating working capital (OWC) is the portion of assets necessary to run short-term operations that has to be financed at a cost. OWC is calculated as minimum cash plus accounts receivable$^+$ plus inventory less accounts payable$^+$.

Having said that, the financial balance sheet shows the portion of the assets that must be funded with costly funds. An important consequence is that OWC can be thought of as the portion of assets necessary to run short-term operations, such as buying and selling, *that has to be financed at a cost*, either from debt or equity.

Put differently, increasing OWC by one dollar on the assets side entails increasing the equities side by one dollar, either in debt, equity, or a combination of the two. In any of the three cases, the firm will have to pay banks, shareholders, or both to keep that extra dollar in place.

A useful relationship that comes directly from the financial balance sheet is:

$$OWC + \text{fixed assets} = \text{debt} + \text{equity}$$

If excess cash is not zero, the expression becomes:

$$\text{excess cash} + OWC + \text{fixed assets} = \text{debt} + \text{equity} \tag{5.1}$$

OWC includes two items that typically belong to operations management's direct responsibilities—inventory and payables—and two items that do not—minimum cash and receivables. Here we use the term *operating* in a broad sense, referring to the daily firm's operations of buying and selling, in contrast to long-term or structural financial decisions made by a firm.

The fact that holding operating working capital over time comes at a cost makes OWC a key element in operations management. In fact, managing OWC is the most important task for a firm's COO, with the exception of managing people. This is especially true for those firms holding significant amounts of inventory, such as manufacturers or retailers.

Chapter 14 and, to some extent, chapter 15 are devoted to illustrating how to effectively manage operating working capital.

On the importance of operating working capital

Managing OWC is the most important task for a firm's chief operations officer—with the exception of managing people—especially if the firm holds significant amounts of inventory.

Exercise

Calculating OWC at TooMuchLeverage Ltd.

TooMuchLeverage's balance sheet is shown below.

Assets		Equities	
Cash	$20,000	Accounts payable	$40,000
Accounts receivable	64,000	Other payables	25,000
Prepaid expenses	4,000	Debt	250,000
Inventory	200,000	Equity	123,000
Fixed assets	150,000		
Total assets	**438,000**	**Total equities**	**438,000**

Calculate TooMuchLeverage's current level of OWC.

Through a simple inspection of the balance sheet, we can assume that there is no excess cash, given the small amount of cash compared to the level of (financial) debt. OWC is then:

$$OWC = \text{minimum cash} + \text{accounts receivable}^{+} + \text{inventory} - \text{accounts payable}^{+}$$

$$= 20{,}000 + (64{,}000 + 4{,}000) + 200{,}000 - (40{,}000 + 25{,}000) = \$223{,}000$$

5.2.1 Discussion: OWC Behavior

Roughly speaking, OWC increases with sales. A mild assumption you can make is that OWC is a percentage of net sales. This is, of course, a simplification: as a firm grows larger, it may have more bargaining power to negotiate payment terms with suppliers, which increase payables and thereby reduces OWC. Also, all other things equal, well-managed inventory should grow less than sales, leading to some economies of scale, reducing the inventory-to-sales ratio (subsection 9.2.3.11 elaborates on this).

Table 5.1
Evolution of selected variables over the year (amounts in $'000 unless otherwise specified).

| | Leveled Ltd. | | | | | | | | | | | |
	Jan	Feb	Mar	Apr	May	Jun	Jul	Aug	Sep	Oct	Nov	Dec
Sales	0	0	0	0	0	0	0	0	300	300	300	300
Production (units)	100	100	100	100	100	100	100	100	100	100	100	100
Purchases	60	60	60	60	60	60	60	60	60	60	60	60
Payables (60 days)	120	120	120	120	120	120	120	120	120	120	120	120
Inventory	100	200	300	400	500	600	700	800	600	400	200	0
Receivables (30 days)	300	0	0	0	0	0	0	0	0	300	300	300

| | Chaser Ltd. | | | | | | | | | | | |
	Jan	Feb	Mar	Apr	May	Jun	Jul	Aug	Sep	Oct	Nov	Dec
Sales	0	0	0	0	0	0	0	0	300	300	300	300
Production (units)	0	0	0	0	0	0	0	300	300	300	300	0
Purchases	0	0	0	0	0	180	180	180	180	0	0	0
Payables (60 days)	0	0	0	0	0	180	360	360	360	180	0	0
Inventory	0	0	0	0	0	0	300	300	300	300	0	0
Receivables (30 days)	300	0	0	0	0	0	0	0	0	300	300	300

Table 5.2
Evolution of OWC over the year (amounts in $'000).

	Jan	Feb	Mar	Apr	May	Jun	Jul	Aug	Sep	Oct	Nov	Dec
Leveled Ltd.	280	80	180	280	380	480	580	680	480	580	380	180
Chaser Ltd.	300	0	0	0	0	−180	−60	−60	−60	420	300	300

Also, OWC depends on the idiosyncrasies of the industry and the firm's strategy. For instance, a manufacturing firm subject to seasonal sales and following a level strategy—that is, producing a constant amount over the year—will see how OWC skyrockets as the selling season approaches, due to large piles of inventory. Another firm in the same seasonal industry following a chasing strategy—that is, adapting production to sales—will have more steady inventories, although payables will increase dramatically after purchases made to cope with the selling season are delivered to start the manufacturing process. Over time, the OWCs of the two firms will be quite different.

Table 5.1 shows the evolution over time of selected variables for firms Leveled Ltd. and Chasing Ltd., which sell widgets at $1,000 with identical sales over the year. Assuming minimum cash is zero, we can calculate OWC over time for both firms (table 5.2).

A graphic representation (figure 5.3) shows that, notably, OWC is on average 375 percent higher for the level strategy ($380,000) than for the chasing strategy ($80,000).

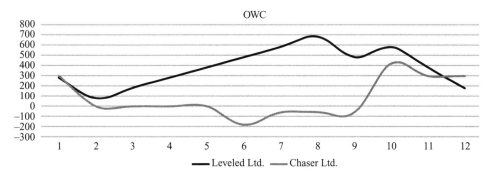

Figure 5.3
Evolution of OWC over the year (smoothed average).

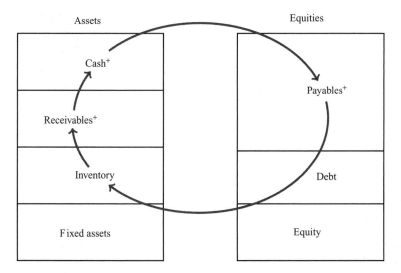

Figure 5.4
An illustration of the involvement of the OWC elements in the operations cycle.

5.3 Operations Cycle and the Cash-to-Cash Cycle

Operating working capital is intimately linked to the operations cycle of a firm. Figure 5.4 illustrates how the elements of operating working capital are involved in the operations cycle.

First, raw materials come from suppliers. Cash will be used to pay for those materials on the due date, decreasing payables. Those raw materials are combined and transformed to obtain the various kinds of inventories. Finished good inventories are sold and then converted into receivables. On the due date, receivables become cash. That cash is further used to pay for new raw materials, closing the operations cycle.

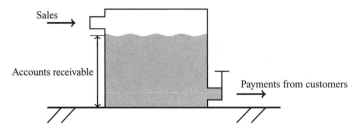

Figure 5.5
A pictorial representation of accounts receivable.

The size of OWC depends on how fast the cash used to pay suppliers of raw materials eventually becomes cash from customers that buy the products manufactured with those raw materials. Obviously, other things equal, the faster the better. However, it is not easy to speed up this process: it takes time to receive goods from suppliers, to convert raw materials into finished products, to persuade customers to buy such products, and finally to collect money from them. Flows of products and money get stuck for a while as stocks at various stages of the value chain. That is why it is so important to manage OWC properly (chapter 14 is entirely devoted to this subject).

Managing OWC effectively implies understanding the various links between the stocks and flows related to OWC. We will next present some of these relationships for the three main elements of OWC: accounts receivable, inventory, and accounts payable. Understanding those will facilitate the comprehension of subsequent topics.

5.3.1 Accounts Receivable

Assuming that sales are paid on account, accounts receivable increase when sales are realized, and decrease later on, when money is actually collected from customers (figure 5.5). The amount of accounts receivable increases with the number of days it takes to collect from customers, the number of units sold, and the price at which units are sold.

The equation that governs the dynamics of accounts receivable is as follows (Subscripts stand for time; for example, acc. receivable$_1$ is the level of accounts receivable at time $= 1$):

$$\text{acc. receivable}_1 = \text{acc. receivable}_0 + \text{sales} - \text{payments from customers} \qquad (5.2)$$

5.3.2 Accounts Payable

Likewise, assuming that purchases are paid on account, accounts payable increase when purchases are realized and decrease later on when money is actually paid to suppliers (figure 5.6).

The equation that governs the dynamics of accounts payable is as follows:

$$\text{acc. payable}_1 = \text{acc. payable}_0 + \text{purchases} - \text{payments to suppliers}$$

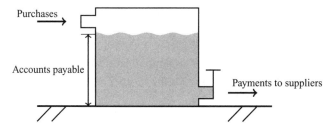

Figure 5.6
A pictorial representation of accounts payable.

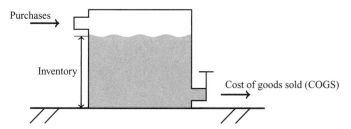

Figure 5.7
A pictorial representation of inventory.

The amount of accounts payable increases with the number of days it takes to pay suppliers, the number of units bought, and the cost at which units are bought.

5.3.3 Inventory

In the case of a retailer, inventory increases when purchases are realized and decreases when the corresponding sale is made (figure 5.7).

In the case of manufacturing firms, inventory increases not only when purchases of raw materials are realized but also when those raw materials are transformed into finished goods. Chapter 8 deals with this situation in detail.

The amount of inventory, as measured in dollars, increases with the number of days physical inventory stays in the firm, the number of units bought, and the cost at which units are bought.

The equation that governs the dynamics of inventory in the case of a retailer is as follows:

$$\text{inventory}_1 = \text{inventory}_0 + \text{purchases} - \text{cost of goods sold} \tag{5.3}$$

Note that the amount of inventory mainly depends on the ability of the firm's management to deal with physical inventory. For instance, better forecasting techniques will reduce uncertainty and thereby physical inventory. This is in contrast with accounts payable and receivable, which mainly depend on the negotiation power of, respectively, suppliers and customers. That means that the number of days to pay suppliers may increase abruptly, say from thirty to sixty, if the buyer's purchasing power is relatively large, as he or she can force the supplier to accept the new conditions. However, things are different regarding inventory, as the number of days of inventory in a supply chain cannot be reduced overnight. Aware of this, some firms resort to reducing inventory on their books and keep the current level of inventory physically—for instance, implementing a vendor-managed inventory program.

5.3.4 OWC Stock and Flows Connections

To appreciate the usefulness of the various relationships just presented, consider the following example.

Exercise

Automoby

Automoby is a retailer in the spare parts auto business. During year 1, the firm has collected $600,000 from customers and has paid $250,000 to suppliers. Additional selected data from the firm's balance sheets is as follows:

Account [$'000]	Dec 31, year 0	Dec 31, year 1
Cash	38	25
Accounts receivable	60	82
Inventory	100	92
Accounts payable	95	85

For year 1, calculate:

1. Sales
2. Purchases
3. Cost of goods sold

To find the required figures, and given that all three (sales, purchases, COGS) are flows, it is useful to think of the stocks on the balance sheet that have a direct relationship with those flows. For instance, sales are directly related to accounts receivable. Therefore we can make use of equation 5.2:

acc. receivable$_1$ = acc. receivable$_0$ + sales − payments from customers

Therefore:

$82,000 = 60,000 + \text{sales} − 600,000 \Rightarrow \text{sales} = \$622,000$

Likewise, purchases are related to accounts payable and inventory. We can consider either one, but calculations are more straightforward if accounts payable are considered.

$$\text{acc. payable}_1 = \text{acc. payable}_0 + \text{purchases} - \text{payments to suppliers}$$

In this case:

$$85,000 = 95,000 + \text{purchases} - 250,000 \Rightarrow \text{purchases} = \$240,000$$

Finally, the cost of goods sold has to do with inventory, thus we can use equation 5.3:

$$\text{inventory}_1 = \text{inventory}_0 + \text{purchases} - \text{cost of goods sold}$$

We have:

$$92,000 = 100,000 + 240,000 - \text{COGS} \Rightarrow \text{COGS} = \$248,000$$

5.4 Why Does Your CFO Go Crazy about OWC?

Operating working capital is, more often than not, a point of friction between the COO and the CFO of a firm. This is true in many companies, manufacturers and retailers, especially in the case of small and medium enterprises (SMEs), which are, on average, more financially constrained than large corporations. The COO may want to work with large production batches and order full trucks worth of raw materials from suppliers to increase production efficiency. Also, he may prefer to have plenty of inventory in the finished good warehouse to guarantee a satisfactory customer service level. All of this may have a large impact on inventory levels, which in turn increases working capital. In contrast, the CFO will typically fiercely push to reduce inventory—and OWC in general—at all levels of the organization: raw materials, work in progress, and finished goods. She will usually put emphasis on the more expensive products, namely finished goods, and A-type products, that is, the most important products in accordance with a Pareto's classification. Frictions between operations and finance have been increasing in the last few decades, given consumers' appetite for a greater variety of products, shorter product cycles, and increasing lead times due to production delocalization. All these trends make inventory grow, as we will see in chapter 15, increasing the financial needs for funding operations.

The truth is that OWC has three undesired effects from the CFO's point of view:

(1) OWC forces the firm to have more debt. As mentioned before, adding one dollar of OWC to the balance sheet entails increasing debt or equity. In the short term, debt is usually the adjustment variable that increases with OWC. Having too much debt increases the firm's risk.

(2) It costs money to keep a given OWC level over time. As mentioned above, one dollar of OWC entails paying interest for one dollar of debt or dividends for one dollar of equity. This has a permanent effect—as long as the OWC level does not change—and erodes the bottom line of the income statement.

(3) OWC prevents cash being used for other purposes—repay debt, pay suppliers, or make additional investments—and therefore decreases liquidity. Also, OWC makes it difficult for the firm to get access to additional funds, thus increasing the risk of the firm not being able to meet its financial obligations on time and eventually going bankrupt.

That is why it is so important that both CFO and COO understand each other's decisions regarding OWC. Also, their incentives should be aligned to prevent unnecessary disputes.

5.5   Operating Working Capital and Working Capital

If you belong to the operations management realm, odds are high that you never heard of *operating* working capital before. Instead, you may be familiar with a related concept, working capital (WC)—also known as net working capital, which is close to OWC but differs from it in subtle but important ways.

We will not be working with WC for the most part. However, since its use is so extended in the financial world, we will devote this section to defining it and noting the differences between WC and OWC. To present the concept of WC, we need first to introduce some new definitions.

We start by splitting debt in the balance sheet into two parts, namely short-term debt and long-term debt. Short-term debt is the portion of the firm's debt that has to be repaid within a year. Likewise, long-term debt is the portion of the firm's debt that has to be repaid in more than one year. The one-year threshold is an artificial convention.

 Short-term debt

> **Short-term debt** is the portion of the firm's (financial) debt that has to be repaid within a year.

 Long-term debt

> **Long-term debt** is the portion of the firm's (financial) debt that has to be repaid in more than one year.

Now that the concept of short-term debt has been introduced, we can define current liabilities as the firm's payment obligations within a year. For the seven-item balance sheet, we would have:

current liabilities $=$ accounts payable$^+$ $+$ short-term debt

Here, we assume that accounts payable$^+$ are also to be paid within a year.

Current liabilities

Current liabilities are the firm's payment obligations within a year. For a seven-account balance sheet, current liabilities is the sum of accounts payable[+] plus short-term debt.

With these definitions in mind, working capital is usually defined as[1]

working capital = current assets − current liabilities

 Working capital

Working capital (WC), or net working capital is the difference between current assets and current liabilities.

That is to say:

working capital = current assets − current liabilities

$$= cash^+ + accounts\ receivable^+ + inventory$$

$$- accounts\ payable^+ - short\text{-}term\ debt$$

The difference between OWC and WC is the short-term debt and excess cash, as the next expression makes explicit.

excess cash + operating working capital = short-term debt + working capital

Figure 5.8 shows both WC and OWC in a balance sheet when excess cash is zero.

If we chop the balance sheet by removing accounts payable[+] (and the corresponding portion in the assets side) as well as fixed assets (and the corresponding portion in the equities side) we obtain a simple relationship between OWC and WC (figure 5.9, left). In the case that the firm has excess cash and no debt, the relationship is as shown in the right. This figure reveals something surprising: Despite its definition, WC lives on the right side of the balance sheet (Aguirreamalloa and Larios 2015) unless it is negative. As such, WC is providing funds to finance OWC. We can see that this is the case by giving an alternative definition for WC (exercise 3 asks you to prove that the following expression is equivalent to the definition):

WC = equity + long-term debt − fixed assets   (5.4)

---

1. To make things confusing, working capital is sometimes defined as receivables plus inventory less payables—that is operating working capital if minimum cash were zero. With this alternative definition, the two concepts, operating working capital and working capital, are synonyms in many instances (as minimum cash = 0 is a mild assumption).

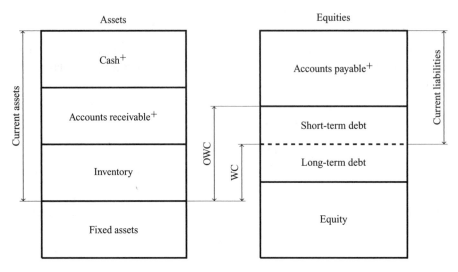

Figure 5.8
Representation of OWC and WC when excess cash is zero.

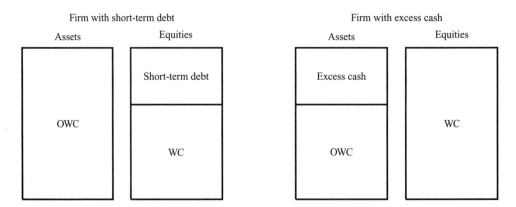

Figure 5.9
Relationship between WC and OWC.

This expression reveals that WC is the portion of long-term financing (that is, equity plus long-term debt) that is available to finance OWC after fixed assets have been financed. An important natural consequence is that liquidity problems in a firm—that is, the need to access short-term debt—manifest themselves when OWC is large, WC small, or both (Aguirreamalloa and Larios 2015).

Also, given the first definition of WC (current assets less current liabilities) you might think that WC fluctuates a lot over time, as it depends on daily payments made and received.

However, given the second definition (equity plus long-term debt less fixed assets) it should be apparent that WC doesn't fluctuate much over time, as all three terms—equity, long-term debt, and fixed assets—move slowly. This apparent contradiction is explained by the fact that short-term debt usually acts as an adjustment variable. It adapts itself by changing heavily over time so that WC stays roughly constant. When short-term debt is zero, excess cash becomes the adjustment variable. As short-term debt is not part of OWC, operating working capital fluctuates much more over time.

5.6 Summary

Operating working capital is defined as minimum cash plus accounts receivable$^+$ plus inventory less accounts payable$^+$. As such, it is the portion of assets necessary to run short-term, daily operations. Because holding OWC over time comes at a cost, OWC is a key concept in operations management. In fact, the management of OWC is the most important task for the COO of a firm—with the exception of managing people—especially if the firm holds significant amounts of inventory.

Exercises

1. What are the elements that conform OWC?

2. What is the relationship between WC and OWC?

3. Equation 5.4 claims that working capital is equity plus long-term debt less fixed assets. Show that this expression is equivalent to the initial definition of working capital—the difference between current assets and current liabilities.

4. Give conditions for OWC to be negative.

5. Can WC be larger than OWC? If so, under which circumstances? If not, why not?

6. When are WC and OWC identical?

7. Why is OWC undesirable from a financial point of view?

8. What is the operations cycle? Which financial stocks from the balance sheet are directly involved in the operations cycle?

9. Other things equal, which of the following stocks in the balance sheet—payables, inventory, receivables, if any—will increase/decrease when:

    a. Inventory in units is reduced.

    b. Payments to suppliers are delayed.

    c. The selling price decreases.

    d. The cost of raw materials increases.

    e. The suppliers' lead-time increases.

    f. Customers decide to accept early-payment discounts.

10. Give conditions for OWC to approximately be receivables plus inventory less payables.

11. Indicate whether each of the following statements is true or false.

   a. OWC is only made of receivables$^+$, inventory, and payables$^+$.

   b. The amounts needed to compute a firm's OWC come only from the balance sheet.

   c. If minimum cash is zero, when a $30,000 account receivable is collected, OWC will decrease by $30,000.

   d. If suppliers are paid on account, when $20,000 worth of inventory is acquired and recorded in the firm's books, OWC will increase by $20,000.

   e. When a firm sells some of its products, liquidity always increases.

12. Following is the detail of all current assets and liabilities on a firm's balance sheet but inventory and short-term debt. Find the levels of inventory and short-term debt if working capital is $200,000 and operating working capital is $320,000.

Cash	$80,000
Accounts receivable	240,000
Accounts payable	180,000
Accrued salaries (not paid)	40,000
Prepaid expenses	30,000

Reference

Aguirreamalloa, Javier, and Pedro Larios. 2015. *Finanzas de empresa*, 2nd ed. Madrid, Spain: Epalsa.

6   Measuring Shareholders' Happiness: The Income Statement

Profit is sweet, even if it comes from deception.
—Sophocles, ancient Greek tragedian

This chapter presents the income statement, without a doubt the most popular financial statement among operations and supply chain practitioners. Its popularity stems from the fact that it contains valuable information for managers and investors and is relatively easy to interpret. However, only relying on the income statement to assess the performance of a firm would be too simplistic. Instead, it should at least be interpreted alongside the balance sheet and the statement of cash flows. We will present the income statement and its elements as well as specific financial jargon along the way.

6.1   Definition

Having described in detail the mechanics of financial accounting in previous chapters, it is quite straightforward to define what the income statement represents. In a nutshell, it is a *summary* of the changes in profit (informally, shareholders' happiness) during a period of time.

 Income statement

> The **income statement** (also known as statement of profit or loss, P&L account, or simply P&L) is a summary of the changes in profit (informally, shareholders' happiness) during a period of time, typically a year, a quarter, or a month. It gives a dynamic view of the firm, as its elements are flows (flows of shareholders' happiness!).

In other words, the income statement is the financial statement that compiles all the elements of the revenue and expenses account of the general ledger in a structured way. Note that both definitions, changes in shareholders' happiness and the elements of the revenue

Revenue and expenses (Shareholders' happiness)			
:☹		:☺	
COGS	60,000	Sales	100,000
SGA-salary	2,200		
SGA-utilities	700		
Interest	184		
SGA-rent	4,000		
Depreciation	556		

Figure 6.1
January's revenue and expense account.

and expense account, are identical, as the revenue and expense account contains exactly the items that make shareholders happier or sadder.

The last line of the income statement, the net profit, also known as the bottom line, gives the ultimate answer to the question initially answered by Luca Pacioli: How did the business do? If net profit is positive, shareholders are happy because the business did well during the period. If net profit is negative, shareholders are unhappy because the business did badly. Therefore, the main goal of the income statement is to find out whether shareholders should be happy or sad in accordance with the accounting criterion.

As an example, we can prepare the income statement of Ethan and Ryan's new firm for January, based on the revenue and expense account (figure 6.1.) Strictly speaking, this figure shows the income statement from January 9 to January 31. However, since shareholders' happiness did not change during the first eight days of January, the figure also represents the changes in shareholders' happiness for the whole month.

6.2   Elements

To prepare a simple income statement, we start by making note of some good news (it is good to be optimistic!): sales in January totaled $100,000 (table 6.1). Sales are part of the revenue of a firm. Revenue is a broader item that includes other sources of wealth, mainly from operating activities, such as rendering of services, lease income, and royalties. *Revenue* comes from Latin *re* (back) and *venire* (come), as it is money that will come back to the firm after investing it in facilities, equipment, and materials.

 Revenue

> **Revenue** is the increase of shareholders' happiness through operating activities, such as sales of goods and rendering of services.

Table 6.1
Revenue makes up the top line of the income statement.

January's Income Statement ($)	
Revenue	100,000
Cost of goods sold	(60,000)
Gross profit	40,000
...	...

Next, we have to take care of the bad news: we acknowledge first the cost of goods sold (COGS; in general, cost of sales). COGS usually includes variable costs (such as purchasing cost) and other direct costs, together with the portion of indirect costs that can reasonably be allocated to the products; chapters 8 and 11 elaborate on this. A fundamental accounting rule requires that the good news (a product has been sold) and the bad news (the firm does not have the product any longer) are recognized in the books at the same time. This is an accounting practice known as the matching principle.

 Matching principle

The **matching principle** requires revenues and expenses to be recorded in the same time period. When revenue is recognized in a period, expenses incurred to generate that revenue should be recorded in the same period.

The difference between revenue and COGS is called gross profit.

 Gross profit

Gross profit is the difference between revenue and the cost of goods sold.

You may have noticed that the $60,000 in table 6.1 appears in parentheses. This is usually the case in accounting when negative figures are represented. It is not that accountants want to hide the bad news (is it?), but just a matter of convenience, to easily distinguish good from bad news in a report. Another way to achieve the same effect would be to print negative figures in red.

Selling, general, and administrative (SGA) expenses are annotated next. In our example:

$$\text{SGA expenses} = \$2,200 + \$700 + \$4,000 = \$6,900$$

SGA expenses usually include all indirect costs that cannot reasonably be allocated to the products sold. Whether a cost should be part of COGS or SGA is at times a topic of debate and may vary greatly from industry to industry and from company to company. For instance,

Table 6.2
EBITDA is the difference between gross profit and SGA expenses.

January's Income Statement ($)	
Sales	100,000
Cost of goods sold	(60,000)
Gross profit	40,000
SGA expenses	(6,900)
EBITDA	33,100
…	…

the blue-collar workers' salary in a factory is part of COGS. The sales force salary is part of SGA though. But in which category should the COO's salary be? Can this cost be reasonably allocated to the products sold? Chapter 11 elaborates on this. A key point is that, once a criterion has been defined to allocate expenses to either COGS or SGA, that criterion must be maintained over time. This is in accordance with the so-called consistency principle.

 Consistency principle

The **consistency principle** states that a firm should apply the accounting procedures uniformly across periods.

The difference between gross profit and SGA expenses is usually referred to as EBITDA (table 6.2).

EBITDA stands for earnings before interest, tax, depreciation, and amortization. Another name for EBITDA is operating profit, which suggests that this intermediate profit (sales less COGS less SGA) is mainly under the purview of the firm's COO, whereas the remaining items in the income statement (depreciation, interest expenses, and tax) are mainly someone else's responsibility.

 EBITDA

EBITDA, or operating profit, stands for earnings before interest, tax, depreciation, and amortization. EBITDA is the difference between gross profit and SGA expenses.

After EBITDA, depreciation is deducted. Sometimes portions of EBITDA are included somewhere else in the income statement; also, some firms do not report depreciation in isolation. For instance, depreciation of machines and other manufacturing fixed assets may be part of COGS (see chapter 8 for details). In this case, only the remaining part of depreciation is annotated below EBITDA.

Table 6.3
Ethan and Ryan's new firm income statement in January.

January's Income Statement ($)	
Sales	100,000
Cost of goods sold	(60,000)
Gross profit	40,000
SGA expenses	(6,900)
EBITDA	33,100
Depreciation	(556)
EBIT	32,544
Interest expenses	(184)
EBT	32,360
Tax	(0)
Net profit	32,360

The difference between EBITDA and depreciation is usually called, not surprisingly, EBIT (earnings before interest and tax).

 EBIT

EBIT stands for earnings before interest and tax. It can be obtained by deducting depreciation (and amortization) from EBITDA.

Interest expenses are deducted next to obtain EBT (earnings before tax).

 EBT

EBT stands for earnings before tax. It can be obtained by deducting taxes from EBIT.

Finally, corporate taxes are deducted to obtain the net profit of the period, also referred to as the bottom line, after-tax profit, net income, or net earnings (table 6.3.) Corporate taxes are usually a fixed percentage of EBT (e.g., 25 percent), although much more intricate schemes exist, especially for large corporations.

All these measures of income on top of net profit—gross profit, EBITDA, EBIT, and EBT—are not part of the Internal Financial Reporting Standards (IFRS). However, these additional measures can benefit investors by giving them greater insight into how firms are managed.[1]

1. PriceWaterhouseCoopers (PWC) 2007.

Table 6.4
Ethan and Ryan's new firm seven-item income statement in January.

Sales	100,000
Cost of goods sold	(60,000)
SGA expenses	(6,900)
Depreciation	(556)
Interest expenses	(184)
Tax	(0)
Net profit	32,360

If we remove the partial totals—for example, EBITDA, EBIT, and so on—we will end up with what we call the seven-item income statement (figure 6.4), the simplest version of an income statement, much like the seven-item balance sheet presented in chapter 4.

6.3   OPEX and CAPEX

OPEX (operating expenses) and CAPEX (capital expenses) are terms sometimes used in connection with the income statement. Although the terms are not included in the IFRS, they are becoming more and more popular in business, as figure 6.2 shows.

6.3.1   OPEX

Operating expenses refer to the money a firm spends on daily operations. OPEX usually include COGS and SGA expenses, although some items (i.e., machine depreciation that is part of COGS) are not usually considered part of OPEX.

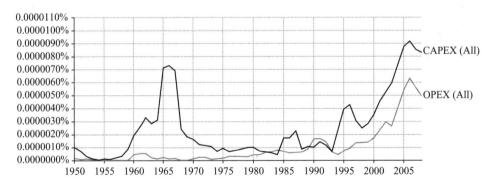

Figure 6.2
Relative prevalence of the terms *OPEX* and *CAPEX* over time.
Source: Ngram Viewer; parameters: case insensitive, smooth = 1.

6.3.2 CAPEX

As opposed to OPEX, capital expenses refer to the money a firm uses to buy and maintain its fixed assets. CAPEX examples include plants, equipment, vehicles, or hardware. It is considered a capital expenditure in the period where the asset is purchased or when money is used to maintain the asset.

We find the name rather confusing, as expenses by definition are items that belong to the revenue and expenses account. However, CAPEX items only become actual expenses when they are depreciated.

6.4 Interpretation

The income statement offers a dynamic view of the firm during the period considered. It is a sort of video clip that explains how and why shareholders' happiness changed during the period. This is in contrast to the balance sheet, which is made up of stocks and shows a static snapshot of the firm but is not concerned with changes within the period.

An important observation is that the income statement deals with happiness flows—or, more formally, changes in equity—not with cash flows. To believe that the elements of the income statement are cash flows is a mistake that many nontrained professionals make. Net profit is *not* the additional cash that is available in the firm at the end of the period with respect to the level of cash at the beginning of the period. It does not measure the change in cash but the change in shareholders' happiness. The difference stems from the fact that shareholders' happiness in the accounting world (i.e., in accordance with the accounting criterion) is linked to the accrual principle, not to cash changes. For instance, sales make shareholders happy, even if customers do not pay at the time of the sale. As we will see in chapter 7, the statement of cash flows will concern itself with cash flows.

Income statement is not about cash

The elements of the income statement are *not* flows of cash, but flows of shareholders' happiness.

Also, net profit is additional happiness for shareholders in accordance with the accounting criterion. Therefore, net profit is not value created to shareholders. Value creation has to do with the market value of the firm, not the book value.

 Net profit

Net profit measures shareholders' additional happiness in accordance with the accounting criterion. It gives the answer to Pacioli's ultimate question: How well has the firm done during the last period?

Last but not least, net profit is subject to managers' opinions. For instance, remember Ryan's estimate that the equipment would last three years. How accurate is this estimate? Why is residual value assumed to be zero? Furthermore, Ryan's estimate is a point-wise estimate. He certainly could have done better than this and could have come up with a number of possible scenarios (e.g., pessimistic, most likely, optimistic) or even a continuous distribution estimate. Unfortunately, accounting only deals with point-wise estimates. This means that the same events, when estimated by different managers, may well lead to different net profits.

That example focused on fixed assets, but it can be extrapolated to any other accounts in the balance sheet. For example, managers have to estimate if old inventory in the distribution center should be removed from the books or if there is still a chance that customers will buy it, if customers will pay for products already delivered, if legal issues will be solved favorably, and so on. We are not talking about distorting reality but about having different perceptions of the future. Therefore, net profit is subject to a great deal of subjectivity and so we can conclude with Fernández (2012) that net profit is "just an opinion." Moreover, only in rare cases, net profit will coincide with increasing cash flows during the period. This is why an income statement should not be interpreted in isolation but together with the balance sheet and the statement of cash flows, and bearing in mind the firm's strategy and the industry in which it operates.

6.5   Example: Understanding Toyota's Income Statement

Having presented the major elements in a standard income statement, we will now proceed to comment on the peculiarities of a real firm. We have chosen Toyota Motor Corporation, the largest Japanese firm by market capitalization. Table 6.5 shows the consolidated income statement as presented in Toyota 2017 annual report (Toyota 2017).

We will go now through each line.

Net revenues   The sum of sales of products and financing operations is net revenues. As said, *revenues* is a more general term than *sales* as it may include income other than product sales. In this case, financing operations is the revenue that Toyota earned from providing financial services, mainly auto loans and leasing, to more than 26 million customers across its network (Toyota 2017, 49).

Costs and expenses   Costs and expenses refer to operating costs.

Cost of products sold   Another term for cost of goods sold is cost of products sold.

Cost of financing operations   This is another term for the cost of selling financial services.

Selling, general, and administrative expenses   These expenses are not separated from the previous costs. Still, we can calculate gross profit as net revenue less cost of products sold

Table 6.5
Toyota Motor Corporation income statement for financial year 2017 (yen in millions).

Consolidated statements of income	FY 2017
Net revenues	**27,597,193**
Sales of products	25,813,496
Financing operations	1,783,697
Costs and expenses	**25,602,821**
Costs of products sold	21,543,035
Cost of financing operations	1,191,301
Selling, general and administrative	2,868,485
Operating income	**1,994,372**
Other income	**199,453**
Interest and dividend income	158,983
Interest expense	(29,353)
Foreign exchange gain (loos), net	36,222
Income before income taxes and equity in earnings of affiliated companies	**2,193,825**
Provision for income taxes	**628,900**
Equity in earnings of affiliated companies	**362,060**
Net income	**1,926,985**

less cost of financing operations—that is: $¥27,597,193 - ¥21,543,035 - ¥1,191,301$, or ¥4.86 million.

Operating income An alternative name for EBITDA is operating income.

Other income (expense) This includes interest and other (net) expenses. Interest income is the money earned from cash deposits, while interest expense is the money paid for financial debt. Dividend income is money Toyota has earned through dividends made by companies of which Toyota has shares.

Foreign exchange gain Foreign exchange gain is a consequence of fluctuating exchange rates. For instance, say that Toyota sells a car in the United States at $30,000. When the sale is recognized, the exchange rate at that moment (say $1 = ¥110$) is used to increase receivables by ¥3,300,000.[2] At the end of the quarter, if the corresponding money has not been collected, the receivable should be valued at the closing rate (i.e., the exchange rate at the end of the quarter). If the closing rate is, say, $1 = ¥115$, an additional profit of ¥150,000 has been earned due to exchange rate fluctuation.

Income before income taxes and equity in earnings of affiliated companies This is a long name for the difference between operating income and other expenses.

2. IRFS Foundation 2018.

Provision for income taxes An estimate for corporate taxes, in this case roughly 28.7 percent of profit before taxes.

Equity in earnings of affiliated companies This is the stake Toyota makes from subsidiaries (after subsidiaries have paid taxes).

Net income Another name for net profit.

6.6 Summary

The income statement of a firm during a period is a collection of changes in shareholders' happiness (or more formally, changes in equity due to the business cycle). A such, it provides a dynamic view of a firm during a period. The last line of the income statement, the net profit, provides an answer to the question first answered by Luca Pacioli: How well did the business do? Other measures of income, such as gross profit or EBITDA, help investors and managers assess the evolution of the business over time and compare a firm's financial performance with its competitors. The income statement alone does not contain all the relevant information to be able to judge a firm's performance: a combined study of the three main financial statements—balance sheet, income statement, and statement of cash flows—is required to make a sound analysis of a firm at any point in time.

Exercises

1. Name the three main financial statements.

2. Does the income statement provide a static or dynamic view of a firm? If static, what are the stocks? If dynamic, what are the flows?

3. Give two additional names for the income statement.

4. What are the seven elements of the seven-item income statement?

5. How are the balance sheet and the income statement of a firm connected?

6. What does EBITDA mean?

7. Which function in a firm is mainly accountable for EBITDA?

8. What is the difference between operating profit and net profit?

9. Are these magnitudes stocks or flows? increasing equity, dividends, net profit, issued shares. Connect them algebraically in an single identity assuming they refer to the same accounting period.

10. Transportation firm A owns its fleet of trucks. Transportation firm B rents an identical fleet of trucks through a leasing contract. As long as the fleet of trucks is concerned:

    a. Which firm has most likely the highest COGS and why?

    b. Which firm most likely depreciates the most, and why?

11. Depreciation is said to be a noncash item in the income statement. What does it mean? Is this really the case?

12. Depreciation is considered after operating profit is calculated. Is this reasonable? Should depreciation have an impact on a firm's operating profit instead?

13. Name three items in the income statement that may be subjective—that is, contingent upon managers' opinion.

14. Can EBIT be larger than EBITDA in a given period?

15. True or false?

    a. The income statement is composed of cash flows.

    b. EBITDA and operating profit represent the same accounting concept.

    c. If depreciation increases, other things equal, EBITDA will decrease.

    d. Even if sales are zero in a period, the cost of goods sold may be different from zero in that period.

    e. If purchases are larger than COGS in a period, other things equal, net profit of that period will decrease.

    f. A period's net profit represents the amount of additional cash that a firm has obtained during that period.

    g. Except for sales, all items in the income statement are negative amounts.

16. Mini-case study: Vending machines[3]

    During his stay in Switzerland in 2017, when he was about to finish his MBA, Sanjay Menon had the idea of starting a new business back home in India. At several European airports, he had seen some vending machines selling electronics (such as iPods) rather than soft drinks or other inexpensive products. He thought that importing and selling those new-generation vending machines in India could be a good idea, especially when some of his relatives were already involved in the industry.

    However, Sanjay did not have much money, so he showed his business plan to his rich uncle Anoop Patnaik, with the aim of involving him in the new firm as the main shareholder. Anoop agreed to invest in the business, so they both went ahead and made a bank deposit of $120,000 (Sanjay invested $20,000, his uncle $100,000) as equity for the new firm. Additionally, at the end of the year, they took out a bank loan ($40,000, 10 percent per year) to avoid potential cash tension.

    On December 30, they bought a small warehouse to store the machines for $100,000 ($40,000 land, $60,000 building). Sanjay paid $80,000 cash; the remaining amount was agreed to be paid on December 30 the following year. Both shareholders estimated the life of the warehouse to be an additional twenty years.

    The same day, Anoop bought some furniture necessary to run the business, paying $4,000 cash, with an estimates life of five years.

    The last day of the year, Sanjay and Anoop met to assess the situation of the firm. No machines had been sold yet. Sanjay had prepared the cash report shown below.

3. Inspired by the case study, Pereira 1969.

INPUTS	
Sanjay	$20,000
Anoop	$100,000
Loan	$40,000
TOTAL	$160,000

OUPUTS	
Warehouse	$80,000
Payment to supplier when buying the first machines	$20,000
Furniture	$4,000
Trips to Switzerland	$6,000
Cash position on December 31, 2017	$50,000
TOTAL	$160,000

Sanjay also mentioned that there were twenty machines in the warehouse, whose total cost had been $2,000 each.

Anoop read the report and told Sanjay that the information was insufficient. He then asked for the balance sheet of the firm (December 31, 2017). Sanjay did not know exactly how to prepare it, but did his best.

During 2018, Sanjay was in charge of the business, taking care of cash flows (i.e., cash inputs and outputs), but not really paying attention to the financial situation of the firm. Time went by quickly. At the beginning of December 2018, Sanjay got an e-mail from his uncle requiring the following information for year 2018:

- Balance sheet (December 31)
- Income statement
- Statement of cash flows

Sanjay gathered all the information he was able to find regarding operations during 2018 and summarized it as follows:

1. The firm imported 150 machines (on account, i.e., using trade credit) at $2,000 each.
2. Fifty machines were sold (cash) at $3,000 each.
3. One hundred machines were sold (on account) at $3,300 each.
4. During 2018, $250,000 was collected from customers who had not paid cash.
5. Likewise, the firm paid the cost of 140 machines to the supplier.
6. General and administrative expenses totaled $20,000 (cash).
7. The remaining money corresponding to the warehouse was paid.
8. On Dec 31, 2018, the bank debt was repaid.
9. Interest of the loan was paid.

    a. Prepare the balance sheet as of Dec 31, 2017.

b. Prepare the balance sheet as of Dec 31, 2018.

c. Prepare the income statement for 2018.

17. Mini-case study: Aida and Maria.

Aida and Maria decided to start selling food and drinks on a street next to the university campus. Read the facts described below, and then answer the questions provided.

1. On September 1st, using all their savings ($12,000) and a bank loan ($8,000, 9 percent per year), they bought a second-hand van (price $10,000, 60 percent paid in cash, the rest due in two months) and some inventory (soft drinks, bread, sausages, and the like) total value $500.

2. On the same day, Aida took an old fridge from her place, which was installed in the van.

3. On September, Aida and Maria started selling to students. The business went well, and, at the end of the year, Aida and Maria had already sold $18,000 in food and drinks, all in cash payments.

4. On September 15 local taxes were paid ($400).

5. On October 20 some maintenance expenses for the van were paid ($200).

6. On November, Aida and Maria decided to pay back a quarter of the outstanding debt, since the business was already generating fresh cash.

7. On December 30, they bought an additional fridge for drinks ($600 cash).

8. Inventory at the end of the year was $1,100.

9. Total purchases of inventory (from September 1 included) totaled $12,000 and were made on account.

10. On December 31, only $1,000 had to be paid to the supplier and nothing to the former owner of the van.

11. On the same day, interest expenses were paid.

12. The van was expected to last three more years, with zero expected scrap value.

13. Corporate tax rate was 40 percent, taxes to be paid the following year.

a. Prepare the balance sheet for Aida and Maria's firm as of September (right after fact #2).

b. Prepare the balance sheet as of December 31.

c. Prepare the income statement for the quarter.

d. What conclusions can be reached from the financial statements you prepared?

18. (Adapted from IFRS Foundation 2014.) A firm owns and operates a ferry that transports passengers, their motor vehicles, and goods between the mainland and an island. The ferry service is the main business of the firm. Given the following facts:

• On 1 January 2016 the firm purchases a new ferry for $1 million cash. The ferry comprises two main components—the main structure (cost $800,000) and the engine (cost $200,000).

• The firm's management expect that after operating the ferry for twenty years the ferry will be scrapped. However, management expect to replace the ferry's engine after operating it for ten years. No proceeds are expected from the scrapping of both the old engine (after ten years) and the ferry and its replacement engine (after twenty years).

• The ferry's passenger carrying capacity is constant over its twenty-year economic life.

- On December 31, 2019 a storm severely damages the engine. Consequently, the firm scraps the engine. On January 1, 2020 the firm replaces the engine at a cost of $300,000. The new engine is expected to propel the ferry for the rest of its estimated useful life, after which the ferry and the engine will be scrapped.

- On December 2020, in response to an unsolicited offer, the firm disposes of the ferry for $910,000.

1. What information about that firm's ferry would a potential investor find useful? Why do you think that information would be useful?

2. Is the ferry an asset of the firm?

3. Prepare accounting entries relating to the ferry from January 1, 2016 to December 31, 2020.

4. List some of the estimates and judgments that the management of the firm would have made in accounting for the ferry.

References

Fernández, Pablo. 2012. "Cash flow is cash and is a fact: Net income is just an opinion." Working paper, n. 629.

IFRS Foundation. 2018. *IFRS Standards 2018*. Part A (red books), IAS 21.

Pereira, Fernando. "Jacinto Basch (A)." IESE, C-266, 01/1969.

PriceWaterhouseCoopers. 2007. "Presentation of income under IFRS: Flexibility and consistency explored."

Toyota. 2017. "Annual report 2017." https://www.toyota-global.com/pages/contents/investors/ir_library/annual /pdf/2017/annual_report_2017_fie.pdf.

7   Tracking Money Changes: The Statement of Cash Flows

The fact is that one of the earliest lessons I learned in business was that balance sheets and income statements are fiction, cash flow is reality.
—Chris Chocola, businessman

The third and last financial statement that we will be dealing with is the statement of cash flows. As its names suggests, it is a summary of the cash flows occurring during a given period within the firm. The importance of the statement of cash flows stems from the fact that it is concerned with the firm's liquidity, a topic of paramount importance that is addressed in chapter 10. The statement of cash flows together with the balance sheet and the income statement enable investors and managers to obtain an overall picture of the financial performance of a firm.

7.1   Definition and Derivation

The statement of cash flows is based on the fact that money neither appears nor disappears out of the blue, which leads us to state that, for any period of time, in a company:

sources of money = uses of money

For instance, remember event 1 in the Sharon the Shareholder example in section 3.1. Money went from Sharon's pocket to the firm's cash box. The statement of cash flows for that transaction would just state that:

money coming from Sharon's pocket (source) = money going into the cash box (use)

or: $1,000 = $1,000; as simple as that.

Admittedly, it would be of more interest to perform the same exercise for a whole period, such as a year or a quarter, to understand the various sources and uses of money within it. To do so, we will first find out which items should be involved in the statement of cash flows. We will do it using two approaches: first, algebraically; second, using sheer logic and common sense. But before we do that, we need to introduce two new concepts.

7.1.1 Funds from Operations and Cash Generated from Operations

For a seven-item income statement, we will define funds from operations (or FFO for short) as net profit adjusted by expenses (or revenues) that do not involve cash, such as depreciation. We will only focus on depreciation, but other adjustments are possible (see section 7.5.1).

$$\text{funds from operations} = \text{net profit} + \text{depreciation}$$

$$+ \text{other noncash items (usually expenses)}$$

Funds from operations can also be thought of as the cash generated from operations (i.e., the net cash flow generated by daily operations through buying and selling) conditional on that all payments—sales from customers, purchases to suppliers, payroll to employees, tax to the government, etc.—were made in cash. More precisely, conditional on the amount in the income statement, but depreciation and other noncash expenses, would imply necessarily a cash flow by the same amount. For instance, if sales totaled $100, a cash flow of $100 would have entered the firm during the period, as customers would pay cash. Likewise, the firm would pay all expenses—COGS, SGA, interest, and taxes—in cash, at the time of recognition in the books.

 Funds from operations

> **Funds from operations** is the sum of net profit plus depreciation and other noncash expenses. It is the cash operations would bring to the firm if all payments were made in cash.

A less restrictive condition for funds from operations to coincide with the cash generated from operations is that OWC doesn't change during the period. In fact,

$$\text{cash generated from operations} = \text{funds from operations} - \Delta\text{OWC} \qquad (7.1)$$

In this equation (Δ) denotes a change—either positive or negative—in the corresponding stock (e.g., ΔOWC is the change in the level of OWC). When more accuracy is needed, an up arrow ($\uparrow$) will denote an increasing stock and a down arrow ($\downarrow$) a decreasing stock.

This equation holds if all payments were made in cash (keeping minimum cash constant), as that implies that OWC doesn't change. But it will hold as well even if payments are not made in cash as long as OWC doesn't change. For instance, that will be the case if payables and receivables increase by the same amount, or if receivables increase as much as inventory decreases.

Although there is no a widespread name in the literature for funds from operations, other proposed names include cash flow earnings (Anthony and Reece 1983, p. 343), accounting cash flow (Fernández 2012), net cash flow (Higgins 2012, p. 22), and cash earnings (Mulford and Jayko 2006).

 Cash generated from operations

Cash generated from operations is funds from operations less increasing operating working capital.

7.1.2 Algebraic Derivation

Having defined funds from operations, we are ready to derive the expression that connects the various sources and uses of cash. We will do it first algebraically.

Let's start with the accounting identity:

$$\text{assets} = \text{equities}$$

As this identity holds at any point in time, it will hold in particular at the beginning (say $t = 0$) and at the end of period ($t = 1$). Thus we can write:

$$\left.\begin{array}{l} \text{assets}_0 = \text{equities}_0 \\ \text{assets}_1 = \text{equities}_1 \end{array}\right\} \Rightarrow \Delta\text{assets} = \Delta\text{equities}$$

It follows from equation 5.1 that:

$$\Delta\text{excess cash} + \Delta\text{OWC} + \Delta\text{fixed assets} = \Delta\text{debt} + \Delta\text{equity}$$

The change in fixed assets can be expressed as:

$$\begin{aligned} \Delta\text{fixed assets} &= \Delta(\text{gross fixed assets} - \text{accumulated depreciation}) \\ &= \Delta\text{gross fixed assets} - \Delta\text{accumulated depreciation} \\ &= \text{investment in fixed assets} - \text{depreciation} \end{aligned}$$

Note that gross fixed assets and accumulated depreciation are stocks, while investment and depreciation are flows. Specifically, the term Δgross FA is the change in fixed assets net of depreciation; that is, the additional investment in fixed assets during the period or, simply, the period investment. Similarly, depreciation is the change in accumulated depreciation during the period; that is to say, the period's depreciation.

Equity increases either due to money flowing from shareholders' pockets (issued equity) or due to the realization of a (positive) net profit during the period. Equity decreases due to money flowing towards shareholders' pockets (dividends). Mathematically:

$$\Delta\text{equity} = \text{issued equity} + \text{net profit} - \text{dividends}$$

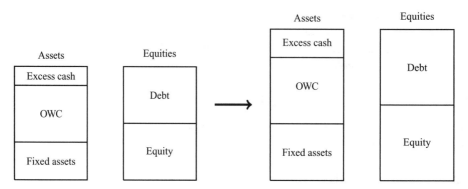

Figure 7.1
The financial balance sheet typically grows with the firm's sales.

Given these derivations, expression 7.1 becomes:

$$\Delta \text{excess cash} + \Delta \text{OWC} + \text{investment}^1 - \text{depreciation}$$

$$= \Delta \text{debt} + \text{issued equity} - \text{dividends} + \text{net profit}$$

Finally, recall the definition of funds from operations (FFO) as net profit plus depreciation. The identity becomes

$$\Delta \text{excess cash} + \text{investment} + \text{dividends} + \Delta \text{OWC} = \Delta \text{debt} + \text{issued equity} + \text{FFO} \quad (7.2)$$

The relationship between the seven items in expression 7.2 forms the core of the statement of cash flows.

7.1.3   Common-Sense Derivation

In order to gain more intuition, we will derive expression 7.2 again by using sheer logic and common sense.

Consider a growing profitable firm. Its (financial) balance sheet would normally grow with the firm's sales (figure 7.1). This will be the case, for instance, for a retailer that increases the number of stores she has in order to boost sales—which increases fixed assets and inventory level alike.

Where can the firm get additional funds to finance growth? Basically there are two options: either operations generates funds through buying and selling, or funds are obtained from outside the firm's operations, either from banks or from shareholders' pockets (i.e., from the right-hand side of the *financial* balance sheet).

---

1. From now on, *investment* will refer to "investment in fixed assets."

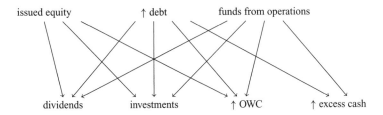

Figure 7.2
Cash movements between sources and uses of funds.

Therefore, it has to be that:

fund sources = funds from operations + Δ debt + issued equity

What are these funds used for? There are three possibilities: (1) either money is paid to the outside (as dividends paid to shareholders), (2) is re-invested in the business to enable future growth, either as OWC or fixed assets (i.e., the left-hand side of the financial balance sheet), or (3) cash increases. Adding up those three amounts yields:

fund uses = dividends + Δ OWC + investment + Δ excess cash

As the sum of sources and uses of funds must be identical, it has to be that:

$$\text{FFO} + \uparrow \text{debt} + \text{issued equity} = \text{dividends} + \uparrow \text{OWC} + \text{investment} + \Delta\text{excess cash} \quad (7.3)$$

This is identical to expression 7.2 when Δ debt and Δ OWC are positive.

Given equation 7.1, an equivalent expression is:

cash generated from operations + $\uparrow$ debt + issued equity

   = dividends + investment + Δ excess cash

which makes it explicit whether operations has actually generated cash.

We can represent the seven items in expression 7.3 pictorially (figure 7.2), which reinforces the message that cash doesn't appear out of the blue.

7.2   The Seven-Item Statement of Cash Flows

The seven-item statement of cash flows is just an arrangement of the seven elements of the last expression (figure 7.3), where the sum of the two columns must be identical, according to expression (7.3).

The statement of cash flows shows how the firm has financed its operations during a period of time. As in the case of the income statement, the statement of cash flows represents

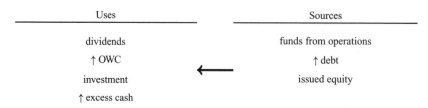

Figure 7.3
A representation of the seven-item statement of cash flows. Funds flow from right to left.

a dynamic view of the firm, as all its elements are flows. But these are flows of cash, in contrast with the income statement, whose elements are flows of shareholders' happiness.

 Statement of cash flows

> The **statement of cash flows** shows the changes in cash within a firm during a period. Changes are grouped according to their nature: operations, investment, financing. The statement of cash flows gives a dynamic view of the firm, as its elements are flows of cash.

Note that figure 7.3 corresponds to a profitable firm that is growing. That would most likely mean that all seven items in the statement of cash flows will be nonnegative. But what if a firm's sales decrease during a period? What if a firm loses money? Some of the sources of funds may become uses and vice versa. In fact, all elements of the statement of cash flows (but dividends) can be positive or negative, hence they can be in either column.

When this is the case, the corresponding item will change columns accordingly. For instance, a firm that does not grow may use the cash flow provided by operations to repay the principal of the debt; thus, if cash doesn't change, Δdebt becomes negative. Debt would show up in the left column of the statement of cash flows with a down arrow ($\downarrow$) next to it (figure 7.4).

Something enticing about the statement of cash flows is that, in contrast to the other two financial statements, the statement of cash flows is not that dependent on managers'

Figure 7.4
Elements of the statement of cash flows change columns if they are negative.

(or anybody else's) opinions. Five (of seven) items of the statement of cash flows—issued equity, Δdebt, dividends, cash, and investments—are irrefutable facts, which is of undoubtful help when assessing the financial performance of a firm.

The paradox is that, according to our experience, and despite its utility, the statement of cash flows is the least known of the three main financial statements among operations and supply chain managers.

7.3   Ethan and Ryan's New Firm Revisited

To get some practice and additional intuition, we will derive in this section the statement of cash flows of Ethan and Ryan's new firm for the period elapsed between January 8 and January 31. In order to do so, it will be convenient to take a number of preparation steps.

7.3.1   Derivation

First, we can rearrange the two balance sheets, at the beginning and at the end of the relevant period, as in table 7.1.

Second, we will reduce the number of accounts by merging similar accounts as described in section 4.2:

- accounts receivable$^+$ = accounts receivable + prepaid expenses
- accounts payable$^+$ = accounts payable + accrued not paid

We will also calculate OWC at the beginning and at the end of the period. To do so, we will assume that minimum cash is zero. Finally, we will insert an additional column with the relevant changes in each account during the period (table 7.2).

Table 7.1
Balance sheets of Ethan and Ryan's new firm as of January 8 and January 31.

	January 8	January 31
Cash	10,000	59,300
Accounts receivable	0	8,000
Prepaid expenses	12,000	8,000
Inventory	60,000	40,000
Fixed assets	20,000	19,444
Total assets	**102,000**	**134,744**
Accounts payable	38,000	50,000
Accrued not paid	0	384
Debt	24,000	12,000
Equity	40,000	40,000
Retained earnings	0	32,360
Total equities	**102,000**	**134,744**

Table 7.2
Ethan and Ryan's new firm's difference of balance sheets.

	January 8	January 31	Difference
Cash	10,000	59,300	49,300
Accounts receivable[+]	12,000	16,000	4,000
Inventory	60,000	40,000	(20,000)
Fixed assets (gross)	20,000	20,000	0
Accumulated depreciation	0	(556)	
Total assets	**102,000**	**134,744**	
Accounts payable[+]	38,000	50,384	12,384
Debt	24,000	12,000	(12,000)
Equity (common stock)	40,000	40,000	0
Retained earnings	0	32,360	
Total equities	**102,000**	**134,744**	
OWC[a]	34,000	5,616	(28,384)

a. OWC = accounts receivable[+] + inventory − accounts payable[+], as minimum cash is assumed to be zero.

The fixed assets account has been unfolded to keep track of potential changes in gross fixed assets (such as investments in new fixed assets during the period). Likewise, the equity (common stock) and retained earnings accounts have not been merged to keep track of potential changes in issued equity.

Inspection of table 7.2 will help us conclude that only four items are relevant in this example, since no new equity has been issued, no investments have been made, and no dividends have been paid. Also, as debt has decreased during the period, the change in debt will appear on the left-hand side of the report as decreasing debt (figure 7.5).

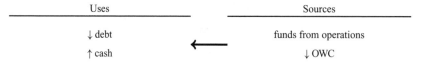

Uses	Sources
↓ debt	funds from operations
↑ cash	↓ OWC

Figure 7.5
Only four items are relevant in this case.

Funds from operations can be calculated as:

$$\text{funds from operations} = \text{net profit} + \text{depreciation}$$
$$= \$32,360 + \$556 = \$32,916$$

Finally, the statement of cash flows is shown in figure 7.6. Note that, as expected, the sums of two columns match.

Uses		Sources	
↓ debt	12,000	funds from operations	32,916
↑ cash	49,300	↓ OWC	28,384
Total uses	**61,300**	**Total sources**	**61,300**

Figure 7.6
Ethan and Ryan's new firm statement of cash flows from January 9 to January 31.

7.3.2 Interpretation and OWC Breakdown

The statement of cash flows contains relevant information about what occurred during the last twenty-three days of January: the firm did pretty well, as funds from operations totaled $32,916; that money together with additional $28,384 freed up by *decreasing* OWC was used to reduce the principal of the bank loan by $12,000. The remaining money just increased the cash by $49,300. This information can be confronted with the original plans and the strategy of the firms to reach further conclusions.

The connection between OWC and cash flows

An increase (decrease) of OWC is equivalent to a negative (positive) cash flow.

A useful exercise at this point may be to break down OWC so as to get additional information about changes of their constituents. As someone working in the operations or supply chain realm, you should understand why OWC changed, and take action if there are unexpected deviations. Figure 7.7 gives the detail of OWC changes. Note that, as expected, the difference between the two totals of both columns coincide with decreasing OWC in figure 7.6.

OWC increases		OWC decreases	
↑ acc. receivable[+]	4,000	↓ inventory	20,000
		↑ acc. payable[+]	12,384
Total	**4,000**	**Total**	**32,384**

Figure 7.7
Ethan and Ryan's new firm statement of cash flows from January 9 to January 31: OWC breakdown.

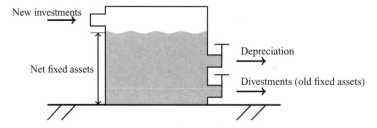

Figure 7.8
A pictorial representation of net fixed assets (a stock in the balance sheet) and the related flows.

7.4   Calculating the Level of New Investments

Some people struggle calculating this item of the statement of cash flows. To avoid confusion, it may be a good idea to resort to use a container simile again (figure 7.8).

As the figure suggests, net fixed assets change only due to investments/divestments or depreciation. More specifically, we can write:

$$\text{net fixed assets}_t = \text{net fixed assets}_{t-1} + \text{new investments}_t - \text{divestments}_t - \text{depreciation}_t$$

where divestments are valued at book value; for instance, acquisition cost less accumulated depreciation.

7.5   Reconciliation of Statement of Cash Flows

The statement of cash flows presented in the previous section is not presented in a standard way, as you would find it in a firm's annual report. Had we followed the standard structure of a statement of cash flows in an annual report, Ethan and Ryan's new firm statement of cash flows would have been something like the report shown in table 7.3.

The data is the same, but it is organized in a different way. The sum of the two first items, net profit and depreciation, is what we called funds from operations. This is further adjusted by the changes in OWC to obtain cash generated from operations. As said, this item tells whether operations generated cash during the period or not, an aspect carefully scrutinized by investors.

Investing activities describes any changes in gross fixed assets, none in the example. Finally, financing activities takes care of the changes in debt or equity—such as share issues or dividend payment but not net profit. The sum of these three items, namely cash provided by operations, investing activities, and financing activities, gives the net increase of cash during the period.

The focus of the first method is on OWC, which may be very useful to address operational issues, while this alternative, standard version focuses on explaining why the level of cash

Table 7.3
An alternative statement of cash flows.

Net profit		32,360
Depreciation		556
Changes in operating assets & equities		
	Receivables[+]	−4,000
	Inventory	20,000
	Payables[+]	12,384
Cash generated from operations[a]		**61,300**
Investing activities		
	New equipment	0
Financing activities		
	Debt repayment	−12,000
Net increase in cash		**49,300**
Initial cash		10,000
Final cash		59,300

a. cash generated from operations $= 32{,}360 + 556 - 4{,}000 + 20{,}000 + 12{,}384$.

changed during the period. All in all, both methods may be useful to represent the statement of cash flows, as they complement each other. We will be using either one throughout the book.

7.5.1 Example: Understanding Tata Motors' Statement of Cash Flows

In this section we comment on the statement of cash flows of Indian automotive company Tata Motors, one of the largest Indian companies (table 7.4). We will also derive the seven-item statement of cash flows.

The most important line in the report is the first line of the last block: "Net increase /(decrease) cash and cash equivalents" (Tata Motors 2017, 194). It tells that cash[+] of Tata Motors increased by 318 crore from April 1, 2016 (229 crore) to March 31, 2017 (547 crore).[2] The rest of the report explains why cash[+] increased by that amount:

• The first block (first six lines, seventeen in the original report) is devoted to calculate "cash flows from operating activities before changes in following assets and liabilities" (Tata Motors 2017, 194), or funds from operations, as we called it. Net profit (net loss in this case at -1,034) is adjusted for noncash items such as depreciation. The resulting figure, 4,091 crore, is the cash operations had generated if OWC were zero.

• The second block gives the detail of the changes in operating working capital: these are of great importance in operations management; therefore we show the complete list as in

2. 1 crore $=$ US\$145,000 as of May 2019.

Table 7.4
Tata Motors statements of cash flows for 2017 in crores, 1 crore = 10,000,000 rupees (abridged).

Cash flows from operating activities:	
Profit/loss after tax	−1,034
Adjustments for:	
Depreciation and amortization expense	3,102
Other non-cash items (12 items)	2,024
(Total adjustments)	5,126
Cash flows from operating activities before changes in following assets and liabilities	4,091
Trade receivables	−1,217
Loans and advances and other financial assets	−1,092
Other current and non-current assets	430
Inventories	−278
Trade payables and acceptances	2,764
Other current and non-current liabilities	−139
Other financial liabilities	−957
Provisions	541
Cash generated from operations	4,142
Income taxes credit/(paid) (net)	−8
Net cash from operating activities	4,134
Cash flows from investing activities	
Payments for property, plant and equipments	−1,379
Other items (15 items)	669
Net cash used in investing activities	−710
Cash flows from financing activities	
Proceeds from long-term borrowings	1,622
Other items (6 items)	−4,728
Net cash (used in) / from financing activities	−3,106
Net increase /(decrease) cash and cash equivalents	318
Cash and cash equivalents as at April 1, (opening balance)	229
Cash and cash equivalents as at March 31, (closing balance)	547

Source: https://www.tatamotors.com/wp-content/uploads/2018/07/27060927/jlr-annual-report-2017-18.pdf.

the original report. The final line of the block, net cash from operating activities at 4,134 crore, is the cash generated by operating activities.

• Next is the detail of investing activities in fixed assets: 710 crore have been used (net) to pay for investments in fixed assets, such as property, plant, and equipments. The figure provided is *net* cash, as some fixed assets may have been sold—hence generated cash inflows.

• Finally, financing activities are detailed. These include increases and decreases in financial debt and equity. For instance, proceeds from long-term borrowings tells that 1,622 crore went from a lender (e.g., a bank) to the firm's cash box. Overall, net cash used in financing

Table 7.5
Tata Motors seven-item statements of cash flows.

Funds uses		Funds sources	
↓ debt	3,106	funds from operations	4,091
investments in fixed assets	710	↓ OWC	51
↑ cash	318		
other	8		
Total	4,142	Total	4,142

activities adds up to 3,106 crore, which means that a good portion of cash generated by the business has been used to repay outstanding debt.

Deducting cash used for investing and financing activities from the cash generated by operations gives exactly 318 crore, which is the amount by which the cash has increased during the fiscal year. Numerically:

$$4,134 - 710 - 3,106 = 318$$

An alternative to the previous report is the one we propose in this chapter (table 7.5).

This report has a number of characteristics that make it suitable for operations management and, in general, for managers outside the finance realm:

• It has no more than seven items, which makes it easier to understand. The original statement of cash flows from Tata has *sixty-five* lines, which may be simply much more information than operations or supply chain managers need.

• The most important piece of information, namely the change in cash, is explicitly shown.

• The fact that items are classified in columns depending on whether the item contributes in cash to the firm or makes use of it facilitates the interpretation of the report. For instance, in the case of Tata, a quick interpretation would go as follows: Tata's operations generated some 4,000 crore during the period. That cash, together with additional 50 crore due to reducing OWC, has been used mainly to repay existing debt (some three quarters) and to invest in new fixed assets. The remaining amount has contributed to increase the cash in some 300 crore.

• Emphasis is made in the change of OWC, the key operations variable. Given the position of ΔOWC in the report (left or right) and its magnitude shows very quickly how well OWC has been managed during the period.

In order to explain in detail the changes in OWC, the report in table 7.6 shows increases and decreases in the three main elements of OWC (as usual, minimum cash is assumed constant).

Table 7.6
Tata Motors seven-item statements of cash flows for 2017: Detail of operating working capital (in crores).

OWC increases		OWC decreases	
Trade receivables	1,217	Trade payables and acceptances	2,764
Other receivables[+] (e.g., governm. grants)	662		
Inventories	278		
Other payables[+] (e.g., provisions)	556		
Total	2,713	Total	2,764

As expected, the difference between the two totals in the report is exactly the amount reported as ΔOWC, that is: $2{,}764 - 2{,}713 = 51$ crore. This report may nicely complement the one in table 7.5, as it provides additional operational information: in the case of Tata, it is clear that OWC has released some money mainly because of the growth of trade payables, that is, payments to suppliers have been delayed on average. This seems to be good news other things equal. On the contrary, accounts receivable and inventory have grown during the period, which is not a good thing other things equal. Other receivables[+] include money to be received, for example from governments or insurance companies (see notes 10 to 14 in the annual report); other payables[+] include items such as provisions for employee benefit obligations, that is, already accrued money to be paid in the future to employees (see notes 27 and 28).

7.6 Summary

This chapter has presented the statement of cash flows, the third major financial statement that, together with the balance sheet and the income statement, gives an overall view of the financial status of a firm. The statement of cash flows gives a dynamic view of the firm, explaining which flows of cash have occurred during a given period.

A good feature of the statement of cash flows is that is based on irrefutable facts for the most part, hence it is more difficult to manipulate. This is in contrast with the other two financial statements, balance sheet and income statement, which are more subject to management judgment.

Two versions of the statement of cash flows are presented: the standard one, as is usually communicated by firms' annual reports, and an alternative one, more succinct, which focuses more on the important items for operations, such as OWC.

Exercises

1. What are the seven elements of the seven-item statement of cash flows?

2. Does the statement of cash flows give a static or a dynamic perspective of a firm? If static, how is it different from the balance sheet? If dynamic, how is it different from the income statement?

3. Indicate whether each of he following items is a source or a use of cash:

  a. A decrease in inventory

  b. An increase in accounts payable

  c. A decrease in accounts receivable

  d. An increase in depreciation

  e. The repayment of a loan

  f. The payment of dividends to shareholders

  g. The purchase of new equipment

  h. The payment of new equipment

  i. The payment of taxes

4. Prepare the 2018 seven-item statement of cash flows for the Vending Machines exercise (number 16) in the previous chapter.

5. Prepare the seven-item statement of cash flows for the Aida and Maria exercise from chapter 6 (number 17) between September 1 and December 31.

6. Given the following balance sheets for a company:

Year	2019	2020
Assets		
Cash	30	6
Receivables	20	55
Inventory	40	50
Fixed assets (gross)	100	225
Accumulated depreciation	(30)	(40)
Equities		
Suppliers	40	62
Salaries	5	6
Debt	0	100
Common stock	100	100
Retained earnings	15	28

and knowing that: (a) the firm didn't pay dividends, (b) it didn't sell any fixed assets in 2018, and (c) minimum cash is six in both years:

  a. Calculate OWC for years 2019 and 2020.

  b. Calculate funds from operations in year 2020.

  c. Prepare the seven-item statement of cash flows for year 2020.

7. Given the following balance sheets:

Year	2019	2020
Assets		
Cash	100	60
Marketable securities	10	10
Receivables	20	60
Inventory	40	155
Fixed assets (net)	400	500
Equities		
Suppliers	40	25
Taxes payable	20	30
Debt, short-term	100	210
Debt, long-term	0	100
Equity	410	420

and knowing that the firm didn't pay dividends, didn't sell any fixed assets in 2018; and minimum cash is zero:

    a. Prepare the seven-item statement of cash flows for year 2020.

    b. What can you infer from the statement of cash flows?

8. Starting at $3 million, a firm's net fixed assets has increased by 20 percent for three consecutive years. If depreciation has been $250,000 every year, how much has the firm invested in fixed assets in each of the three years? (Assume that no fixed assets have been sold.)

9. Which of these two magnitudes, FFO (funds from operations) or CGO (cash generated from operations), is most important to control when it comes to liquidity?

10. Give conditions under which FFO and CGO are identical during a period.

11. Give conditions under which FFO may be negative during a period.

12. True or false? If inventory obsolescence is very high in a given year, FFO will most likely be larger than CGO.

References

Anthony, R. N., and James S. Reece. 1983. *Management accounting: Text and cases*. Homewood, IL: The Willard J. Graham series.

Fernández, Pablo. 2012. "Cash flow is cash and is a fact: Net income is just an opinion." Working paper, n. 629.

Higgins, Robert C. 2012. *Analysis for financial management*, 10th ed. New York: McGraw-Hill.

Mulford, Charles W., and James Jayko. 2006. "Net income plus depreciation, operating cash flow, and buildups in operating working capital." Working paper, Georgia Tech Financial Analysis Lab.

8 Accounting for Inventory

Inventory? Oh, so sweet—It's what it's all about!
—David Berman, founder and general partner, Durban Capital L.P.

Inventory refers to any tangible item held by a company to sell, support production, or consume in the course of business. Typically, inventory represents the largest current asset in manufacturing and retail firms. Based on historical data from the United States Census Bureau (2019) at the end of 2017 the total investment in inventory for U.S. firms was equal to $1.9 trillion, representing about $1.35 investment in inventory for every dollar of sales made. Given the considerable amount of cash tied up in inventory, the potential impact of good management of this asset in the bottom line can be significant. In this chapter we will show that in addition to operational excellence in inventory control, the accounting practices that a company utilizes for pricing inventory may also have a substantial impact on the firm's net income and working capital measurements. To that end, accounting for inventory represents an important element in a firm's accounting strategy.

In this chapter, we present the basic accounting methods for inventory valuation and discuss how managerial discretion in the selection of these methods can affect a firm's financial results. Our goal is to understand: (a) what the inventory categories are, (b) how the value of inventory is calculated in manufacturing firms, (c) what inventory assumptions are available to determine ending inventory and cost of goods sold, and (d) what the impact of these assumptions is on net income and taxes.

8.1 Inventory Valuation in Retailing and Manufacturing

There are several drivers that encourage companies to hold inventory, such as economies of scale, demand variability, lead time, or production smoothing. Depending on its intended use and its stage within a firm, inventory can be classified into four categories: finished goods, work in progress, raw materials, and consumables (or manufacturing supplies).

Retailers' main business is to purchase finished goods that are then sold to customers. Hence, inventory in merchandising companies typically falls under the first category.

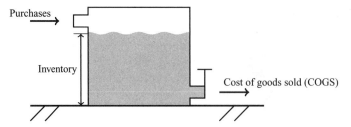

Figure 8.1
Retailer's inventory can be represented by the level of water in the tank.

As figure 8.1 suggests, we can think of the inventory account in retailing as a quantity stored in a tank with two valves (see also section 2.5.7 on stocks and flows). The level of water in the tank increases during a specific period of time when an inflow takes place and decreases whenever we have an outflow. In the physical world, if we consider retailer's inventory as a stock, then an inflow would correspond to items purchased, while an outflow would be items sold. In the accounting domain, inventory can be represented by the quantity in the container, while the inflows and outflows correspond to the monetary value of purchases and the cost of goods sold, respectively.

That is, there is a clear correspondence between the movement of goods in and out of a firm's physical inventory and the interpretation of these movements as accounting transactions. Consequently, the basic equation that links stocks and flows in a retailer's inventory account is as follows:

end inventory = beginning inventory + purchases − cost of goods sold

The only complication arises from the difference in the timing between when these movements take place in the physical and accounting worlds. For example, while goods flow in and out of a firm's physical inventory continuously, the accounting reporting of these movements usually takes place in predetermined intervals (e.g., monthly or quarterly). But, as business conditions (e.g., purchasing cost of a good) might be subject to frequent changes, this introduces managerial discretion in the accounting reporting of inventory movements. In section 8.3 we discuss how a firm's assumptions regarding inventory flows might affect its reported net income and working capital.

In manufacturing companies, things are a bit more nuanced. As a manufacturing firm is defined by the process of transforming raw material into finished goods, inventory in these firms includes all four categories. In a typical manufacturing firm, raw materials are purchased and enter the raw material inventory until they are released to production—that is, when they enter the work-in-progress inventory. At this stage, the costs of direct labor and manufacturing overhead (which also usually includes consumption of manufacturing supplies) are added. Upon completion of the production process, the finished items enter

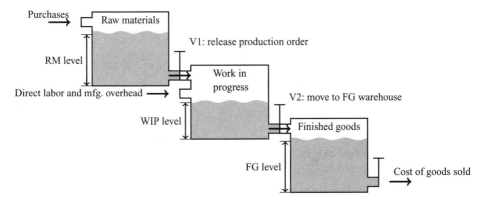

Figure 8.2
A more detailed view of manufacturing inventories, including raw materials (RM), work in progress (WIP), and finished goods (FG).

the finished goods inventory until they are sold to customers. Since the balance sheet is a snapshot in time while production process is a continuous process, we expect all three types of inventory described above to be present at any point of time.

A key question for manufacturing firms is how to calculate the value of inventory in each of these stages. While the allocation of direct material and direct labor costs (i.e., material and labor that can be directly linked to the products) is straightforward, allocating manufacturing overhead requires a cost system. For example, how should the salaries of plant engineers be allocated to the different products manufactured in the plant? The procedures that can be used for this purpose are presented in section 8.2. Nevertheless, given some valuation method of the work-in-progress inventory, the process of calculating the value of inventory and cost of goods sold follows the same stock-and-flow logic that has been shown above for merchandising firms.

We can zoom in to obtain a more detailed view of manufacturing inventories (figure 8.2). When an order is released to production, valve V1 opens and raw materials to produce such production order are moved to work in progress inventory. As raw materials get processed, additional value is added to inventory as direct labor and manufacturing overhead (e.g., supervisory labor, insurance, depreciation of equipment, utilities). A key point is that these indirect costs are not considered expenses yet but increase the book value of inventory. Once the order is finished, valve V2 opens and inventory becomes finished goods. Only when inventory is sold, all costs involved in the production of that inventory being sold are at once considered expenses (cost of goods sold).

As it can be observed in figure 8.2, the basic equations that link stocks and flows in a manufacturer's inventory accounts are as follows:

end RM inventory = beginning RM inventory + purchases − releases to production

end WIP inventory = beginning WIP inventory + released RM + direct labor

$$+ \text{ manufacturing overhead} - \text{releases to FG inventory}$$

end FG inventory = beginning FG inventory + released from production

$$- \text{cost of goods sold} \tag{8.1}$$

It follows that in addition to the timing problem (i.e., changes in business conditions) discussed above, which might be responsible for variations in the cost of different items over time, valuing inventory in manufacturing firms is also subject to managerial discretion regarding allocation of manufacturing expenses to the different products.

Before closing this section, we would like to make a quick note on services companies. Two characteristic attributes of these firms are that the product (service) is typically intangible and that the service is produced and consumed at the same time. The only feature that resembles the role of inventory in merchandising or manufacturing firms is the capacity (i.e., the number of employees participating in the service delivery process). However, since the salaries of these employees are considered a period's expenses, the only type of inventory in the balance sheets of services companies is consumables. Consequently, the cost of services (i.e., cost of sales) in these firms includes the salaries of the employees who directly provide the service and perhaps some allocation of the overhead that can be related to the service delivery process.

The key questions associated with a firm's inventory valuation

• How to allocate the business costs to the company's products?

• When do costs from the inventory accounts become period expenses?

As it is clear from our discussion above, inventory valuation involves two fundamental decisions: product costing and inventory cost flow assumptions. Product costing is the accounting process of determining the cost of inventory that is available for sale or manufactured. The inventory cost flow assumptions answer the question of which costs are moved first from the inventory account to become period expenses (i.e., COGS) when inventory is sold and delivered to customers. Next, we discuss each of these processes and the managerial discretion behind them.

8.2   Product Costing

Product costing is a very important process not only for the accounting reporting of the value of inventory but also for supporting core managerial decisions such as production planning and budgeting, pricing, and determination of production mix. Actually, cost accounting—which deals with the recording and analysis of all the costs incurred in a business—is a discipline on its own concerned with facilitating cost-informed decision making. While this section inevitably uses terminology and basic concepts from cost accounting, our main focus here is on how product costing affects the financial reporting of inventory value. We revisit most of these concepts later in chapter 11, which focuses on the use of accounting information for managerial decision making.

Product costing takes place through a costing system whose main features are the identification and classification of the different cost elements, their measurement, and their allocation to an organization's cost centers (i.e., products, business units, manufacturing sites, etc.). Due to the focus of this chapter on inventory, in what follows we will only consider products as cost centers.

In a manufacturing context, inventory cost is the sum of the applicable expenses directly or indirectly incurred in bringing an article to its existing condition and location. The main types of costs that are associated with the production of a good generally include material, labor, and overhead. These costs can be classified as either variable—if costs increase with the level of activity (i.e., production quantity)—or fixed—if they stay constant. Likewise, they can be categorized as direct—when they can be fully allocated to a cost center (i.e., a specific product)—or indirect—otherwise.

 Product costing in manufacturing

Product costing in manufacturing involves the measurement and allocation of direct and indirect material, labor, and overhead expenses into the different products.

The allocation of costs to different products would be a relatively easy process, if only direct or variable costs were allocated to the products they can be traced to. However, for reporting purposes, the accounting standards (including GAAP and IFRS) require the incorporation of manufacturing expenses in the cost of inventory. That is, even if a cost element is not directly associated with each of the products manufactured in a plant, it should still be allocated to the cost of inventory of these products. This accounting requirement is referred to as absorption costing (also known as full costing) and is mandatory for both external financial reporting and income tax reporting.

 Absorption costing

Absorption costing is a method of calculating the cost of a product by taking into account production costs—direct and indirect.

Due to the absorption costing requirement, manufacturing firms need to determine a basis for the allocation of the overhead to the products' inventory cost (and consequently, to cost of goods sold). This can be quite challenging when it comes to allocation of fixed overhead costs such as salaries of plant administrative staff, rent, depreciation of equipment, and so on. Next, we will discuss the application of different rules for allocating manufacturing overhead through an example of a firm that manufactures and sells two product models.

 Exercise

Inglass Inc.

Inglass Inc. is an interior door glass supplier to oven manufacturers. The company currently produces two models, Model A and Model B, in a single plant located in North Carolina. For financial reporting purposes, but also in order to make better pricing and production decisions, management would like to estimate the full cost and assess the profitability per unit of each product. In one accounting period the firm produced 700,000 units of product A and 1,900,000 units of product B, while the selling price has respectively been $45.00 and $30.00 per unit. The following table shows the resulting direct costs for the period.

	Model A	Model B	Total
Units produced	700,000	1,900,000	2,600,000
Direct materials cost per unit	13.93	7.70	
Direct labor cost per unit	9.00	7.11	
Direct materials cost	9,750,000	14,625,000	24,375,000
Direct labor cost	6,300,000	13,500,000	19,800,000
Total direct costs	16,050,000	28,125,000	44,175,000

Direct material costs include costs of silica sand, soda ash, and other chemicals used in the production of the two models. These raw materials are considered direct as they can be easily identified, conveniently measured, and directly allocated to the cost of producing the company's finished goods. Direct labor costs include the cost of person-hours for running the production machines (furnace, forming, internal treatment, and annealing). Similarly, these labor costs are considered direct as the efforts of the production line workers can be directly traced to the manufacturing process of the company's products. In addition to direct material and direct labor, 384 and 716 hours of machinery run time can be directly allocated to products A and B, respectively.

The company's cost accountants have also identified cost totals for the period's production support activities and other overhead, which are shown in the table below.

Cost category	Indirect costs	As % of total indirect
Material purchasing	950,000	6.4
Machine setup, testing, and calibration	2,625,000	17.7
Product packaging	1,200,000	8.1
Production supervision	1,000,000	6.7
Quality assurance	1,305,000	8.8
Plant administration	1,850,000	12.5
Utilities	3,075,000	20.7
Supplies	1,345,000	9.1
Depreciation of equipment	1,500,000	10.1
Total indirect costs	14,850,000	100.0

The indirect cost components include costs that cannot be directly assigned to specific product units, but they relate to specific production runs, batches, or time periods, such as expenses for material purchasing, machine setup, testing and calibration, utilities, and supplies. They also include manufacturing overhead, such as depreciation of equipment and the salaries of quality assurance staff, supervisors, and employees working in the plant administration offices.

As the company follows the IFRS standards for financial reporting, these indirect costs cannot be reported as expenses when they are incurred; instead, they need to be included as cost of inventory. While the direct costs per unit were easily attributed to the two products, the allocation of the indirect costs requires the application of a costing methodology. Traditionally, Inglass Inc. has used predetermined overhead rates for allocating the total indirect cost to each product, A or B. In particular, these rules have been based on factors, or cost drivers, such as:

a. the proportion of units of each product over the total output.

b. the proportion of direct labor costs used by each product.

c. the proportion of production machine time used by each product.

1. Allocate indirect costs according to the above mentioned rules.

2. What are the implications for the profitability of each product?

Table 8.1 shows the allocation percentages as suggested by the three rules.
The resulting unit cost estimates, along with the gross profit and gross margin per product, are shown in table 8.2.

Table 8.1
Allocation percentages according to the three cost drivers.

Cost driver	Model A		Model B		Total	
	units measured	%	units measured	%	units measured	%
(a) Production (units)	700,000	26.9	1,900,000	73.1	2,600,000	100
(b) Direct labor cost ($)	6,300,000	31.8	13,500,000	68.2	19,800,000	100
(c) Production machine time (h.)	384	34.9	716	65.1	1100	100

Table 8.2
Gross profit and gross margin calculations for each product of Inglass Inc. (US$).

	Method (a)		Method (b)		Method (c)	
	Model A	Model B	Model A	Model B	Model A	Model B
Selling price	45	30	45	30	45	30
Total direct cost / unit	22.93	14.81	22.93	14.81	22.93	14.81
Allocated indirect cost / unit	5.71	5.71	6.75	5.33	7.41	5.09
Total cost / unit	28.64	20.51	29.68	20.13	30.34	19.89
Gross profit / unit	16.36	9.49	15.32	9.87	14.66	10.11
Gross margin (%)	36.4	31.6	34.0	32.9	32.6	33.7

In table 8.2, the allocation of indirect cost to each unit of the two models, A and B, is done by applying the corresponding allocation percentages from table 8.1 to the total indirect cost and dividing by the number of units produced of each product. For example, the allocated indirect cost per unit of model A under the direct labor method (b) is $31.8\% \cdot 14,850,000/700,000 = \$6.75$.

Table 8.2 suggests that the three different methods considered by Inglass Inc. for the allocation of indirect costs would result in three different figures for the cost per unit of model A and B produced. For instance, on a basis of proportion of direct labor, the unit costs (gross margins) of models A and B are, respectively, $29.68 (34.0 percent) and $20.13 (32.9 percent). The corresponding values under a production machine time basis are $30.34 (32.6 percent) and $19.89 (33.7 percent). The management wonders which of the three methods provides a more accurate approximation for the period studied of the real cost per unit for the two models produced by Inglass Inc. Is there a better alternative?

From the Inglass Inc. example it becomes obvious that—due to the absorption costing requirement—the selection of a method for the allocation of the indirect costs to the different products produced by a manufacturing firm might indeed have implications on the company's balance sheet (inventory account) and income statement (cost of goods sold and, consequently, gross profit). Consider, for example, the quite common case that a period's sales are lower than the period's production output. In this case, the allocation rule used by the firm will determine the amount of manufacturing overhead that will be absorbed by sales (through cost of goods sold) and the amount that will appear in the balance sheet as cost of inventory. Consequently, under certain conditions, a firm's selection of cost allocation rules might determine whether it will report profit or loss in a given period.

This case also brings up another important consideration: how accurate are the calculated costs in table 8.2 if, for example, the production of model A is characterized by more frequent ordering of raw materials or smaller production batches? This question introduces us to another methodology for allocating overhead costs to different products, namely activity-based costing, which is discussed next.

8.2.1 Use of Activity-Based Costing (ABC) Principles for Allocating Overhead

Activity-based costing (or ABC for short) is a costing method that assigns indirect costs to products based on the activities that go into them (Kaplan and Cooper 1997). In particular, ABC first assigns costs to the activities that are the real cause of the overhead; then it assigns the cost of the resources consumed by these activities only to the products that do make use of them. For example, the activity of running machinery might be the key driver of power cost; hence, machine operating hours can be the basis for the allocation of this cost to different products based on their share of machine running time. By recognizing the relationships among costs, activities, and products, ABC allocates indirect costs to products less arbitrarily than conventional methods. As a result, ABC and traditional cost accounting can give quite different estimates for the cost of inventory and cost of goods sold for different products.

Improving costing accuracy and assessing the true profitability of individual products are the main incentives for firms to adopt ABC. As ABC is more useful in environments with many machines, multitasking labor, and processes and products that consume common resources, this method is widely used in the manufacturing sector. Another reason for the prevalence of ABC is that manufacturing indirect costs—as percentage of overall production costs—have significantly increased over the decades. This has created a need to properly allocate those costs.

 Activity-based costing

> **Activity-based costing** is an accounting method that identifies and assigns costs to overhead activities and then allocates those costs to different products on the basis of each product's consumption of overhead activities.

Before moving on with describing how the ABC method works, we should mention that ABC is a discipline on its own, often used by firms as a decision support tool. Actually, activity-based management (ABM) is a management system which uses ABC to evaluate activities that a company performs with the objective of improving strategic and operational decision-making in the organization. Such decisions may include closing a business unit or initiating a new one, adding or removing products from the product portfolio, adjusting pricing models, streamlining departments, assessing customer profitability, evaluating total cost of doing business with suppliers, and so on. We will discuss how accounting can help support such decisions in chapter 11. As our focus here is on accounting for inventory, this section discusses how incorporating the principles of ABC into their costing systems may help companies allocate their manufacturing overhead to the cost of inventory more accurately than traditional methods.

Activities in ABC are those tasks (referred to as cost objects) that consume indirect resources. Unlike conventional cost measurement systems that depend on volume count (such as machine hours and/or direct labor hours) to allocate indirect or overhead costs to products, the ABC system recognizes that the cost of some activities may relate to other factors, such as the number of batches, number of product lines, and so on. To that end, ABC assigns activities to one of four categories.

Unit-level activities   Unit-level activities occur every time a product is made or a service is performed. Direct materials and direct labor are clear examples of costs associated with unit-level activities.

Batch-level activities   These occur every time a group of units is produced or a series of process steps is performed. Examples of batch-level activities include setting up machines for production, placing purchase orders, running quality tests, and so on.

Product-level activities   Those activities that support an entire product line but not necessarily each individual unit are called product-level activities. Engineering changes in the production line, developing product design changes, and maintaining special storage facilities are examples of product-level activities.

Facility-level (or organization-sustaining) activities   These activities refer to support activities that are necessary for production to take place. The cost of these activities are administrative in nature and include building depreciation and maintenance, plant security, salaries of management and support staff, and so on.

Associated with activities are the cost drivers (or activity drivers), which describe the transactions or events that drive the cost of an activity and form the allocation base. In other words, a cost driver is the unit of an activity that causes the change in its cost. Examples of cost drivers include machine setups, machine running time, purchase orders, quality inspections, maintenance requests, product design changes, and so forth. Based on the unit of measurement applied, there are two categories of activity measures: transaction drivers, which require counting how many times an activity occurs, and duration drivers, which measure how long an activity takes to complete. Table 8.3 presents commonly used cost drivers for some activity cost pools.

The selection of a particular cost driver over another is very context-specific. For example, if it takes the same time to set the machines for the production of different products, then the number of machine setups (i.e., a transaction driver) can be a suitable cost driver for the activity of setting up machines. Otherwise, it might be more appropriate to use

Table 8.3
Common activity cost pools and cost drivers.

Activity cost pools	Activity cost drivers
Schedule production jobs	Number of production runs
Set up machines	Number of setups
Run machines	Machine hours
Process purchasing orders	Number of purchasing orders
Quality assurance	Number of quality inspections
Engineering department	Number of engineering change orders
Production supervision	Number of direct labor hours
Product design	Number of design changes
Customer service	Number of customer requests attended

machine setup hours (i.e., a duration driver) as a cost driver for the allocation of the same activity.

Notice that all examples in table 8.3 refer to activities that are either unit-level, batch-level, or product-level. The costs of such activities can be relatively easily allocated to individual product units. In contrast, the facility-level activities cannot be directly traced to products because there is no meaningful method. For instance, how can a plant manager's salary or a building's depreciation be allocated to individual product units? Obviously, these costs would have to be assigned on an arbitrary basis, such as the number of product lines or the area occupied by each product in the production facility. When ABC is applied as a decision support tool, the cost of organization-sustaining activities is often treated as period expenses and is not allocated to products. For accounting purposes, though, this lump of overhead costs must still be assigned to products.

Exercise

Inglass Inc. (revisited)

Calculate total unit cost for products A and B using activity-based costing.

Data for starting the analysis include the indirect cost components shown in the original case, which, in the ABC terminology, are viewed as activity cost pools. Next, ABC requires the identification of the cost drivers for each cost pool. In the operating environment of Inglass Inc., the total cost of the activity "setting up and testing machines," for instance, is driven by the number of machine setups, while the total cost of the activity "quality assurance" is driven by the number of quality inspections. Table 8.4 shows the cost drivers and the allocation of the total cost driver unit count among the two products, A and B.

Table 8.4
Activity cost drivers and allocation of their unit count to each product of Inglass Inc.

			Model A		Model B	
Activity cost pool	Cost driver	Total cost driver Unit count	Cost driver Unit count	%	Cost driver Unit count	%
Material purchasing	# purch. orders	235	140	59.6	95	40.4
Machine setup and testing	# setups	186	96	51.6	90	48.4
Product packaging	# packages	1,175,000	700,000	59.6	475,000	40.4
Production supervision	Direct labor	$19,800,000	$6,300,000	31.8	$13,500,000	68.2
Quality assurance	# inspections	117	72	61.5	45	38.5
Plant administration	Direct labor	$19,800,000	$6,300,000	31.8	$13,500,000	68.2
Utilities	Machine-time	1,100	384	34.9	716	65.1
Supplies	# units	2,600,000	700,000	26.9	1,900,000	73.1
Depreciation of equipment	Machine-time	1,100	384	34.9	716	65.1

Table 8.5
Allocation of activity cost pools to each product of Inglass Inc.

Activity cost pool	Measured cost	Model A	%	Model B	%
Material purchasing	950,000	565,957	59.6	384,043	40.4
Machine setup and testing	2,625,000	1,354,839	51.6	1,270,161	48.4
Product packaging	1,200,000	714,894	59.6	485,106	40.4
Production supervision	1,000,000	318,182	31.8	681,818	68.2
Quality assurance	1,305,000	803,077	61.5	501,923	38.5
Plant administration	1,850,000	588,636	31.8	1,261,364	68.2
Utilities	3,075,000	1,073,455	34.9	2,001,545	65.1
Supplies	1,345,000	362,115	26.9	982,885	73.1
Depreciation of equipment	1,500,000	523,636	34.9	976,364	65.1
Total cost	14,850,000	6,304,791		8,545,209	

Again, note that the selection of a cost driver for a particular activity is dependent on the specific context of the manufacturing environment. Transaction drivers are suitable if the processes associated with some activity are standardized and have the same duration among different products, while duration drivers are better suited for time-intensive processes. Note also that Inglass Inc. uses direct labor as a cost driver for plant administration (a facility-level activity). This is an arbitrary selection made in order to assign this cost to products for accounting purposes.

Based on the allocation of the cost driver unit counts to the different products, the assignment of the activity costs to the two models, A and B, is done on the basis of their proportional consumption of each activity. This is calculated in table 8.5.

Once the activity cost pools have been allocated to the two products, the computation of the allocated cost per unit of product is done by simply dividing the total allocated cost per product category (last line in table 8.5) by the quantity produced of each product. This

Table 8.6
Gross profit and gross margin calculation for each product of Inglass Inc. under ABC.

	Direct labor		ABC	
	Model A	Model B	Model A	Model B
Selling price	45.00	30.00	45.00	30.00
Total direct cost / unit	22.93	14.80	22.93	14.80
Allocated indirect cost / unit	6.75	5.33	9.01	4.50
Total cost / unit	29.68	20.13	31.94	19.30
Gross profit / unit	15.32	9.87	13.06	10.70
Gross margin (%)	34.0	32.9	29.0	35.7

is given under "allocated indirect cost per unit" in table 8.6, which shows how these costs contribute to the new version of profitability calculations for each product.

By applying an ABC approach to the product costing problem of Inglass Inc., it becomes clear that model A consumes more resources than model B. Consequently, the total unit cost for model A is higher than the cost obtained under the traditional costing approaches. Also, in contrast to the direct-labor basis for overhead allocation, ABC suggests that model B is actually more profitable than model A (gross margin of 35.7 percent for B over 29.0 percent for A). These differences result from the different treatment of overhead costs by the two methods, as in ABC the allocation of these costs is done in a less arbitrary manner.

What is also implied in the Inglass Inc. case is that costing inventory with ABC requires more data and more detailed analysis compared to conventional cost accounting methods. In particular, ABC involves a thorough understanding of the resources that are consumed by supporting (overhead) activities, identification of appropriate activity cost drivers, measurement of activity consumption (i.e., number of transactions for transaction drivers or duration of activity for duration drivers), and tracing of activity consumption per product. Hence, there is a clear trade-off between obtaining more accurate estimates of the true production cost for the different products and the higher cost associated with ABC implementation. Actually, applicability of ABC is often bound by the cost of collecting the required data. Hence, the key point is to set up a targeted ABC system that provides the most critical information at a reasonable cost.

In general, firms may find value in adopting ABC under some circumstances. First, it might make sense to consider ABC if the cost of indirect and support activities within an organization is relatively high compared to direct expenses but also if this cost pool does not correlate with machine hours or direct labor hours. Second, the potential benefit of ABC might be large if there is high diversity within an organization in terms of product mix, production quantities, product demand and demand variability, manufacturing and production support processes, storing requirements, etc. Whatever the case, management still needs to investigate whether the benefit of improved cost accuracy is worth the cost of ABC before implementing the new costing method.

Finally, it must be noted that from a purely accounting perspective, how accurately overhead has been allocated to the different products is not of huge importance. What absorption
costing requires is for the entire manufacturing overhead to be allocated as cost of inventory.
In that sense, ABC might have little impact on a firm's financial reports, as both ABC and
traditional costing allocate the same costs to the same accounts—the two methods simply
use a different approach to do so. For example, in the trivial case where Inglass Inc. begins
the accounting period with zero inventory and sells the entire production quantity during
the period, the two methods would give the same aggregate calculation of cost of goods sold
and would have no impact at the bottom line. Nevertheless, having in place a sophisticated
costing system can support important managerial decisions with regard to pricing, product
mix, facility selection, and so forth (addressed in chapter 11).

8.2.2 Inventory Valuation Debate: Absorption versus Direct Costing

As we have discussed in section 8.2, the accounting standards require that the full cost of
manufacturing products be reported as product costs in the financial statements, irrespective
of their classification as variable, fixed, or mixed. We have referred to this cost accumulation method as absorption costing, since each unit produced within an accounting period
essentially absorbs part of the total manufacturing cost incurred in that period. The underlying accounting principle of absorption costing is the matching principle, which requires
that expenses be reported on a firm's income statement in the same period as the revenue
generated by those expenses. Conceptually, since fixed manufacturing costs generate revenue only when manufactured goods are actually sold, they should initially be incorporated
as cost of inventory and then be expensed when inventory is sold.

Direct (or variable) costing, on the other hand, is based on the classification of costs as
variable and fixed. In direct costing, product costs include only the direct material, direct
labor, and the variable portion of manufacturing overhead costs. Fixed manufacturing overhead costs are excluded from product costs (i.e., they are not allocated as cost of inventory)
and are charged instead to the income statement as a period expense. Direct costing is not
accepted by accounting standards (GAAP and IFRS) for external financial reporting or
income tax reporting as, in the view of the standard setters, it violates the matching principle of accounting. However, this method is sometimes used for internal accounting (i.e.,
decision-making) purposes because it provides management with a more realistic picture
of the relationships among volume, costs, and profits.

Main difference between absorption and direct costing
Absorption costing allocates both fixed and variable manufacturing overhead into the
different products, while direct costing assigns into product costs only the latter.

The main difference between absorption costing and direct costing is how fixed manufacturing overhead costs are treated. This can have a substantial impact in the measurement
of net income. Basically, the two cost accumulation methods of inventory valuation have

different answers to the question of which costs are relevant to future periods (and thus should be included in product valuation) and which should be charged against current income. This question has been the focus of extensive debate among accounting theorists and professionals, the origin of which can be traced back to the 1930s and 1940s.

Proponents of absorption costing argue that allocating the full manufacturing expenses to product cost is better aligned with the definition of inventory cost, and it does not violate fundamental principles of accrual accounting. Proponents of direct costing, on the other hand, argue that as fixed manufacturing overhead costs do not change with production volume and tend to remain the same from period to period, they should be reported on the income statement as period expenses. They further claim that a firm's income should depend on sales and not on production that is stored in inventory. Is there any merit to those arguments? Consider, for example, the trivial case of a firm that for some reason does not produce anything in a particular period. However, as fixed manufacturing overhead would still be incurred, this cost can obviously only be reported as period expenses (since it cannot be allocated to any produced items).

Despite the prevalence of absorption costing as the single acceptable product valuation method for external reporting, managers still need to have a good understanding of the differences between the two approaches in their computations of inventory value and net income. To illustrate the broader idea, let's take a look at the following exercise.

 Exercise

Smart Widgets Inc.

Smart Widgets Inc. is a small manufacturing firm that produces a single widget. Building one product unit requires $4 worth of raw materials, $3 in direct (variable) labor and $1 in variable overhead costs (mainly electricity consumed by the production equipment). The fixed manufacturing overhead is equal to $12,000 per quarter and includes equipment depreciation, rent, and salaries of supervisors and administrative staff. In the first quarter of 2019, Smart Widgets produced 5,000 units and incurred $8,000 in operating expenses (i.e., SGA charges). In the same period, total sales were 4,600 units at a unit price of $14. Also, at the beginning of the quarter the firm was not holding any inventory and had zero debt. Prepare the income statements and determine the finished goods inventory for the first quarter of 2019 under both the absorption and variable costing methods.

Based on the information given, the income statements under the two methods are shown in the table 8.7.

Note that the two methods provide a different picture regarding the firm's performance in the first quarter of 2019. This is a consequence of the different approaches followed by the two methods for calculating period product cost per unit. Under absorption costing, each

Table 8.7
Smart Widgets Inc. income statement for Q1 of 2019 under absorption versus direct costing.

| | Income statement | |
	Absorption costing	Direct costing
Sales revenue	64,400	64,400
Cost of goods sold	47,840	36,800
Gross profit	16,560	27,600
Operating expenses	8,000	20,000
Net operating income	8,560	7,600
Net operating margin (%)	13.3	11.8

unit has a reported cost of $10.40; that is, $4 direct material plus $3 direct labor plus $1 variable overhead plus $2.40 worth of the fixed overhead ($12,000 / 5,000 units = $2.40 per unit). Under direct costing, each unit produced has a reported cost of $8; that is, $4 direct material plus $3 direct labor plus $1 variable overhead. In the meantime, the $12,000 in fixed manufacturing overhead is treated as a quarterly expense (is added to the operating expenses). As a result, the net operating income under absorption costing is $8,560, while the same figure under direct costing is equal to $7,600.

A natural question, then, would be what happened to the $960 difference in net operating income derived by absorption costing? Does the firm indeed perform better under the absorption costing method? Obviously, this cannot be the case as the only thing that is different in the two calculations of net operating income is the product valuation method applied. We must remember that, at the end, net income is just an opinion. This difference is due to the fact that the portion of fixed manufacturing overhead related to the units produced but not sold during the period will be reported as value of inventory in the balance sheet. Under absorption costing, finished goods inventory has a reported value of $4,160; i.e., 400 units (produced, but not sold) times $10.40 (unit cost). The reported value under direct costing is equal to $3,200; that is, 400 units times $8. Therefore, the difference in reported income between the two methods is reconciled by their difference in inventory valuation in the balance sheet.

So, finally which method provides a more accurate picture of a firm's performance? This is a rather rhetorical question as each method serves a different purpose. Absorption costing ensures that financial statements reflect the full cost of products and thus provide a more accurate estimate of inventory value. In our example, the fact that some units were produced but not sold does not mean they have lost their value. Direct costing, on the other hand, may provide a more valuable picture to the management of how well the firm has actually performed in the particular period. First, it provides a more accurate picture of the cash flow. Note that the net operating income derived by the direct costing method in our example is the actual cash flow for the period. Second, from a purely operational perspective, it doesn't provide operations and supply chain managers with the wrong incentive to manipulate reported income by increasing production. We leave it as an exercise to verify that had the firm produced 8,000 instead of 5,000 units, under absorption costing the reported net operating income would have been $12,700 (i.e., $4,140 more than in the current situation), while the direct costing income statement would have been exactly the same.

As illustrated in our example above, the major weakness of absorption costing is that reported income with this method becomes a function of both production and sales. Aside from the risk of inducing managerial misbehavior, it is out of the question that a firm's profit should come from sales, not from production. To that end, special caution is needed when interpreting financial reports, especially in periods when firms are building up inventory. On the other hand, by separating fixed and variable costs, direct costing can better support managerial decision making, particularly when it comes to production planning and budgeting. Despite the fact that only absorption costing is allowed by accounting standards for external reporting, firms can gain insight from also maintaining direct costing records, making the extra cost of doing so often well worth the benefit.

8.3   Inventory Cost Flow Assumptions

In parallel with product costing decisions, companies use cost flow assumptions to determine the cost of goods sold and inventory value. These assumptions are necessary for accounting purposes because of the difficulty of monitoring the physical flow of inventory. They are particularly useful in cases where companies experience variations in the prices for buying or producing the same item in inventory over the course of an accounting period. In the previous analysis, to simplify the presentation of the different concepts, we were assuming that the cost of all inventory items was constant over time. But, is this a realistic assumption? Consider, for example, a retailer who replenishes inventory of a particular item on a monthly basis and for the first quarter paid a $45 purchasing price per unit in January, $44 in February, and $46 in March. Therefore, there are three layers of inventory, each lot acquired at a different price. As it may be hard to keep track of which layer the exact items that have been sold in the quarter come from, the retailer needs a method for determining which goods are sold and which goods remain in inventory. Hence, cost flow assumptions in retailing refer to the methods available for moving the cost of a company's products from the inventory account to the revenue and expenses account. In addition to that, manufacturing firms use cost flow assumptions to also determine the movement from one inventory account to another (i.e., from raw materials to work-in-progress to finished goods inventory).

 Inventory cost flow assumptions

The **inventory cost flow assumptions** define the methods available for moving the cost of a company's products from the inventory account to the revenue and expenses account.

The methods that firms select regarding their inventory cost flow do not have to agree with the actual movement of goods. What *is* necessary, though, is that cost of goods sold plus the cost of goods remaining in ending inventory be equal to the total cost of inventory for the accounting period. Also, companies are allowed to use different cost flow assumptions for different types of products in inventory. For example, a firm might use a particular method for valuing inventory of its high-end product categories and a different method for its low-end ones. Finally, firms shall consistently use the same cost flow assumptions over time, although changes are allowed under specific conditions (and usually upon permission by the tax authorities).

Before introducing the various cost flow assumptions, it would be useful first to present a basic rule, one that is based on the recognition that the value of goods in inventory can often change over time due to damage, obsolescence, or market price decline. The *lower-of-cost-or-market rule* states that a company must record the cost of inventory at the lower of two costs: the item's historical cost or its net realizable value. Historical cost is the cost at which the inventory was purchased or manufactured. Net realizable value (or market value) of an item is defined as the estimated selling price minus estimated costs to complete and sell the item. If the net realizable value of an item falls below its historical cost resulting in a loss to the company, the lower of cost or market method can be applied to record the loss either under cost of goods sold or in a separate loss account (e.g., write-down of inventory).

 Lower of cost or net realizable value

According to the **lower of cost or net realizable value** accounting principle, if a firm's inventory is carried on the accounting records at greater than its net realizable value, a write-down from the recorded cost to the lower net realizable value should be made.

 Exercise

Swift Fashion Ltd.

After the spring selling season, Swift Fashion has leftovers as follows:

Category	Leftovers (units)	Cost	Price	Discount
Jackets and coats	5,000	$45	$60	30%
Trousers and shorts	4,000	25	40	30%
Suits	3,000	90	120	20%
Skirts and dresses	12,000	30	45	60%
Shoes, boots, and slippers	13,000	35	50	60%
Sweaters and waistcoats	5,000	20	30	50%

where "cost" is the average unit purchasing cost and "price" the average unit list price. The last column includes the management's estimate of the average discount that has to be applied to each category to sell the season's leftovers in the market. It includes the estimated costs that will be incurred to sell the item, such as distribution cost.

What is the value of inventory to be written off by the firm after the selling season?

According to the lower of cost or net realizable value accounting principle, the new book value per unit for the jackets and coats category should be:

$$\min(45, 60 \cdot (1 - 0.3)) = \min(45, 42) = 42$$

Therefore, the level of inventory to write off is:

$$5,000 \cdot (45 - 42) = \$15,000$$

In the case of trousers and shorts, the book value should not change, given that:

$$\min(25, 40 \cdot (1 - 0.3)) = \min(25, 28) = 25$$

and no inventory should be written off.

Working in this fashion, you can check that the value of inventory to write off for all categories totals $379,000. This value should be deducted from the inventory account on the assets side and added to the period's expenses.

The application of this rule prevents a company from carrying forward any losses for recognition in some future period and is in accordance with the matching and conservatism principles of accounting. As the discounts are subjective estimates made by managers, you should realize that they have the key that opens the door of creative accounting of inventories.

Next, we introduce the most commonly used cost flow assumptions in inventory valuation.

8.3.1 Specific Identification

Under the specific identification method, each time an item is sold its actual cost is charged as cost of goods sold. Think of this method as having a virtual sticker on each item tracing its actual cost throughout the selling cycle. Literally speaking, specific identification is more of a cost flow method than an assumption (as no assumption is really made with regard to the physical flow of inventory). Obviously, this method is not practical for most businesses. For conventional firms selling identical items, such as grocery goods, apparel, books, low-cost devices, and tools, the cost of maintaining a record-keeping system to track each individual item of inventory would most likely outweigh any potential benefit. However, the specific identification method is suitable for high-value, low-volume items that can be assigned their own identification numbers (e.g., serial numbers), such as automobiles, specialized equipment, jewelry, art pieces, and so on. It follows that the application of this method has no implications on the reported cost of goods sold and value of ending inventory, as it keeps track of the exact relevant costs associated with the physical flow of inventory.

8.3.2   Standard Costing Method

Standard costing is a method that assigns predetermined (named standard) costs to all inventory items purchased or produced during an accounting period. This method is more convenient for manufacturing firms where it might be too time-consuming to collect actual costs associated with different layers of inventory produced. Standard costs can be calculated by averaging the actual production costs for a particular period (e.g., past few months), taking into consideration factors that may influence these costs in the near future. Such factors might include equipment efficiency (e.g., due to installation of new machines or aging issues of current machines), labor efficiency (e.g., due to learning curve effects or production process changes), purchasing prices (e.g., due to switching suppliers, inflation or buying in different quantities), and so on. Apparently, standard costing is preferable in low-volatility production environments. The more stable the production plans and processes are within a company, the less time is needed to calculate standard costs and the less disposed to errors these costs will be. Since standard costs are usually different from actual costs, any realized difference between these two costs, if small, is usually recorded as a period expense, namely, assigned to cost of goods sold. If the variance is relatively large, however, the practice is to allocate it among the cost of goods sold and the ending inventory account. Due to the inevitable variances between standard and actual costs, the former need to be reevaluated on a regular basis in order to be more aligned with actual costs.

In addition to the convenience and potentially lower cost from the implementation of standard costing, there are more advantages associated with this method, even if it is not used for external reporting. In particular, keeping track of standard costs can be used as a benchmark for a facility's operational performance. More importantly, standard costs are useful inputs to core business processes that take place well in advance of any actual costs realization, such as budgeting and product pricing.

Despite the advantages mentioned above, though, there are situations where standard costing can be quite problematic. If there is high volatility in the production processes and in the external business environment, standard costs would need frequent updating and might be prone to large errors. Moreover, as the variances reported by a standard costing system are usually decomposed into their components (i.e., cost of raw material, direct labor, overhead), this might drive improper actions by management. For example, managers might place large orders for raw materials to take advantage of discounts or run large production batches to reduce allocated overhead per unit. However, while such actions could potentially create favorable variances with regard to standard cost performance, they can also have a large impact on a firm's total inventory and working capital, which eventually might deteriorate its financial and operational performance.

8.3.3   Average Cost Flow Assumption

The average cost flow method assumes that all goods of a certain type are interchangeable (in the physical sense) and only differ in their purchase price or production cost. In contrast to the specific identification method where the identity and cost of each item is precisely known, the average cost flow assumption considers all items of the same type as equivalent and assigns as unit cost their average purchase or production cost over the accounting period. Once the cost per unit has been established, the ending inventory (cost of goods sold) is determined by simply multiplying the number of units left in inventory (number of units sold) by the average cost per unit. That is, while this method uses in its calculations the actual costs per layer of inventory, it assumes that the flow of cost is not related to the actual physical flow of goods.

 Exercise

Wok & Roll (1 of 3)

Wok & Roll, a chain of fast-food restaurants in InflationLand, needs help to quantify the value of inventory in an inflationary environment. As a sample, they have sent you some information about the last purchases and sales of spring roll boxes:

	Units	Unit cost	Total
Beginning inventory	20	$8	$160
Purchases			
#1	20	$10	$200
#2	10	$11	$110
#3	20	$15	$300
Total units available for sale	70		$770
Total units sold in the period	45		
Ending inventory	25		

Find the cost of goods sold and the value of ending inventory under the average cost flow assumption.

Given this information, we can find the required values knowing that:

average cost per unit = total cost of units available for sale/total units available for sale

COGS = total units sold in the period · average cost per unit

ending inventory = units in ending inventory · average cost per unit

By performing these calculations, we find that the average cost per unit is equal to $11 (770/70); the cost of goods sold is $495 (45 · $11); and the ending inventory is $275 (25 · $11). Note that the cost of goods sold plus the cost of goods remaining in ending inventory is equal to the total cost of inventory available for sale, as it should be for cost balancing purposes.

Apart from some computational convenience, the weighted average valuation method might be suitable for companies that face high cost-volatility (e.g., in raw material prices) and opt for consistency in their reported income. On the other hand, the proportional treatment of both cost of goods sold and ending inventory by the average cost flow assumption may lead to a situation in which neither of the two is representative of their true cost.

8.3.4   First-In, First-Out (FIFO) Assumption

The first-in, first-out cost flow (FIFO) assumption assigns to cost of goods sold the oldest layers of inventory. In other words, the items purchased first are assumed to have been sold first, while goods purchased at the end of the accounting period remain in ending inventory. In many businesses this is in fact what happens in the physical world, regardless of the accounting method. In grocery stores, for example, a common practice is to place older items in front of newer ones on the shelf in order to sell them first before they lose freshness. Similar inventory placement practices are followed in most warehouses, particularly for products with expiration dates or products that can decay or be damaged. Nevertheless, it must be noted that under the FIFO method it is not necessarily the oldest item that is sold but rather it is the oldest cost that is moved from the inventory account to cost of goods sold. Hence, under the FIFO cost flow assumption, the cost of goods sold and value of ending inventory are calculated as follows:

$$COGS = \text{cost of the first units sold in the period}$$

$$\text{ending inventory} = \text{total cost of units available for sale} - COGS$$

 Exercise

Wok & Roll (2 of 3)

Find the cost of goods sold and the value of ending inventory under the first-in, first-out cost flow assumption.

Under the FIFO cost flow assumption, the cost of goods sold is $415 (20 · $8 + 20 · $10 + 5 · $11); and the ending inventory is $355 ($770 − $415).

Notice that the cost of goods sold includes the cost of the two oldest layers of inventory (i.e., beginning inventory and purchase #1) plus the cost of five units from purchase #2. Similarly, the ending inventory reflects the value of the last twenty-five items that entered inventory during the accounting period.

The FIFO method has two main advantages: First, the assumed flow of costs is more aligned with the actual physical flows of goods. Second, FIFO provides a more accurate figure of the inventory account in the balance sheet (as the unit cost of items in ending inventory is closer to current market value). However, in periods when prices increase (as is usually the case), applying FIFO for inventory valuation yields higher profits, which might seem good for the stock price but are potentially unrealistic. For the same reason, FIFO has a clear tax disadvantage due to inflated profit results.

8.3.5 Last-In, First-Out (LIFO) Assumption

In contrast to the FIFO rule, the last-in first-out (LIFO) cost flow assumption assigns to cost of goods sold the costs that reflect the most recent layers of inventory. In other words, the items purchased last are assumed to have been sold first; that is, it is the newest cost that is moved from the inventory account to cost of goods sold. As a result, the ending inventory may include items that have been purchased several accounting periods back. In most cases, LIFO is not aligned with the physical flow of goods in and out of the inventory account. It must be noted also that while LIFO is permitted under the US GAAP, it is prohibited under the IFRS standards; hence, it is rarely used outside the United States. Nevertheless, a large percentage of US firms use the LIFO method for external and tax reporting purposes due to some advantages that will be discussed later in this section.

Under the LIFO cost flow assumption, the cost of goods sold and value of ending inventory are calculated as follows:

$$COGS = \text{cost of the last units sold in the period}$$

$$\text{Ending inventory} = \text{total cost of units available for sale} - COGS$$

Exercise

Wok & Roll (3 of 3)

Find the cost of goods sold and the value of ending inventory under the last-in, first-out cost flow assumption.

Under the LIFO cost flow assumption, the cost of goods sold is $560 ($20 \cdot \$15 + 10 \cdot \$11 + 15 \cdot \$10$); and the ending inventory is $210 ($770 - $560).

Table 8.8
COGS and ending inventory under average cost flow, FIFO, and LIFO for Wok & Roll.

	Cost flow method		
	Average cost flow	FIFO	LIFO
Cost of goods sold	495	415	560
Ending inventory	275	355	210

Notice that the cost of goods sold includes the cost of the two latest layers of inventory (i.e., purchases #2 and #3) plus the cost of fifteen units from purchase #1. Similarly, the ending inventory reflects the value of the oldest twenty-five items in inventory. Table 8.8 summarizes the results obtained for Wok & Roll under average cost flow, FIFO and LIFO.

The LIFO cost flow assumption provides a more updated estimate of cost of goods sold as it assigns to it relatively current costs of items purchased/produced rather than outdated figures. For that reason, the LIFO assumption is often considered as more compliant with the matching principle. A direct consequence is that during periods of rising prices LIFO understates a firm's gross profit. While this distortion to income might seem undesirable for management, the actual advantage of LIFO lies in the cash flow benefit from the subsequent decrease in tax liabilities. Notice in our example Wok & Roll that the cost of goods sold under LIFO is 35 percent larger than the same figure calculated under FIFO (as shown in table 8.8), which might considerably lower the firm's taxable income and, consequently, its tax burden.

Despite the tax benefits associated with LIFO, this method has some serious disadvantages: First, it requires significant book keeping to track purchases that have taken place several accounting periods back in time. Second, LIFO does not provide an accurate estimate of the true value of inventory on the balance sheet. Actually, in periods of high inflation, the reported inventory value may be heavily outdated and useless. This can in turn create issues for companies that wish to maintain a relatively strong balance sheet to qualify for loans, entice investors, or convey positive signals to analysts. The major disadvantage of LIFO, though, is that it creates opportunities for managers to artificially inflate earnings by dipping into old layers of inventory. This practice is often referred to as LIFO liquidation. Take for example the case of Wok & Roll discussed before. What if, for some reason, the firm's management wanted to show higher earnings for the accounting period? They could simply delay the placement (or transfer of inventory ownership) of purchase #3 and report a cost of goods sold of $430 ($10 \cdot \$11 + 20 \cdot \$10 + 15 \cdot \$8$), namely, about 23 percent lower than the current $560. Finally, note that LIFO liquidation might have further implications of an ethical nature, as firms can postpone the timing of liquidation to coincide with favorable taxation conditions (i.e., they can hold up on out-of-date priced inventory, waiting for favorable changes in taxing legislation).

Table 8.9
Example of LIFO reserve reporting.

December 31 (in millions)	2017	2016
Raw materials and work in process	11,757	12,636
Finished goods	9,169	8,798
Unbilled shipments	481	536
	21,407	21,971
Revaluation to LIFO	516	383
Total inventories	21,923	22,354

Source: General Electric 2017, p. 140, n. 5.

Due to potential distortions of a firm's profitability and financial statements, LIFO is not allowed by IFRS. The main reason is that IFRS places more focus on the balance sheet rather than on the income statement. Specifically, IFRS requires that the figures in the statement of the balance sheet should be measured according to up-to-date information (i.e., should reflect current market conditions). Despite the fact that LIFO is prohibited in most countries outside the United States (which have adopted IFSR), about 36 percent of major US firms still apply this inventory valuation method. These firms, however, are subject to some restrictions on the use of LIFO (imposed by the US tax code and GAAP): First, the LIFO conformity rule requires firms that use LIFO for tax reporting purposes to use also LIFO for external reporting. Second, companies that have decided to use LIFO must also provide FIFO figures in their financial statements. In particular, a revaluation to LIFO, commonly known as LIFO reserve, shall be disclosed in the firms' financial reports, which when added to the reported inventory value would give its FIFO equivalent.

Consider the following note (table 8.9) taken from General Electric (GE) Company's 2017 annual report. According to the report, a portion of the firm's U.S. inventories (accounting for 32 percent of GE's global inventory) is determined on a LIFO basis. It follows that GE's inventory valuation in 2017, had the firm used FIFO instead of LIFO, would have been $21,923 million, while $516 million represents the total difference in inventory costs under LIFO versus FIFO (since the time that LIFO was adopted by the company for some inventory items). The change in the LIFO reserve balance of $133 million ($516 − $383) corresponds to the increase of cost of goods sold in 2017 due to LIFO reporting. As this amount is also equivalent to the decrease in the firm's taxable income for 2017 due to LIFO, by multiplying by the income tax rate we can get the tax savings for the same year. Consequently, the total LIFO reserve of $516 million times the income tax rate can be considered as GE's total deferred income tax since the adoption of LIFO.

The disclosure of LIFO reserve by companies—as demonstrated in the GE example— facilitates a fair presentation of inventory value in financial reports, which allows investors and analysts make more accurate comparisons of financial performance among firms using different methods. For example, being provided with the LIFO reserve figure, analysts can calculate the tax benefits of using LIFO, adjust important inventory ratios (i.e., inventory turnover and GMROI), and assess whether or not a LIFO liquidation has occurred in an accounting period.

From our discussion so far, it becomes clear that the selection of inventory cost flow assumptions represents an important managerial decision with implications that extend beyond reported income and inventory value to actual cash flows (or, at least, their timing). If the costs faced by a company are steady, it doesn't matter which valuation method is followed, as all would give similar results. So, the question of which method should firms use becomes relevant for companies whose costs change. In general, companies that use LIFO inventory valuations are typically those with relatively large inventories and increasing costs. Also, fast-growing firms might benefit from LIFO due to their reliance on cash flows for supporting their growth (while outside analysts evaluate them on sales growth rather than reported income). On the other hand, if such circumstances do not hold, FIFO is probably the most suitable method because it is convenient (from the book-keeping point of view), provides an accurate picture of the balance sheet, does not allow space for profit manipulation, and is the method preferred by the IFRS standards.

We close this section by presenting an excerpt from Procter & Gamble's 2012 annual report: "Inventories are valued at the lower of cost or market value. Product-related inventories are primarily maintained on the first-in, first-out method. Minor amounts of product inventories, including certain cosmetics and commodities, are maintained on the last-in, first-out method. The cost of spare part inventories is maintained using the average-cost method" (Procter & Gamble 2012, 54). Here we can see that firms can use different cost flow assumptions for different types of inventory. It's worth investigating, though, what might have been the criteria behind Procter & Gamble's selection.

8.4   Application of Cost Flow Assumption in Manufacturing Firms

Most of the discussion in our presentation of the different cost flow assumptions has focused on inventory valuation for merchandising companies. We have not yet considered the implications of cost flow assumptions in the computation of inventory value and cost of goods sold for manufacturing firms. However, both product costing and cost flow assumptions are relevant for inventory valuation in production environments. In the Inglass Inc. case, for instance, how would the firm account for the cost of silica sand if there were several batches of this material purchased over the accounting period at different prices? In this section, we shift our focus to the application of the different cost flow methods in manufacturing. Consider the following example.

Exercise

Accounting for Inventory in AFC

Company AFC manufactures a single product according to the two-stage production process shown in the figure below. At the first stage, two units of raw material (RM) are going through the assembly process for producing one unit of intermediate product (WIP). At the second stage, the assembled item goes through the finishing process to produce one unit of finished goods (FG). The assembly process consumes $10 of direct labor cost per unit of intermediate product, while the same cost for the finishing process is $5 per unit of finished good. Also, based on historical data, the firm has found that each unit of finished good consumes about $2 of manufacturing overhead. The validity of this assumption is evaluated periodically and any minor divergence is considered as period expenses. Finally, for overhead cost allocation purposes, any WIP item that has gone through the assembly stage but has not yet completed the finishing stage is considered equivalent to 0.5 units of FG.

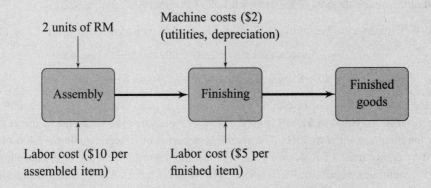

At the beginning of the month, company AFC has thirty units of RM inventory, each worth $20. The beginning WIP and FG inventory is zero. Then, during the month the following events take place:

1. The firm purchases fifty units of RM at $22 each.

2. The firm purchases forty units of RM at $25 each.

3. Eighty units of RM go through the assembly process during the month.

4. Thirty units of final product are completed.

5. Twenty-five units of final product are sold at $120 each.

Due to the fact that the prices of RM are quite volatile, company AFC applies the LIFO assumption in the valuation of its inventory. Our task is to compute the values of RM, WIP, and FG inventory at the end of the period, as well as the cost of goods sold and gross profit for the period.

To calculate these figures, we will use the equations presented in section 8.1, considering also the relevant cost flow assumptions. We have:

end RM Inventory = beginning RM inventory + purchases − releases to production

$$= \$600 + \$2,100 - \$1,880 = \$820$$

The cost of the beginning RM inventory is $600 (30 · $20), while the total purchases for the period are equal to $2,100 (50 · $22 + 40 · $25). Then, using the LIFO assumption, the units that enter the RM inventory last are released to production first. That is, the cost of the RM units released to production is equal to $1,880 (40 · $25 + 40 · $22). Hence, at the end of the month the cost of the units left in RM inventory is equal to $820.

end WIP inventory = beginning WIP inventory + released RM + direct labor

+ manufacturing overhead − releases to FG inventory

$$= \$0 + \$1,880 + \$550 + \$70 - \$1,950 = \$550$$

In the above calculation, beginning WIP inventory is zero and the cost of released RM has been found equal to $1,880 from the previous analysis. The total cost of direct labor for the month is equal to $550. The assembly department is accountable for $400 of this cost as eighty units of RM have gone through the assembly process in the month (i.e., forty assemblies were made, each costing $10 in direct labor). The finishing department's contribution is equal to $150 (i.e., completion of thirty units of final product, each costing $5 in direct labor). Similarly, the manufacturing overhead cost is equal to $70, from which $60 correspond to the production of thirty units of FG (each of which incurs a predetermined overhead allocation of $2), and $10 to the completion of the assembly process for ten items of WIP (i.e., the equivalent of five units of FG).

To compute the cost of releases to FG inventory, we apply the following process. We know that thirty units of FG were completed and released to FG inventory. Each of these units will take with them some of the production cost for the month (i.e., RM, direct labor, and overhead). The allocation of the direct labor and overhead to the items completed is straight, as these costs are assumed to be constant during the month. That is, each of the thirty units completed will absorb $300 of assembly direct labor (30 · $10); $150 of finishing direct labor (30 · $5); and $60 manufacturing overhead (30 · $2). To allocate the RM cost, however, we will make use of the LIFO assumption; namely, we assume that the last items that enter RM are the first ones to leave the production process as FG. Therefore, the RM portion of the thirty units completed will include forty units of RM priced at $25 and twenty units of RM priced at $22; that is, a total of $1,440. Consequently, the total cost of releases to FG inventory is equal to $1,950 ($1,440 + $300 + $150 + $60), resulting to cost of end WIP inventory of $550.

$$\text{end FG inventory} = \text{beginning FG inventory} + \text{released from production} - \text{COGS}$$

$$= \$0 + \$1,950 - \$1,645 = \$305$$

To calculate the portion of FG inventory that will be assigned to cost of goods sold, we need to again use the LIFO cost flow assumption. The direct labor and manufacturing overhead cost of the twenty-five units sold can easily be found equal to $425 ($25 \cdot \$10 + 25 \cdot \$5 + 25 \cdot \$2$). The RM cost corresponds to the last units that have entered the RM inventory; that is, this is equal to $1,220 ($40 \cdot \$25 + 10 \cdot \$22$). Therefore, under the company's cost flow assumption, the cost of goods sold and end FG inventory are found to equal $1,645 and $305, respectively.

How would our results vary if the firm followed a different cost flow assumption (FIFO or average cost)? See exercise 14.

8.5   Inventory Write-Offs and Its Impact on the Firm's Value

We close this chapter by addressing the subject of inventory write-offs and how they impact the value of a firm. This is of paramount importance for manufacturers and retailers alike, as writing off inventory from the balance sheet may have a substantial impact on the income statement as well as in the value of the firm.

Accounting rules on inventory are apparently simple: inventory should initially be registered at acquisition cost, including items such as inbound transport or import duties. If there is a decrease on the market value below acquisition cost, the new book value of inventory should be that of the market (convention of conservatism). In other words:

inventory book value = min(acquisition cost, current market value)

IFRS standards have refined this definition and suggest firms now be more prudent by using the following metric:

inventory book value = min(acquisition cost, expected net realizable value)

where net realizable value is market value less inventory-related costs to be incurred by the firm until inventory is sold, such as distribution or advertising costs.

In practice, though, things turn out to be more involved: for instance, when inventory becomes obsolete, managers should recognize that fact in the books in accordance with the convention of conservatism by writing off the value of inventory involved. Net profit will decrease accordingly, as a write-off is an expense, which goes directly to the revenue and expenses account. Therefore, bad managers may be tempted not to recognize the loss and pretend that inventory is still saleable. Obsolete inventory may then physically remain in the warehouse—and virtually in the balance sheet—for months, even years, until it is finally declared obsolete. (That is why warehouses are sometimes ironically called cemeteries of working capital.) It doesn't help that auditors cannot easily judge inventory as obsolete, as obsolescence is often subject to management subjectivity.

To make things worse, not writing off inventory on time will distort the value of the firm much more than the value of inventory not written off. For instance, if the value of obsolete inventory is, say, $1 million, not writing if off on time may inflate the value of the firm, not by $1 million, as you might expect, but by, say, $4 million. This unexpected discrepancy stems from the methods analysts use to value companies. A popular method is that of multiples, where the value of the firm is assumed to be a multiple of the current year's EBITDA or net profit. If this year's EBITDA or net profit is inflated due to not writing off inventory, the value of the firm will be wrongly assumed to be the not-executed write-off times the multiple, a number usually much larger than one. The qualitative effect is the same when the firm's value is calculated using cash flows discounting, another well-known method to value firms. ("David Berman," a case from Harvard Business School, abounds in this methodology [Raman, Gaur, and Kesavan 2005].)

No matter which method is used to value a firm, the incentive for bad managers not to write off inventory on time is even stronger. Being aware of this fact, good management practices should articulate control tools to avoid these behaviors. Frequently tracking ratios such as the ones presented in section 9.2.3 may help.

 Exercise

Inventory Obsolescence at FancyStuff

FancyStuff is a firm that manufactures and sells trendy products in the apparel industry. Fashion trends change quickly, leading some of their products to become obsolete in every season. Record the following facts in the firm's books:

1. Before the selling season started, 800 jackets were bought on account from a Bangladeshi supplier. The cost was $100 per jacket.

2. Soon after the selling season started, the firm realized that it would be very difficult to sell those jackets at the regular price, as the customers' taste had changed for more vivid colors. The expected price at which the jackets could be sold on average was now $60 per unit.

3. At the end of the season, however, only a portion of the jackets could be sold, resulting in a total sale of $28,000 in cash. The firm decided to throw away the remaining unsold jackets.

? Event 1

Before the selling season started, 800 jackets were bought on account from a Bangladeshi supplier. The cost was $100 per jacket.

The firm acquired inventory worth $800 \cdot \$100 = \$80,000$. Two accounts, inventory in the assets side and payables in the equities side, should be increased by $80,000.

? Event 2

Soon after the selling season started, the firm realized that it would be very difficult to sell those jackets at the regular price, as the customers' taste had changed for more vivid colors. The expected price at which the jackets could be sold on average was now $60 per unit.

According to the accounting rule for inventory described above, the firm should recognize a loss, as the expected selling price ($\$60 \cdot 800 = \$48,000$) is now lower than the inventory cost. As the firm still holds the inventory, it will make a provision of $\$80,000 - \$48,000 = \$32,000$ using the contra account "allowance for obsolete inventory." The new book value of inventory is $48,000. Figure 8.3 shows the annotations made in the previous and this event.

? Event 3

At the end of the season, however, only a portion of the jackets could be sold, resulting in a total sale of $28,000 in cash. The firm decided to throw away the remaining unsold jackets.

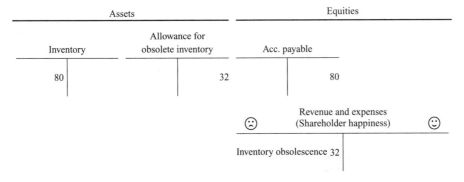

Figure 8.3
Annotations in the general ledger at FancyStuff after event 2 (in thousands).

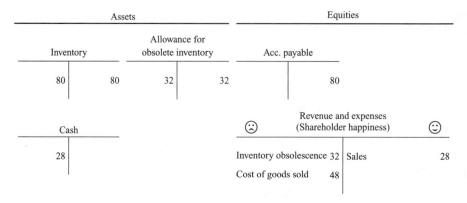

Figure 8.4
Annotations in the general ledger at FancyStuff after event 3.

The firm should recognize the sale ($28,000) and the COGS ($48,000) on the one hand, and zero the inventory and the allowance for obsolete inventory accounts on the other hand. Figure 8.4 shows the result of all these transactions.

8.6   Summary

In this chapter we have presented the managerial decisions associated with the financial accounting of inventory, namely inventory costing and inventory cost flow assumption. Through using several case studies, we have illustrated how the selection of methods generates various trade-offs between the reported inventory value in the balance sheet and the cost of goods sold in the income statement.

8.7   Suggested Reading

• Eldon S. Hendriksen and Michael F. Van Breda. 1992. *Accounting theory*, 5th ed. Homewood, IL: Irwin.

• Raman, Ananth, Vishal Gaur, and Saravanan Kesavan."David Berman." Harvard Business School Case 9-605-081, April 2005. (Revised October 2006.)

Exercises

1. Which are the two fundamental decisions associated with inventory valuation of a manufacturing firm? What are the key questions they answer?

2. Which are the main cost types in inventory valuation for manufacturing companies? What are the criteria for their classification?

3. In financial reporting of inventory for a manufacturing company, which of the following statements is true or false? Please explain.

a. Both fixed and variable manufacturing overhead costs are allocated to inventory value.

b. Only variable manufacturing overhead costs are allocated to inventory value.

c. If the firm builds up inventory over a single accounting period, else being equal, the gross profit per unit (as derived from the income statement) increases.

4. Under what conditions may a lithium-ion battery pack for electric vehicles be considered as raw material, work in progress, or a finished good?

5. The following data relate to the manufacturing activities of MilTech company during November:

1. Sales $400,000

2. Purchases $60,700

3. Expenses include:
   - Light and power for manufacturing: $2,700
   - Depreciation of machines for manufacturing: see accounts below
   - Rent for manufacturing: $4,100
   - Selling, general, and administrative expenses: $125,000
   - Salaries of fifty manufacturing workers who work eight hours per day (assume twenty working days in a month) and have an average salary of $16.25 per hour

4. General ledger accounts as of October 31 include (assume linear depreciation, no scrap value, all equipment started working on October 31, last year):
   - Equipment: $108,000
   - Accumulated depreciation: $21,600
   - Raw materials: $42,400
   - Work in progress: $75,800
   - Finished goods: $44,200

5. General ledger accounts as of November 30 include:
   - Raw materials: $46,900
   - Work in progress: $63,200
   - Finished goods: $46,300

Calculate for the month of November:

a. Cost of raw materials used

b. Cost of units completed and transferred to the finished goods warehouse

c. Cost of goods sold

d. Earnings before interest and taxes (EBIT)

6. CardioMed Inc. is a manufacturer of wearable heart monitoring products that automatically detect, record, and transmit abnormal heart rhythms for up to thirty days. In one accounting period the firm produced in its plant in San Jose, California, 220,000 units of model A and 140,000 units of

model B. The selling prices of models A and B are respectively $160 and $190, while the direct costs for the period are shown in the table below:

	Model A	Model B
Units produced	220,000	140,000
Direct materials cost	$6,340,000	$4,120,000
Direct labor cost	$7,260,000	$6,870,000

If total manufacturing overhead expenses for the same period have been equal to $14,460,000, what would be the unit cost and gross profit margin per model if the company uses an allocation rule based on: (a) the proportion of each product over the total output (in units) and (b) the proportion of direct labor costs used by each product. Which allocation basis do you think is more representative of the actual overhead consumption of the two models? Please explain briefly.

7. Continuing problem 6, CardioMed's cost accountants have identified cost totals for the period's production support activities and other overhead. The table below provides this information, along with activity cost drivers and allocation of their unit count to each model:

Cost category	Indirect costs	Cost driver	Cost driver unit count Model A	Model B
Material purchasing	$770,000	# purchase orders	64	96
Machine setup, testing, and calibration	$3,725,000	# setups	64	128
Production supervision	$1,180,000	Direct labor	$7,260,000	$6,870,000
Quality assurance	$1,807,000	# inspections	42	86
Plant administration	$1,440,000	Direct labor	$7,260,000	$6,870,000
Utilities	$2,595,000	Machine-time	600	360
Supplies	$1,143,000	# units	220,000	140,000
Depreciation of equipment	$1,800,000	Machine-time	600	360

What would be the unit cost and gross profit margin per model if the company was using ABC principles for the allocation of its manufacturing overhead expenses? Under what conditions would you advice CardioMed's management to adopt an ABC approach for product costing?

8. Go back to problem 6. For the sake of simplicity let's assume that the entire manufacturing overhead cost is fixed. This assumption is quite reasonable—at least in the short-term—given that the largest portion of this cost entails salaries. If CardioMed's sales in the given accounting period consisted of 198,000 units of Model A and 122,000 units of Model B, and the company's operating expenses were equal to $14.5 million:

a. What would be CardioMed's net operating income under absorption costing with direct labor as allocation base?

b. What would be CardioMed's operating income under direct costing?

Please briefly explain how you would use the additional insight provided by direct costing if you were managers in CardioMed.

9. What is the underlying accounting principle of absorption costing? What is the major weakness of this method?

10. In the Smart Widgets Inc. example in section 8.2.2 what would be the company's net operating profit had the firm produced 8,000 instead of 5,000 units? How does this compare with the current results?

11. Given the following data for retailer ABC in a given period:

		Units	Unit cost ($)
Beginning inventory		20	40
Purchases			
	#1	20	50
	#2	10	55
	#3	70	59
	#4	20	64

If the firm sold sixty units during the period, calculate the cost of goods sold using FIFO, LIFO, and weighted-average cost flow assumptions.

12. For a firm operating in an economy facing inflation, which of the following is true or false regarding its inventory cost flow assumption? Please explain briefly.

a. Cost of goods sold is more accurate under a LIFO cost flow assumption.

b. Value of inventory is more accurate under a FIFO cost flow assumption.

c. EBIT is higher under a LIFO cost flow assumption.

13. Given the following financial statements for a retailer firm:

Balance sheets ($'000)			
		2018	2017
Assets			
	Cash	52	40
	Accounts receivable	156	143
	Inventories	302	285
	Fixed assets	290	282
	TOTAL	800	750
Equities			
	Accounts payable	85	92
	Debt	190	222
	Equity	525	436
	TOTAL	800	750

Income statements ($'000)

	2018	2017
Revenue	1,100	1,000
Cost of goods sold	600	550
Gross profit	500	450
SGA expenses	210	200
Depreciation	85	80
Interest	24	22
EBT	181	148
Taxes	72	59
Net profit	109	89

Inventories have been evaluated under LIFO assumption. Under FIFO, inventories would be eighty and sixty higher in 2018 and 2017, respectively.

a. What would gross profit have been in 2018 had the firm used the FIFO assumption? Show your work.

b. How many taxes did the firm save in 2018 because of the LIFO assumption?

c. Under which method (FIFO or LIFO) is it easier to manipulate net profit? Why? What is/are the lever(s) managers have in order to do so?

14. For the company AFC in section 8.4, compute the values of RM, WIP, and FG inventory at the end of the period, as well as the cost of goods sold and gross profit for the period, assuming (a) a FIFO and (b) an average cost flow assumption.

15. After the holiday season, at the end of its annual reporting period, a toy manufacturer estimates that some of the toys it holds with a historical cost of $700,000 are unsaleable. Which entries, if any, should be recorded given that estimate? Why would it make sense to value inventory at the lower of cost or market? What is the underlying accounting principle that motivates this decision?

References

General Electric. 2017. "Annual report 2017," 140, n. 5. Accessed June 1, 2019. https://www.ge.com /investor-relations/sites/default/files/GE_AR17.pdf.

Kaplan, Robert S., and Robin Cooper. 1997. *Cost & effect: Using integrated cost systems to drive profitability and performance.* Cambridge, MA: Harvard Business School Press.

Procter & Gamble. 2012. "Annual report 2012," 54. Accessed June 1, 2019. https://annualreport.pg.com /annualreport2012/files/PG_2012_AnnualReport.pdf.

Raman, Ananth, Vishal Gaur, and Saravanan Kesavan. 2005. "David Berman." *HBS* 9-605-081.

9 Interpreting Financial Statements for Operations

Tell me how you measure me, and I will tell you how I will behave.
—Eliyahu Goldratt, operations guru

The main purpose of financial statements is to provide stakeholders with relevant information in order to make sound decisions: for instance, managers may look for opportunities to reduce inventory costs further; investors may be interested to know why sales have grown in the last years; suppliers may want to know how long it takes the firm to pay its existing suppliers before reaching a commercial agreement with the firm; and competitors may want to compare themselves with the industry leader to close the most relevant performance gaps. With the information in hand, decisions are made to, respectively, rationalize inventory, launch a new marketing campaign to boost sales, sign a commercial long-term contract with a new customer, or adopt new forecasting techniques in order to improve gross profit. Therefore, as illustrated in figure 9.1, financial statements are—among other things—tools designed for managers to make better decisions.

A problem with raw financial statements is that they do not provide the desired information directly. The statements must be combined to obtain the information desired. Financial ratios are one tool typically used for further analysis of financial statements: they combine information from the balance sheet and the income statement, or normalize quantities—usually through percentages—so that they are comparable. In addition to ratios, there are other tools, such as visual financial statements or Dupont's analysis, which also make it easier to evaluate the firm's performance and strategy.

By presenting these tools, this chapter shows how to analyze financial statements in order to provide managers with relevant information so that they can make better decisions. As you might expect, the emphasis is on those financial ratios that are most relevant to operations and supply chain management.

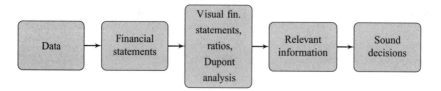

Figure 9.1
From data to decisions. The ultimate goal of interpreting financial statements is to make better decisions.

9.1 More Intuitive Financial Statements

The adage goes: "a picture is worth one thousand words." When interpreting financial statements, we could restate it as: "a picture is worth one thousand numbers." A major difficulty faced by managers without a financial background is that they get overwhelmed by numbers when trying to interpret the usually dry financial information contained in firms' annual reports. An attempt is made in this section to make that information more understandable. First, we will present visual financial statements; afterwards, we will discuss the use of ratios.

9.1.1 Visual Balance Sheet

Table 9.1 shows a simplified version of the balance sheet of Inditex at the end of fiscal year 2016. One should read and internalize the figures to determine their importance and relative magnitude. Even if the amount of data is relatively small, this requires great deal of mental effort.

A better way to quickly grasp the relative importance of each account in the balance sheet is to express all amounts as percentages of total assets, as shown in table 9.2. Percentages are easier to internalize, as the reference to compare each figure (100 percent, in contrast to total assets) is always the same and is a straight number. This is especially true when assessing the evolution of accounts over time. For instance, table 9.1 shows that Inditex's fixed assets have increased from the end of 2015 to 2016 when measured in euros, but table 9.2 shows that fixed assets have actually decreased when measured as a percentage of total assets. This means that fixed assets have grown at a slower pace than sales, a symptom that may lead to an analysis of the causes.

Finally, we can represent the information in the balance sheet pictorially, as in figure 9.2. The height of each account box is proportional to the percentage value shown in table 9.2. For instance, the height of the cash$^+$ box at the end of 2016 is 31.3 percent, or almost one-third, of the total height of the balance sheet. Representing accounts in this fashion gives an immediate idea of which accounts are important and which are not. For instance, in the case of Inditex, cash and fixed assets on the assets side and payables and equity on the equities side are much more relevant than the rest. What can we infer from this

Table 9.1
Inditex's simplified balance sheet 2015–2016 at the end of fiscal year.

(Amounts in billions of euros)

	2016	2015		2016	2015
Cash+	6.15	5.31	A/P+	5.33	4.59
Other current assets	0.23	0.18	Other liabilities	1.42	1.24
A/R+	0.97	0.76	Debt	0.12	0.08
Inventory	2.55	2.20	Equity	12.75	11.45
Fixed Assets	9.72	8.91			
Total assets	**19.62**	**17.36**	**Total equities**	**19.62**	**17.36**

Source: Authors' elaboration based on Inditex (2016, p. 242).

Table 9.2
Inditex's abridged balance sheet at the end of 2015–2016, measured as percentage of total assets.[a]

(Percentage of total assets)

	2016	2015		2016	2015
Cash+	31.3	30.6	A/P+	27.2	26.4
Other current assets	1.2	1.0	Other liabilities	7.2	7.1
A/R+	5.0	4.4	Debt	0.6	0.5
Inventory	13.0	12.7	Equity	65.0	65.6
Fixed assets	49.5	51.3			
Total assets	**100.0**	**100.0**	**Total equities**	**100.0**	**100.0**

a. Total assets: €19.62 billion (2016) and €17.36 billion (2015).

observation? The fact that the cash account is so large, together with nonexisting debt and very large equity, indicates that the Inditex's balance sheet is very robust, most likely the consequence of a prudent financial policy. Large fixed assets suggest that Inditex usually owns its stores, in contrast to other retailers that may resort to franchising or joint ventures. Likewise, payables are large, indicating that it pays its suppliers relatively late (more on this later), a common practice in the industry.

Also, there are two accounts—other current assets and debt—that do not even have room for their names in our diagram. It is therefore not worth devoting too much time to them. Receivables are small, as one might expect from a retailer that sells directly to end users. Finally, inventory is significant, but actually quite small by retailer standards. This is a consequence of Inditex's fast-fashion approach, for which the firm is well known in the industry. When comparing the evolution of accounts over time, it can be easily observed in the figure that the structures of both balance sheets at the end of 2015 and 2016 are almost identical, suggesting there have not been any notable changes (e.g., a major acquisition) during 2016.

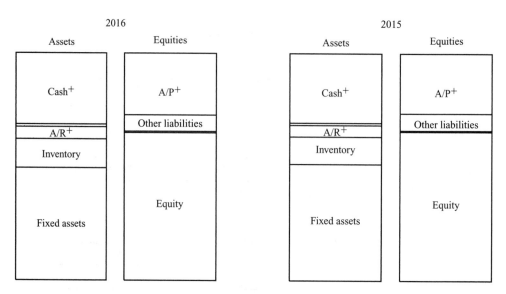

Figure 9.2
Pictorial representation of Inditex's balance sheet at the end of fiscal years 2015–2016.

Of course, more analysis is needed to ascertain that our conclusions are correct, but a quick and dirty analysis may be all that is needed in many cases. Notably, all these conclusions can be obtained without seeing the numbers; a picture of the balance sheet and some knowledge of the industry is enough to make a rough analysis of the financial status of a firm.

9.1.2 Visual Income Statement

Likewise, we can present the income statement using alternative formats. Inditex's income statement for years 2015 and 2016 is presented in table 9.3. In fashion retail, gross profit is an important measure of performance, as it captures to some extent how well a company does selecting an assortment of goods. An adequate assortment selection guarantees that prices will be relatively high—leading to higher sales—and inventory write-offs relatively low—leading to lower COGS. Combine the two effects and you end up with a higher gross profit. The argument, of course, can be reversed. So, how well did Inditex do in terms of gross profit in 2016 compared to 2015? Table 9.3 shows that gross profit increased from €12.1 billion to €13.3 billion, but, given that sales increase, does this gross profit increase signal an improvement in performance? To answer this question, it would be better to look at gross margin, that is, the ratio gross profit to sales. In fact, we can divide every number in table 9.3 by the amount of sales to obtain the relative importance of each account in the income statement. This is shown in table 9.4. We can see that Inditex's gross profit actually decreased as a percentage of sales, from 57.9 percent to 57.1 percent, a consequence of

Table 9.3
Inditex's simplified income statement in years 2015–2016.

(Billions of euros)

	2016	2015
Sales	23.3	20.9
Cost of goods sold	(10)	(8.8)
Gross profit	13.3	12.1
Selling, general, and administrative expenses[+]	(8.2)	(7.4)
EBITDA	5.1	4.7
Depreciation	(1.1)	(1.0)
EBIT	4	3.7
Other	0.1	0.1
Earnings before taxes	4.1	3.8
Tax	(0.9)	(0.9)
Net profit	3.2	2.9

Source: Inditex (2016, 240)

Table 9.4
Inditex's simplified income statement in 2015–2016.[a]

(Percentage of sales)

	2016	2015
Sales	100	100
COGS	(42.9)	(42.1)
Gross profit	57.1	57.9
SGA[+]	(35.2)	(35.4)
EBITDA	21.9	22.5
Depreciation	(4.7)	(4.8)
EBIT	17.2	17.7
Other	0.4	0.4
EBT	17.6	18.2
Tax	(3.9)	(4.3)
Net profit	13.7	13.9

a. Sales: €23.3 billion (2016) and €20.9 billion (2015).

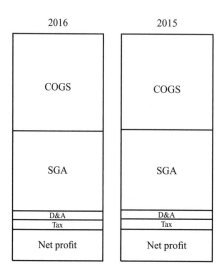

Figure 9.3
Pictorial representation of Inditex's income statement in years 2015–2016.

an increase in COGS from 42.1 percent to 42.9 percent. Likewise, net profit increased in euros but decreased in percentage. A quick analysis of table 9.4 reveals that the main reason for lower net profit in 2016 is in fact an increase in COGS, despite the reduction in SGA, depreciation, and tax.

Finally, we can also represent the income statement pictorially, as we did with the balance sheet (figure 9.3). Here, the total height of the figure should be proportional to sales. In the particular case of Inditex, however, we encounter a small difficulty: the account labeled "other" is €0.1 billion, or 0.4 percent of sales, a positive amount. This is due to the fact that this account includes net financial results. Since Inditex has no financial debt, but a large cash account (figure 9.1), it makes sense that deposit returns are larger than financial expenses. Since the amount is so small (lower than 0.5 percent) we can just ignore it, as the picture is not going to change. Had the difference been significant, we could have set the reference 100 percent to be sales plus other, rather than just sales.

9.1.3   Visual Statement of Cash Flows

We close this section by presenting the third major financial statement—the statement of cash flows—in alternative formats.

Table 9.5 shows the sources and uses of funds for Inditex in years 2015 and 2016. The original report has been converted into a seven-item statement of cash flows, as presented in chapter 7. Table 9.6 presents the statement of cash flows expressed in percentages by dividing every figure by total uses (equivalently, total sources).

Table 9.5
Inditex's simplified statement of cash flows in years 2015 and 2016.

(Billions of euros)

Uses	2016	2015	Sources	2016	2015
Dividends	1.87	1.63	Funds from operations	4.40	3.91
Investments	2.40	2.42	↑ Debt	0.02	0.00
↑ OWC	0.27	—	↓ OWC	—	0.60
↑ Cash	—	0.46	↓ Cash	0.12	—
Total uses	**4.54**	**4.51**	**Total sources**	**4.54**	**4.51**

Source: Inditex (2016, p. 243).

Table 9.6
Inditex's simplified statement of cash flows in years 2015 and 2016.[a]

(Percentage of total)

Uses	2016	2015	Sources	2016	2015
Dividends	41.2	36.1	Funds from operations	97.0	86.7
Investments	52.9	53.7	↑ Debt	0.4	0.0
↑ OWC	5.9	—	↓ OWC	—	13.3
↑ Cash	—	10.2	↓ Cash	2.6	—
Total uses	**100.0**	**100.0**	**Total sources**	**100.0**	**100.0**

a. Total uses are €4.54 billion (2016) and €4.51 billion (2015).

A quick review of percentages allows us to summarize the big picture of Inditex's movements of funds in 2016 in a very simple way: Money coming from sales (ultimately customers) is split between shareholders (a bit more than 40 percent) and new investments to sustain growth (a bit more than 50 percent). The rest of the money is used to increase operating working capital (roughly 6 percent). This conclusion is much more evident when figures are shown in percentages rather than euros. Trying to obtain this very same information from Inditex's original report is a much harder task unless you are very familiar with cash flows statements.

The corresponding pictorial version of the statement of cash flows is shown in figure 9.4. This picture offers the simplest interpretation of funds movements for the company in 2016. Isn't it nice?

9.2   Financial Ratios

The previous section has already illustrated why ratios are very useful to describe firms' performance, such as profitability or liquidity. For instance, knowing that a firm has made $1 million in the last year does not mean much. If sales were $4 million it would be great news, if sales were $1 billion it would be a completely different story. Ratios combine

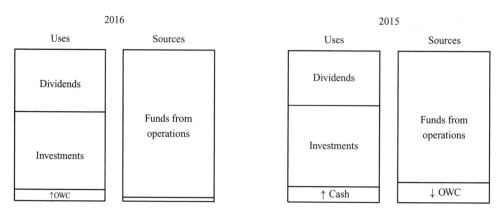

Figure 9.4
Pictorial representation of Inditex's statement of cash flows in 2015–2016.

different amounts from the financial statements to provide the reader with various measurements of performance. This section presents the most common financial ratios, focusing on those that measure operations performance. The list of ratios presented is not by any means comprehensive.

9.2.1   Why Financial Ratios?

As with most key-performance indicators (KPIs), there are two things that financial ratios do well:

Track performance over time A ratio value in isolation may not be meaningful, but, when compared to previous values, it indicates whether the measured magnitude has improved or worsened. A such, financial ratios are a formidable control tool and should be essential elements of your firm's control tower. In order to achieve this goal, ratios should be measured in a consistent way over time. Any changes in accounting practices or in the company strategy should be accounted for before reaching conclusions about performance. For instance, a company may make a strategic decision to increase service level at the store level. Once the policy has been implemented, the inventory turns ratio (to be presented very soon) may experience a drastic decrease. Is this a bad signal? Not necessarily, as lower inventory turns is a natural consequence of increasing customer service level.

Establish comparisons with other firms in the industry A careful ratio analysis of companies in the industry may unveil formidable opportunities for self-improvement. How is it possible that the leader of the industry gets away with so few days of inventory? What are we doing differently that we cannot achieve the same number of days of inventory, or even lower? Why is a competitor paying its suppliers later and later? Is it part of her strategy or is she going through liquidity problems? These and similar questions should be triggered when making a healthy analysis. Again, ratio comparison across firms should be done bearing in mind that different competitive strategies lead to some ratios looking better, some others worse. Ratio analysis should never be done in isolation from the context. That said, it may not be wise to compare with other companies in different industries, as the rules that govern each industry are generally different. For instance, holding six months of inventory can be satisfactory for a retailer selling car spare parts but totally inadmissible for a firm that manufactures and sells smartphones.

9.2.2 Overall Performance Ratios (CEO)

We begin by presenting those ratios related to overall performance, that is, those under the purview of the firm's chief executive officer (CEO). Of course, not only the CEO is accountable for these, but he or she is typically assumed to be the main proprietor of the ratio.

9.2.2.1 Return on equity (ROE)

Return on equity is the most common ratio to measure overall profitability for shareholders. A possible definition is

$$\text{ROE}_1 = \frac{\text{net profit}_t}{\text{equity}_{t-1}}$$

Other definitions include

$$\text{ROE}_2 = \frac{\text{net profit}_t}{\frac{\text{equity}_{t-1} + \text{equity}_t}{2}} \quad \text{or even} \quad \text{ROE}_3 = \frac{\text{net profit}_t}{\text{equity}_t}$$

All three definitions are used in practice. The first definition is based on the following logic: If you buy one share of a company priced at $100 on January 1 and net profit per share during the year is $20, your share will be worth $120 at the end of the year. If you sell the share on December 31 you will get $120 cash. The yield obtained is $\frac{20}{100}$, or 20 percent, exactly the value of ROE for the same period. The second definition makes an estimate of the average level of equity during the year by taking the average of equity at $t-1$ and t. Finally, the third definition is the most convenient to calculate, as it only uses financial data from one period. For other ratios, similar arguments are possible. Irrespective of which alternative is chosen, the choice should be consistent across ratios and over time.

Coming back to ROE, there are three limitations that are worth emphasizing: First, ROE compares two accounting amounts (one from the income statement, one from the balance sheet). As such, it cannot capture facts that impact the value of a firm but are not recorded by the accounting system. In particular, any future benefits are ignored. For instance, if the firm signs a five-year contract or obtains a ten-year patent, ROE will remain the same. This is a limitation of accounting and therefore a limitation of ROE. Second, recall that net profit is not a fact but an opinion (Fernández 2012). As such, ROE is subject to the opinions of the firm's managers, specially in the short term, as profits can be moved from one year to the following (whether acting in good faith or not is a different story). Third, ROE decreases if dividends are paid to shareholders, as dividends decrease the period's net profit. Given these three limitations, it should be apparent that ROE does *not* actually measure value created for shareholders. Despite this fact, ROE is closely scrutinized by analysts and managers altogether.

As an example of ROE calculation, combine net profit from Inditex's income statement in 2016 (table 9.3) with equity from the balance sheet in 2015 (table 9.1) to obtain:

$$\text{ROE} = \frac{3.2}{11.45} \approx 0.279 = 27.9\%$$

9.2.2.2 Sales growth

Sales growth is a simple ratio than links the current year's sales to the previous year's sales. It can be defined as

$$\text{sales growth} = \frac{\text{current year's sales} - \text{previous year's sales}}{\text{previous year's sales}}$$

It is usually expressed as a percentage, and sales are measured in monetary units (e.g., dollars). Although sales growth in dollars may not be an accurate measure of the growth of the firm's activity in periods of significant price or exchange rate changes. For instance, if sales in units increase by 10 percent and prices of those units sold have decreased on average 15 percent, sales growth in dollars will be -6.5 percent (that is, $110 \cdot 0.85 - 100$), possibly a misleading figure. Therefore, firms may prefer to use other growth measures in addition of sales growth measured in dollars, such as units sold or number of stores.

In the case of Inditex, sales growth in 2016 was (data from figure 9.3)

$$\text{sales growth in dollars} = \frac{23.3 - 20.9}{20.9} \approx 0.115 = 11.5\%$$

For a retailer such as Inditex, it may make sense to calculate what is known as like-for-like sales growth. This measures the efficiency of the average store at making sales by ignoring changes in the number of stores. For instance, Inditex had 7,013 stores at the end of 2015 and 7,292 stores at the end of 2016. Therefore, its like-for-like sales growth in 2016 was:

$$\text{like-for-like sales growth} = \frac{23.3 - 20.9}{20.9} \cdot \frac{7,013}{7,292} \approx 0.111 = 11.1\%$$

Assuming Inditex's new openings occur steadily over time, had Inditex had 7,013 stores in 2016, its sales growth would have been not 11.5 percent, but 11.1 percent. That means that more units per store were sold, or that the average price increased, or (most likely) a combination of the two. Various methods of like-for-like measurement exist, making it difficult to compare this ratio across competitors.

We will finish our discussion on sales growth by saying that investors and analysts alike love growth. The main reason may be that the value of an investment increases drastically with growth. As a simple illustration of this fact, consider a perpetual dividend of $200 paid every year discounted[1] at 10 percent, which is worth

$$\sum_{t=1}^{\infty} \frac{200}{(1+0.01)^t} = \frac{200}{0.1} = \$2,000$$

If the same dividend increases by a modest 2 percent every year (say, as a consequence of 2 percent sales growth), the perpetual dividend discounted at 10 percent is now:

$$\sum_{t=1}^{\infty} \frac{200 \cdot 1.02^{t-1}}{(1+0.01)^t} = \frac{200}{0.1 - 0.02} = \$2,500$$

A small 2 percent increase in dividends leads to a significant 25 percent increase in value! Furthermore, assuming a 10 percent discount rate, in order to double the investment value (from $2,000 to $4,000) dividends should only increase by 5 percent per year!

The example provided may make you understand the analysts and investors' appetite for growth. This includes not only sales growth but almost anything that can be linked to dividends, such as stores, share price, cash flows, gross profit, or EBITDA.

9.2.2.3   Net margin and gross margin

Net margin (also known as ROS—return on sales) is an intuitive indicator that measures profitability by linking two figures from the income statement: net profit and sales. The definition is as follows:

$$\text{net margin} = \frac{\text{net profit}_t}{\text{sales}_t}$$

Net margin is usually given as a percentage of sales. In this case, the same year's data is used, as it makes no sense no compare profits and sales for different years. As with ROE, net margin compares two accounting figures. As such, both can be subject to managers' biases.

For instance, Inditex's net margin in 2016 was (data from table 9.3)

$$\text{net margin} = \frac{3.2}{23.3} \approx 0.137 = 13.7\%$$

Note that the number coincides with the one on the bottom line in table 9.4, as percentages in that table are calculated by dividing by sales. Sometimes the fancier acronym ROS (return on sales) is used instead of sheer net margin.

Similarly to net margin, gross margin is defined as the ratio gross profit to sales.

---

1. See chapter 12 for details.

9.2.2.4   Leverage as a measure of the firm's risk

A CEO's concerns should include the exposition of the firm to risk. Measuring risk is very difficult, both in operations and finance. What is undeniable is that both operating and financial decisions not only impact a firm's financial statements but also the amount of risk faced by the firm.

Although many sources of risk have been identified, most of them boil down to only three: industry risk, operational risk, and financial risk. For instance, a major disruption of components supply is an examples of industry risk; a strike that affects only a firm's workers is an example of operational risk.

(1) Industry risk is related to demand variability, that is, how much demand fluctuates over time. It can be measured, for instance, by the coefficient of variation of the demand.

(2) Operational risk depends on operating leverage, that is, on how sensitive EBIT is to changes in sales (in dollars). It can be measured using the following expression:

$$\text{operating leverage} = \frac{\text{percentage change in EBIT}}{\text{percentage change in sales}} = \frac{\%\,\Delta\,\text{EBIT}}{\%\,\Delta\,\text{sales}}$$

For instance, other things equal, if EBIT increases (decreases) by 15 percent when sales increase (decrease) by 10 percent, the operating leverage would be $\frac{15}{10} = 1.5$.

Operating leverage mainly depends on the percentage of fixed costs over total operational costs. The higher the percentage of fixed costs, the higher the operational risk. For instance, if a firm heavily invests in new manufacturing fixed assets, a fixed cost will be incurred and the operating leverage will increase. Therefore, it should be clear that not only the CEO but also the COO have access to the levers that modify operating risk.

(3) Financial risk depends on financial leverage—that is, on how sensitive net profit is to changes in EBIT. It can be measured by an analogue expression.

$$\text{financial leverage} = \frac{\text{percentage change in net profit}}{\text{percentage change in EBIT}} = \frac{\%\,\Delta\,\text{net profit}}{\%\,\Delta\,\text{EBIT}}$$

For instance, if net profit increases (decreases) by 18 percent when EBIT increases (decreases) by 10 percent, the operating leverage would be $\frac{18}{10} = 1.8$.

Financial risk mainly depends on the amount of debt the company holds and its price, as the resulting regularly paid interest is clearly a fixed cost that doesn't increase with sales. Similar to operating risk, both CEO and CFO have the ability to change financial risk by deciding on the capital structure (i.e., the amount of debt with respect to the sum of debt plus equity) of the firm.

The multiplication of both operational and financial leverage measures the joint effect of both risks and can be defined as total leverage. We have:

$$\text{total leverage} = \frac{\%\,\Delta\,\text{EBIT}}{\%\,\Delta\,\text{sales}} \cdot \frac{\%\,\Delta\,\text{net profit}}{\%\,\Delta\,\text{EBIT}} = \frac{\%\,\Delta\,\text{net profit}}{\%\,\Delta\,\text{sales}}$$

The following exercise elaborates on this.

 Exercise

Operating versus Financial Risk

Consider the income statement of a firm whose COGS is made only of variable costs and SGA expenses are made only of fixed costs. Tax rate is 30 percent.

Sales	20,000
COGS (variable)	(17,000)
Gross Profit	3,000
SGA (fixed)	0
EBIT	3,000
Interest	0
EBT	3,000
Tax	(900)
Net profit	2,100

1. By how much will net profit increase if sales increase by 10 percent?
2. Let's now suppose that COGS is only $13,000 and SGA is $4,000 such that EBIT is $3,000, exactly as in the base case. By how much will net profit increase if sales increase/decrease by 10 percent?
3. Assume now that the firm has to pay $500,000 in interest expenses while keeping operational fixed costs null. What is the impact of increasing sales by 10 percent on net profit now?
4. Finally, let's combine scenarios #2 and #3: in scenario #4, fixed operational costs add up to $4,000, as in scenario #2, and interest expenses are $500,000, as in scenario #3. What is the combined impact on net profit of both operational and financial leverage? What if sales increase/decrease by 20 percent?

? Question 1

By how much will net profit increase if sales increase by 10 percent?

If sales increase by 10 percent, net profit will also increase by 10 percent. This is due to the fact that all costs in the income statement are variable, as they increase with sales. The resulting income statement is presented in table 9.7 (scenario #1, right column).

Table 9.7
Impact of operational and financial leverage on net profit.

Scenario	#1 (base case)		#2 (op. leverage)		#3 (fin. leverage)		#4 (op. & fin. lev.)	
Sales increase	+10%		+10%		+10%		+10%	
Sales	20,000	22,000	20,000	22,000	20,000	22,000	20,000	22,000
COGS (variable)	(17,000)	(18,700)	(13,000)	(14,300)	(17,000)	(18,700)	(13,000)	(14,300)
Gross profit	3,000	3,300	7,000	7,700	3,000	3,300	7,000	7,700
SGA (fixed)	0	0	(4,000)	(4,000)	0	0	(4,000)	(4,000)
EBIT	3,000	3,300	3,000	3,700	3,000	3,300	3,000	3,700
Interest	0	0	0	0	(500)	(500)	(500)	(500)
EBT	3,000	3,300	3,000	3,700	2,500	2,800	2,500	3,200
Tax	(900)	(990)	(900)	(1,110)	(750)	(840)	(750)	(960)
Net profit	2,100	2,310	2,100	2,590	1,750	1,960	1,750	2,240
EBIT increase	+10.0%		+23.3%		+10.0%		+23.3%	
Net profit increase	+10.0%		+23.3%		+12.0%		+28.0%	

❓ Question 2

Let's now suppose that COGS is only $13,000 and SGA is $4,000 such that EBIT is $3,000, exactly as in the base case. By how much will net profit increase if sales increase/decrease by 10 percent?

If sales increase by 10 percent, net profit will increase by 23.3 percent (scenario #2). This is due to the fact that operational leverage has increased (specifically, fixed costs have increased from 0 to $4,000), while keeping total costs constant. As 23 percent is much larger than 10 percent, we might wrongly infer that increased operational leverage is a good thing. However, how will net profit change if sales *decrease* by 10 percent? You can check that net profit will go down by 23.3 percent (exercise 2 asks you to perform the calculations). Therefore, by increasing operating leverage, expected profit doesn't change but risk increases.

❓ Question 3

Assume now that the firm has to pay $500 in interest expenses while keeping operational fixed costs null. What is the impact of increasing sales by 10 percent on net profit now?

In this case, net profit increases by 12 percent (scenario #3, right column), again a number larger than 10 percent. This situation is identical to the one in scenario #2 at the qualitative level. However, the source of the increase of net profit comes only from the financial side of the firm, as financial leverage has increased: a fixed payment of $500 has to be made each period irrespective of the level of sales.

? Question 4

Finally, let's combine scenarios #2 and #3: in scenario #4, fixed operational costs add up to $4,000, as in scenario #2, and interest expenses are $500, as in scenario #3. What is the combined impact on net profit of both operational and financial leverage? What if sales increase/decrease by 20 percent?

In this last case, you can see (scenario #4, right column) that net profit increases by 28 percent, more than either 23.3 percent or 12 percent. A key point is that both operational and financial leverages become amplified when they coincide. More specifically, as mentioned, total leverage becomes the multiplication of operating leverage and financial leverage. Indeed:

$$\frac{\%\Delta \text{net profit}}{\%\Delta \text{sales}}\bigg|_{\text{scenario \#4}} = \frac{\%\Delta \text{EBIT}}{\%\Delta \text{sales}}\bigg|_{\text{scenario \#2}} \cdot \frac{\%\Delta \text{net profit}}{\%\Delta \text{EBIT}}\bigg|_{\text{scenario \#3}} \Rightarrow$$

$$\frac{28}{10} = \frac{100 \cdot \left(\frac{3,700}{3,000} - 1\right)}{10} \cdot \frac{12}{100 \cdot \left(\frac{3,300}{3,000} - 1\right)} \Rightarrow$$

$$\frac{28}{10} = \frac{23.33}{10} \cdot \frac{12}{10} \tag{9.1}$$

Now, what if the sales increase (decrease) doubles to 20 percent? Net profit will increase (decrease) by 56 percent, twice as much as before!

The simple calculations performed should be enough to realize that the total amount of risk a firm bears should be carefully planned and limited. What should be the limit? Of course, it depends on the specific situation of the firm, but here are two rules of thumb:

(1) The higher the industry risk is, the lower operational and financial risks should be. That means that a firm running, say, windmill farms, may take more debt from a bank (and therefore bear fixed interest payments) than a technological start-up. (The industry risk for wind mills is relatively low, as the annual amount of electricity generated from wind doesn't change much across years—although it may vary greatly across months.)

(2) Operational and financial leverages should not both be simultaneously large, as their effects get multiplied. Figure 9.5 illustrates the fact that a firm cannot have too much operating leverage and financial leverage simultaneously, or the bar will break.

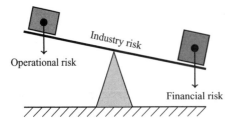

Figure 9.5
A representation of operational risk (left weight), financial risk (right weight), and industry risk (bar strength).

 Too much of two good things

Operational and financial leverages should not both be simultaneously large, as their effects on the firm's risk get multiplied.

9.2.3   Operational Performance Ratios (COO)

Having discussed some ratios that measure overall performance, we now turn our attention to operational ratios, those mainly under the purview of the chief operations officer (COO).

9.2.3.1   Return on assets (ROA)

We start our discussion by presenting ROA, the COO's counterpart to the CEO's ROE. Return on assets may be defined as follows:

$$\text{ROA} = \frac{\text{EBITDA}_t}{\text{total assets}_{t-1}}$$

As with ROE, alternative denominators can be used, such as total assets$_t$ or $\frac{1}{2}$(total assets$_{t-1}$ + total assets$_t$). In this case, the numerator can also change to include other measures of profit, such as net profit or EBIT. We claim that using EBIT or EBITDA is more appropriate than net profit when measuring the firm's performance in operations, as net profit is affected by financial expenses and corporate taxes, accounts typically under the purview of the CFO. Likewise, if the bulk of depreciation is mainly made up of manufacturing buildings and equipments rather than corporate buildings, the COO may be accountable for depreciation (D&A) and then EBIT is preferable to EBITDA in the ROA definition.

Using the data from tables 9.1 and 9.3, we can see that Inditex's ROA in 2016, defined as $\frac{\text{EBITDA}_t}{\text{total assets}_{t-1}}$, is:

$$\text{ROA} = \frac{5.1}{17.36} \approx 0.294 = 29.4\%$$

Table 9.8
NOPAT calculation example.

Detail of income statement

EBIT	100
Interest expense	(20)
EBT	80
Tax (30%)	(24)
Net profit	56

9.2.3.2 Return on net assets (RONA)

In our search for a good measure of operations performance, we can refine ROA further, and use RONA (also known as ROIC—return on invested capital) instead. Its definition is:

$$RONA = \frac{NOPAT_t}{\text{net assets}_{t-1}}$$

where NOPAT stands for net operating profit after tax, and is defined as:

$$NOPAT = \text{net profit} + \text{interest expense} \cdot (1 - t)$$

where t is the tax rate. An equivalent definition is:

$$NOPAT = EBIT \cdot (1 - t)$$

In other words, NOPAT is the net profit the firm would have had in the absence of interest expenses. The following example will show that all three definitions given are equivalent. Given the detail of an income statement in table 9.8, the two first definitions of NOPAT give identical results:

$$NOPAT_1 = \text{ net profit} + \text{interest expense} \cdot (1 - t) = 56 + 20 \cdot (1 - 0.3) = 70$$

$$NOPAT_2 = \text{ EBIT} \cdot (1 - t) = 100 \cdot (1 - 0.3) = 70$$

As for the third definition, let's build the income statement as if the firm did not have any interest expenses (figure 9.9). As expected, net profit ($70) coincides with NOPAT. In the unusual case that interest expenses are negative, the three definitions are still equivalent (see Inditex example below).

The denominator of RONA is net assets, defined as:

$$\text{net assets} = \text{assets} - \text{accounts payable}^+$$

Using net assets rather than total assets in the definition of RONA may seem strange: Why are accounts payable subtracted from total assets? The answer has to do with the fact that funds from suppliers (accounts payable) are claimed not to have a cost to the firm. Recall

Table 9.9
NOPAT calculation example (cont.).
Detail of income statement

EBIT	100
Interest expense	(0)
EBT	100
Tax (30%)	(30)
Net profit	70

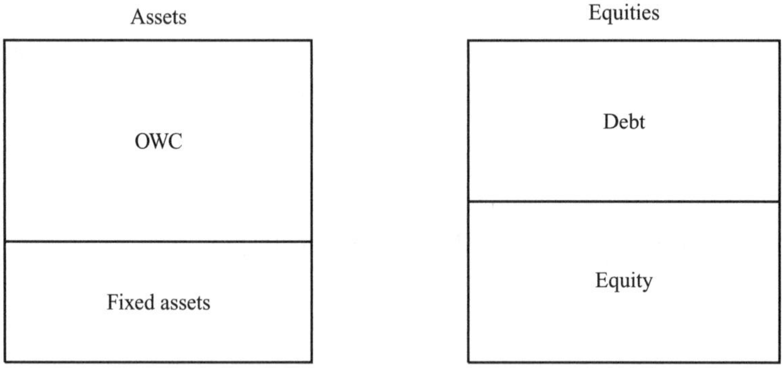

Figure 9.6
Financial balance sheet when excess cash is zero.

the financial balance sheet when excess cash is zero presented in 5.2. Net assets are OWC plus fixed assets, or, equivalently, debt plus equity.

RONA compares NOPAT to the portion of costly assets, those that have to be funded through debt and equity, and which require paying, respectively, interest and dividends.

RONA can help compare firms that have different leverage strategies, something that is not possible with ROE. For example, consider two identical firms, operating in the same industry and having the same net profit margin but following different leverage strategies (i.e., having different Debt/Equity ratios). What the RONA ratio measures is each firm's capability to generate returns on its assets, assuming that none of the firms is carrying any debt. Hence, by eliminating the impact of their leverage policies, RONA facilitates comparison of the two firms in similar terms.

Using the data from tables 9.1 and 9.3, we can see that Inditex's RONA in 2016 is:

$$\text{RONA} = \frac{\text{NOPAT}_t}{\text{net assets}_{t-1}} = \frac{\text{EBIT}_t(1-t)}{\text{debt}_{t-1}+\text{equity}_{t-1}} = \frac{4(1-0.22)}{0.08+11.45} \approx 27.1\%$$

where the average tax rate has been calculated by dividing tax by EBT in 2016. Alternative measures of profit to NOPAT to calculate RONA include EBITDA and EBIT. Also, similar ratios to RONA are ROCE (return on capital employed), defined as the ratio EBIT to net assets or ROI (return on investment), defined as the ratio net profit to net assets. The link between RONA and ROCE is:

$$RONA = ROCE(1 - t)$$

9.2.3.3   Days of inventory outstanding and inventory turns

Days of inventory outstanding (DIO) measures the number of days on average inventory stays on the firm's premises. Similarly, inventory turns (IT) measures how many times on average the firm's warehouses are filled (and emptied) every year. For instance, thirty days of inventory are roughly equivalent to twelve turns per year, as inventory leaves the warehouse one month after arriving, and this cycle repeats twelve times a year. DIO or IT are maybe the most important performance operational measures for a firm that holds significant amounts of inventory.

DIO is defined as:

$$DIO = \frac{inventory_t}{cost\ of\ goods\ sold_t} \cdot 365$$

First, note that the denominator is *not* sales but cost of goods sold. This is because inventory is measured in terms of cost (mainly acquisition cost plus operating cost), but sales are measured in terms of price. Using sales would be like comparing apples and oranges. Also, note that we are comparing a stock from the balance sheet in the numerator to a flow from the income statement in the denominator. The inventory is measured in dollars, COGS in dollars per year, therefore our final ratio is measured in years. In order to get days, we multiply the result by 365 (days in a year). Finally, note that the numerator is a snapshot of inventory at the end of the year. This might not be representative of inventory throughout the year (in contrast to COGS, which does tell the story of the whole year). We could use instead average inventory at the end of each quarter or, even better, at the end of each month to avoid what we call the end-of-the-period syndrome (see section 9.5).

Exercise
Inventory Turns

Given the following selected data for a company:

	Year 1	Year 2
Inventory	120	80
COGS	1,200	1,000

Calculate inventory turns for year 2.

Inventory turns is simply:

$$IT = \frac{COGS_2}{inventory_2} = \frac{1,000}{80} = 15 \text{ turns per year}$$

or, using the best available measure of average inventory over year 2:

$$IT = \frac{COGS_2}{\text{average inventory during year 2}} = \frac{1,000}{\frac{120+80}{2}} = 10 \text{ turns per year.}$$

Other things equal, it is better to have fewer DIO, as inventory increases OWC. However, note that "other things equal" in this context may mean, for instance, maintaining the same customer service level in terms of both availability and lead-time. Therefore, reducing inventory too much will erode service level. Because of these considerations a firm's goal should not be to reach zero inventory, but the right amount of inventory such that the firm can accomplish its competitive strategy.

Using the data from tables 9.1 and 9.3, we can see that Inditex's DIO in 2016 turns out to be:

$$DIO = \frac{inventory_t}{\text{cost of goods sold}_t} \cdot 365 = \frac{2.55}{10} \cdot 365 \approx 93 \text{ days}$$

Of course this is an approximation, as inventory level at the end of the fiscal year (January 31 in the case of Inditex) may not be a good representative of inventory level during the year.

9.2.3.4 Days of payables

Similarly to DIO, days of payables outstanding (DPO) measure how many days on average it takes a firm to pay its suppliers. The count usually begins when the goods arrive or when the service is delivered. For instance, if DPO is forty-five days, it means that, on average, it takes a firm to pay suppliers one month and a half. DPO may be under the purview of the COO—for instance, when purchasing reports to the COO. But it could also be the case that DPO falls under the CFO's umbrella. We include DPO (and DSO) here to keep consistency, given the parallelism of DIO, DPO, and DSO, and the fact that all three make up the so-called cash conversion cycle.

DPO is defined as:

$$DPO = \frac{\text{accounts payable}_t}{purchases_t} \cdot 365$$

Note that we are using purchases in the denominator, and not sales (valued at price, not cost) nor COGS (which may include production costs not related to suppliers). As with DIO, we are comparing a stock in the balance sheet (accounts payable) with the corresponding flow (purchases). Also, we are using accounts payable at the end of the year to calculate DPO. We are therefore assuming that the amount of payments outstanding is roughly the same over the year. This is not necessarily the case: if sales (and therefore purchases) are seasonal, or if the firm suffers from end-of-the-period syndrome, then payments outstanding may be a more variable figure over time. If so, we would have to modify our calculations in order not to achieve the wrong conclusions. For instance, according to its 2016 annual report (note 6.19), in 2016 Inditex made payments to suppliers and creditors in Spain worth €2.9 billion. Outstanding payments at the end of fiscal year 2016 were €199,000. DPO was then:

$$\text{DPO} = \frac{\text{accounts payable}_t}{\text{purchases}_t} \cdot 365 = \frac{199}{2,920} \cdot 365 \approx 25 \text{ days.}$$

However, according to the very same source, the comparable average period of payments to suppliers was roughly thirty-six days. The fact that these two numbers are significantly different may signal that either Inditex sales are seasonal, or that Inditex suffers from end-of-the-year syndrome, or, most likely, a mix of both.

Other things equal, it seems better to have more DPO, as accounts payable decreases OWC. However, other things equal in this context means, among other things, maintaining supplier's price, quality, and service throughout a measurement period. For instance, consistently paying a supplier too late may lead to the supplier not having enough funds to invest in R&D, something that may erode both the supplier's and the firm's competitive edge over time. In more extreme cases, paying a supplier late may drag the supplier to bankruptcy, especially in the case of small, financially-weak suppliers.

9.2.3.5 Days of receivables

Much like DIO and DPO above, days of sales outstanding (DSO) measures how many days on average it takes a firm to collect money from its customers after a sale has been made. For consistency, the name should be "days of *receivables* outstanding," but this notation is much less used, maybe because the acronym DRO is already in use within finance. (DRO stands for debt relief order, a concept we won't be discussing here.) As with DPO, the level of DSO may be under the COO's jurisdiction; for instance, if he negotiates agreements with franchisees, but it may well be the case that the CFO takes full responsibility.

DSO is defined as:

$$\text{DSO} = \frac{\text{accounts receivable}_t}{\text{sales}_t} \cdot 365$$

which again compares a stock in the numerator with a flow in the denominator. Unsurprisingly, we are using sales in the denominator this time, as both accounts receivable and sales are measured in selling price. Other things equal, it is better to have fewer DSO, as accounts receivables increase OWC.

DSO sometimes measures the relative purchasing power of buyers and sellers. A small firm selling to a multinational company usually has no bargaining power and will accept the

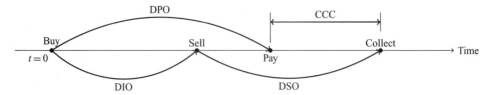

Figure 9.7
Representation of cash conversion cycle (CCC) on a time line.

(usually long) payment terms imposed by the large multinational. Likewise, in a business to consumer (B2C) environment, firms selling to individuals will typically collect money very quickly, as end consumers will typically pay cash or credit card. This is especially true in e-commerce, where customers typically pay first to receive the purchased goods days later. In this case, DSO becomes negative.

To return to our Inditex case study, sales in 2016 were €23.3 billion (table 9.3) and accounts receivable totaled €0.86 billion,[2] hence DSO are:

$$DSO = \frac{accounts\ receivable_t}{sales_t} \cdot 365 = \frac{0.86}{23.3} \cdot 365 \approx 13\ days.$$

It makes sense that the collection period is relatively small, as customers in stores pay cash or with credit card and online customers pay before even receiving the goods acquired. Note that DSO would most likely be even smaller if Inditex had no franchises.

9.2.3.6 Cash conversion cycle or cash to cash cycle

Having defined DIO, DPO, and DSO, we are ready to present the notion of the cash conversion cycle (CCC), also known as the cash to cash cycle. It is defined as:

cash conversion cycle = DIO + DSO − DPO

This ratio measures the lapse of time from the moment cash is paid to suppliers until cash is collected from customers. During that time, the firm is relatively more vulnerable, as money to suppliers has already left the firm and many things may go wrong until money is collected from the customers that will buy those goods. Given this definition, there is no need to say that, other things equal, CCC should be as small as possible, even negative. Figure 9.7 shows a pictorial representation of CCC.

We can calculate CCC for Inditex, assuming that DPO, which was calculated for Spanish suppliers, can be extrapolated to its entire base of suppliers (admittedly, a big assumption):

cash conversion cycle = DIO + DSO − DPO = 93 + 13 − 25 = 81 days

---

2. Trade and other receivables were €861,027, of which €0.46 billion correspond to trade receivables and receivables due to sales to franchises (Inditex 2016, n. 6.11). Income tax receivable were €107,473, therefore accounts receivable[+] were roughly €0.97 billion, as shown in figure 9.3.

Therefore, money paid to suppliers today will return to the firm from customers in roughly three months (together with additional gross profit).

9.2.3.7 Asset turnover and other turnover ratios

Asset turnover measures the utilization of total assets by computing how many times they are included in sales. That is to say:

$$\text{asset turnover} = \frac{\text{sales}_t}{\text{assets}_t}$$

The ratio compares a flow from the income statement in the numerator and a stock from the balance sheet in the denominator.

For instance, Inditex's asset turnover in 2016 was:

$$\text{asset turnover} = \frac{\text{sales}_t}{\text{assets}_t} = \frac{23.3}{19.62} \approx 1.19$$

Therefore, in one year Inditex was able to sell 1.19 dollars of merchandise per dollar of assets. Think about it: assets are needed resources that the firm holds to run operations. It includes things like factories, machines, trucks, and inventory. If the firm could sell the same amount of items while holding fewer assets and keeping *everything else* constant (that includes, for instance, risk), then profitability would increase, as holding assets has a cost (well, holding equities does, but assets = equities). We can then conclude that, other things equal, the higher the asset turnover, the better.

Asset turnover can be refined in two ways at least: First, we can use net assets rather than total assets. That is to say, we can remove from assets a large portion, such as payables$^+$, which is assumed to be free funds (We did exactly this when we defined RONA). For instance, in the case of Inditex:

$$\text{asset turnover}_2 = \frac{\text{sales}_t}{\text{net assets}_t} = \frac{23.3}{19.62 - 5.33} \approx 1.63$$

Second, by the same token, we can remove excess cash from total assets. Recall that excess cash is the level of cash in excess of the required cash for operations. For instance, Inditex ended 2016 with a pile of cash and cash equivalents of €6.15 billion. How much of that is required cash can only be answered (if anyone) by Inditex management. If, say, half of existing cash were excess cash, asset turnover would be:

$$\text{asset turnover}_3 = \frac{\text{sales}_t}{\text{assets}_t - \text{excess cash}_t} = \frac{23.3}{19.62 - 0.5 \cdot 6.15} \approx 1.41$$

We can combine the last two definitions and subtract both payables$^+$ and excess cash from total assets:

$$\text{asset turnover}_4 = \frac{\text{sales}_t}{\text{net assets}_t - \text{excess cash}_t} = \frac{23.3}{19.62 - 5.33 - 0.5 \cdot 6.15} \approx 2.08$$

Granted, all these refinements are attempts to be more fair when comparing the ratio with past periods or competitors.

There are many other stocks in the balance sheet that can be compared to annual sales in order to get the corresponding turnover ratios, such as accounts receivable, inventory, fixed assets, or even working capital. For instance, inventory turnover is defined as:

$$\text{inventory turnover} = \frac{\text{sales}_t}{\text{inventory}_t}$$

Inditex's inventory turnover ratio in 2016 (which is $23.3/2.55 = 9.1$) shows that the firm sells 9.1 dollars per dollar of inventory held.

Accounts receivable turnover, fixed asset turnover, or working capital turnover can be similarly defined.

9.2.3.8   Gross margin return on inventory

The operational ratios presented so far are quite standard and usually found in most financial analysis books. That is not the case for the remaining three ratios, as they are specific for inventory, a stock on the balance sheet that does not usually get much attention in finance literature.

The first ratio on the short list is gross margin return on inventory, or GMROI for short (pronounced "jimroy"). GMROI is defined as:

$$\text{GMROI} = \frac{\text{gross profit}_t}{\text{inventory}_t}$$

It measures gross margin per dollar of held inventory. This ratio is of great importance in retailing, as it links gross margin and inventory, two of the most powerful drivers of profitability for retailers. Note that each of the two elements of GMROI, gross margin and inventory, can be improved at the expense of the other. For instance, it is relatively easy to get rid of inventory by selling goods at a deep discount, which would erode gross margin. But it is not easy to keep gross margin high and inventory low simultaneously. As such, GMROI is a key figure that measures how well firms in general and retailers in particular handle inventory-related functions. These include:

Assortment selection Retailers typically choose items in their portfolios following rules of thumb, as assortment selection is still more of an art than a science (see Fisher and Raman [2010] for state-of-the-art methods on portfolio selection). Bad assortment selection leads to high inventories and subsequent discounts, which erode gross profit, hence GMROI.

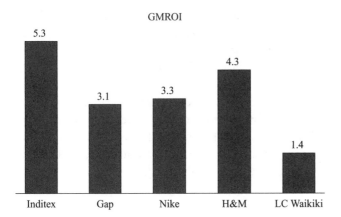

Figure 9.8
GMROI for selected retailers in 2015.
Source: Authors' elaboration from the firms' financial statements.

Forecasting accuracy In make-to-stock environments, forecasting is a key driver of profitability. Good forecasting decreases excess inventory, making it unnecessary to reduce prices significantly, leading to higher GMROI.

Replenishment policies Setting the right levels of safety inventory and purchasing lot size, as well as choosing reliable and well-located suppliers will also have a large impact on GMROI. For instance, selecting a far-away supplier because a lower unit cost will improve the gross margin, other things equal, but it will also entail higher levels of safety and cycle stock, which increases overall inventory holding cost. The level of GMROI will depend on how this trade-off is worked out.

Transhipments policies Likewise, moving inventory between sister stores reduces inventory and may increase sales, but transportation cost erodes gross margin. Solving this trade-off correctly will make GMROI look better.

Figure 9.8 shows the value of GMROI in 2015 for a selection of retailers in the fashion industry. Inditex's GMROI stands out as the company is known for pioneering so-called fast fashion. They are adept at reacting very quickly to market trends by working with relatively close suppliers, moving goods by air, using lab stores, and various other strategies. The graph suggests that these work well for Inditex.

9.2.3.9 Inventory-to-payables

The inventory-to-payables (ITP) ratio compares inventory and payables, two amounts from the balance sheet. This dimensionless ratio is defined as:

$$\text{inventory-to-payables} = \frac{\text{inventory}_t}{\text{accounts payable}_t}$$

where both amounts are measured in *dollars*, not in days. This is an important distinction because this ratio should not be confused with the payables-to-inventory ratio (PTI), where payables and inventory are measured in days, that is, the ratio DPO to DIO, which measures the fraction of held inventory unpaid. Note that ITP $\neq$ 1/PTI, as the two ratios contain different information.

The goal of the ITP ratio is to detect inventory obsolescence, which makes this ratio particularly useful, especially when there is no data to calculate the average age of inventory. Indeed, when inventory is bought and sold normally, the ratio does not change in the long run, once inventory has been sold and the supplier has received its payment. However, if inventory is not sold, the ratio will increase over time. This is best illustrated by one example.

 Exercise

Detecting Obsolescence Using the Inventory-to-Payables Ratio

Consider a retailer that holds inventory for sixty days on average and pays suppliers in forty-five days. Average levels of inventory and payables are 2,000 and 1,000 monetary units respectively. Therefore, COGS and purchases will be roughly 12,000 and 8,000 respectively.

1. How will the inventory-to-payables ratio evolve over time in normal conditions?
2. What if there is obsolescence?

Figure 9.9 shows the levels of inventory, accounts payable, and the inventory-to-payables ratio over time for two scenarios: on the left, inventory is bought and sold normally; on the right, inventory cannot be sold because of obsolescence.

In the first case, inventory worth 500 arrives to the warehouse on day zero, then both inventory and A/P levels increase by 500. Forty-five days later, 500 is paid to the supplier so payables go down to 1,000 again, but inventory does not change. On day sixty inventory worth 500 is sold and inventory level goes down to 2,000. Therefore, after paying the supplier and selling the acquired inventory, the ITP ratio goes back to its original value after some fluctuations.

In the second case, inventory cannot be sold due to obsolescence, so inventory remains abnormally high after sixty days. The ITP ratio has increased from 2.0 to 2.5. This should be a signal for management to find out what's wrong with the level of inventory.

The ratio will fluctuate normally due to buying, paying, and selling inventory. However, in the absence of obsolescence, it should remain fairly constant. Of course, the ratio should be recalibrated if either payment terms or inventory strategies (e.g., the addition of a warehouse) change significantly.

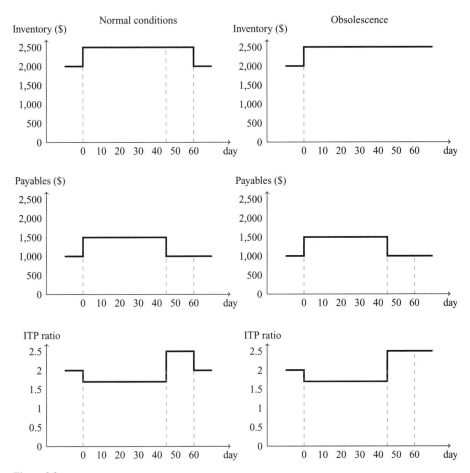

Figure 9.9
Evolution of inventory-to-payables ratio in normal conditions (left panel) and in the presence of obsolescence (right panel).

9.2.3.10   Age of inventory

As mentioned, the average age of inventory may be a good indicator for obsolescence, provided that data is available to calculate it. In order to be able to compute it, the ERP system should keep track of when each unit of inventory arrived at the firm premises. For average inventory to be of practical help, calculations should be done for each family of products or even per SKU. For instance, it would not make much sense to mix electronic cards (an expensive item subject to obsolescence) and screws (a cheap item that will not become obsolete) in the same calculation.

Exercise

Dating Inventory

Inventory records of a seller of bearings in the after-sales market for family A (made of items A1 and A2) are shown in the following table:

Lot	Item	Date	Quantity
1	A1	March 2	240
2	A2	March 18	150
3	A1	April 4	240
4	A1	April 14	120
5	A2	April 16	250

If today is April 26:

1. What is the average age of item A1?
2. What is the average age of items in family A?

Lot 1 has been in the firm for $29 + 26 = 55$ days. Likewise, lots 3 and 4 have been around for 22 and 12 days respectively. On average, the age of item A1 is

$$\text{average age of item A1} = \frac{240 \cdot 55 + 240 \cdot 22 + 120 \cdot 12}{240 + 240 + 120} = 33.2 \text{ days.}$$

Similarly, average age for items in family A is:

$$\frac{240 \cdot 55 + 150 \cdot 39 + 240 \cdot 22 + 120 \cdot 12 + 250 \cdot 10}{240 + 150 + 240 + 120 + 250} \approx 28.3 \text{ days.}$$

9.2.3.11   David Berman (DB) ratio

As of 2019, David Berman was a senior managing director at Macquarie Capital, a large investment company. Over the years, Berman devised an investment methodology based on the relationship between sales and inventory growth. His main idea was that sales and inventory should grow roughly at the same rate. If inventory steadily increases at a higher rate than sales, it most likely means that useless inventory is piling up and, sooner or later, that useless inventory will have to be written off (i.e., removed from assets, hence incurring expenses). Tracking the connection between sales and inventory over time allowed him to estimate when write-offs would occur. He would then short-sell stocks prior to inventory write-offs, making a profit once the stock price had plunged (Raman, Gaur, and Kesavan 2005).

The DB ratio is defined as

$$DB = \frac{\text{inventory growth}}{\text{sales growth}}$$

where both growths are percentages, that is:

$$\text{inventory growth} = \frac{\text{inventory}_t - \text{inventory}_{t-1}}{\text{inventory}_{t-1}}$$

$$\text{sales growth} = \frac{\text{sales}_t - \text{sales}_{t-1}}{\text{sales}_{t-1}}$$

According to Berman, the ratio should not be significantly above 1 for several consecutive periods. If so, the ratio would signal the existence of too much inventory, maybe due to obsolescence. Of course, any significant changes in the firm's inventory strategy or selling prices should lead to the recalibration of the index.

In the case of Inditex, sales increased from €20.9 billion in 2015 to €23.3 billion in 2016, or 11.5 percent; inventory increased from €2.2 billion to €2.55 billion in the same period, or 15.9 percent. DB ratio in 2016 is then 15.9/11.5 = 1.38. There is not much we can say about the quality of this value. We could have obtained a more accurate result had we used average inventory during the year—for instance, using data at the end of each quarter—rather than inventory at the end of the year. In addition, to reach conclusions from this ratio we should have data for at least a few consecutive periods.

Using inventory theory, we can refine Berman's approach to be more precise about how much additional inventory a healthy firm should have when sales increase. For instance, if market demand for units doubles (100 percent increase) keeping everything else constant (that is, selling price, cost structure, number of SKUs, lead-time, number of warehouses), total inventory should go up by about 40 percent. Why? Well, both cycle and safety inventory can be shown to increase with the square root of demand under mild conditions (see appendix C), so if demand doubles, inventory should increase by $\sqrt{2} - 1 \approx 0.4$, or 40 percent. Therefore, if demand doubles a fair DB ratio is not 1 but 0.4! Other things equal, a DB ratio much higher than 0.4 would most likely signal excess inventory. In general, if demand increases by x percent, inventory should increase by $100 \cdot \left(\sqrt{1 + \frac{x}{100}} - 1 \right)$ percent, and DB ratio should be $\frac{100}{x} \cdot \left(\sqrt{1 + \frac{x}{100}} - 1 \right)$. Exercise 16 asks you to show this.

9.2.4 Financial Performance Ratios (CFO)

After having presented the CEO and COO's ratios, we finally turn our attention to the CFO's performance. Some of the ratios already presented, such as DPO or DSO, may also belong to the CFO's realm, and the same can be said for some of the ratios presented next, which may be the responsibility of the CEO (e.g., financial leverage) or the COO (e.g., current ratio). We will present only a few ratios, those which will be used later in the book, as they are related to operations.

9.2.4.1 Debt / equity and assets / equity

These ratios measure financial leverage, that is, the relative amount of debt in the balance sheet. The first ratio measures only financial debt—that is, money owed to banks—while the second measures the amount of money owed to both banks and suppliers. The definitions are as follows

$$\text{debt equity} = \frac{\text{debt}_t}{\text{equity}_t} \tag{9.2}$$

$$\text{assets equity} = \frac{\text{assets}_t}{\text{equity}_t} \tag{9.3}$$

The first expression directly compares the amounts of debt and equity. Unlike previous ratios, it is not clear what the right value of this ratio should be. If the value is large, it means the firm has a great deal of debt, which may be good as debt is cheaper than equity.[3]

However, having too much debt is risky, because it entails paying interest, a fixed cost. If a firm cannot pay its interest on the due date, it may go bankrupt.

On the other hand, if the value of the ratio is small, it means the firm has a great deal of equity. Having a lot of equity is good in terms of risk, although it means shareholders should be rewarded through dividends or increasing stock price. And (rational) shareholders are more expensive to satisfy than banks, as the former bear more risk. Despite this fact, some companies have more conservative financial policies and do not have debt in their balance sheets (e.g., Apple, Inditex) while others decide to be more financially aggressive or simply do not have the option to reduce debt because the business does not generate enough cash to do so.

For instance, for Inditex in 2016, the debt/equity ratio is simply

$$\text{debt / equity} = \frac{\text{debt}_t}{\text{equity}_t} = \frac{0.12}{12.75} \approx 0.0$$

The second ratio should be worked out to understand what it does:

$$\text{assets / equity} = \frac{\text{assets}_t}{\text{equity}_t} = \frac{\text{equities}_t}{\text{equity}_t} = \frac{\text{A/P}^+_t + \text{debt}_t + \text{equity}_t}{\text{equity}_t} = \frac{\text{A/P}^+_t + \text{debt}_t}{\text{equity}_t} + 1$$

Therefore, this ratio compares the sum of money owed to banks and suppliers (more precisely, interest-bearing and noninterest-bearing creditors) to equity. Therefore, it complements

---

3. If shareholders are rational, they should ask for higher returns (dividends) than debt holders (banks) to make up for the higher risk they bear. This is because, in contrast to banks who receive *certain* returns (interest) periodically, shareholders are uncertain about the time and the quantity of money that they will receive. Also, in the case of bankruptcy, banks collect money earlier than shareholders, making shareholders' investment even riskier.

the information given by the first ratio and adds information about suppliers and other creditors. Neither ratio is inherently better—you probably want to have both in your dashboard.

In the case of Inditex in 2016:

$$\text{assets / equity} = \frac{19.62}{12.75} \approx 1.5$$

9.2.4.2 Current ratio

Current ratio measures liquidity by estimating the ability of the firm to pay its creditors given the amount of assets that will be converted to cash in the short term (within one year). Its definition is

$$\text{current ratio} = \frac{\text{current assets}_t}{\text{current liabilities}_t} \tag{9.4}$$

In a seven-item balance sheet, the current assets category is composed of cash[+], A/R[+], and inventory; current liabilities of A/P[+] and short-term debt. Most finance books will tell you that this ratio should be greater than one. If the ratio is lower than one, the firm may go bankrupt because of lack of cash. The logic goes as follows: within a year, the firm has to pay suppliers (assuming the firm pays suppliers within a year) and repay short-term debt. To do so, the firm can use the available cash at the moment, receivables that will become cash at maturity (assuming customers pay within one year), and inventory that will be sold and subsequently collected within one year. An issue with this logic is that it ignores the firm dynamics within the year: customers will keep buying and paying and workers will keep asking for payrolls at the end of the month. Therefore, a current ratio lower that one is not necessarily a bad sign. In fact, it can be a good sign under some circumstances! For instance, Walmart consistently has a current ratio below one, as table 9.10 shows.

Walmart collects money from clients rather quickly, does not hold much inventory or cash in relative terms, and pays suppliers late. Overall, current assets are always below current liabilities. This is fine for a company such as Walmart, as the industry risk is low,

Table 9.10
Evolution of current ratio for Walmart, years 2011–2016.

	2016	2015	2014	2013	2012	2011
Current assets	60,239	63,278	61,185	59,940	54,975	52,012
Current liabilities	64,619	65,253	69,345	71,818	62,300	58,603
Current ratio	0.93	0.97	0.88	0.83	0.88	0.89

Source: Authors' elaboration from Walmart's annual reports.

which guarantees future inflows of cash at a steady rate. That cash can also be used to pay for future obligations, something that does not appear in the static picture of the balance sheet and therefore cannot be captured by the current ratio. This balance sheet structure is part of Walmart's strategy.

 Should the current ratio always be larger than one?

A current ratio lower than one is *not* necessarily a bad sign.

A firm that cannot pay suppliers on time because of lack of cash would be a different story entirely. A/P would start increasing and current ratio would decline in this case. Current ratio below one would be worrisome, as the chance of bankruptcy would be large. So it matters whether the firm has been forced to reduce current ratio below one or whether does so as part of its financial strategy.

9.2.4.3 Debt to EBITDA ratio

The (net) debt-to-EBITDA ratio is defined as:

$$\text{debt to EBITDA ratio} = \frac{\text{debt}_t - \text{cash}_t}{\text{EBITDA}_t} \tag{9.5}$$

This ratio combines two magnitudes, one from the balance sheet (net debt) and one from the income statement. Some banks measure the ability of their clients to repay outstanding debt using this or similar ratios. The logic is that EBITDA roughly measures the cash available for the firm to pay interest to the bank. A large value of this ratio may signal that the firm has problems paying back financial debt in the future. Therefore, this ratio may be used by banks, among other measurements, to decide whether to grant loans to clients. Some practitioners from the baking industry even suggested that a ratio equal to three may be used as a rough threshold to make a decision (i.e., approve the loan application if the ratio is lower than three, reject it otherwise), although the number may heavily change depending on the company and the industry.

In the case of Inditex, the ratio debt-to-EBITDA was a mere 0.02 in 2016, given that Inditex's financial debt is almost nonexistent.

This ratio has two limitations: First, it doesn't take the interest rate into account. Second, since EBITDA is not cash, EBITDA might be significantly larger than cash available if, for instance, OWC has increased during the period. To get around the latter difficulty, an alternative ratio to be used when the change in OWC is large is:

$$\text{CGO to EBITDA ratio} = \frac{\text{cash generated from operations}_t}{\text{EBITDA}_t} \tag{9.6}$$

9.3   Breaking Down and Combining Ratios

When keeping track of your KPIs in your firm's dashboard, you may notice a ratio begins to slip down, but you don't understand exactly why. For instance, ROA may decrease due to the deterioration of margins or the addition of brand new equipment. Only the first case may be a point of concern. But looking at ROA alone is not enough to know whether the root cause is margins or fixed assets. In order to have a greater understanding of ratios, firms typically resort to breaking down certain ratios into smaller pieces. We present here the most common, emphasizing those related to operations.

9.3.1   ROE Breakdown

We first pay attention to ROE. Recall its (third) definition:

$$\text{ROE} = \frac{\text{net profit}_t}{\text{equity}_t}$$

Multiplying twice by one, we obtain

$$\text{ROE} = \frac{\text{net profit}_t}{\text{equity}_t} \cdot \frac{\text{sales}_t}{\text{sales}_t} \cdot \frac{\text{assets}_t}{\text{assets}_t}$$

or, rearranging terms

$$\text{ROE} = \left(\frac{\text{net profit}_t}{\text{sales}_t}\right) \cdot \left(\frac{\text{sales}_t}{\text{assets}_t}\right) \cdot \left(\frac{\text{assets}_t}{\text{equity}_t}\right)$$

$$= \text{net margin}_t \cdot \text{asset turnover}_t \cdot \text{financial leverage}_t \tag{9.7}$$

This breakdown for ROE can be represented pictorially by means of a mind map (figure 9.10).

The expression above shows the factors that explain ROE:

Net margin As ROE measures profitability, it makes sense that it depends on net margin, another measure for profitability.

Asset turnover Other things equal, high asset turnover contributes to ROE: indeed, relative low assets or high traffic both contribute to higher profitability.

Financial leverage More surprisingly, other things equal, financial leverage has a direct impact on ROE. If the debt is relatively large for a given level of assets, equity will be relatively small, thus increasing ROE. Note how dangerous this is. A way to increase ROE artificially would be to take additional debt from a bank to pay dividends to shareholders. Indeed, debt would increase and equity would decrease simultaneously, boosting ROE but significantly increasing the risk of the firm. This is one of the reasons why ROE should not be judged in isolation but as part of a set of well-pondered KPIs.

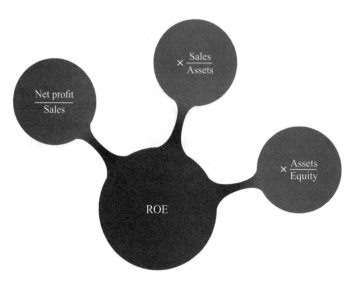

Figure 9.10
ROE breakdown into three factors: net margin, assets turnover, and financial leverage.

A firm may focus on one of the three factors to achieve high ROE. For instance, Lover's Deep Luxury Submarine in St. Lucia claims to be the most expensive hotel in the world, at \$175,000 per night. Even if client traffic is scarce, the exorbitant rate will make the net margins boost ROE. On the other side of the spectrum, a fast-food franchise restaurant gets almost zero net margin but achieves a decent ROE through daily customer traffic in the hundreds, if not thousands.

Inditex's ROE in 2016 can be broken down as:

$$25.1\% = \text{net margin}_t \cdot \text{asset turnover}_t \cdot \text{financial leverage}_t$$

$$= 13.7\% \cdot \frac{23.3}{19.62} \cdot \frac{19.62}{12.75} = 13.7\% \cdot 1.19 \cdot 1.54$$

To get some perspective on this analysis, we can compare with a direct competitor, such as H&M, the Swedish fashion company (data from annual report 2016; money in Swedish kronor).

$$30.4\% = 8.3\% \cdot \frac{222.9}{98.6} \cdot \frac{98.6}{61.2} = 8.3\% \cdot 2.26 \cdot 1.61$$

This break-down reveals that, even though Inditex's net margin is substantially larger, H&M's ROE is larger than Inditex's. The key point is that H&M's asset turnover is almost twice as large as Inditex's, mainly due to its relatively lighter fixed-assets policy.

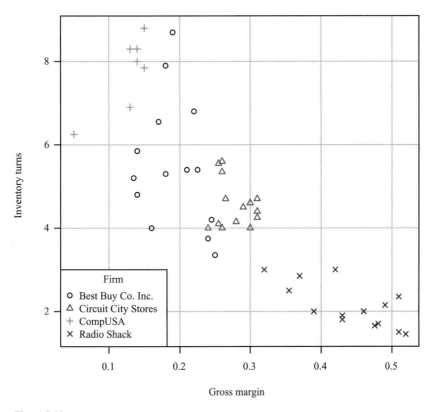

Figure 9.11
Inventory turns versus gross margin for four consumer electronics retailers (1987–2000).
Source: Gaur, Fisher, and Raman (2003).

9.3.2 GMROI Breakdown

Gaur, Fisher, and Raman (2003) show that GMROI can also be broken down into three factors as follows:

$$\text{GMROI}_t = \frac{\text{gross profit}_t}{\text{inventory}_t} = \frac{\text{gross profit}_t}{\text{sales}_t} \cdot \frac{\text{sales}_t}{\text{COGS}_t} \cdot \frac{\text{COGS}_t}{\text{inventory}_t}$$

$$= \text{gross margin}_t \cdot \left(\frac{\text{sales}_t}{\text{COGS}_t}\right) \cdot \text{inventory turns}_t. \tag{9.8}$$

This breakdown shows the existing trade-off between gross margin and inventory turns. Figure 9.11 shows that trade-off for four consumer electronics retailers.

We can go one step further:

$$\text{GMROI}_t = \text{gross margin}_t \cdot \left(\frac{\text{sales}_t}{\text{sales}_t - \text{gross profit}_t}\right) \cdot \text{inventory turns}_t$$

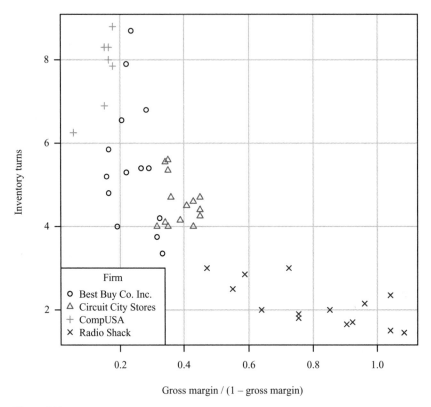

Figure 9.12
Inventory turns versus gross margin / (1−gross margin) for four consumer electronics retailers (1987–2000).

$$= \text{gross margin}_t \cdot \frac{1}{\frac{\text{sales}_t - \text{gross profit}_t}{\text{sales}_t}} \cdot \text{inventory turns}_t$$

$$= \left(\frac{\text{gross margin}_t}{1 - \text{gross margin}_t} \right) \cdot \text{inventory turns}_t \tag{9.9}$$

Figure 9.12 provides a slightly better fit than figure 9.11 as, in contrast to the previous figure, GMROI in this case is *entirely* explained by the two variables included in the graph.

In both cases, the figures show that it is not easy to achieve high profitability and high inventory turns at the same time.

9.3.3   ROA Breakdown

Much like we did for ROE, ROA can also be broken down into factors.

$$\text{ROA} = \left(\frac{\text{EBITDA}_t}{\text{sales}_t} \right) \cdot \left(\frac{\text{sales}_t}{\text{assets}_t} \right)$$

$$= (\text{EBITDA margin})_t \cdot \text{asset turnover}_t \tag{9.10}$$

Here, EBITDA margin is defined as the ratio of EBITDA to sales. This expression is already useful and shows ROA as a key figure of merit, depending on two factors: profitability and asset turnover. But the expression can be worked out further. For instance (Gaur, Fisher, and Raman 2003):

$$\begin{aligned}
\text{ROA} &= \left(\frac{\text{EBITDA}_t}{\text{sales}_t}\right) \cdot \left(\frac{\text{sales}_t}{\text{assets}_t}\right) = \left(\frac{\text{gross profit}_t - \text{SGA}_t}{\text{sales}_t}\right) \cdot \frac{\text{sales}_t}{\text{assets}_t} \\[2mm]
&= \frac{\text{gross profit}_t}{\text{sales}_t} \cdot \left(1 - \frac{\text{SGA}_t}{\text{gross profit}_t}\right) \cdot \frac{\text{sales}_t}{\text{assets}_t} \\[2mm]
&= \text{gross margin}_t \cdot \left(1 - \frac{\text{SGA}_t}{\text{gross profit}_t}\right) \cdot \frac{\text{sales}_t}{\text{COGS}_t} \cdot \frac{\text{COGS}_t}{\text{inventory}_t} \cdot \frac{\text{inventory}_t}{\text{assets}_t} \\[2mm]
&= \left(\text{gross margin}_t \cdot \frac{\text{sales}_t}{\text{COGS}_t} \cdot \text{inventory turns}_t\right) \cdot \left(1 - \frac{\text{SGA}_t}{\text{gross profit}_t}\right) \cdot \frac{\text{inventory}_t}{\text{assets}_t}
\end{aligned}$$

Using equation 9.8, we finally obtain:

$$\text{ROA} = \text{GMROI}_t \cdot \left(1 - \frac{\text{SGA}_t}{\text{gross profit}_t}\right) \cdot \frac{\text{inventory}_t}{\text{assets}_t} \tag{9.11}$$

This expression is certainly interesting for operations and supply chain management, as it connects ROA with measurements closer to operations, namely gross profit, SGA, inventory, and assets; but sales does not appear in the expression. Therefore, ROA (recall, defined as EBITDA/assets) increases with:

(1) High GMROI, that is, good inventory management practices.

(2) Low proportion of general expenses with regard to gross profit.

(3) Low level of assets other than inventory.

In the case of Inditex, we can break down ROA as follows:

$$\begin{aligned}
\text{ROA} &= \frac{13.3}{2.5} \cdot \left(1 - \frac{8.2}{13.3}\right) \cdot \frac{2.55}{19.62} \\[2mm]
&= 5.32 \cdot 0.38 \cdot 0.13 \tag{9.12}
\end{aligned}$$

9.3.4 Relationship between ROE and RONA

We close this section by breaking down ROE as a function of RONA and financial leverage.

$$\text{ROE} = \frac{\text{net profit}_t}{\text{equity}_t} = \frac{(\text{EBIT}_t - i\text{D}_t)(1 - t)}{\text{E}_t} = \frac{\text{NOPAT}_t - i\text{D}_t(1 - t)}{\text{E}_t}$$

$$= \frac{\text{NOPAT}_t}{E_{t-1}} \cdot \frac{(E+D)_t}{(E+D)_t} - \frac{iD_t(1-t)}{E_t} = \text{RONA}_t \frac{(E+D)_t}{E_t} - \frac{iD_t(1-t)}{E_t}$$

$$= \text{RONA}_t \left(1 + \frac{D_t}{E_t}\right) - \frac{iD_t(1-t)}{E_t}$$

to obtain finally:

$$\text{ROE}_t = \text{RONA}_t + \frac{D_t}{E_t}(\text{RONA}_t - i(1-t)) \tag{9.13}$$

where i is the cost of debt and t the corporate tax rate.

This expression is interesting in the sense that it connects ROE, RONA, and financial leverage—ratios mainly under the purview, respectively, of the CEO, COO, and CFO of the firm. Indeed, the expression says that ROE is the sum of RONA plus financial leverage. But note that financial leverage is multiplied by the factor $(\text{RONA} - i(1-t))$, a factor that may be negative. This means that financial leverage contributes positively to ROE only if $\text{RONA} > i(1-t)$; that is to say, only if operational performance, as measured by RONA, is at least as large as the true cost of debt (i.e., the nominal cost of debt after taxes). This condition makes much sense: The firm goes to the bank to get some money at cost $i(1-t)$ (the factor 1–t takes care of the tax shield[4] here), which is used to run operations. If profitability from operations does not cover the cost of debt, it would be better not to take on debt to begin with $(D=0)$. Overall, financial leverage may improve or worsen ROE.

9.3.5   Further Breakdown of Ratios

By working recursively, financial ratios can be broken down to the operating levers that ultimately define a firm's financial performance. For instance, figure 9.13 shows the breakdown of RONA, defined as the ratio of EBITDA to net assets, for a third-party logistics firm. The firm charges its customers for storing their pallets at the distribution centers, performing the picking and packing, and dispatching goods from the warehouse. The figure, although not comprehensive, shows the relationship between RONA and the firm's operational drivers, such as the salary of workers or the number of fork-lift trucks. Similar representations can be found in Cachon and Terwiesch (2013, chap. 6) and Lai (2013, app. A).

9.4   Using Ratios to Obtain Information from Financial Statements

In this section, we will present two examples illustrating how ratios can be used to obtain relevant information from financial statements.

---

4. A tax shield refers to the protection a firm has when corporate taxes are reduced, usually due to interest expenses.

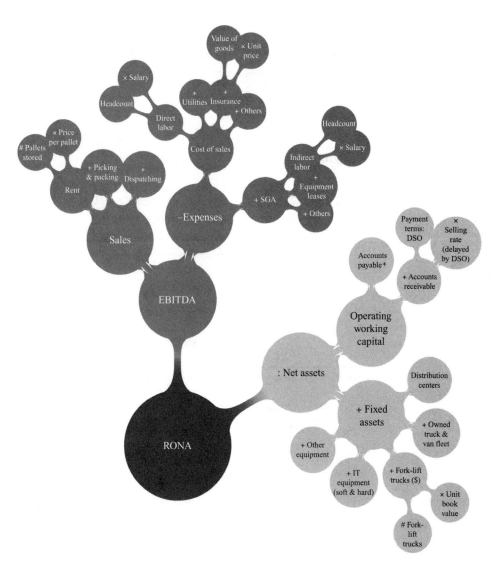

Figure 9.13
RONA breakdown for a third-party logistics firm, where financial data is linked to operational variables.

9.4.1   Groupe Casino

Groupe Casino is a French multinational in the mass retail industry. It has more than 12,000 stores worldwide (supermarkets, convenience stores, etc.), mainly in France and Latin America.

Exercise

Interpreting Groupe Casino Financial Statements

Analyze the financial statements given below, then answer the questions provided. The seven-account income statement is:

(Millions of euros)

	2017	2016
Revenue	38,236	36,572
Cost of goods sold	(28,694)	(27,364)
SGA expenses	(8,299)	(8,174)
Depreciation and others	(481)	(625)
Financial expenses (net)	(445)	(359)
Taxes	(56)	(34)
Profit after taxes[a]	260	16

a. It doesn't include discounted operations and equity-accounted investees profits.

The seven-account version of the balance sheet is:

	2017	2016		2017	2016
Cash+	3,391	5,750	Payables+	16,422	17,386
Receivables+	2,356	2,552	Debt	8,722	10,215
Inventory	3,871	3,990	Equity	13,057	14,440
Fixed assets	28,583	29,749			
Total assets	**38,201**	**42,041**	**Total equities**	**38,201**	**42,041**

Source: Authors' elaboration based on Groupe Casino's Annual Report 2017, pp. 39–41.

1. Analyze the evolution of the firm's profitability in terms of net and gross margins.

2. Did GMROI increase in the last year?

3. Assess the contribution of financial leverage to shareholders' returns.

4. Is the following statement true? "As for any firm, as Groupe Casino continues to grow, cash tensions will appear, since the amount of operating working capital will increase."

? Question 1

Analyze the evolution of the firm's profitability in terms of net and gross margins.

Looking at the income statement, it is clear that net margins are really small: in 2016, net margin was:

$$100 \cdot \frac{16}{36,572} = 0.04\%$$

In 2017, it went up to:

$$100 \cdot \frac{260}{38,236} = 0.68\%$$

still a discrete result, even for an industry such as mass retail.

Gross margins are carefully monitored in this industry, given the large impact of the cost of goods sold and the importance of selling price. Gross margin slightly decreased from

$$100 \cdot \frac{36,572 - 27,364}{36,572} = 25.2\%$$

in 2016 to

$$100 \cdot \frac{38,236 - 28,694}{38,236} = 25.0\%$$

in 2017.

? Question 2

Did GMROI increase in the last year?

Combining information from the income statement and the balance sheet, we will find that GMROI in 2016 was

$$\frac{\text{gross margin}}{\text{inventory}} = \frac{36,572 - 27,364}{3,990} = 2.31,$$

and

$$\frac{38,236 - 28,694}{3,871} = 2.46$$

in 2017. Therefore, GMROI increased by roughly 6 percent in the last year.

Question 3

Assess the contribution of financial leverage to shareholders' returns.

We can calculate the elements of equation 9.13 for year 2017:

$$\text{ROE} = 100 \cdot \frac{260}{13{,}057} = 1.99\%$$

$$t = 100 \cdot \frac{56}{56 + 260} = 17.7\%$$

$$i = 100 \cdot \frac{\text{interest}_t}{D_t} = 100 \cdot \frac{445}{8{,}722} = 5.10\%$$

$$\text{RONA} = 100 \cdot \frac{\text{EBIT}_t(1 - t)}{(D + E)_t} = 100 \cdot \frac{(445 + 56 + 260)(1 - 0.177)}{(8{,}722 + 13{,}057)} = 2.88\%$$

And now it is easy to check that the equation holds:

$$1.99\% = 2.88\% + \frac{8{,}722}{13{,}057}(2.88\% - 5.10\%(1 - 0.177))$$

Interestingly, RONA is larger than ROE, which means that financial leverage is actually eroding ROE. RONA turns out to be smaller than the cost of debt after taxes, which means that the return obtained from net assets (2.88 percent) doesn't even compensate for the actual cost of debt (which is $5.10\%(1 - 0.177) = 4.20\%$).

Question 4

Is the following statement true? "As for any firm, as Groupe Casino continues to grow, cash tensions will appear, since the amount of operating working capital will increase."

The statement is *usually* true for many firms that need additional funds to keep growing. However, Groupe Casino is an exception to the rule, as its operating working capital is negative. Indeed, in 2017, assuming excess cash is zero (a fair assumption, given the level of debt), we have that OWC = $3,391 + 2,356 + 3,871 - 16,422 = -\$6,804$. Therefore, the more Groupe Casino grows, the *lower* the cash tensions will be.

9.4.2   Who Is Who?

The next exercise is proposed to illustrate how ratios can be used to infere important financial conditions of companies—such as profitability, liquidity, fiancial leverage, as well as to compare financial performance across companies.

Exercise

Who Is Who?

Below are the income statements and balance sheets of five companies in 2017.

Amounts have been disguised by multiplying by a constant (each firm by a different one).

	Firm A	Firm B	Firm C	Firm D	Firm E
Sales	77,871	99,770	37,870	83,479	47,440
Cost of sales	23,656	41,025	31,271	54,579	33,743
SGA & depreciation	33,984	33,982	4,820	21,928	10,846
Financial cost	1,055	289	675	651	442
Taxes	4,497	13,078	281	1,898	474
Net profit	14,679	11,396	823	5,688	1,936
Total assets	105,232	177,566	27,654	121,762	25,739
Cash+	16,414	91,684	2,322	52,967	1,744
Receivables+	12,000	19,598	8,981	5,352	834
Inventory	10,860	674	6,206	4,425	5,714
Fixed assets	65,958	65,610	10,146	59,018	17,447
Payables+	38,516	36,714	12,487	28,331	11,110
Debt	30,548	3,600	9,205	1,562	6,901
Equity	36,167	137,252	5,962	91,869	7,728

A short description of the five firms follows:

1. A first-tier manufacturer in the automotive industry
2. A leading pharmaceutical company
3. A retailer in the department and discount industry with market share of 6 percent
4. A technology conglomerate
5. A leading furniture retailer

Link each firm to its financial statements above.

The first step to identify which financial statements correspond to each firm should be to present the financial statements in percentages. This will allow us to compare across firms and to eliminate the confusion introduced by so many meaningless figures. To do so, we will divide all items in the income statement by the level of sales and all items in the balance sheet by total assets. For instance, the cost of sales (COGS) for Firm A is $23,656/77,871 = 0.304$, or 30.4 percent. The result of this first step is shown in table 9.11.

Table 9.11
Income statements and balance sheets in percentage.

	A	B	C	D	E
Sales	100.0	100.0	100.0	100.0	100.0
Cost of sales	30.4	41.1	82.6	65.4	71.1
SGA & depreciation	43.6	34.1	12.7	26.3	22.9
Financial cost	1.4	0.3	1.8	0.8	0.9
Taxes	5.8	13.1	0.7	2.3	1.0
Net profit	18.9	11.4	2.2	6.8	4.1
Total assets	100.0	100.0	100.0	100.0	100.0
Cash$^+$	15.6	51.6	8.4	43.5	6.8
Receivables$^+$	11.4	11.0	32.5	4.4	3.2
Inventory	10.3	0.4	22.4	3.6	22.2
Fixed assets	62.7	36.9	36.7	48.5	67.8
Payables$^+$	36.6	20.7	45.2	23.3	43.2
Debt	29.0	2.0	33.3	1.3	26.8
Equity	34.4	77.3	21.6	75.4	30.0

Given the percentage figures, we can focus now on the salient differences across companies:

Inventory Dividing inventory level by COGS in the previous table and multiplying by 365 we can obtain DOI for each firm: 168, 6, 72, 30, and 62 days respectively. It is very likely that the only firm that is neither a manufacturer nor a retailer (firm 4) holds the fewest days worth of inventory. Therefore, 4B is the first answer.

Receivables Dividing receivables$^+$ by sales and multiplying by 365 is an approximation of the number of days it takes to collect money from customers. These are, respectively, 56, 72, 87, 23, and 6 days. It seems plausible that the two retailers are the ones with the shortest number of days, as, in contrast to manufacturers, they sell directly to final users, who have no bargaining power. That gives two possible combinations: either 3D and 5E, or 3E and 5D.

Balance sheet robustness To distinguish between the two possible combinations, note first that the income statement of firms D and E are quite similar, although operating margin of firm E is 6.0 percent, lower than that of firm D at 8.3 percent. This suggests that firm D is more profitable than firm E. The equities side of the balance sheet comes to confirm this fact: the financial position of firm D is much more robust than that of firm E, in that equity represent roughly three quarters of total equities, compared to 30 percent in the case of firm E. Also, financial leverage of firm D measured as the ratio D/E is a mere 1.7 percent compared with 89.3 percent for firm E. These figures suggest that firm D has been profitable over the years and, as a result, it has a much more robust balance sheet than firm E. So we can infer that firm D is the furniture retailer, as it has a leading position in the industry; and that firm E is the retailer in the department and discount industry with a low market share. Odd are high that the latter retailer's profitability is eroded by tough competition from large competitors.

Profitability Finally, we focus on profitability of remaining firms A and C. Clearly, firm A is much more profitable as measured by net margin for instance (a solid 18.9 percent versus a thin 2.2 percent). That leads to infer that firm A is the pharmaceutical company—high profitability is a feature among pharma industry leaders—and that firm C is the auto manufacturer. Moreover, firm C has the highest financial leverage of all firms and collects money the latest, two distinct aspects of most first-tier suppliers who serve almighty OEMs, who pay relatively little and late.

In sum, we can assert with confidence that the right match is 1C, 2A, 3E, 4B, and 5D. Of course, a different approach could have been followed to reach the same conclusions, as there are no strict rules to follow when doing this type of analysis, only guidelines and rough rules of thumb.

9.5 Final Words on the Use of Ratios

In this chapter we have presented some of the ratios most used by finance people with a focus on operational ratios. If appropriately used, ratios may be great control tools in your dashboard. However, ratios can also be misleading. In order not to be misled by the use of ratios, recall some of the points mentioned.

(1) Ratios can be only properly compared other things equal. For instance, if you increase the number of SKUs in your warehouse, inventory turns will deteriorate. However, worsening is not a signal of bad practices, it is just that some of the extant conditions (number of SKUs) have changed, making the comparison a skewed one.

(2) Ratios should be read as part of the big picture, not in isolation. A single ratio doesn't mean much. In order to judge a ratio value, you have to look at the remaining related ratios first and keep in mind the strategy of the firm. For instance, increasing DSO may be ok if your strategy is to grow aggressively. Likewise, if DSO increases and your sales are stuck, some of your customers may not be paying you on time.

(3) The same ratio may mean opposite things depending on the context. For instance, large DPO may be good if that is part of your purchasing strategy, but it is definitely a point of concern if it grows because you don't have cash to pay your suppliers on time.

Ratios are often used to reward managers when business's goals are met. However, if ratios are not well defined, they may fire back. That is exactly what happened in Hanoi,

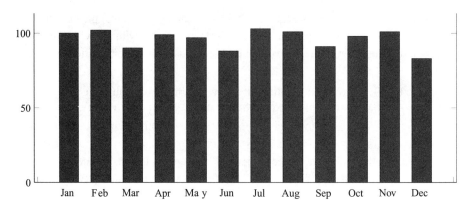

Figure 9.14
Inventory level at the end of the month ($'000).

Vietnam, a city infested with rats during the French colonial rule. The regime was so overwhelmed trying to get rid of rats that they asked citizens for help. They decided to reward citizens for every tail of rat they provide. What happened? The population of rats fell very quickly as people hunted and killed rats to get the bounty. However, some time later the population of rats increased dramatically. Why? Well, smart Vietnamese would capture rats, cut off their tails, and release them so that they could procreate![5]

As Goldratt (1990, 26) put it, "tell me how you measure me, I will tell you how I will behave." When people are measured with ratios, it is tempting for managers to cook the numbers at the end of the measuring period (a month, a quarter, a year) such that numbers look artificially better. For instance, monthly inventory may look as shown in figure 9.14.

How to interpret this graph? Well, it may be the case that the manager in charge of inventory artificially reduces inventory at the end of each quarter to increase his or her bonus. They may be telling suppliers to stop sending raw materials for a couple of days at the end of each quarter, or even for a couple of weeks at the end of the year. Of course, these bad practices should be eliminated.

Another issue that may arise when measuring managers' performance with ratios is that this may cause managers to lose the big picture of the business and acquire a narrow-minded focus on the ratio. For instance, an operations or supply chain manager may have a goal to improve EBITDA by 5 percent. One way to achieve this is to move expenses from above to below the EBITDA line in the income statement. A manager in a transportation company with five hundred trucks may decide to terminate the existing leasing contracts for trucks and acquire all of them. Suddenly, SGA will decrease and EBITDA will rise (which

5. See "The cobra effect," https://en.wikipedia.org/wiki/Cobra_effect.

seems good from the point of view of the manager's bonus) at the expense of depreciation. Is this a good idea from the point of view of the business? Probably not, as buying the trucks may dramatically increase operational leverage and entails paying a considerable amount of money, possibly jeopardizing needed cash in the firm.

Last, but not least, assigning unaligned ratios to measure performance in related departments or business units may lead to bitter confrontation between departments. If the COO of a manufacturing company is measured by deliveries on time to customers, he may want to increase inventory to make sure there are plenty of raw materials to meet demand when orders arrive. If the CFO is measured by OWC, she will want to reduce inventory. Confrontation between COO and CFO will be almost inevitable.

9.6   Summary

This chapter has presented the usual ratios that firms use to evaluate their performance. Although ratios are defined to help managers make better decisions, they can be misleading at times. They should be interpreted bearing in mind the strategy of the firm and the industry in which it operates. Ratios can be used to evaluate managers' performance, but those should be defined very carefully so that people don't get the wrong incentives.

Exercises

1. Indicate which category (profitability, liquidity, financial leverage) the following ratios belong to.

   a. Return on equity   b. Cash/Assets

   c. Debt/Equity   d. Return on assets

   e. Current ratio   f. Assets/Equity

2. Describe two uses of ratios.

3. Does annual ROE quantify value creation for shareholders during the year?

4. What is the optimal value for inventory turns?

5. If sales in year 2 were $43 million and in year 7 $98 million, what has been the average annual sales increase in five years?

6. If sales were $13 million last year, and sales are expected to grow 23 percent for four consecutive years, what is the level of expected sales in year 4?

7. What is the most likely impact on ROA of the following events?

   a. Open three new regional warehouses   b. Change from own fleet of trucks to leasing contracts

   c. Start paying suppliers fifteen days later   d. Use a third-party logistics provider to take care of warehousing and transportation

8. Should a current ratio lower than one be a point of concern for management? If so, explain under which circumstances. If not, explain why.

9. Given the financial statements of a firm, is it true that RONA is never smaller than ROA? If so, explain why. If not, under which circumstances?

10. Calculate NOPAT knowing that: EBITDA = 800, depreciation = 200, tax rate = 25%.

11. Does a negative OWC imply negative CCC? If so, why? If not, under which conditions?

12. How would table 9.7 change if sales decrease by 10 percent in each of the four scenarios considered?

13. Can a firm with negative ROE pay dividends to their shareholders?

14. What is GMROI mainly useful for?

15. Can ROE be smaller than RONA? If yes, under which conditions? If not, why not?

16. Show that, when demand increases by x percent, other things equal, inventory increases by $100 \cdot \left(\sqrt{1 + \frac{x}{100}} - 1 \right)$% and DB ratio is $\frac{100}{x} \cdot \left(\sqrt{1 + \frac{x}{100}} - 1 \right)$.

17. For a company that pays cash to its suppliers, what is the relationship between the two ratios that measure financial leverage?

18. Find last year's balance sheet and income statement of Amazon on the internet, and calculate the following ratios.

a. ROE
b. RONA
c. Current ratio
d. CCC
e. NOPAT
f. GMROI
g. Sales growth
h. Financial leverage
i. Inventory-to-payables
j. DB ratio

19. Match the following companies with their corresponding balance sheets and financial ratios.[6] In doing the exercise, consider the operating and competitive characteristics of the industry and their implications for (1) the collection period; (2) the inventory turnover; (3) the amount of plant and equipment; (4) the profit margins and profitability; and (5) the appropriate financing structure. Then identify which one of the five sets of balance sheets and financial ratios best match your expectations.

a. Electric utility
b. Japanese automobile manufacturer
c. Discount general merchandise retailer
d. Automated test equipment / systems company
e. Upscale apparel retailer

6. Original exercise: Piper 2012.

(Balance sheet percentages)	A	B	C	D	E
Cash	1.5	14.4	12.1	13.3	11
Receivables	4.6	3.8	30.9	39.8	11.8
Inventories	1.8	24.6	13.7	4.7	16.7
Other current assets	2	4.3	5	3.8	10
Property and equipment (net)	74.5	49.6	34.1	22.1	20.3
Other assets	15.6	3.4	4.3	16.3	30.2
Total assets	100.0	100.0	100.0	100.0	100.0
Notes payable	5.3	0.4	5.4	18.2	1.4
Accounts payable	2.1	24.8	11	8.3	8.8
Other current liabilities	5.9	17	14.2	8.7	16.5
Long-term debt	33.6	10	34.3	23.1	21.7
Other liabilities	26.3	2.2	11.2	5.6	2
Owners' equity	26.8	45.6	23.9	36.1	49.6
Total	100.0	100.0	100.0	100.0	100.0
Net profit / Net sales	10.30%	1.50%	5.10%	1.30%	−5.80%
Return on capital	6.80%	9.20%	12.60%	0.90%	−3.10%
Return on equity	12.50%	10.80%	28.10%	2.20%	−7.60%
Sales / Total assets	0.32	3.25	1.31	0.63	0.65
Collection period (days)	52	4	86	232	43
Days of inventory	43	32	62	31	147
Sales / Net property & equipment	0.43	6.7	3.8	2.9	3.6
Total assets / Equity	3.73	2.19	4.19	2.79	2.01
Total liabilities / Total assets	0.73	0.54	0.76	0.66	0.5
Interest-bearing debt / Total capital	59%	19%	62%	53%	32%
Times interest earned	3.2	16	6	4.4	NM
Current assets / Current liabilities	0.67	1.11	2.01	1.22	1.85

20. Given the financial statements of an American retailer provided below, calculate:

	Year 2	Year 1
Sales	30,000	-
Cost of sales	(18,000)	-
SGA & depreciation	(7,000)	-
Financial cost	(700)	-
Taxes	(1,300)	-
Net profit	3,000	-

	Year 2	Year 1
Cash[+]	1,130	900
Receivables[+]	4,300	3,600
Inventory	7,900	5,600
Fixed assets (net)	10,670	9,900
Total assets	24,000	20,000
Payables[+]	3,300	3,500
Debt (short-term)	1,900	1,500
Debt (long-term)	6,800	6,000
Equity	12,000	9,000
Total equities	24,000	20,000

a. Cash-to-cash cycle   b. Inventory turns

c. Return on equity   d. Return on net assets

e. Financial leverage   f. GMROI

21. Prepare the income statement for scenario #2 in table 9.7 when sales decrease by 10 percent with respect to scenario #1. By how much does net profit decrease?

References

Cachon, Gérard, and Christian Terwiesch. 2013. *Matching supply with demand: An introduction to operations management*, 3rd ed. New York: McGraw Hill.

Fernández, Pablo. 2012. "Cash flow is cash and is a fact: Net income is just an opinion." Working paper, n. 629.

Fisher, Marshall, and Ananth Raman. 2010. *The new science of retailing: How analytics are transforming the supply chain and improving performance.* Boston: Harvard Business Press.

Gaur, Vishal, Marshall Fisher, and Ananth Raman. 2003. "An econometric analysis of inventory turnover in retail services." *Management Science* 51 (2): 181–94.

Goldratt, Eliyahu M. 1990. *The haystack syndrome: Sifting information out of the data ocean.* Croton-on-Hudson, NY: North River Press.

Groupe Casino. 2017. "Annual report 2017," 39–41.

Inditex. 2016. "Annual report 2016." Accessed May 9, 2019. https://www.inditex.com/documents/10279/319575/Inditex+Annual+Report+2016/6f8a6f55-ed5b-41f4-b043-6c104a305035.

Lai, Richard. 2013. *Operations forensics: Business performance analysis using operations measures and tools.* Cambridge, MA: MIT Press.

Piper, Thomas. 2012. "Assessing a firm's future financial health." *HBS* 9-911-412.

Raman, Ananth, Vishal Gaur, and Saravanan Kesavan. 2005. "David Berman." *HBS* 9-605-081.

10 Financial Forecasting

It is tough to make predictions, especially about the future.
—Anonymous Danish parliamentarian

In business, planning is a process that helps a firm determine a course of action in order to achieve future objectives, given limited resources. Financial planning is an integral part of this process, concerned with how a firm can best use its financial resources in pursuit of the organization's goals. Financial planning takes place periodically (usually once a year or quarter) and can cover different planning horizons, either short-term (twelve months) or long-term (two to five years) in support of the company's operating and strategic business plans. It also requires the collaboration between finance and other key functions in an organization, such as operations and marketing, so that realistic plans can be developed on the basis of well-aligned business assumptions and objectives.

A typical financial planning process begins with evaluating the market environment and past performance in order to identify business strategic and operating priorities. This is followed by determining and quantifying the resources needed, within the planning horizon, to achieve the business goals. Finally, detailed budgets are developed, augmented by risk analyses and contingency (scenario) plans for determining actions in case of changes in the external market environment and deviations between projected and actual business results. Nevertheless, financial planning is not easy because of the number of variables that affect a firm's performance. For example, due to changing market conditions, it is hard for a company to predict how well customers will respond to its products and prices, while costs can also be quite volatile due to changes in commodity prices. For that reason, financial forecasting is at the core of the financial planning process.

Financial forecasting estimates a company's future financial outcomes—in line with the financial planning horizon—on the basis of historical accounting and sales data, external market and economic indicators, and assumptions about company variables linked to specific operating plans. A financial forecast allows management teams to estimate the firm's future needs for external funding, determine how they should allocate their budgets, and calculate the cost of capital. Financial forecasts are regularly updated to capture changes in the firm's competitive environment or operations so that adjustments can be made in the marketing and production plans on the basis of variance analysis. To that end, financial forecasting can be used for preparing and testing different scenarios (what if analyses) and evaluating managerial options for dealing with these scenarios.

In this chapter we discuss financial forecasting through the use of pro forma statements and reflect on its implication in a firm's financial and operations planning.

10.1   Pro Forma Financial Statements

Pro forma financial statements are financial reports issued by a company on the basis of historical data and assumptions that present the projected financial results of an organization for given future periods. Apart from providing valuable information to management in developing the firm's operations plans, these statements are also useful in conveying information to outside entities (e.g., investors and creditors) in support of investment, acquisition, or financing proposals. Pro forma financial statements are often used by organizations to evaluate different financing options, allowing them to see the diverse impacts such options might have on the firm's balance sheet, income statement, and statement of cash flows. They can also be valuable tools when performing risk management exercises by modeling best-case and worst-case scenarios and testing the financial impact of different managerial decisions in response to these scenarios.

Next, we present the mechanics of pro forma financial statements construction in the frame of a manufacturing SME firm case study.

 Exercise

Financial Forecasting at Bathline Inc.

Steve Lafon, founder and CEO of Bathline Inc., a manufacturing SME specializing in bathroom furniture units, is sitting in his office looking at the company's 2017 year-end financial reports he has just received from his financial director (see table below). The firm started operations in early 2010 and has since achieved remarkable growth, closing year 2017 with a record annual increase in sales of 28 percent. Located in a growing suburb of a large city in California, the company mainly serves the local market, where its products can be found in several general merchandise and bathroom specialty stores.

To penetrate the market, Bathline has focused its strategy on two pillars. First, its designs are carefully selected to combine functionality with aesthetics that match the style, colors, and general trends of modern Californian houses. Second, the company's products are offered at competitive prices in their respective categories. Low pricing is possible through operational efficiency—facilitated by investment in some automation and special tooling in a traditionally labor-intensive industry—and by taking advantage of quantity and early payment discounts in purchases of raw materials. This strategy, along with the state's favorable market environment over the last few years in terms of economic and job growth, has helped the company to establish itself and gain market share in a highly competitive industry. The end of 2017 has found the firm with several new potential customers lining up to discuss trading agreements to retail Bathline's products.

Balance sheet ($'000)	2014	2015	2016	2017
Assets				
Cash and cash equivalents	$241	$243	$219	$183
Accounts receivable	873	1,051	1,344	1,759
Inventory	910	1,154	1,487	1,804
Total current assets	2,024	2,448	3,050	3,746
Fixed assets (net)	582	621	666	724
Total assets	$2,606	$3,069	$3,715	$4,470
Equities				
Accounts payable	$352	$582	$911	$1,424
Accrued expenses	13	15	17	29
Bank loan (short-term)	79	140	275	299
Long-term debt, short portion	40	40	40	40
Total current liabilities	484	777	1,243	1,792
Long-term debt	760	720	680	640
Shareholders' equity	1,361	1,572	1,792	2,038
Total equities	$2,606	$3,069	$3,715	$4,470

Income statement ($'000)	2014	2015	2016	2017
Revenue	$7,460	$8,877	$11,097	$14,204
Cost of goods sold	6,058	7,227	9,155	11,860
Beginning inventory	819	910	1,154	1,487
+ Purchases	4,150	5,057	6,398	8,145
+ Manufacturing expenses	1,999	2,414	3,090	4,032
− Ending inventory	910	1,154	1,487	1,804
Gross profit	1,402	1,650	1,942	2,344
Selling, general, and admin. expenses	903	1,083	1,354	1,747
Earnings before interest and tax	500	567	588	597
Interest expenses	21	30	49	52
Earnings before tax	479	538	540	545
Tax	192	215	216	218
Earnings after tax	$287	$323	$324	$327

Looking at the numbers, Steve has the feeling that the company is generally going in the right direction. On top of the notable sales growth, the firm's ROE was also quite satisfactory and consistently higher than 15 percent throughout the years. Moreover, dividends of more than 20 percent of net profit were paid to the small group of investors—mostly friends and family members—whose funds, along with Steve's savings, had helped him start his business. Finally, the new inventory management system they had installed last year seems to be working well, as inventory appears to grow at a lower rate than sales.

On the flip side, Steve is concerned by the low cash level, which may cause problems to the firm's capability to meet payment obligations as they are due. In pursuit of additional sources of cash, in 2017 the company had to forego early payment discounts and delay payments to suppliers for as long as possible, resulting to a considerable increase in the firm's accounts payable. However, Steve is aware that the company cannot rely on trade credit anymore to fund its growth, and that more reliable and stable sources of financing are needed.

A few years ago, Bathline had raised funds through a mortgage of $800,000—repayable at a rate of $40,000 and bearing a flat interest of $10,000 per year until the debt is completely repaid—secured by the company's land and buildings. In addition, the firm has in place a short-term, renewable loan at an interest rate of 14 percent from the Pacific Union Bank; the bank that also maintains the company's deposits since the beginning of operations. The credit line for the last two years was set to $300,000, an amount that the company took full advantage of in 2017.

Steve believes that a credit line double this size (i.e., $600,000) would be sufficient to fund the firm's escalating need for financing to support its growth. However, he understands that he cannot rely on the good relationship he has with the bank to extend the current credit limit. Any loan beyond $300,000 would require higher authorization by the bank's central credit committee on the basis of a thorough evaluation of the firm's financial projections. For that purpose, and before filing his credit extension request with the bank, Steve has arranged a meeting with his finance and operations directors to prepare the pro forma financial statements for year 2018 that will help them derive more accurate estimates of the firm's actual credit needs.

10.1.1   Evaluating Bathline's Performance

Before helping Steve and his team calculate Bathline's actual financing needs, we will start with an evaluation of the firm's performance. This is a necessary step for two reasons: First, one of the purposes of financial planning is to help the firm achieve its goals; thus, evaluating the direction of the company is an important input to the process. Second,

Table 10.1
Selected financial ratios for Bathline Inc., 2014–2017.

	2014	2015	2016	2017
Sales growth		19%	25%	28%
ROE (same year equity)	21.1%	20.5%	18.1%	16.0%
Cost of goods sold (% of sales)	81.2%	81.4%	82.5%	83.5%
SGA (% of sales)	12.1%	12.2%	12.2%	12.3%
Net profit (% of sales)	3.8%	3.6%	2.9%	2.3%
Days sales in cash	11.8	10.0	7.2	4.7
Days receivable	42.7	43.2	44.2	45.2
Days payable	31.0	42.2	52.0	63.8
Days inventory	54.8	58.3	59.3	55.5
Cash conversion cycle (days)	66.5	59.5	51.5	36.9
Total assets growth		17.8%	21.1%	20.3%
Current ratio	4.2	3.2	2.5	2.1
Leverage (debt / equity)	64.6%	57.2%	55.5%	48.0%
Retained earnings (% of net earnings)		65.4%	67.8%	75.4%
RONA (same year equity and debt)	13.4%	13.8%	12.7%	11.9%

financial planning is based on assumptions, which, as we will show, are made on the basis of particular financial performance figures and ratios.

Table 10.1 provides selective ratios derived from Bathline's financial statements, as given in the case. Let us start with ROE, which attempts to measure overall profitability for share-holders. We can see that ROE is decreasing, although it is still a large number. So, is this good or bad? To answer this question, we will need to consider (a) the industry character-istics and (b) the firm's strategy. The bathroom furniture industry can be considered as a mature industry with commodity products, which probably is characterized by low growth and low entry barriers. Thus, we can assume that there are already many players in the industry who mainly compete on price to gain customer orders. On the other hand, as Bath-line is a relatively new player and eager to establish itself in this industry, it makes sense to have growth as a central element of its strategy. Yet the only way to grow in such an industry is to steal market-share to competition by offering lower prices to attract customers; that is, reducing its margins (consequently, the numerator in the ROE ratio). Under this prism, and assuming that the firm's shareholders cannot gain better returns for the same level of risk, Bathline's ROE can be considered quite satisfactory, given the firm's high growth. A similar argument holds for RONA.

A second observation in table 10.1 is the increase in cost of goods sold as percentage of sales. Most likely, this is mainly due to the fact that the company had to forgo early payment discounts from its suppliers—as also reflected in the large increase in days payable—in order to secure additional sources of cash. The firm's inability to take advantage of supplier discounts might also be responsible for the downward trend observed in gross and net profit margins.

Table 10.2
Statements of cash flows for Bathline Inc., 2015–2017. (Data for 2014 cannot be calculated.)

Statements of cash flow	2014	2015	2016	2017
Cash flow from operating activities				
Net profit		$323	$324	$327
Decrease (increase) in A/R+		−178	−293	−415
Decrease (increase) in inventory		−244	−333	−317
Increase (decrease) in A/P+		231	332	524
Cash provided (used) by operating activities		**132**	**29**	**119**
Cash flow from investing activities				
Capital expenditures		−40	−44	−59
Cash provided (used) by investing activities		**−40**	**−44**	**−59**
Cash flow from financing activities				
Borrowing (repayment) of debt		21	95	−16
Cash dividends		−112	−104	−80
Net cash from financing activities		**−91**	**−9**	**−96**
Net increase (decrease) in cash[a]		2	−24	−36
Cash at the beginning of the year		241	243	219
Cash at the end of the year		243	219	183

a. For instance, in 2017: $-36 = 119 - 59 - 96$.

Finally, the selling, general, and administrative expenses (as percentage of sales), as well as the days receivable, both showed an upward trend, which might have been due to additional complexity in managing a larger customer base. Regarding the increase in days receivable, this might also have been the result of better payment conditions offered to some customers for gaining market share.

Our brief analysis shows that, apart from the need to secure additional funding, the firm appears to be doing quite well. Over the last years, it has achieved high growth in a competitive industry, while, with the right financial resources in place, it can improve its margins and restore its return ratios' performance.

However, how is it possible for the company to have remarkable growth and positive net earnings every single year, while at the same time facing such liquidity problems? This question might be best answered by taking a look at the statements of cash flows, which can be constructed using the information provided in the case (table 10.2). Looking at the big picture, the statements of cash flow show that as Bathline grows, the cash decreases year after year as long as the firm maintains the current policies for dividends, capital investments, and payment terms.

Table 10.3
WC and OWC metrics for Bathline Inc., 2014–2017.

	2014	2015	2016	2017
Working capital	1,540	1,671	1,806	1,954
Change in WC		131	135	148
% growth of WC		8.5%	8.1%	8.2%
Operating working capital	1,659	1,851	2,121	2,293
Change in OWC		192	270	172
% growth of OWC		11.6%	14.6%	8.1%

Table 10.4
Statements of cash flows for Bathline Inc., 2015–2017 (alternative).

	2015	2016	2017		2015	2016	2017
Dividends	112	104	80	Funds from operations	323	324	327
Decreasing debt	0	0	16	Increasing debt	21	95	0
Increasing OWC	192	271	171				
Investments	40	44	60				
Total	344	419	327	Total	344	419	327

> **How to identify a firm's liquidity problems.**
> The statement of cash flows is very useful to identify potential liquidity problems, as it shows the changes in cash together with an explanation for that.

Notice in the firm's balance sheets that both accounts receivable and inventory increase at a similar rate to sales growth, which is naturally the case with these accounts. But together with these accounts, so do the firm's working capital and OWC. Table 10.3 shows the evolution of the firm's working capital and OWC since 2014.

Considering working capital, we can observe that as long as the firm's access to external financing is not constrained (i.e., in the period 2014–2016), the increase in this metric appears to be under control and a reasonable result of the firm's growth. On the other hand, OWC (for the same period) appears to increase at a much higher rate, which reflects the firm's escalating needs for external financing as a consequence of its growth. This signal—which is not captured by simply looking at the firm's working capital changes—would be even stronger if Bathline were not capable of delaying its payments to its suppliers.

Table 10.4 shows the alternative version of the statement of cash flows, where OWC stand out as a point of concern.

OWC versus WC

OWC reflects the needs for external financing better than WC—as WC is oblivious to the increases of short-term debt.

To fund its sales (receivables) and production (inventory), the company will need to make use of some sources of cash, these generally being profit from operations, proceeds from sales of fixed assets, suppliers' credit, bank loan, or shareholders' equity. Let's examine each of these potential sources separately.

Profit from operations Due to the low margins and the relatively long cash conversion cycle in the industry, the company's sales cannot generate the funds required for financing operations fast enough.

Proceeds from sales of fixed assets Apart from being an asset-light company, there is no indication in this case that selling assets is an option for Bathline.

Suppliers' credit Despite the fact that taking advantage of early payment discounts is one of its strategic goals, the firm has made extensive use of suppliers' credit, to the extent that days payable have more than doubled in the last four years. It is doubtful that the suppliers will be willing to continue financing Bathline's operations.

Bank loan The company has already reached the limits of the available credit line and is in the process of requesting its extension. The amount of credit that is actually needed is discussed later in the section.

Shareholders' equity There is no indication in the case that this is an option; however, even if the equity holders forego their dividends for 2017, this will not solve the firm's liquidity problem.

From our discussion above, it can be inferred that the combination of (a) large growth, (b) small net margin, and (c) large OWC (equivalently, long cash conversion cycle), is a dangerous one. Actually, firms that have all three and no access to external financing may soon be facing the stares of bankruptcy lawyers.

 A recipe for disaster

As a rule of thumb, the combination of the following three elements:

1. Large growth

2. Small net margin (even if positive)

3. Large operating working capital

is not sustainable over time and will eventually drag the firm into bankruptcy.

Our analysis brings up some interesting questions. How serious is Bathline's liquidity problem? How fast can the firm grow without going bankrupt? The subsequent sections will provide answers to these questions.

10.1.2   Estimating Bathline's Financing Needs

To estimate Bathline's actual financing needs, we will construct the firm's pro forma statements for 2018. For that purpose we need to make some assumptions, the most important of which are presented next.

Sales growth   The firm will keep growing at the current rate of 28 percent.

Cost of goods sold   This cost as a percentage of sales will decrease by 1 percent to match the 2016 figure (the underlying reasoning is that, with fresh financing, the company will gradually return to its strategy of taking advantage of early payment discounts from its suppliers).

Cash   The firm will hold ten days of sales in cash (i.e., match the 2015 figure) to exit the dangerous state of low liquidity.

Fixed assets   Following the pattern observed in years 2014–2017, fixed assets for year 2018 will be equal to 4.5 percent of sales.

Days payable   This metric will decrease to fifty days to match the 2016 figure (see argument made above for cost of goods sold).

Retained earnings   The firm will increase this figure to 80 percent to signal to the bank that it does not intend to use debt to pay generous dividends.

In addition to the above assumptions, it is reasonable to expect that other ratios will not show any change compared to 2017 figures. Therefore, we assume that days of inventory and days receivable will remain the same, as will manufacturing and general, selling, and administrative expenses as percentage of sales. Finally, the tax rate is assumed to remain the same, and an arbitrary value is assigned as accrued expenses. The resulting pro forma statements are shown in table 10.5.

First, notice that interest expenses (income statement) and short-term bank loan (balance sheet) are both highlighted in gray. This is because the interest paid will be connected to the debt level, in order to have an accurate forecasting of the firm's financial needs. In this case, we know that the annual interest paid by Bathline is equal to the $10,000 payment for long-term debt (given in the case) plus an estimated 14 percent on the end-of-year value of short-term debt. So once the values for the pro forma items have been introduced according to the assumptions (including the above formula for interest expenses), the last item to be entered is the short-term bank loan. The latter is then determined by trial-and-error until a value is reached that balances total assets with total equities.

Table 10.5
Pro forma financial statements for Bathline Inc., December 31, 2018 ($'000).

Income statement	2017	2018	Assumptions
Revenue	$14,204	$18,181	28% growth
Cost of goods sold	11,860	14,999	82.5% of sales
Beginning inventory	1,487	1,804	
+ Purchases	8,145	10,386	
+ Manufacturing expenses	4,032	5,091	28.0% of sales
− Ending inventory	1,804	2,383	
Gross profit	2,344	3,182	
Selling, general, and admin. expenses	1,747	2,236	12.3% of sales
Earnings before interest and tax	597	945	
Interest expenses	52	213	$10,000 + 14\% \cdot$ short-term debt
Earnings before tax	545	732	
Tax	218	293	40% tax rate
Earnings after tax	$327	$439	

Balance sheet	2017	2018	Assumptions
Assets			
Cash and cash equivalents	$183	$498	10 days of sales
Accounts receivable	1,759	2,241	45 days receivable
Inventory	1,804	2,383	55.5 days inventory
Total current assets	3,746	5,123	
Fixed assets (net)	724	818	4.5% of sales
Total Assets	$4,470	$5,941	

Equities			
Accounts payable	$1,424	$1,423	50.0 days payable
Accrued expenses	29	35	
Bank loan (short-term)	299	1,453	
Long-term debt, short portion	40	40	
Total current liabilities	1,792	2,951	
Long-term debt	640	600	
Shareholders' equity	2,038	2,390	80% retained earnings
Total equities	$4,470	$5,941	

Second, notice that the firm's actual bank credit needs are much higher than what Steve was expecting them to be. Actually, even if the firm was following the same policy for accounts payable (i.e., days payable equal to sixty-three) and assuming that it could improve the cost of goods sold ratio without using early payment discounts (e.g., to 82.5 percent of sales), the short-term bank loan would still need to be over $1 million. Later in this section, we will discuss the usefulness of pro forma statements in testing different scenarios for financial planning. With $1,453 short-term debt, the firm's leverage (as measured by the ratio of debt to equity) rises to about 70 percent, while ROE is estimated to 20 percent.

As we have already discussed, the combination of high growth, low margin, and large OWC can be quite toxic. Assuming that Bathline has little control over the margins and the cash conversion cycle—as both, to a large extent, depend on market forces—the only element that is under the company's control is growth. This leads us to the question: What is the right level of sales growth? Or more formally, what is a sustainable growth rate for the Bathline company? This will be the topic of the next section.

10.2 Sustainable Growth

Sustainable growth is a rate of sales growth that a company can maintain that is consistent with a defined financial policy. In general, as a firm increases its sales, it will require more assets of all types to support this growth. A reasonable starting assumption is that the firm's assets increase proportionally to sales. That is, the same growth rate that applies to sales also applies to total assets. A second assumption is that paying dividends or issuing new equity are not available options. Cash-constrained firms do not usually have the luxury of paying dividends. Also, issuing new equity is not so common for many firms, as this is almost always the most costly option for raising funds and can be quite time-consuming.

Let's denote the growth rate as $g = \Delta S / S_0$, where S_0 is the base year's sales and ΔS is the planned increase in sales. Then, by the fundamental balance sheet identity as applied to the financial balance sheet (see chapter 4), we have:

Increase in total assets = Increase in total equities, or

$$g \cdot (\text{OWC}_0 + \text{FA}_0) = \Delta D + \Delta E, \text{ or}$$

$$g \cdot (D_0 + E_0) = \Delta D + \text{net profit}$$

We will consider two cases for debt—although more can be applicable.

Case 1: The firm has no access to new debt. In this case $\Delta D = 0$ and we get the following expression for sustainable growth:

$$g = \frac{\text{net profit}}{D_0 + E_0}$$

Sustainable growth when the level of debt is constant
> If a firm's outstanding debt is to be maintained constant, the firm's growth is limited
> by the ratio net profit to net assets.

Case 2: The firm's leverage cannot go beyond a threshold expressed by the D/E ratio.
This is a quite common risk management strategy applied by firms and can also be con-
tractually imposed by debt holders in the form of covenants. In this case D/E shall remain
constant (consequently, $\Delta D =$ net profit $\cdot$ D_0/E_0), resulting in the following formula for
sustainable growth:

$$g = \frac{\text{net profit}}{E_0}$$

In this case, if the firm does not distribute any dividends, its sustainable growth rate is
determined by the company's projected ROE (evaluated at the starting value of equity).

 Sustainable growth when the financial leverage is constant
> If a firm's current financial leverage (D/E) is to be maintained constant, the firm's
> growth is limited by its ROE.

Returning to Bathline's problem, can these two formulas be directly applied to suggest
what the firm's sustainable growth rate should be? By using the actual 2017 net profit (in the
numerator) and the end-of-2016 values for debt and equity (in the denominator), these formulas would suggest a growth rate of 11.7 percent and 18.2 percent for cases 1 and 2,
respectively (see Bathline's financial statements). Actually, these values represent the maximum sustainable growth rates that can be achieved under the two scenarios if the company
pays no dividends. However, as the company has been growing, over the last two years, by
relying heavily on suppliers' credit, it has achieved higher growth rates than the maximum
sustainable ones. By doing so, it has reached a point where further supplier credit might
not be possible, while its cash balance has been decreased to dangerously low levels. This
is not uncommon for many small firms. Being driven by an urge to establish themselves in
the market, these firms place emphasis on their growth without planning carefully for the
necessary funds to support this growth, just to end up growing bankrupt.

Obviously, it is necessary for Bathline to reevaluate its operating plans in light of the new
information obtained from financial forecasting. Next, we will present financial planning
as an activity that brings together the firm's operating and financial plans (considering the
limitations associated with the latter) and discuss what type of actions Bathline can take to
manage its growth and stay in business.

10.3   Financial Planning at Bathline Inc.

Exercise

Considering Alternative Operational Policies at Bathline Inc.

Assume that Steve Lafon (correctly) believes that the bank would be unwilling to extend the firm's short-term credit line beyond $600,000. Given this constraint, how should the company adapt its operating plans without completely halting its growth?

Currently, there is momentum for 28 percent growth in sales—which, as we have seen, would get Bathline into severe liquidity problems. The company should probably reconsider some of its policies so that it can be able to achieve some growth without risking going out of its financial limitations. Next, we discuss some potential changes that Bathline can make in its operations:

Pricing and trade credit policies   As Bathline's products are relatively differentiated, we expect that a small increase in prices will not have a great impact on demand. Another action that would help the company decrease its operating working capital is to shorten the credit period it offers to its customers, or simply intensify its receivable collection efforts. For the purpose of this exercise, we assume that by increasing the prices 2 percent (which roughly translates into 18.5 percent gross margin, similar to the 2015 figure) and reducing the days receivable to forty days, the company will hold its growth potential down to 18 percent (i.e., 10 percent reduction relative to the current momentum).

Cash and dividend policies   Regarding cash, while the firm's overall goal is to hold ten days of sales in cash, it can achieve this more gradually by setting its cash balance for 2018 to 7.2 days (i.e., match the 2016 figure). To achieve this target, the company could increase its retained earnings to 100 percent for one year. While the shareholders might not be happy with not receiving any dividends next year, given that they are a group of family and friends, Steve could explain the criticality of the situation, promising larger dividends in the years to come once the company is under control.

Accounts payable policy   To evaluate the policy for accounts payable, it would be useful to first calculate the cost of foregoing early payment discounts.

Let's assume that Bathline is offered 2/10 net 45 trade credit terms by its suppliers. That is, the firm earns a 2 percent discount on an invoice if paid within ten days of its issuance, or can pay the full invoice amount in forty-five days. Now consider the case that the firm foregoes the $20 discount associated with a $1,000 invoice issued ten days ago. This means that it can use $980 for thirty-five days; namely, incur an interest rate of 2.04 percent ($= 20/980$)

for the same period. This roughly translates into a 21.3 percent ($= 2.04\% \cdot 365/35$) interest in annual terms.[1]

Given the above calculation, it would be beneficial for Bathline to use bank credit to take advantage of early payment discounts, as the interest rate paid to the bank is lower than 21.3 percent. However, notice that the firm's current figure for days payable is 63.8 days, which would translate into an actual annual interest rate for suppliers' credit of 13.8 percent ($= 2.04\% \cdot 365/53.8$). Assuming that the company can maintain its days payable at similar levels without facing any problems from suppliers, then, given its current liquidity problems, it might be a good idea to keep doing so.

Applying these changes, the resulting updated pro forma statements for year 2018 are shown in table 10.6. The updated pro forma financial statements suggest that if Bathline can successfully implement the actions outlined above, it can still achieve considerable growth without increasing its external funding needs to undesirable or infeasible levels. With this plan, the company's short-term debt is estimated as $414,000 (well below the $600,000 credit limit), resulting in a leverage ratio of 40 percent and an estimated ROE of 22 percent.

However, notice that the updated pro forma financial statements are based less on historical data and more on our (management's) assumptions about the impact of particular operational changes in the firm's performance. As these projections are more prone to judgmental mistakes, it is important to make sure that the assumptions made do not create any inconsistencies in the overall picture. For example, a forecast for growth in revenue shall be accompanied by corresponding increases in working capital, fixed assets, and associated financing. Additionally, a sensitivity analysis of these assumptions is equally important to identify the range and variance of the target outcomes but also to drive managerial action in a timely manner. For example, what if the customer demand is more price-sensitive than initially anticipated, resulting in slower than expected sales growth? Or, what if the company is not so successful in collecting its accounts receivable faster? A sensitivity analysis of the model's outcomes to its key input elements can be done either through simulation or scenario testing. As financial forecasting through pro forma statements is mostly spreadsheet-based, both approaches are quite straightforward. Table 10.7 shows the pro forma statements for year 2018 for a best-case and a worst-case scenario.

While these scenarios are not exhaustive in capturing the potential implications for the firm's performance from the aforementioned operational changes, they can still be valuable input in management's effort to keep the business under control. For example, the worst-case scenario suggests that the potential credit limit of $600,000 might not be sufficient to cover the firm's funding needs. However, with an awareness of this projection, the firm's management can be better prepared to react accordingly in case the analysis of actual over forecast performance suggests that the worst-case scenario is materializing. For example,

---

1. See "Shortofcash Inc." example in section 14.3.1 for more precise calculations using compound interest.

Table 10.6
Updated pro forma financial statements for Bathline Inc., December 31, 2018 ($'000).

Income statement	2017	2018	Assumptions
Revenue	$14,204	$16,761	18% growth
Cost of goods sold	11,860	13,660	81.5% of sales
Beginning inventory	1,487	1,804	
+ Purchases	8,145	9,241	
+ Manufacturing expenses	4,032	4,693	28.0% of sales
− Ending inventory	1,804	2,383	
Gross profit	2,344	3,101	
Selling, general, and admin. expenses	1,747	2,062	12.3% of sales
Earnings before interest and tax	597	1,039	
Interest expenses	52	68	$10,000 + 14\% \cdot$ short-term debt
Earnings before tax	545	971	
Tax	218	388	40% tax rate
Earnings after tax	$327	$583	

Balance sheet	2017	2018	Assumptions
Assets			
Cash and cash equivalents	$183	$331	7.2 days of sales
Accounts receivable	1,759	1,837	40.0 days receivable
Inventory	1,804	2,383	55.5 days inventory
Total current assets	3,746	4,551	
Fixed assets (net)	724	754	4.5% of sales
Total assets	$4,470	$5,305	
Equities			
Accounts payable	$1,424	$1,595	63.0 days payable
Accrued expenses	29	35	
Bank loan (short-term)	299	414	
Long-term debt, short portion	40	40	
Total current liabilities	1,792	2,084	
Long-term debt	640	600	
Shareholders' equity	2,038	2,621	100% retained earnings
Total equities	$4,470	$5,305	

they can start discussions with new investors to provide fresh funding in exchange for company shares. They can also consider alternative ways to control operating working capital, such as by reducing inventory through longer promised lead times and/or lower customer service levels.

Table 10.7
Pro forma financial statements for best-case and worst-case scenarios for Bathline Inc., December 31, 2018 (values in $'000).

Income statement	2018 Worst case	2018 Best case	Assumptions Worst (best) case
Revenue	$15,624	$18,181	10% (28%) growth
Cost of goods sold	12,890	14,817	82.5% (81.5%) of sales
Beginning inventory	1,804	1,804	
+ Purchases	8,672	10,177	
+ Manufacturing expenses	4,375	5,091	28.0% of sales
− Ending inventory	2,383	2,383	
Gross profit	2,734	3,363	
Selling, general, and admin. expenses	1,922	2,236	12.3% of sales
Earnings before interest and tax	812	1,127	
Interest expenses	124	73	$10,000 + 15\% (14\%) \cdot$ short-term debt
Earnings before tax	688	1,054	
Tax	275	422	40% tax rate
Earnings after tax	$413	$633	

Balance sheet	2018 Worst case	2018 Best case	Assumptions Worst (best) case
Assets			
Cash and cash equivalents	$308	$359	7.2 days of sales
Accounts receivable	1,798	1,992	42.0 (40.0) days receivable
Inventory	2,383	2,383	55.5 days inventory
Total current assets	4,490	4,735	
Fixed assets (net)	703	818	4.5% of sales
Total assets	$5,193	$5,553	
Equities			
Accounts payable	$1,307	$1,757	55.0 (63.0) days payable
Accrued expenses	35	35	
Bank loan (short-term)	760	450	
Long-term debt, short portion	40	40	
Total current liabilities	2,142	2,282	
Long-term debt	600	600	
Shareholders' equity	2,452	2,671	100% retained earnings
Total equities	$5,193	$5,553	

10.4 Summary

In this chapter we have shown how financial forecasting techniques can be used to reconcile a firm's operations and financial plans in a coherent way. However, the pro forma financial statements we have used only present a snapshot of a company's financials at the end of the time period they refer to. While this approach can be appropriate for companies with stable operations, it is not sufficient for firms that are in a growing phase or face seasonality in their operations with significantly fluctuating cash levels. In this case, cash budgets should be constructed to reveal the funding needs of the company throughout the planning horizon, on the basis of actual monthly cash receipts and disbursements, rather than their accrual interpretation. We return to this issue in chapter 15, where we discuss the challenges faced by a company with highly seasonal demand.

Exercises

1. Why is the analysis of a firm's historical performance necessary before constructing pro forma financial statements?

2. Roughly speaking, if a firm's sales is forecast to increase 30 percent:

   a. By how much will accounts receivable increase?

   b. By how much will DSO increase?

3. Calculate an expression for sustainable sales growth rate when leverage is constant as measured by D/E and pay-out ratio is p (that is, for each dollar of net profit, p dollars are paid as dividends, with $0 < p < 1$).

4. Tables 9.1, 9.3, and 9.5 in the previous chapter present Inditex's financial statements for years 2015 and 2016. Use the information in these tables to answer the following questions:

   a. What is Inditex's sustainable growth rate for year 2016?

   b. How does this compare with the actual growth rate for the same year?

5. Are the following statements true or false? Please explain briefly.

   a. Financial forecasting helps management anticipate differences between actual and sustainable growth rates and develop contingency plans for managing those differences.

   b. If the ratio debt to equity cannot be further increased AND issuing new equity or paying dividends is not an option AND there are neither economies nor diseconomies of scale, the sales growth rate of a firm is limited by ROE.

   c. Rapidly growing firms are more likely to face liquidity problems if their net margin is small and they have a long cash-to-cash cycle.

6. The management of Green Staples Inc., a wholesale distributor of office supplies on the East Coast of the United States, is in the process of developing the firm's financial plans for year 2019. The company has met its goal of expanding its market coverage, having increased its 2018 sales by 8.1 percent, a growth much higher than the industry average. The management believes that 2019 will

bring opportunities for further expansion, as one of the local key players is preparing to exit the market (due to the owner's retirement). However, they also understand that they need to secure in advance the necessary financing sources in order to prudently meet the new target of 11 percent sales growth in 2019. The following charts show the company's year-end financial statements for the last three years.

Income statement ($'000)	2016	2017	2018
Sales	$13,280	$14,090	$15,231
Cost of goods sold	10,916	11,638	12,612
Beginning inventory	1,554	1,726	1,860
+ Purchases	11,089	11,772	12,777
− Ending inventory	1,726	1,860	2,026
Gross profit	2,364	2,452	2,620
Selling, general, and administrative expenses	1,607	1,719	1,858
Earnings before interest and tax	757	733	762
Interest expenses	19	15	25
Earnings before tax	738	717	737
Tax	258	251	258
Earnings after tax	$480	$466	$479

Balance sheets ($'000)	2016	2017	2018
Assets			
Cash and cash equivalents	$437	$463	$501
Accounts receivable	1,062	1,131	1,260
Inventory	1,726	1,860	2,026
Total current assets	3,225	3,454	3,787
Fixed assets (net)	1,036	1,099	1,203
Total assets	$4,261	$4,553	$4,990
Equities			
Accounts payable	$942	$1,009	$1,120
Bank loan (short-term)	78	52	121
Long-term debt, short portion	30	30	30
Total current liabilities	1,050	1,091	1,271
Long-term debt	360	330	300
Shareholders' equity	2,851	3,131	3,419
Total equities	$4,261	$4,553	$4,990

a. Construct the firm's statement of cash flows and compute its basic ratios. What can you infer about the firm's historical performance? Are there any ratios that require management's attention? Please explain briefly.

b. What is your guess about the firm's short-term debt needs to support its 2019 growth target? To answer this question, please assume that Green Staples Inc. does not intent to change its earnings retention policy and has no access to shareholder equity or long-term debt (due to covenants from the current debt-holders).

7. Continuing problem 6, use the financial statements and the following list of assumptions to construct the firm's pro forma financial statements for 2019.

Green Staples Inc. assumptions for 2019			
Sales growth rate	11.0%	Cash	12.0 days in sales
Cost of goods sold	82.8% of sales	Accounts receivable	30.3 days receivable
SGAs	12.3% of sales	Inventory	60 days inventory
Interest expenses	$8,000 + 14% short-term debt	Fixed assets (net)	$1,336,000
Tax rate	35%	Accounts payable	32.0 days payable
Retained earnings	60.0% of net profit	Current portion long-term debt	$30,000

a. What is Green Staples's projected short-term debt financing in 2019? How does this number compare with the 2018 figure?

b. Perform a sensitivity analysis on the short-term debt requirement projection by considering each of the following changes:

- What would happen if sales increase by 14 percent instead of 11 percent?

- What if selling, general, and administrative expenses decline from 12.3 percent to 11.0 percent of sales?

- What would be the impact of an increase of days of inventory to sixty-three days?

8. Continuing problem 7, now assume that the bank is not willing to extend short-term debt by more than $200,000. What policy changes would you recommend to Green Staples so that it can meet its growth target while remaining within the short-term financing limitations?

11 Tools to Improve Operating Margin: Introduction to Cost Accounting

Almost all decisions based on cost accounting are utterly wrong.
—Eliyahu Goldratt, operations guru

Consider a company that is pondering reassessing (a euphemism for closing) one of its subsidiaries. The net profit of the subsidiary under scrutiny has been consistently negative in the last ten quarters. Should it be closed in accordance with an economic criterion? From the point of view of financial accounting, the right answer seems to be "yes," or even "absolutely." However, it may be the case that closing the subsidiary is not a good idea after all, even from a purely economic point of view. It turns out there is another angle from which to look at the situation, the one offered by cost accounting.

This chapter explains how cost accounting can, based on the information provided by financial accounting, help managers improve their decisions. More formally, we can define cost accounting (also known as managerial accounting) as the field within accounting that is concerned with the use of financial accounting to provide managers with relevant information so that they can make better, more informed, decisions. In simple terms, cost accounting processes financial data using additional (possibly confidential) data to extract relevant information from it. As such, in contrast to financial accounting, cost accounting doesn't use financial accounting standards but adapts itself to the managers' needs. As a consequence, cost accounting is not intended to be used by other stakeholders, such as shareholders or regulators.

We will start by classifying costs and defining the key notion of contribution margin, or simply contribution. Through a number of examples, we will explain why contribution is usually the right criterion to use when making business decisions. We will move then to explaining how decisions may change in the presence of bottlenecks, a topic of great importance in operations management. We will close by illustrating the use of an activity-based costing (ABC) system to allocate fixed costs.

11.1 Simple Cost Taxonomies

The main purpose of classifying costs is two-fold: First, it helps to organize the financial information better. Second, it helps managers make more informed decisions. These two goals will be illustrated throughout the chapter by a number of examples.

11.1.1 Variable and Fixed Costs

We will start by defining the main types of cost depending on the activity level. See figure 11.1 for a simple representation.

Variable cost A cost is said to be variable when it increases with the level of activity and is zero if the level of activity is zero. Purchasing cost of raw materials or subassemblies may be a good example of variable cost.

Fixed cost A cost is fixed when it does not change with the level of activity. Examples include the plant manager and the plant administration staff's salaries, depreciation, or a storefront rent. All these costs are typically independent of the level of production at the plant or the level of sales at the store.

Semivariable cost A cost is semivariable when it increases with the level of activity and is not zero if the level of activity is zero. The cost of electricity in a factory may be a good example of semivariable cost. No matter how many units are produced, the fixed portion

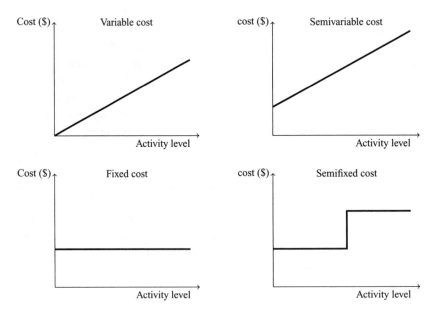

Figure 11.1
Types of cost based on activity level.

of the electricity bill has to be paid. This fixed portion may depend, for example, on the amount of contracted power. In addition to that, electricity cost will increase with every unit produced, due to the energy requirement of machines.

Semifixed cost A cost is semifixed when it is fixed within a range, but there are several ranges that each incur a different cost. For instance, when a plant manager decides to go from one to two (or three) working shifts, some semifixed costs are incurred, such as foremen and security personnel salaries or lighting.

Having defined the main types of cost, some comments are in order.

How the level of activity is measured should be specified Examples include level of demand, sales, purchases, production, inventory, overtime, or number of batches produced. As such, we can say that the (variable) cost of a product is $10 per unit bought or $15 per unit produced. Moreover, note that even the nature of a cost may change depending of the unit of measurement of the activity level. For instance, consider a production phase where parts are cured in an oven in batches. The cost of processing a batch (i.e., the cost of keeping the oven hot during the, say, ten-minute process time) is approximately the same irrespective of the number of units in the batch. Therefore, that cost is *semifixed* in the number of units, but *variable* in the number of batches. Sometimes the level of activity is implicit, while not defining others may lead to misunderstandings.

The nature of a cost depends on the range considered A store rent is fixed insofar as a single store is enough to cope with sales. If the level of sales increases by, say, 80 percent, a second store may be needed and an additional rent cost is incurred; hence, a fixed cost becomes semifixed outside of a reasonable range. The span of the range of course depends on the specific cost considered.

The time horizon is also relevant to determine the nature of a cost For instance, fixed costs become variable for a sufficiently long time horizon, as any cost will increase with the level of activity (e.g., if one more production plant is needed, it will be built).

The nature of a cost depends on the decision under scrutiny Consider a firm where firing workers is not an option due to an agreement with unions. If the firm is pondering opening a new factory and hiring new workers, the salary of workers will be variable in the number of workers hired. However, if the firm is considering closing an existing factory, the salary of workers will be fixed. This asymmetry may have a large impact on decisions.

 On the nature of costs

> The nature of a cost depends on how the level of activity is measured, the range considered, the time horizon, and the decision being made.

11.1.2 Direct and Indirect Costs

Another classification of costs includes direct and indirect costs. A direct cost is the one entirely incurred at a given unit of reference. For instance, the head of production's salary in a manufacturing plant producing items A and B is direct to the production department, but it is indirect to the production of item A (or B). Note that this classification is conceptually different from the previous one, which distinguished between variable and fixed costs. Therefore, a cost may be both direct and fixed (e.g., the salary of the supervisor of the section where only item A is produced) or indirect and variable (e.g., the cost of radio spots to advertise products A and B grows with the number of spots broadcast, but it is indirect to product A). However, some people tend to link direct costs to variable costs as well as indirect costs and fixed costs. As we have seen, this is not generally true.

11.2 Contribution Margin and Break-Even

The contribution margin or, simply, contribution, is a straightforward but powerful concept. It can be applied to a product unit or an entire company. In the first case, its definition is

$$\text{(unit) contribution} = \text{net price} - \text{sum of unit variable costs} \tag{11.1}$$

For instance, if the unit cost of product A is $10, its price $11, and 60 percent of the total cost is variable, the unit contribution of A is:

$$\text{unit contribution} = \$11 - 0.6 \cdot \$10 = \$5$$

This means that selling one more unit of A contributes not one (that is, $11–$10), but five additional dollars to EBT (earnings before taxes). This makes sense: the total cost of the product is $20 because $4 of fixed costs have been allocated to the product. But those costs are fixed: they will *not* increase if we produce and sell one more unit of A. Therefore, shareholders' happiness will increase by $11 due to sales and decrease by $6 due to variable costs. Overall, shareholders' happiness (if taxes are zero) increases by $5.

In the case of an entire firm, the definition of contribution during a period changes as:

$$\text{(total) contribution during a period} = \text{net sales} - \text{sum of variable costs} \tag{11.2}$$

In other words, total contribution is the sum of the individual contribution of all units sold during the period.

 Contribution margin

Contribution margin is the difference between sales and the sum of variable costs. Likewise, unit contribution margin is the difference between unit price and unit variable cost.

Total contribution is connected to the important concept of the break-even point. A crucial question for managers is: How many units should we sell such that net profit is zero? The answer gives a threshold above which the company starts making money. That leads to the definition of break-even point, or simply break-even, which is the level of sales required to achieve zero profit. In other words, the break-even point is achieved when sales exactly compensate total costs incurred. As total cost can be split into variable and fixed categories, the condition for break-even can be written as:

sales $=$ variable costs $+$ fixed costs $\Longrightarrow$

sales $-$ variable costs $=$ fixed costs $\Longrightarrow$

total contribution $=$ fixed costs   (11.3)

Break-even point

The **break-even point** refers to the number of units that have to be sold during a period so that net profit is zero.

As the last equality suggests, in order to reach zero profit, total contribution should be enough to cover total fixed costs.

Having presented the concepts of contribution margin and break-even, let's start understanding their usefulness in making economic decisions through a simple example.

Exercise

Selling Bicycles

Imagine you buy and sell bicycles from your small store. One day, you receive a customer, Yuya, who tells you the following: "I want to buy a bicycle whose price is $200, but I am only willing to pay $100 for it." You know that the total cost of each bicycle is $160, with $70 the sum of variable costs and $90 the sum of *allocated* fixed costs.

1. Would you sell the bicycle for $100? (Ignore taxes when making your calculations.)

Maybe your immediate answer is "no!" since $100 is not enough to cover the total cost of the bicycle, which is $160, so you think you will lose $60 by selling at that price. However, there is a better way to answer this question. The contribution of selling one bicycle at $100 is $100 − $70 = $30, which is positive, so you will be better off if you sell the bicycle at

$100! The key point is that, again, fixed costs are allocated, but since they are fixed, they will not increase if one more bicycle is produced and sold.

Exercise

Selling Bicycles (cont'd)

You accepted and sold the bicycle to Yuya for $100. It turns out that she happens to be a popular YouTube star. She immediately told her millions of followers that you had sold her a great $200 bicycle for half its price. The following day you had some 1,000 new customers at your store willing to buy the very same bicycle at $100. Suddenly, you have enough customers to cover one year of demand and book your annual production capacity!

2. Would you sell them 1,000 bicycles at $100 each?

3. Assuming fixed costs do not change for any range of production, how many bicycles would you have to sell at $100 to reach break-even?

Given the answer to question 1. above, you might be tempted to say "yes" again. Well, that would be a big mistake! Admittedly, the contribution of selling 1,000 bicycles is $30 · 1,000 = $30,000. However, this is not enough to cover your fixed costs. Assuming you can produce and sell 1,000 bicycles a year, your fixed costs are approximately $90 · 1,000 = $90,000, a number much larger than $30,000. There is no way you can make up for the remaining $60,000, which leads to annual losses of $60,000 before taxes. A small disaster given your sales will be just $100,000!

Note that to reach break-even, you would need to sell:

$$\frac{\text{fixed costs}}{\text{unit contribution margin at } \$100} = \frac{90,000}{30} = 3,000 \text{ bicycles}$$

without increasing fixed costs, something that doesn't seem plausible. Moreover, you don't even have capacity to produce so many bicycles....

This simple example illustrates how contribution margin and net margin should both be considered when making business decisions. Forgetting about one of them may lead you to make the wrong decision.

On net margin and contribution margin

When it comes to making operational decisions, the net margin does not provide all the answers. In fact, the contribution margin provides many more answers than net margin.

The next example shows how to calculate the break-even point in a slightly more complex setting.

Exercise

Calculating Break-Even Points: GettingThere Inc.

The monthly income statements of GettingThere Inc. in Notaxland during the first four months of the year are given in the following table:

	Jan	Feb	Mar	Apr
Sales	31,000	28,500	32,150	34,775
COGS	18,600	17,100	19,290	20,865
Salaries	5,500	5,500	5,500	5,500
Rent	2,000	2,000	2,000	2,000
Utilities	6,450	6,160	6,604	7,164
Net profit	−1,550	−2,260	−1,244	−754

As a manager of GettingThere, you should be concerned about the situation of your firm because net profit has been negative for four consecutive months. You wonder how many units the firm had to sell such that break-even is reached. You consider three scenarios:

1. Price is held constant at $25 per unit.
2. Price increases by 10 percent.
3. Price decreases by 10 percent.

Which scenario might bring you more easily to the desired break-even point?

(1) In order to calculate the break-even point, we need first to identify variable and fixed costs. A quick inspection of income statements reveals that salaries and rent are fixed. Also, COGS is variable at 60 percent of sales (e.g., in January, $18,600 = 31,000 \cdot 0.6$). However, whether utilities is fixed or variable is not that clear, as it changes over time, but the cost is not proportional to sales (you can check that). The data suggests that utilities' cost might be semivariable. To see if that is the case, we can plot utilities expenses (Y axis) versus the number of units sold (X axis), as in figure 11.2. To calculate units sold per month, just divide monthly sales by the unit price, $25. The figure can be done in MS Excel using an XY (scatter) chart.[1]

1. To plot the line that tries to connect all four points, right click on the graph and click Add trendline, making sure you tick the Display equation on chart option.

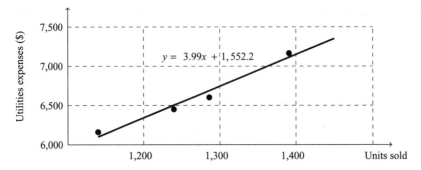

Figure 11.2
Relationship between utilities expenses incurred and units sold (each point represents a month).

The equation displayed says that the utilities expenses increase by $3.99, or roughly $4, every time an additional unit is sold. So the unit variable cost is approximately $15 + $4 = $19, and the unit contribution margin $25 − $19 = $6. Likewise, the intercept of the line is roughly $1,552. Therefore total fixed costs per month total $5,500 + $2,000 + $1,552 = $9,052. From equation 11.3, the number of units x to sell to reach break-even is:

$$\$6 \cdot x = \$9,052 \implies x \approx 1,509 \text{ units}$$

that is, 8.5 percent more than sales in April (We sold $34,775 / $25 = 1,391 units in April).

(2) If the price is reduced 10 percent, the new solution is

$$(\$25 \cdot 0.9 - \$19) \cdot x = \$9,052 \implies x \approx 2,587 \text{ units}$$

Therefore, a 10 percent price reduction requires that we sell 86 percent more units than in April to reach break-even.

(3) If the price is increased 10 percent, the number of units to break-even becomes:

$$(\$25 \cdot 1.1 - \$19) \cdot x = \$9,052 \implies x \approx 1,065 \text{ units}$$

In this case, a 10 percent price increase requires that demand decreases by no more than 23.4 percent with respect to April in order not to lose money.

Given the notably asymmetrical results in parts 2 and 3, it seems that increasing the price by 10 percent might be a better approach to try to reach the break-even point, although the actual answer will depend on the price elasticity of the demand.

Again, combining break-even and contribution margin we have come up with what seems to be the right pricing policy for the firm, at least in the short run.

11.3 Decisions at Capacity

When maximizing contribution margin in operations management, many times there are internal constraints that limit the output of a firm, which we call bottlenecks. In those cases, the decisions that optimize contribution margin, thus profit, may change dramatically. We can illustrate this point by means of the following exercise.

11.3.1 Decisions at Capacity: An Enlightening Exercise

The following exercise is a sloppy proof that the epigraph by Eliyahu Goldratt at the beginning of the chapter is true (see the original exercise that inspired the first part of this one in Corbett [1999]).

 Exercise

A Tough Managerial Decision

You have recently been hired as a manager to run a production plant facing serious financial problems. The plant runs sixteen hours per day (two shifts), five days per week, and produces two products, P1 and P2. Demand for both products is known and constant: 250 units of each product per week. Prices are dictated by competition, and they are not likely to change: P1 is sold at $120 per unit, P2 at $140 per unit. The production process requires raw materials, machine time, and labor. There are four types of raw materials: RM1, RM2, RM3, RM4. Unit prices of raw materials are constant and known: RM1 ($35), RM2 ($15), RM3 ($20), RM4 ($30). Producing one unit of P1 requires one unit each of raw materials RM1, RM2, and RM3. Producing one unit of P2 requires two units each of RM2 and one unit of raw materials RM3 and RM4. There are four types of machines (MA, MB, MC, MD), one of each type, that can work simultaneously. Ignore setup times and overlapping times between machines. The number of minutes required at each machine to produce one unit of product is shown in the following table.

	P1	P2
MA	10	4
MB	7	10
MC	8	14
MD	4	15

Labor costs are fixed. Total fixed costs (including labor) equal $24,000 per week.

1. How many units of each product should you produce to maximize profit?

2. If the situation described above cannot be changed even in the long run (i.e., shifts or machines cannot be added, costs cannot be reduced, etc.), would you recommend shutting down the plant?

The first thing we have to check is if we have capacity at all four machines to produce the demand we face. Total capacity in minutes per week *at each machine* is 16 hours · 60 minutes per hour · 5 days per week = 4,800 minutes. Now, time required at machine MA to produce the existing demand is 250 · 10 + 250 · 4 = 3,500 minutes per week. As this amount is not larger than capacity (4,800 minutes per week), we have no capacity problems at machine MA. Proceeding identically with the remaining machines, workload turns out to be, respectively 4,250, 5,500, and 4,750 minutes at machines MB, MC, and MD. Clearly, only machine MC does not have the capacity to produce all the demand, as 5,500 > 4,800. That means we cannot satisfy all the demand. Therefore, we have to find out what is the most profitable product in order to produce 250 units of that product, and devote the remaining capacity at machine MC to produce the less profitable product. If we use unit contribution margin to determine which is the most profitable product, we obtain:

	P1	P2
Price	$120	$140
Sum of unit variable costs	$70	$80
Unit contribution margin	$50	$60

Therefore, it seems that we should produce as many units as possible of P2 and use the remaining capacity at machine MC, if any, to produce P1. Producing 250 units of P2 requires 250 · 14 = 3,500 minutes at machine MC. The remaining time is 4,800 less 3,500 minutes, or 1,300 minutes. Using that remaining capacity, 162 units of part P1 can be produced (as 1,300 / 8 = 162.5). Therefore, the best production plan requires manufacturing 162 P1 and 250 P2. Given those production levels, the total contribution margin is 162 · $50 + 250 · $60 = $23,100. Unfortunately, this amount is not enough to compensate for fixed costs at $24,000, meaning that net profit is −$900 < 0. If the situation cannot be reversed, we are facing a serious problem in the long run.

 Exercise

A Tough Managerial Decision (2)

Just out of curiosity: What would net profit have been had we produced 250 P1 and as many P2 as possible given the remaining capacity at machine MC?

The weekly time required at MC to produce 250 P1 is $250 \cdot 8 = 2{,}000$ minutes. Remaining time at MC is $4{,}800 - 2{,}000 = 2{,}800$ minutes. In that time, we can produce $2{,}800 / 14 = 200$ units, leading to a production plan of 250 P1 and 200 P2. Total contribution margin is $250 \cdot \$50 + 200 \cdot \$60 = \$24{,}500$, hence net profit is $\$24{,}500 - \$24{,}000 = \$500 > 0$. Wait a minute! How is this possible? The second production plan is supposed to yield an even more negative net profit, since we are producing *more* of the product with the *lowest* unit contribution margin. However, net profit is now positive! Did we make any mistakes in the calculations? Not really. The reason for this apparent contradiction has to do with the fact that we have a bottleneck in machine MC. Therefore, we should look for the production plan that gets the most out of each minute at the bottleneck. That means that we have to maximize the unit contribution margin *per minute of capacity of machine MC*. Or more generally, we have to maximize the unit contribution margin per unit of scarce resource.

Maximizing profit with constraints

To maximize profit in the presence of a bottleneck, the unit contribution margin *per unit of scarce resource* should be maximized.

Let's apply this criterion to the example. In one minute at machine MC, P1 generates $\$50 / 8 = \$6.25$ of contribution, while P2 generates only $\$60 / 14 \approx \$4.29$. Therefore, it is better to produce all the P1s, even if P1 has the lowest unit contribution margin. The optimal production plan is then to produce 250 units of P1 and 200 units of P2, leading to a profit of $500.

It should be clear that maximizing the contribution margin works only in the particular case when there are no internal bottlenecks; namely, when the bottleneck is in the market. When this is the case, the scarce resource is market demand, and so "maximizing the unit contribution margin per unit of scarce resource" means "maximizing the unit contribution margin per unit sold," equivalent to "maximizing the unit contribution margin."

 Exercise

A Tough Managerial Decision (3)

What would the most profitable product be if there is ample machine capacity, but there is a scarcity of RM2 (say, kilos of polyethylene pellets) in the market, such that not all the demand can be satisfied?

Given the new assumptions, the bottleneck is not machine MC anymore but rather the amount of polyethylene (PE) available in the market. Therefore in this case maximizing the unit contribution margin per unit of scarce resource leads to maximizing unit the contribution margin per kilo of PE used. In the case of product P1, we generate $50 of contribution per kilo of PE, as one kilo of PE (i.e., one unit of RM2) is needed to produce P1. However, in order to produce one P2, we need two kilos of PE, thus we generate: $60 / 2 = $30 of contribution per kilo of PE. Since $50 > $30, product P1 is more profitable if there is a scarcity of PE in the market.

11.3.2   Maximizing Profit Using Linear Programming

We will now present a different approach to solving the previous exercise using linear programming techniques for constrained problems, as they are usually taught in undergraduate linear programming or microeconomics courses. An issue with this approach is that, although the solution achieved is indeed optimal, it doesn't give any managerial insights of why the solution found is optimal.

The linear program can be defined as:

$$\max \pi (q_1, q_2) = 120q_1 + 140q_2 - 70q_1 - 80q_2 - 24,000$$

$s.t.$

$10q_1 + 4q_2 \leq 4,800$ (machine A constraint)

$7q_1 + 10q_2 \leq 4,800$

$8q_1 + 14q_2 \leq 4,800$

$4q_1 + 15q_2 \leq 4,800$

$0 \leq q_i \leq 250,$ with $i = 1, 2$

where the objective function π is profit and the decision variables q_1 and q_2 are the quantities of P1 and P2 to produce.

Such a program can be solved using the Solver tool in MS Excel or any other optimization program. In this case, as the problem is relatively simple, it can also be solved pictorially, as shown in figure 11.3. The two dotted lines (one horizontal, one vertical) represent the demand constraints. The solid lines represent the machine's time constraints: the solution should be to the southwest of these four lines and within the rectangle defined by the dotted lines and the axes. The feasible area is shown shaded. Finally, the dashed lines are isoprofit lines, whose equations are of the type: $50q_1 + 60q_2 =$ constant. As profit grows when we move northeast, the optimal solution will be the point where an isoprofit line touches the feasible area only once, as shown in the figure. We then obtain a corner solution, where $q_1 = 200$, $q_2 = 250$, exactly as calculated before.

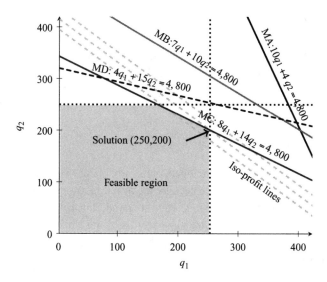

Figure 11.3
Pictorial solution of the maximization problem "A Tough Managerial Decision."

11.3.3 Some Tips on Bottlenecks

Given the solution of the exercise above, it should be apparent how important it is to have in mind where the bottleneck is. Sometimes bottlenecks are difficult to identify, so here are some guidelines that may help identifying them:

(1) In a system, there is only one bottleneck at a time. In practice, you cannot have two simultaneous bottlenecks.

(2) Inventory (e.g., raw materials in a job shop, patients in an emergency room) tends to grow at the entrance of a bottleneck. Inspection of the levels of inventory may help to quickly identify bottleneck candidates.

(3) Bottlenecks may change over time. For instance, due to raw materials scarcity, a bottleneck may change from one raw material to another throughout the year. Due to changing demand in an emergency room, a bottleneck may change from one doctor to another throughout the day.

(4) Managers' precious time may also be a bottleneck. Sometimes, managers devote their time to the most profitable projects, irrespective of how much time those actually require from them. In light of the criterion presented in this section (maximize contribution per unit of scarce resource) that is clearly a mistake. Managers should confront the expected contribution of a project with their required time to execute it. Undertaking a less profitable but less demanding project in terms of management time may be preferred.

11.4   Unleashing the Power of Contribution Margin

In this section we make use of contribution margin (again!) to address important managerial questions in a realistic setting where a firm seems to be in trouble.

 Exercise

Makepad in Trouble

The company Makepad produces three types of widgets in its only plant: W1, W2, and W3. The management of the firm is concerned because the firm is losing money. No major bottlenecks limit the production of widgets. They are pondering a number of potential solutions to reach the break-even point. Last year the firm sold 23,800 W1s; 10,200 W2s; and 9,400 W3s. The income statement broken down by product was as follows. (All dollar values are in thousands.)

	W1	W2	W3	Total
Sales	535.9	269.4	276.6	1081.8
Materials	184.3	83.4	71.3	339.0
Direct labor	89.9	49.0	59.4	198.3
Power	2.3	2.6	3.1	8.0
Gross profit	259.3	134.4	142.7	536.5
Insurance	5.4	4.1	5.5	15.0
Rent	29.5	16.3	44.3	90.1
Indirect labor	23.8	22.0	35.4	81.2
Light and heat	1.5	1.3	1.1	3.9
Building service	1.0	0.8	0.8	2.6
Maintenance	1.8	1.5	1.1	4.4
Selling expenses	64.0	47.5	48.7	160.2
General administration	35.7	13.5	18.4	67.6
EBITDA	96.5	27.4	−12.4	111.4
Depreciation	58.6	44.4	37.9	140.8
EBIT	37.9	−17.0	−50.3	−29.4
Interest	5.4	4.1	5.5	15.0
Profit	32.5	−21.1	−55.8	−44.4

Regarding costs, assume that only materials and power are variable in the level of sales; the rest can be considered fixed.

1. What would have been the impact on the bottom line of dropping product W3?

2. Increasing the marketing budget by $20,000 to advertise W2 is expected to increase sales of W2 by 20 percent. Is this a wise investment?

3. If the price of W1 increases by 10 percent sales of W1 are expected to decrease by 20 percent. Is increasing the price of W1 a good idea?

4. Overall, how bad is the firm's situation?

Source: This exercise was inspired by Bruns (1991).

? Question 1

| What would have been the impact on the bottom line of dropping product W3?

A quick inspection of the income statement provided above suggests that, in order to improve profit, we should focus first on product W3, the product with the lowest profit, and possibly drop it. If W3 is dropped, the good news is that we will not incur the variable costs of W3, namely materials and power. Therefore, we will save $71,300 + $3,100 = $74,400. The bad news is that we will not realize W3 sales at $276,600. Overall, we will incur a net cost of $202,200. (Note that this value is exactly the contribution margin of product W3!) As a result, the total profit if W3 had been dropped would have been −$44,400 − $202,200 = −$246,600. So, not a good idea.

Obviously, the *fixed costs of product W3 will still be incurred if W3 is dropped, since those costs are allocated*, including the direct and indirect cost of product W3. In other words, if W3 is dropped, then remaining products W1 and W2 will have to absorb the fixed costs previously allocated to W3. For instance, if W3's fixed costs are split in half between W1 and W2, the resulting income statement would be that shown in table 11.1. In sum, dropping W3 doesn't seem like a sound business decision.

Now, if some of the fixed costs could be avoided, would the answer change? Well, it might change, but only if the additional costs to be saved by dropping W3 can compensate for the contribution of W3 ($202,200.) For instance, some direct costs to W3, such as, say, the salary of the production foreman in charge of section where only W3 is produced, could be saved. However, after inspecting the income statement, saving more than $200,000 doesn't seem achievable.

Net margin may be misleading

| Removing a product whose net margin is negative from the portfolio is *not* necessarily a good idea.

Table 11.1
Income statement if W3 had been dropped.

	W1	W2	Total
Sales	535.9	269.4	805.2
Materials	184.3	83.4	267.7
Direct labor	119.6	78.7	198.3
Power	2.3	2.6	4.9
Gross profit	229.6	104.7	334.3
Insurance	8.2	6.9	15.0
Rent	51.7	38.4	90.1
Indirect labor	41.5	39.7	81.2
Light and heat	2.1	1.8	3.9
Building service	1.4	1.2	2.6
Maintenance	2.4	2.1	4.4
Selling expenses	88.4	71.8	160.2
General administration	44.9	22.7	67.6
EBITDA	−10.8	−79.9	−90.7
Depreciation	77.5	63.3	140.8
EBIT	−88.3	−143.2	−231.5
Interest	8.2	6.9	15.0
Profit	−96.5	−150.1	−246.5

? Question 2

Increasing the marketing budget by $20,000 to advertise W2 is expected to increase sales of W2 by 20 percent. Is this a wise investment?

Let's calculate the additional contribution of W2. The unit price of W2 is $269,400 / 10,200 = $26.41; and the unit variable cost of W2 is ($83,400 + $2,600) / 10,200 = $86,000 / 10,200 = $8.43. Therefore, the unit contribution margin of W2 is $26.41 − $8.43 = $17.98. Now, if sales of W2 increase by 20 percent, the number of additional units expected to be sold is 10,200 · 0.2 = 2,040 units. It follows that the total contribution of additional sales of W2 is $17.98 · 2,040 = $36,700. We have to compare this number with the initial investment in marketing. Since $36,700 > $20,000, investing in marketing seems like a good idea, although it is not enough to reach break-even: overall profit would become −$44,400 + ($36,700 − $20,000) = −$27,700.

? Question 3

If the price of W1 increases by 10 percent, sales of W1 are expected to decrease by 20 percent. Is increasing the price of W1 a good idea?

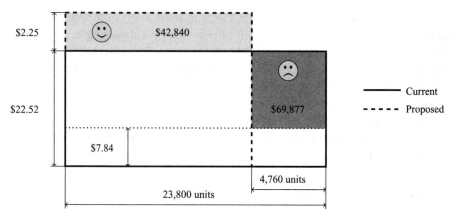

Figure 11.4
A representation of differential total contribution as a function of units sold (horizontal axis) and price (vertical axis) for question 3.

The unit price of W1 is $535,900/23,800 = 22.52; its unit variable cost is ($184,300 + $2,300)/23,800 = 7.84. In this case, if the price of W1 increases by 10 percent, the unit contribution margin will increase as much as price, that is to say, 10 percent of $22.52, or $2.25 per unit. On the other hand, the number of units will be reduced by $23,800 \cdot 0.2 = 4,760$ units. Therefore, additional contribution due to larger unit contribution will be $(23,800 - 4,760) \cdot \$2.25 = \$42,840$ (see light shaded area in figure 11.4). Lost contribution due to fewer units sold will be $4,760 \cdot (\$22.52 - \$7.84) = \$69,877$ (dark shaded area). Overall, total contribution will decrease by $69,877 - $42,840 = $27,037$. Therefore, other things equal, it doesn't make economic sense to increase the price of W1.

? Question 4

Overall, how bad is the situation?

Suppose you have examined all potential actions, and only the one described in question 2 above is expected to have a positive impact on profit. Assuming your estimates are correct, the firm is still losing money. Can the firm survive in the short and medium term? The first thing we have to do is to assess the size of expected losses with regard to total sales: expected net margin is $-\$27,700 / \$1081,800 = -2.6$ percent, a relatively small number. Another key question would be how long these losses can last without dragging the firm into bankruptcy. Well, recall that a firm goes bankrupt not because net profit is negative, but because it runs out of cash. Therefore, we should estimate cash flows to answer the question. Assuming the firm pays and collects money as usual, funds from operations is $-27,700 + 140,800 = \$113,100$, or roughly 10 percent of sales. This is money that the

firm has available to pay for additional investments in fixed assets or to repay outstanding debt. Assuming a cost of debt of, say, 10 percent, current outstanding debt would be
roughly $150,000 (as total interest paid is $15,000, which is 10 percent of $150,000), a
moderate number compared to $113,100. Consequently, the firm should be fine if it makes
conservative investments in the short and medium terms.

The answers to questions 1 to 3 above have illustrated the power of contribution margin
to help managers make decisions in accordance with an economic criterion. Also, it should
be apparent that profits don't mean much, especially when fixed costs represent a large
proportion of operational costs.

11.5   Improving Makepad's Decisions Using Activity-Based Costing

Admittedly, there are more decisions to make based on financial information that those
considered in the example Makepad in Trouble. One of these—a very important one—is
how to price the various products offered. One common approach to come up with the price
of products is to calculate the total cost of the product and add a fixed markup percentage.
(Sometimes this method is referred to as cost plus pricing.) For instance, the total cost of
product W1 in the example above is $(535,900 - 32,500) / 23,800 = \$21.15$ per unit. This
cost includes the unit variable cost ($7.84, as seen before) and the allocated fixed cost,
$21.15 - \$7.84 = \$13.31$. We can now add, say, a 5 percent markup to define the price of
W1: $\$21.15 \cdot 1.05 = \$22.21$. Working in this fashion, we can define the prices for all three
products, as shown in table 11.2.

In a competitive market, margins are relatively small and customers are price-sensitive, so
it is of paramount importance that prices are well-calculated. More so when the percentage
of fixed costs over total cost is large, as in this case. That means that the allocation of
fixed costs is extremely important to guarantee that prices make economic sense. The key
question is then: How should fixed costs be allocated? The importance of this question has
grown over the years, since manufacturing and handling costs have shifted (are shifting)
from variable to fixed, mainly due to automation and the prevalence of unions. Offhand
approaches include allocating fixed costs depending on sales, the number of units sold, net

Table 11.2
Price calculation for products W1, W2, W3 using cost plus pricing ($ per unit).

	W1	W2	W3
Variable cost	7.84	8.43	7.92
Fixed cost (allocated)	13.31	20.05	27.44
Total cost	21.15	28.48	35.35
Markup (5%)	1.06	1.42	1.77
Price	22.21	29.90	37.12

Table 11.3
Fixed costs and associated cost drivers ($'000).

Item	Fixed cost	%	Cumulative %	Cost driver(s)
Direct labor	198.3	25.5	25.5	Headcount
Selling expenses	160.2	20.6	46.0	Sales force salaries
				Media spots
Depreciation	140.8	18.1	64.1	Machine use
Rent	90.1	11.6	75.6	Space
Indirect labor	81.1	10.4	86.1	Salaries
General administration	67.6	8.7	94.7	Sales
Insurance	15.0	1.9	96.7	Sales
Interest	15.0	1.9	98.6	Sales
Maintenance	4.4	0.6	99.2	Machine use
Light and heat	3.9	0.5	99.7	Space
Building service	2.6	0.3	100.0	Space
Total	779.2	100.0		

margin, or contribution margin. These are fine only if fixed costs represent a small portion of total costs but not otherwise. We will follow the steps of the ABC approach described in chapter 8:

Define a cost driver for each fixed cost The first step involves identifying one or more cost drivers for each fixed cost. Table 11.3 shows all fixed costs and the cost drivers chosen. Items have been sorted according to their importance, As the table shows, the first five items account for more than 85 percent of total fixed costs. Accordingly, those are the items that require most of our attention. Let's now justify the selection of drivers: Direct labor (roughly, blue-collar workers' salaries) will be allocated according to headcount, assuming that blue-collar workers' salaries are similar. Selling expenses are made of two main accounts: sales force salaries (say 60 percent) and media spots to advertise the products (40 percent). We don't use headcount in this case because there are large differences between sales people's salaries. Next, depreciation and maintenance are assumed to be proportional to machine use. Rent, light and heat, and building service are roughly proportional to plant space. We could have used volume (m^3) for light and heat rather than surface (m^2) if, for instance, there were large differences in heights across plant sections. Finally, general administration expenses, insurance, and interest will be allocated according to sales.

Estimate percentage use of resources Once cost drivers have been identified, the second step requires determining the amount of resources used by each product as determined by cost drivers. For instance, suppose the firm has eight blue-collar workers: three work for product W1; two for products W2 and W3; and one, in charge of inspection, splits her time evenly among all three products. Therefore, headcount for W1, W2, and W3 would be, respectively, 3.34, 2.33, and 2.33 workers. Since the total cost of direct labor is $198,300,

Table 11.4
Use of resources per product and rates ($ per unit).

Item	Driver	Units	W1	W2	W3	Total	Rate
Direct labor	Headcount	People	3.34	2.33	2.33	8.0	24,788
Selling expenses	Sales force salaries	$000	38.4	28.8	28.8	96.1	1,000
	Media spots	Spots	40	70	70	180	356.1
Depreciation	Machine use	Hours	3,800	2,000	2,200	8,000	17.6
Rent	Space	m^2	2,000	1,800	1,200	5,000	18.0
Indirect labor	Salaries	$000	40.6	20.3	20.3	81.2	1,000
General admin.	Sales	$000	33.5	16.8	17.3	67.6	1,000
Insurance	Sales	$000	8.2	3.7	3.2	15.0	1,000
Interest	Sales	$000	6.8	3.7	4.5	15.0	1,000
Maintenance	Machine use	Hours	3,800	2,000	2,200	8,000	0.6
Light and heat	Space	m^2	2,000	1,800	1,200	5,000	0.8
Building service	Space	m^2	2,000	1,800	1,200	5,000	0.5

the resulting rate per worker is $198,300 / 8 = \$24,787$ per worker (table 11.4). Similarly, the 180 media spots cost 40 percent of $160,200, or $64,080. The resulting rate is $64,080 / 180 = \$356.1$ per spot. Allocating indirect labor and sales force salaries may be trickier. A good idea may be to ask every person in the firm to allocate his or her time to the products. Calculating space and use of machines is usually easier. Table 11.4 shows the allocation of resources for all three products.

Allocate fixed costs accordingly The final step converts the use of resources calculated in step 2 into dollars. To do so, the number of units used should be multiplied by the rate in the last column. For instance, direct labor allocated to W1 is 3.34 people $\cdot \$24,788 = \$82,00$. Likewise, the insurance expense allocated to W2 is $\$3.7 \cdot 1,000 = \$3,700$. As expected, the sum of all allocated costs matches the figures in the initial income statement, except for rounding errors. The resulting costs measured in thousands of dollars are given in table 11.5.

We are now ready to write the income statement of Makepad with the new allocation of fixed costs (table 11.6). Comparing the new income statement with the original one, we can see that the results are similar in that product W1 yields a positive profit and products W2 and W3 don't. However, profit is much lower now for W2 and higher for W3. This suggests that prices should be changed, such that profit becomes positive for all three products. The new unit cost and suggested prices are as shown in table 11.7.

In an industry where margins are relatively small, changes in the prices of products W2 and W3 are large enough to create a reaction in competitors. For instance, dropping the price of product W3 by 11.3 percent may attract additional (elastic) demand from customers, but it may also induce a competitor to reduce its prices as well. This may even trigger a

Table 11.5
Summary of allocated fixed costs to the products ($'000).

	W1	W2	W3	Total
Direct labor	82.8	57.8	57.8	198.4
Selling expenses	52.6	53.7	53.7	160.0
Depreciation	66.9	35.2	38.7	140.8
Rent	36	32.4	21.6	90
Indirect labor	40.6	20.3	20.3	81.2
General admin.	33.5	16.8	17.3	67.6
Insurance	8.2	3.7	3.2	15.1
Interest	6.8	3.7	4.5	15
Maintenance	2.1	1.1	1.2	4.4
Light and heat	1.6	1.4	1.0	4.0
Building service	1.0	0.9	0.6	2.5

Table 11.6
Income statement of Makepad with the new allocation of fixed costs.

	W1	W2	W3	Total
Sales	535.9	269.4	276.6	1081.8
Materials	184.3	83.4	71.3	339.0
Direct labor	82.7	57.8	57.8	198.3
Power	2.3	2.6	3.1	8.0
Gross profit	266.5	125.6	144.3	536.5
Insurance	8.1	3.7	3.2	15.0
Rent	36.1	32.4	21.6	90.1
Indirect labor	40.6	20.3	20.3	81.2
Light and heat	1.6	1.4	1.0	4.0
Building service	1.0	0.9	0.6	2.5
Maintenance	2.1	1.1	1.2	4.4
Selling expenses	52.6	53.8	53.8	160.2
General administration	33.5	16.8	17.3	67.6
EBITDA	90.9	−4.8	25.3	111.5
Depreciation	66.9	35.2	38.7	140.8
EBIT	24.0	−40.0	−13.4	−29.3
Interest	6.8	3.7	4.5	15.0
Profit	17.2	−43.7	−17.9	−44.3

Table 11.7
New cost structure and price for Makepad ($ per unit).

	W1	W2	W3
Variable cost	7.84	8.43	7.92
Fixed cost (allocated)	13.95	22.26	23.41
Total cost	21.79	30.69	31.33
Markup (5%)	1.09	1.53	1.57
Price	22.88	32.22	32.90
Suggested price change	2.9%	7.7%	−11.3%

price war. Likewise, increasing the price of product W2 may induce some customers to buy from competitors, but competitors may also decide to follow suit and increase prices as well. These strategic aspects should be carefully pondered before making price decisions.

11.6 Summary

This chapter has introduced the basic ideas of cost accounting. We have stated that costs can be classified as variable and fixed, or direct and indirect. We have pointed out that the nature of costs depends on the activity considered, the range, the time horizon considered, and the decision under scrutiny. Also, we have presented contribution margin as a key decision variable for firms. It is normally more useful than net profit for making many decisions. For instance, if the net profit of a product is negative, it doesn't necessarily mean that dropping the product will improve profitability. Contribution margin should be used instead to know how much profit will change by if a product is dropped.

Exercises

1. Give two examples of each of the following cost categories.

   a. Variable   b. Fixed

   c. Semivariable   d. Semifixed

2. A supplier sells an item at $200 per unit, but offers a 10 percent discount per each unit exceeding 1,000 (i.e., the 1,000-th unit costs $200, the 1,001-th costs $180).

   a. Plot the total cost for the buyer as a function of the numbers of units bought in the range $[0 - 2,000$ units].

   b. Can this cost be classified in any of the cost categories presented—variable, semivariable, fixed, semifixed?

3. Are gross margin and contribution margin the same concept? If so, why? If not, what is the difference?

4. Are the following statements true or false?

   a. COGS is made only of variable costs.

   b. SGA is made only of fixed costs.

   c. A firm fixed costs appear only above EBITDA in the income statement.

   d. The percentage of fixed costs usually increases with operations automation.

   e. The very same cost may be fixed or variable, depending on the decision under consideration.

5. At 50,000 units, a company loses $45,000. If it produced 10,000 additional units, it would do $13,000 better. Assuming the firm's costs are either variable or fixed (i.e., no semifixed costs):

   a. What is the contribution margin per unit?

   b. What is the level of fixed costs?

   c. What is the break-even point in units?

6. Single Mixers manufactures and sells a single model of kitchen mixer at $800 per unit. The firm's sales and cost figures (in thousands of dollars) for January–April 2020 are as follows:

	Jan	Feb	Mar	Apr
Number of units sold	4,200	6,700	5,000	6,000
Cost of goods sold	3,000	4,200	3,500	7,100
Operating expenses	1,000	1,450	1,000	1,250

   a. Using linear regression, calculate the fixed and variable cost portions for COGS and operating expenses.

   b. Calculate the total contribution margin at each of the four months.

7. (Exercise courtesy of Prof. María Jesús Grandes from IESE Business School.) Firm F produces five products: A, B, C, D, and E. Relevant data for all five products are as follows (figures in millions of dollars).

	A	B	C	D	E
Sales	30	40	20	10	20
Variable cost	12	8	21	8	14
Contribution margin	18	32	−1	2	6
Fixed cost type I	3	3	2	3	4
Fixed cost type II	6	8	4	2	4
Operating margin	9	21	−7	−3	−2

   There are no cross-selling effects (i.e., sales of one product do not affect sales of the other products). If a product is removed, the firm saves fixed costs of type I but not fixed costs of type II. There are no capacity constraints.

   a. If products with negative operating margins are removed, what is the total operating margin?

   b. Which products, if any, should be removed to maximize profit? Explain why.

c. If the products you suggest were removed, what would the total operating margin be?

8. Firm F manufactures and sells two products: A and B. (Exercise courtesy of Prof. María Jesús Grandes from IESE Business School.) Parameters for both products are as follows:

	A	B
Price ($ per unit)	25	35
Variable cost ($ per unit)	17	23
Fixed cost ($ per unit)	2	3
Timer required in machine M (hours per unit)	2	4

Note that fixed costs are allocated. Total fixed costs per month are $50,000. The firm manufactures and sells 10,000 units of each product per month. Sales are very stable and there are no finished goods.

a. At the end of November, a machine breakdown reduces the total number of machine hours available in December to 30,000. Since not all the demand can be satisfied, how many units of product A and product B would you produce to maximize profit? Explain why.

b. On November 30, you find a supplier able to deliver both products A and B while the machine is being repaired. Assume that the capacity of the supplier is infinite. Supplier's prices are $20 per unit of A, and $31 per unit of B. You can still make use of reduced production capacity (30,000 hours). How many units of product A and product B would you buy from the supplier in December to maximize profit? Explain why.

9. Which statement is true regarding which criterion matters when making a decision?

a. Only net margin matters, contribution doesn't.

b. Only contribution matters, net margin doesn't.

c. Either net margin or contribution matter, depending on the specific decision.

d. Both net margin and contribution matter in every decision.

10. Consulting-On-the-Go is a consulting firm that sells three types of projects: simple, long, complex. Average price at which these projects are sold to clients is $180,000, $300,000, and $350,000. Each type of project requires an expected number of hours from a pool of freelancers, whose cost can be considered variable as the firm contracts them on a per-project basis. The following table summarizes the average cost and the number of hours required per type of freelance.

	Cost	Simple	Long	Complex
Project manager	$200	40	80	200
Team leader	150	200	400	500
Senior team member	100	500	800	800
Junior team member	60	1,000	1,400	800

In addition, fixed costs for each type of project are, respectively, $30,000, $40,000, and $70,000.

1. What is the type of project that gives the highest average profit?

2. What is the most profitable type of project?

3. What would be the most profitable type of project if the project leader type were difficult to find (i.e., if the number of hours of project leaders were constrained)?

References

Bruns, William J., Jr. "Hilton Manufacturing Company." HBS Case 192-063, October 1991. (Revised October 2004).

Corbett, Thomas. 1999. *Throughput accounting*. Croton-on-Hudson, NY: North River Press.

12 Operations Investment Assessment: The Basics

Rule number 1 (to make investments): Never lose money.
Rule number 2: Never forget rule number 1.
—Warren Buffett, business magnate

12.1 Introduction

Investment is a central activity to many firms, as a firm is often the result of its previous investments. As such, investment valuation is of paramount importance. This chapter concerns itself with investment valuation. A set of tools to assess the appropriateness of potential investments will be presented. Even if the focus will mainly be on fixed assets—such as building a new factory—we will also discuss what the impact of investing on OWC—such as building up new inventory—will have on the valuation of an investment.

Valuation is a major point of concern for managers, since a firm may go bankrupt because of a single wrong decision on a major investment. The valuation process is tricky because it requires assumptions about the future and, based on those assumptions, the commitment of relatively large amounts of money upfront. A typical investment requires money today to obtain benefits in the future. Today's outlay of money is certain but future returns of money are not. Therefore, managers may want to carefully consider the key assumptions made in order to make good decisions and, in case things go wrong, to justify the decisions that led to an undesired outcome.

In operations, investment decisions typically involve putting money into fixed assets—such as building a new factory or automating a production line—or into OWC—such as increasing inventory by decentralizing distribution centers or shifting from air to sea transportation. In other realms, such as finance, investments may involve buying or selling financial products—such as bonds, shares, or derivatives—or even entire firms.

12.2 Net Present Value

Consider the following investment proposal: Invest, say, $100 today and in one year get $100 for sure. How does it seem to you? Most people would judge this investment to be unwise. Why? Well, consider the alternative of buying $100 worth of US-government bonds. These bonds are papers that compel the US government to pay you back, say, $102 in one year (the actual price depends on when you buy the bonds). We are assuming here that (a) the US-government is sure to pay, that is, the risk of the investment is zero; and (b) there are no transaction costs, namely, there are no fees to be paid when buying or selling. As the risk of the two alternatives is the same and $100 < $102, the proposed investment should be rejected in accordance with an economic criterion. In fact, any return lower than 2 percent, that is to say, $102/100-1$, should not be accepted. This threshold is usually referred to as the risk-free rate.

Likewise, any certain return above the threshold 2 percent in one year should be preferred using an economic criterion. For instance, invest $100 today and get $106 in one year is better than the US-government bond alternative, because $106 > $102. Finally, we should be indifferent between both investment choices if the return is exactly 2 percent. Therefore, we can state that, assuming no risk, $100 today is equivalent to $102 in one year. The time value of money refers to this situation: the value of money changes over time due to the alternatives available.

Assuming no risk, converting next year's money into today's money can be done by dividing next year's money by the the US-government bond yield, in our example, 2 percent. As such, $102 in one year would be equivalent to $\frac{102}{1.02} = \$100$ today. In general, if we want to convert risk-less x dollars from year 1 (i.e., one year down the road) into year 0 (today), we can divide x over $(1 + r_f)$, where r_f is the risk-free rate. The resulting value is called the present value (PV) of x:

$$\text{present value of } \$x \text{ in 1 year} = \frac{x}{1 + r_f}$$

In general, we can take the same approach to move money from year $t + 1$ to year t. We will assume that r_f is constant. Converting future money into today's money is usually referred as discounting.

 Discounting

> **Discounting** is the process of converting tomorrow's money into today's money, such that they are of the same value to a rational investor.

The yield at which we discount future money is called the discount rate.

Discount rate

Discount rate is the rate, r, at which money is discounted. For instance, r_f is a discount rate.

Likewise, if we want to move money forward by one year, we have to multiply the quantity considered by $(1 + r_f)$.

What if we want to move money from year 2 to today (year 0)? We don't know how to do it directly yet, but we can do it in two steps: first, we will move the money to year 1; second, we will move the resulting sum from year 1 to year 0. For instance, if $r_f = 2$ percent, $120 in year 2 is equivalent to $\frac{120}{1.02} \approx \$117.6$ in year 1. In turn, $117.65 in year 1 is equivalent to $\frac{117.6}{1.02} \approx \$115.3$ in year 0. Therefore, to move money directly from year 2 to year 0, we can divide the amount of money considered by the discount rate twice:

$$\text{PV of \$120 in year 2} = \frac{\frac{120}{1+0.02}}{1+0.02} = \frac{120}{(1+0.02)^2} \approx 115.3$$

Working in this fashion, we can discount money from year t to year 0 as follows:

$$\text{PV of \$x in year } t = \frac{x}{(1+r_f)^t}$$

If the time lapse is not an integer number, the expression above is still valid. For instance, to move $120 eighteen months backwards at a 2 percent discount rate, we proceed as follows:

$$\text{PV of \$120 in month 18} = \text{PV of \$120 in year 1.5} = \frac{120}{(1+0.02)^{1.5}} \approx \$116.5$$

What if there are several flows of money involved? How do we calculate the equivalent of the sum of a set of flows in today's money? We can proceed in two steps. First we discount each flow individually to year 0 and then we add the resulting flows algebraically. For instance, if the discount rate is 2 percent, the sum of a risk-less flow of $100 in year 1 and a risk-less flow of $120 in year 2 is equivalent to:

$$\text{PV of \$100 in year 1 and \$120 in year 2} = \frac{100}{1.02} + \frac{120}{1.02^2} \approx 98.0 + 115.3 = \$213.3$$

in year 0. Note that we can add the resulting flows algebraically, 98.0 and 115.3, because they are at the same point in time (year 0). However, it would be incorrect to add flows considered at different points in time because of the time value of money.

In general, for a set of risk-less flows f_t occurring in a horizon of T years we have:

PV of an array f_t in years $t, t = 1, 2, ..., t = \dfrac{f_1}{1 + r_f} + \dfrac{f_2}{(1 + r_f)^2} + ... + \dfrac{f_T}{(1 + r_f)^T}$

or, using a more compact notation:

PV of an array f_t in years $t, t = 1, 2, ..., t = \displaystyle\sum_{t=1}^{T} \dfrac{f_t}{(1 + r_f)^t}$

Present value

> **Present value** is the expected sum of all future cash inflows involved in an investment when previously converted into today's value.

What if future flows are not riskless?   So far, we have assumed that future flows are riskless, but what if the realization of future flows is uncertain? Consider the following investment:

 Exercise

Choosing between a Cash Flow or an Expected Cash Flow

You are given two options to invest your $100 today: (a) invest $100 today and obtain $106 for sure in one year; (b) invest $100 today and in one year, you have an equal chance of getting either 86 or 126.
   Should you be indifferent between the two investments?

The answer to this little dilemma depends on the risk profile of the decision maker: If she is risk-neutral she will be indifferent, given that 106 is the average between 86 and 126, However, if she is risk-prone she will prefer the second option, as *only* playing a lottery opens the door to obtain $126, a higher return. Finally, if she is risk-averse, she will prefer the certain $106.
   It turns out that the overwhelming majority of humans are risk-averse. Therefore, when evaluating future, uncertain cash flows, it makes sense to assign a relatively lower value to them as compared to riskless cash flows.
   The usual approach to reducing the value of an investment subject to uncertain flows is to increase the discount rate. For instance, in the latter example, we could have used a 10 percent discount rate for the risky flow and a mere 2 percent for the risk-less one. Thus:

PV ($106 for sure in 1 year) $= \dfrac{106}{1.02} \approx 103.9$

and

$$\text{PV (\$86 or \$126 with probability 0.5 each in 1 year)} = \frac{\frac{86+126}{2}}{1.10} \approx 96.4$$

As the discount rate in the denominator grows, the present value of the investment decreases.

In sum, when flows are risky, the discount rate should be larger and vice versa. Therefore, other things equal, the higher the risk, the higher the discount rate and the lower the value of the investment.

 Impact of risk on investments

Other things equal, the higher the risk, the higher the discount rate and the lower the value of the investment.

Calculating the discount rate when cash flows are risky is a tricky point that we will briefly touch in the next chapter.

Having argued that the discount rate is a function of the riskiness of future cash flows, we have to conclude that the discount rate should be project-specific, as each project has its own level of risk. For instance, US-government bonds should be discounted at the risk-free rate *irrespective of which firm makes the investment*, either a utilities firm—which usually undertakes low-risk investments—or a biotechnology firm—which undertakes high-risk investments. Likewise, evaluating an investment in research and development (R&D) for a new drug would require the use of a larger discount rate as the risk of such investment is higher. Therefore, investors would require a higher return for undertaking such a risk.

 Discount rate of a firm or a project?

A discount rate should be project-specific, as it depends on the risk of the project.

However, most firms or business units use the same discount rate when valuing investments. Why? The (usually implicit) assumption is that the investments typically assessed by a firm or a business unit have similar levels of risk, so it may be acceptable to use, roughly speaking, the same discount rate. But it is important to understand when this assumption is valid in order to avoid mistakes.

Finally, if we consider the initial money invested, that is f_0, which is an outlay, we can define the net present value (NPV) of a (possibly risky) investment as:

$$\text{NPV of cash flows } f_t \text{ occurring at time } t = f_0 + \frac{f_1}{1+r} + \cdots + \frac{f_T}{(1+r)^T} = \sum_{t=0}^{T} \frac{f_t}{(1+r)^t}$$

	A	B	C	D
1				
2		r	10%	
3		f_0	-100	
4		f_1	50	
5		f_2	50	
6		f_3	50	
7		NPV	$24.3	=C3+NPV(C2,C4:C6)

Figure 12.1
MS Excel function to calculate net present value. The initial flow, f_0, has to be added to the function NPV, which depends on the remaining cash flows $f_1, f_2, \ldots, f_T$.

where the last equality is justified by the fact that f_0 can be written as $\frac{f_0}{(1+r)^0}$

 Net present value

> **Net present value** is the difference between the present value of expected cash *inflows* and the present value of expected cash *outflows* over a period of time. Mathematically:
>
> $$\text{NPV of } \textit{expected} \text{ cash flows } f_t \text{ occurring at time } t = \sum_{t=0}^{T} \frac{f_t}{(1+r)^t}$$

The use of NPV is so generalized that MS Excel has a specific function (called NPV) to compute it. It requires two arguments, namely the discount rate and the array of cash flows to discount. Figure 12.1 illustrates its use for an investment of $100 that gives expected cash flows of $50 in years 1 to 3 when the discount rate is 10 percent. Oddly enough, the arguments of the NPV function do *not* include the initial cash flow, f_0, which has to be added to obtain the actual net present value.

A nice property of NPV is that it tells how much value is expected to be created—or destroyed—if the investment is made. For instance, in the latter example, an expected cash flow of $106 (either $86 or $126 with probability $\frac{1}{2}$ each) in one year will reward the initial $100 investment. Assuming a discount rate of 10 percent, the net present value of the investment is

$$\text{NPV} = -100 + \frac{106}{1+0.1} \approx -\$3.7 < 0$$

suggesting that $3.7 worth of value for shareholders is expected to be destroyed if the investment is undertaken.

A not-so-nice property of NPV is that it is very sensitive to the value chosen for the discount rate, therefore a small change in the discount rate may lead to a large change of NPV. Given the difficulty of calculating or estimating the discount rate, there is usually uncertainty on the accuracy of the NPV calculated. Section 13.4 explains how to deal with this issue.

12.2.1 Example: Calculating Net Present Value

Having presented the basics of net present value calculations, we will make now make use of one example to illustrate how to take advantage of net present value in practice.

 Exercise

Calculating Net Present Value in Practice

Automato Inc. is considering acquiring new manufacturing equipment to produce parts for an original equipment manufacturer (OEM) in the automotive industry under a contract that will expire in five years. After that time, the equipment will be sold. Corporate tax rate is 30 percent and discount rate is 15 percent. Given the information provided:

1. A consulting firm was paid $20,000 to estimate the impact of buying the equipment for the five-year contract.
2. The cost of the equipment is $400,000, half of which will be paid cash and half in one year.
3. Depreciation period is eight years.
4. The market value of the equipment after five years has been estimated to be 40 percent of the acquisition cost.
5. If the equipment is bought, four workers whose actual cost is $35,000 per worker per year will be fired. Firing cost is $10,000 per worker.
6. Given the lack of flexibility of the new equipment, additional inventory—worth $25,000—will be needed during the life of the project.

Note that sales will be identical in either scenario.
   Should the new equipment be acquired in accordance with an economic criterion?

We will go through the six items above to study their impact on cash flows, then we will calculate the NPV of the investment.

Item 1

A consulting firm was paid $20,000 to estimate the impact of buying the equipment for the five-year contract.

We will argue that this piece of information is irrelevant as far as the NPV of the investment is concerned. A key point to bear in mind is that only differential cash flows are relevant. In this context, a cash flow is differential (or incremental) when it is realized in *only one* of the two branches that leave from the decision square in a decision tree (figure 12.3). In this case, the consulting firm already got its money because of a decision made in the past. Past decisions entail cash flows that are never differential. In other words, if the machine is bought, $20,000 will have been paid to the consulting firm; if the machine is not bought, $20,000 will have been paid to the consulting firm as well. Cash flow commitments deriving from past decisions are usually referred to as sunk costs.

 Sunk cost

A **sunk cost** is a cost already incurred as a consequence of a previous decision.

 Impact of sunk costs on net present value

Sunk costs are irrelevant as far as net present value calculations are concerned.

 Item 2

The cost of the equipment is $400,000—half of which will be paid cash and half in one year.

Given the payments scheduled, a negative cash flow of −$200,000 should be considered today (say end of year 0) and additional −$200,000 at the end of year 1 (table 12.1).

Item 3

Depreciation period is eight years.

Table 12.1
Relevant cash flows after item 2 (in $'000).

Category	\multicolumn{6}{c}{Cash flow at the end of year}
	0	1	2	3	4	5
Equipment cost	−200	−200				

Table 12.2
Relevant cash flows after item 3 (in $'000).

Category	Cash flow at the end of year					
	0	1	2	3	4	5
Equipment cost	−200	−200				
Depreciation tax shield		15	15	15	15	15

This piece of information may seem irrelevant as well, as depreciation is not a cash flow. However, depreciation has an indirect impact on cash flows through taxes. To understand why, consider the amount depreciated each year, namely $\$400,000/8 = \$50,000$. As depreciation is a period's expense, it reduces profit before taxes, reducing taxes as well. As an example, say that the profit before taxes if the machine is not bought is $800,000. Taxes due would be 30 percent $\cdot$ $800,000 = $240,000. If the machine is bought, profit before taxes would be $800,000 − $50,000 = $750,000 and taxes due is 30 percent $\cdot$ $750,000 = $225,000. The difference in the taxes paid between the two scenarios is $240,000 − $225,000 = $15,000 (table 12.2).

A more straightforward way to calculate the same amount would be to multiply the amount depreciated times the tax rate, that is to say, $50,000 $\cdot$ 30 percent = $15,000. Since not paying $15,000 in taxes every year is equivalent to receiving the same amount annually from the government, a positive cash flow of $15,000 should be considered every year starting at the end of year 1.

Item 4

The market value of the equipment after five years has been estimated to be 40 percent of the acquisition cost.

An acceptable assumption would be that the equipment will be sold at its market value after five years. If this is the case, a positive cash flow of 40 percent $\cdot$ $400,000 = $160,000 will occur in year 5. Furthermore, an additional cash flow due to the impact of taxes will also take place. Indeed, the book value of the equipment at the end of year 5 will be:

$$\text{book value at the end of year 5} = \$400,000 - 5 \cdot \frac{\$400,000}{8} = \$150,000$$

Since the equipment will be sold at $160,000, the difference between book and market values will create $10,000 worth of additional happiness for shareholders, which should be taxed. In other words, profit before taxes will increase by $10,000 increasing taxes by 30 percent $\cdot$ $10,000, or $3,000. Therefore, the net cash flow at the end of year 5 due to the sale of the equipment will be: $160,000 − $3,000 = $157,000 (table 12.3).

Table 12.3
Relevant cash flows after item 4 (in $'000).

Category	Cash flow at the end of year					
	0	1	2	3	4	5
Equipment cost	−200	−200				
Depreciation tax shield		15	15	15	15	15
Equipment residual value						157

? Item 5

> If the equipment is bought, four workers whose actual cost is $35,000 per worker per year will be fired. Firing cost is $10,000 per worker.

If the tax rate were zero, not paying four workers' salaries for five years is equivalent to receiving $35,000 \cdot 4 = \$140,000$ every year. Since the tax rate is 30 percent, the latter amount will be taxed as profit before taxes will increase by that amount. The resulting cash flows will be $\$140,000 − 30\% \cdot \$140,000 = \$140,000\,(1 − 0.3) = \$98,000$ per year.

Similarly, an outlay of $28,000 (that is, $4 \cdot \$10,000(1 − 0.3)$) has to be considered today to take care of the firing cost (table 12.4).

Table 12.4
Relevant cash flows after item 5 (in $'000).

Category	Cash flow at the end of year					
	0	1	2	3	4	5
Equipment	−200	−200				
Depreciation tax shield		15	15	15	15	15
Equipment residual value						157
Dismissed workers	−28	98	98	98	98	98

? Item 6

> Given the lack of flexibility of the new equipment, additional inventory ($25,000) will be needed during the life of the project.

Again, inventory is a stock, so is this information relevant when computing the NPV, which is a sum of flows? The answer is in the affirmative. To see why, let us first plot the evolution of inventory needed over time.

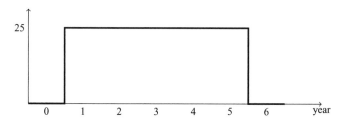

Figure 12.2
Incremental inventory level over time during the five-year contract if the equipment is bought.

Table 12.5
Relevant cash flows after item 6 (in $'000).

Category	Cash flow at the end of year					
	0	1	2	3	4	5
Equipment	−200	−200				
Depreciation tax shield		15	15	15	15	15
Equipment residual value						157
Dismissed workers	−28	98	98	98	98	98
Changing inventory level	−25					25

Note in figure 12.2 that the inventory stock level changes twice. Whenever a stock changes, there should be a cash flow involved. For instance, when inventory increases in year 0, there is a cash flow from the firm to the supplier, so we have to consider a negative cash flow of $25,000 in year 0. Likewise, a decreasing inventory level is equivalent to a positive cash flow, in this case, $25,000 in year 5 (table 12.5).

Recall that inventory is part of OWC. Therefore, we can generalize our inventory example to state that an increase (decrease) of OWC is equivalent to a negative (positive) cash flow.

[**The connection between OWC and cash flows (again!)**

An increase (decrease) of OWC is equivalent to a negative (positive) cash flow.]

Once we have identified all relevant cash flows, we can add them up by columns to obtain the last row in table 12.6.

The last step involves discounting each cash flow such that it becomes equivalent to a cash flow in year 0. To do so, we divide each cash flow by a factor $(1 + r)^t$, where r is the

Table 12.6
Sum of total relevant cash flows (in $'000).

Category	Cash flow at the end of year					
	0	1	2	3	4	5
Equipment	−200	−200				
Depreciation tax shield		15	15	15	15	15
Equipment residual value						157
Dismissed workers	−28	98	98	98	98	98
Changing inventory level	−25					25
Total	−253	−87	113	113	113	295

Table 12.7
Sum of total discounted relevant cash flows (in $'000).

Category	Cash flow at the end of year					
	0	1	2	3	4	5
Equipment	−200	−200				
Depreciation tax shield		15	15	15	15	15
Equipment residual value						157
Dismissed workers	−28	98	98	98	98	98
Changing inventory level	−25					25
Total	−253	−87	113	113	113	295
Factor	1.15^0	1.15^1	1.15^2	1.15^3	1.15^4	1.15^5
Equivalent cash flow in year 0	−253	−76	85	74	65	147

discount rate (15 percent) and t is the time in years (table 12.7). Alternatively, MS Excel NPV function can be used: assuming cash flows $f_0, ..., f_5$ are in cells B8, ..., H8, we have: NPV(0.15, C8:H8) + B8 = $42,000.

The equivalent cash flows in the last row can be added algebraically to obtain the NPV of the investment, which turns out to be $42,000. Since this is a positive figure according to an economic criterion, the equipment should be bought, as value is expected to be created for shareholders if the proposed investment is undertaken.

 Applying the net present value criterion

If net present value is positive, the investment should be undertaken in accordance with an economic criterion, and vice versa.

Some take-aways and important considerations regarding NPV emerge from this example:

Only nondebt-related cash flows must be considered In other words, the NPV calculations are not themselves concerned with the source of funds to pay for the investment. The funds may have come from the cash account of the firm or from a new long-term loan from a bank. In both cases, there is a cost involved. If the money came from cash, there is an opportunity cost, as the money could have been used for something else. If the money came from a bank, some money should have been paid to the bank as interest. In either case, a portion of the money invested came from shareholders, and such money could have been invested somewhere else instead. The cost of all these alternative uses of funds is captured by the discount rate in the denominator, thus cash flows in the numerator should not include any cash flows related to debt—such as interest payments or debt repayments—or equity—such as dividends.

Only differential cash flows are relevant Differential cash flows are those payments incurred—or avoided—if *and only if* the investment is undertaken. In particular, sunk costs, such as the money paid to the consulting firm, are irrelevant, as they are incurred irrespective of whether the investment is made. To figure out if a cash flow is differential, it is helpful to consider a decision tree with two branches, such as the one shown in figure 12.3.

The upper branch corresponds to the investment decision, while the lower branch correspond to the noninvestment decision. Cash flows that show up on either one of the branches are differential, while those who appear in both are not.

> **Only differential cash flows are relevant**
> When calculating the net present value of an investment, only differential cash flows—those incurred *only if* the investment is made—are relevant.

Expected cash flows must be used Instead of optimistic or pessimistic estimates, expected cash flows must be used. Future cash flows are uncertain by definition. When a manager says that next year's sales will be 100, she most likely has in mind that sales will follow

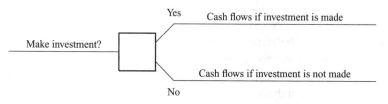

Figure 12.3
A simple investment decision tree (the square on the left represents a decision to make by the decision maker).

a certain probability distribution whose mean is 100. Whether NPV, which is based on expected cash flows, is a valid measure to make decisions is the subject of section 13.3, but the point here is that future cash flows used in NPV analysis should neither be optimistic nor pessimistic. Some managers tend to think that, given that an investment is risky, they should be cautious and use pessimistic figures for future cash flows. This is not correct: as discussed, riskiness is captured by the discount rate in the denominator, so reducing also the magnitude of the cash flows in the numerator is really double counting. Similarly, there are managers that are overly optimistic or are biased because they really want to go ahead with the investment for whatever reasons. Needless to say, optimism in the planning phase of a project may lead to subsequent frustration and regret.

 Investment risk should be captured only once

The investment risk must be captured by the discount rate only. No pessimistic cash flows estimates should be made in addition to adjusting the discount rate for risk.

Corporate taxes are cash flows As such, they should be accounted for in NPV calculations. To check if taxes are relevant, ask yourself if the piece of information you are considering has an impact on the income statement. If so, taxes owed will change and will therefore be relevant. Of course, there may be cases where the tax rate is zero, or the tax rate may not be linear but step-wise, or even negative if a firm has declared losses in the current or previous periods. All these circumstances should be considered and the marginal tax rate (not the average) should be used when computing an investment NPV. In general, from an economic point of view, for a profitable firm that pays taxes on a regular basis, taxes make good news worse and bad news better.

 Taxes flatten both good and bad news

Corporate taxes make good news worse and bad news better.

Discrete discounting is typically used This is done for the sake of simplicity, with periods lasting a year. All flows occurring within a given year are supposed to occur at the end of the current or previous year. For instance, sales (and associated cash flows) may occur evenly during the year, but are usually assumed to collapse into a single big sale on December 31. Likewise, payments of taxes may be deferred until the following year but again are assumed to occur on December 31. Of course, more precision can be achieved by using shorter time buckets, such as quarters or months, or even continuous discount (i.e., zero-length buckets), but all that may lead to analysis paralysis.

Changes in operating working capital (OWC) are cash flows This statement stems from the fact that OWC is a stock, and for a stock to change, a flow is needed. Also note that OWC changes do not have an impact on corporate taxes, as changing OWC does not necessarily have an impact on the income statement. For instance, if inventory is acquired using financial debt (say from a line of credit), OWC will increase as inventory does, and debt will increase as well, but the revenue and expenses account (hence the income statement) will remain untouched.

12.3   Internal Rate of Return (IRR)

A close relative of NPV is the internal rate of return, or IRR for short. It is defined as the discount rate such that NPV is zero. Therefore it solves the equation:

$$\text{NPV}(r) = 0 \Rightarrow \sum_{t=0}^{T} \frac{f_t}{(1+r)^t} = 0 \text{ , or, multiplying by } (1+r)^T: \sum_{t=0}^{T} f_t(1+r)^{T-t} = 0$$

where r, the discount rate, is the unknown.

 Internal rate of return

> The **internal rate of return** is the discount rate that makes the net present value of an investment zero. Mathematically, it is the discount rate, r, that solves:
>
> $$\text{NPV}(r) = 0$$

As the last expression reveals, the equation to solve to find IRR is a polynomial of degree T, thus it may have up to T different solutions. In practice, only one (two at most in rare cases) makes economic sense. As finding the roots of a T-degree polynomial analytically is not easy—sometimes impossible—we will find the solution numerically making use of MS Excel function IRR. The function requires two arguments: the stream of cash flows (this time from $t=0$ in contrast to NPV) and an initial estimate of the solution from which to start the numerical search. The next example illustrates how to do it.

 Exercise

Calculating a Project's Internal Rate of Return

A simple project requires investing $100,000 today and yields expected returns of $50,000 in years 1, 2, and 3. If the discount rate of the project is 10 percent:
Should the project be undertaken in accordance to its internal rate of return?

	A	B	C	D
1				
2				
3		f_0	−100	
4		f_1	50	
5		f_2	50	
6		f_3	50	
7		IRR	23%	= IRR(C3:C6,0.15)

Figure 12.4
MS Excel function to calculate the internal rate of return. The second parameter value of the IRR function (0.15 or 15 percent) tells MS Excel where to start the numerical search of the solution.

Much like NPV, IRR can be used to determine whether the investment is sound in accordance with an economic criterion. If IRR is larger than the project discount rate, then NPV is positive, and the investment should be made. Likewise, If IRR is smaller than the project discount rate, then NPV is negative, and the investment should not be made. The IRR of the project proposed is the discount rate that solves:

$$-100 + \frac{50}{1+r} + \frac{50}{(1+r)^2} + \frac{50}{(1+r)^3} = 0$$

As figure 12.4 shows, the IRR of the project is 23 percent. As this number is larger than the project discount rate, 10 percent, then the investment should be made.

Applying the internal rate of return criterion
If the internal rate of return is larger than the investment discount rate, the investment should be undertaken in accordance with an economic criterion, and vice versa.

The main advantage of using IRR as a criterion for decision making is that computing it doesn't require estimating the discount rate, which for some investment types might be hard to do. The main disadvantage is that it only gives a yes/no type of answer, without quantifying value creation, as NPV does. NPV and IRR can be used together to assess the expected economic impact of an investment, as they provide complementary information. When used properly, NPV and IRR give the same answer to the question of whether an investment should be made. The dichotomy that some present, in which one method is more valid than the other, is simply nonexistent.

12.4   Selecting the Best Project

This section shows how to select a project when facing several mutually exclusive projects. The answer is easy in principle—select the one with the highest NPV—but the question hides some nuances that are worth addressing. We will start with one example.

 Exercise

OMG Inc.

OMG Inc.'s COO has to give his thumbs-up to one of three projects based on three existing technologies, A, B, and C. The technologies are identical in terms of initial investment—$3,456,000 in all three cases—and risk, but differ on the respective expected future cash flows they bring, as show in the following table (cash flows in thousands).

Project	$t=0$	$t=1$	$t=2$	$t=3$
A	−3,456	0	0	6,543
B	−3,456	1,849	1,849	1,849
C	−3,456	849	1,849	3,456

Given that the total amount to invest is set to $3,456,000 (that is, only one project can be undertaken), which project should be chosen?

The main difficulty the COO of OMG Inc. faces is that he doesn't know which discount rate to use to calculate the NPV of each project. He decides to plot NPV as a function of discount rate for each project (figure 12.5).

The graph reveals something very interesting: depending on the discount rate, any of the projects can be the best. Indeed, if the discount rate is (roughly) below 11 percent, project A has the highest NPV, then C, then B. However, if the discount rate is between 11 percent and (roughly) 27 percent, then project C is preferred, as it has the highest NPV. Finally, when the discount rate is above 27 percent, project B is the best.

Also, the fact that the IRRs of projects B and C are higher than the IRR of project A doesn't imply that the former are better. This illustrates that IRR should not be used to compare mutually exclusive projects. This is sometimes a point of confusion: recall that IRR only indicates where NPV is zero, but it does *not* quantify the degree of appropriateness of a project (only NPV does so).

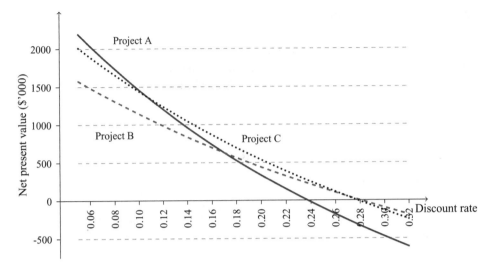

Figure 12.5
NPV as a function of the discount rate for the three competing projects, A, B, and C.

 On the use of IRR to compare projects

That project A's IRR is larger than project B's IRR does *not* imply that project A is better than project B in accordance with an economic criterion.

Therefore, OMG's COO should discuss with the CFO to come up with an estimate of the discount rate. If the discount rate is 11 percent or less, project A should be chosen; if it is between 11 percent and 27 percent, project C should be chosen; otherwise, none of the projects are interesting as all three NPVs are negative for any discount rate higher than 28 percent. Close to the cut-off points, the COO should be indifferent between the two competing projects in accordance with the economic criterion: other noneconomic criteria may be used to make the final decision.

12.5   Other Methods to Value Investments

There is a plethora of criteria that firms use to select projects, such as payback period, economic value added, return on capital employed or accounting rate of return, profitability index, and more. We will briefly comment on the first two criteria and refer the interested reader to Northcott (1998), which discusses several of these methods in detail.

12.5.1 Payback Period

A popular selection method within firms is the payback period criterion. This method asks how long it takes to recover the initial investment. If the time is shorter than a given threshold, the project is accepted; otherwise it is not.

Exercise

OMG Inc.'s Project C Revisited

Given the cash flows involved in OMG Inc.'s project C, if the maximum payback period to accept making an investment is two years:
    Should project C be undertaken?

The cash flows involved are the initial outflow at $-\$3,456,000$ and expected annual cash flows starting at $t=1$ at \$849,000; \$1,849,000; and \$3,456,000. Cumulative annual cash flows starting at $t=1$ are consequently \$849,000; \$2,698,000; and \$6,154,000. Given that the accumulated money earned after two years is lower than the initial outlay ($\$2,698,000 <$ $\$3,456,000$), it follows that the payback period is larger than two years, and the project should not be accepted.

The two main drawbacks of this method are that cash flows are not discounted, and all cash flows expect to occur after the threshold are irrelevant for the valuation of he investment. The main advantages are that calculations are fairly easy and that an estimate of the discount rate is not needed.

12.5.2 Economic Value Added (EVA)

The economic value added (EVA) is an expression that combines book and market values. Formally, EVA is defined as:

$$EVA_t = NOPAT_t - (E_{t-1}^b + D_{t-1}^b) \cdot WACC$$

where NOPAT is the net operating profit after taxes (see section 9.2.3.2), E^b and D^b are, respectively, the values of equity and debt of the firm evaluated at book value, and WACC is the weighted average cost of capital of the firm (to be presented in section 13.2).

Note that EVA is *not* a cash flow but a mix of accounting and market parameters: NOPAT, E, and D are given at book value, but WACC is computed at market value. Subscripts indicate the period at which each variable should be calculated. For instance, at $t=1$, we can write:

$$EVA_1 = NOPAT_1 - (E_0^b + D_0^b) \cdot WACC$$

which shows that the value of EVA in period 1 (say, year 1) will be the NOPAT of period 1 less the money invested in year 0 (today) times the cost of capital of the firm.

To analyze the economic impact of a decision, the stream $EVA_t, t = 1, 2, \ldots$ should be discounted at the WACC to obtain the so-called market value added (MVA), namely, the net present value of all EVAs. A key point is that EVA does not measure value creation, but MVA does (see Fernández 2002 section 14.7, for details).

 EVA and value creation

EVA (economic value added) does *not* measure value creation, MVA (market value added, the net present value of EVAs) does.

12.6   Summary

This chapter has presented the basics of investment valuation, a topic of great importance for managers in operations and supply chain management. Net present value (NPV) is the most important tool to value investments, as it tells how much value is expected to be created or destroyed if the investment is made. NPV is a function of the expected cash flows involved in the investment as well as the discount rate, which measures the risk of the investment. Riskier investments should be evaluated at a higher discount rate.

Calculating the net present value of an investment in operations is not always an easy task, as it presents several issues that should be kept in mind: First, sunk costs should not be considered as they are not differential, and only differential costs should be considered. Second, the risk of the investment should be captured only once by the discount rate. Also, corporate taxes are relevant, as any changes in revenues or expenses will modify the amount of taxes to be paid. Finally, changes in operating working capital have also an impact on NPV, as those changes are effectively cash flows.

Other investment tools exist, such as the internal rate of return (IRR), the payback period, or the EVA. Of these, IRR and discounted EVA (MVA) are always aligned with NPV, in that all three give the same answer given a proposed investment. However, IRR gives only a qualitative answer (yes/no) and therefore can only complement, not substitute NPV.

Additional points regarding investment valuation are addressed in the next chapter.

Exercises

1. A project requiring an initial outlay of $2,200,000 at $t = 0$ is expected to provide the following array of annual cash flows starting at $t = 2$: $400,000, $600,000, $800,000, $1,000,000. Using a discount rate of 12 percent,

   a. Calculate the net present value of the project using a calculator.

   b. Calculate the net present value of the project using a spreadsheet. Check that you got the same result as with the calculator.

c. Without performing any additional calculations, is the IRR of the project larger or smaller than 12 percent?

2. An experimental plant investment plan to generate electricity based on kryptonite requires investing $100 million at $t = 0$ and is expected to generate positive cash flows of $12 million for 25 consecutive years starting at $t = 1$. In year 25, an additional outflow of $-\$220$ million is considered, as it will be very costly to dismantle the plant, taking care of radioactive contaminated materials.

a. Plot in a graph the NPV of the investment as a function of the discount rate.

b. In accordance with an economic criterion, for which range of discount rates does this investment make sense?

c. Would you invest in such an investment plan?

3. Show that the NPV of a perpetuity of f dollars per year (that is, obtaining a cash flow of f dollars at the end of years $1, 2, 3, \ldots$ for ever) is f/r, where r is the discount rate. (Hint: use an expression for the sum of a geometric series.)

4. An investment of c dollars generates an annual return of r. If the generated returns become part of the investment:

a. How many dollars will be available after n years?

b. How many years are needed to double the initial investment if $r = 10$ percent?

5. If the discount rate in exercise Automato Inc. in section 12.2.1 had been 18 percent, the resulting NPV would have been $10,000. Given that the cost of the study made by the consulting firm was $20,000, it seems that the total value of the project would have been negative. Under such circumstances, should the equipment have been acquired?

6. Given two investments, A and B, with identical expected NPV, but different IRR—say $IRR_A > IRR_B$, which project should be chosen in accordance with an economic criterion? Are there any circumstances under which project B should be preferred?

7. Consider the following mutually exclusive projects:

Period	Project 1	Project 2	Project 3
0	−6,800	−6,800	−6,800
1	0	3,740	2,040
2	0	3,740	3,400
3	12,920	3,740	6,568

Amounts are expressed in thousands of dollars and correspond to the cash flows expected to occur at the end of each period. Period 0 is today, period 1 is one year from today, and so on.

a. Which project should be undertaken according to their payback period?

b. Which project should be undertaken according to their NPV if the discount rate is 10 percent?

c. Which project should be undertaken according to their NPV if the discount rate is 15 percent?

d. Which project has the highest IRR?

8. For each project in the previous question, rank the projects according to their NPV as a function of the discount rate.

9. Consider the following expected cash flows from a project:

Period	Cash flows
0	−3,740
1	5,950
2	6,800
3	−10,710

    a. What is the IRR of the project?

    b. Plot the NPV of the project as a function of the discount rate.

10. Consider the following expected cash flows from a project:

Period	Project A	Project B
0	−680	−360
1	425	238
2	510	280

    a. What is the IRR of each project?

    b. If the discount rate is 10 percent, explain why the best project is not the one with the highest IRR.

11. Consider the following expected cash flows from a project:

Period	Project C
0	−320
1	32
2	352

    a. Calculate NPV if discount rate is 10 percent.

    b. Give the reason why you got precisely that result.

12. Consider the following expected cash flows from these projects:

Period	Project A	Project D
0	−680	−680
1	425	270
2	510	632

a. What is the NPV of each project if discount rate is 10 percent?

b. Note that the cash flows from project D are the sum of the cash flows from projects B and C in exercises 10 and 11, and that the NPV of project D is the same as the NPV of project B in exercise 10. Is the latter fact a coincidence? Explain why or why not.

13. Consider the following expected cash flows from these projects:

Period	Project A	Project B
0	−600	−720
1	200	450
2	200	220
3	200	200
4	200	130

a. What is the NPV of each project if discount rate is 10 percent?

b. What is the IRR of each project?

c. Which project/s should be undertaken if the projects are mutually exclusive?

d. Which project/s should be undertaken if the projects are not mutually exclusive?

14. A firm has a capital budget of $111,000 and is considering three potential independent projects: Project A requires investing $44,400 today and yields $15,840 per year for five consecutive years. Project B requires investing $37,000 today and yields $15,481 per year for five consecutive years. Project C requires investing $62,900 today and yields $21,467 per year for ten consecutive years. Money not allocated to the projects can be placed in a bank deposit that gives 15 percent per year.

a. Identify the six combinations of project investments such that the budget is exhausted.

b. Which of the six combinations should the firm choose if the discount rate is:

    1. 15 percent   2. 20 percent

15. If a new project is undertaken, the following items of the balance sheet are expected to change *due to the project* as follows (thousands of dollars):

	Year 1	Year 2	Year 3	Year 4
Accounts receivable	0	290	460	380
Accounts payable	140	280	240	200
Inventory	50	200	400	−100
Minimum cash	0	290	460	380

For instance, in year 3 accounts receivable are expected to be $460,000 larger than today.

a. What is the incremental level of OWC at the end of each year?

b. What is the economic impact of these changes of OWC on the NPV of the project?

16. Siddharth Srivastava, cofounder of Zip Delivery, a B2B bike delivery marketplace in India, is considering investing in a new promotion program to accelerate sales in a particular region.

    The current revenue in the region is 400,000 and is expected to decline 8 percent per year, starting next year. Siddharth is considering a promotion program that costs half a million today and is expected to increase revenue to 600,000 for each of the next two years, followed by a decline of 30 percent per year.

    a. Identify the relevant cash flows that should be evaluated when deciding on making the promotion investment. Ignore taxes and inflation.

    b. Assuming a eight-year horizon, what is the IRR of the investment?

17. You are negotiating with a customer the sale of some equipment whose worth today is $6m. The customer offers to pay 10 percent cash today and make five identical payments x, in the next five years. If your discount rate is 12 percent, what is the value of x that makes you indifferent in accordance with NPV?

18. Given a discount rate of 20 percent, calculate the NPV of the following stream of cash flows starting today: -800, 600, 500.

19. Consider a situation where you have $847 in your pocket that you can invest at a rate of 20 percent. You are required to make a payment of $600 at time $t = 1$ and another $500 at $t = 2$. You decide to spend $47 in a nice restaurant today and invest the rest of the money.

    a. Will you be able to afford the required payments in $t = 1$ and $t = 2$?

    b. Compare your answers to a. and to the previous exercise.

    c. Reflect on the fact that NPV can be defined as the expected value created (today!) for investors.

20. For a discount rate of 10 percent, consider the following two mutually exclusive projects (Adapted from Higgins 2012):

    • Building a steel bridge with initial cost $200,000, annual maintenance expenses $5,000, and useful life of forty years, or:

    • Building a wooden bridge with initial cost $100,000, annual maintenance expenses $10,000, and useful life of ten years.

    a. Which option is preferable from an economic point of view?

    b. Now assume that the firm believes it will need a bridge for twenty years. The company also believes that reconstructing the wooden bridge at the end of ten years would cost $150,000 (due to inflation). Finally, the company estimates that the salvage value of the steel bridge in twenty years will be $90,000. How does this information affect your choice? (Problem adapted from Higgins 2012.)

21. (Adapted from Higgins 2012) Consider the expected cash flows of projects A and B:

Period	Project A	Project B
0	-600	$-1,200$
1	200	400
2	200	400
3	200	400
4	200	400

a. Find the NPV and IRR of each project.

b. What conclusions can you draw in light of the results you obtained?

References

Fernández, Pablo. 2002. *Valuation methods and shareholder value creation.* San Diego, CA: Elsevier Science.

Higgins, Robert C. 2012. *Analysis for financial management*, 10th ed. New York: McGraw-Hill.

Northcott, Deryll. 1998. *Capital investment decision-making*. London: Thomson.

13 Operations Investment Assessment: Some Refinements

Wealth is not about having a lot of money; it's about having a lot of options.
—Chris Rock, comedian

13.1 Introduction

This chapter extends the analysis presented in chapter 12 to discuss additional topics regarding NPV as a decision tool. First, some ideas on how firms calculate discount rates are presented. Then, the appropriateness of NPV is discussed; when NPV is not adequate, an approach based on Monte Carlo simulation is described. The following section goes one step beyond and presents the topic of real options. Sometimes investment decisions are not made at once, but subdecisions can be made over time. Real options enrich the investment valuation process by considering management's discretion to mitigate risk and take advantage of solved uncertainties. While real options can provide additional insights to managers regarding alternative actions in the course of an investment, their valuation can be quite intricate in practice. Some reflections are presented to guide the investment decision process when there are aspects that can be neither calculated nor estimated. The chapter closes with a case study where an operations investment has to be made, and three methodologies are presented: one from the operations area and two from the financial area. The case encourages readers to penetrate the involved relationship between the operations and financial spheres using the tools learned in these two chapters as well as standard operations tools.

13.2 Estimating the Discount Rate

As a manager in operations or supply chain management, you will not have to come up with a discount rate yourself. Someone from the finance department will provide you with such information. Despite that, in this section we give some guidance of how to calculate the discount rate for you to have an idea of what you can expect from your finance peers.

Theoretically speaking, the discount rate for an investment is the required return of the best available alternative having the same risk as the investment under consideration.

Admittedly, given the definition, finding the discount rate is not an easy task. Maybe that is why many firms, from small to large corporations, use a single, constant discount rate for every investment *irrespective of the risk of the investment*. Although this is not correct, it is an extended practice. Some candidates for such a single discount rate include the WACC and the marginal cost of debt, which we will discuss next.

13.2.1 The Weighted Average Cost of Capital (WACC)

The WACC, also known as the cost of capital of the firm, is a weighted average of the required return from rational shareholders, r_e, and the cost of debt after taxes, $r_d(1-t)$, where t is the tax rate (e.g., 25 percent). The weights used to calculate the average rate are $\frac{E}{D+E}$ and $\frac{D}{D+E}$ respectively, where E and D are the market value of equity and debt. Formally:

$$\text{WACC} = \frac{E}{D+E}r_e + \frac{D}{E+D}r_d(1-t)$$

Although the definition is a bit involved, the idea behind the WACC is not: simply speaking, money comes at a cost and WACC captures this cost.

When calculating the WACC, r_e is usually the trickiest parameter to estimate. Sometimes firms use the CAPM model to estimate r_e. This model includes a constant parameter that links the firm returns with the market returns and is difficult to estimate in practice. There are tabulated values for it, which depend on the industry, the size of the firm, and the countries in which the investment will be made. The WACC and the firm's capital structure (i.e., the proportion debt/equity) are at the cornerstone of modern finance, but dealing with these is outside the scope of the book. Further information about the CAPM and the WACC can be found in Brealey, Myers, and Allen (2011).

 Weighted average cost of capital (WACC)

The **WACC** of a firm is a measure of the cost of capital of the firm. It is a weighted average rate between the cost of equity and the cost of debt after taxes.

The main issue with using the WACC of the firm to discount investment cash flows is that the WACC doesn't account for the risks of specific projects. Still, using the WACC might be a good approximation if investments made by the firm are relatively small—so that the capital structure of the firm doesn't change much—and bear a risk similar to most project undertaken by the firm.

13.2.2   The Marginal Cost of Debt

The marginal cost of debt is the cost of new (financial) debt taken by a firm. It may not be the same as the average cost of debt, as the the cost of debt usually increases with the amount of outstanding debt. For instance, a firm may have outstanding debt at \$400,000 whose cost is 6 percent. The firm asks its bank how much it would cost an additional loan of \$100,000. The bank would charge, say, 8 percent. The average cost of debt would be:

$$\frac{400 \cdot 6 + 100 \cdot 8}{400 + 100} = 6.4\%$$

while the marginal cost of debt would be 8 percent.

The issue with using this discounting rate is that it is oblivious to the fact that capital to make investments is provided not only by banks but also shareholders; and rational shareholders ask for larger returns than banks as they bear more risk. Therefore the marginal cost of debt underestimates the discount rate, hence overestimates the value of investments.

13.3   Is NPV Always a Valid Quantitative Measure?

As mentioned in the previous chapter, NPV depends on expected cash flows. A key question is if using NPV is a plausible criterion to make decisions regarding investments. Before answering that question, we propose you to play four very simple consecutive games.

 Exercise

Game #1 Including a Simple Lottery

You are given a choice between two alternatives: either obtaining \$100 for sure now or playing a lottery, where a fair coin is tossed; if it is heads, you obtain \$210 now, if it is tails, you get nothing. Which alternative do you prefer?

The decision tree shown in figure 13.1 illustrates the choices you have in this first game.

If you prefer the branch of the decision tree that gives you the highest NPV, you should choose playing the lottery. Indeed, the NPV of playing the lottery is $0.5 \cdot \$210 + 0.5 \cdot \$0$, or \$105, which is larger than \$100. However, a surprisingly high number of people would prefer \$100 for sure despite that its NPV is lower. As most people are risk-averse, they prefer certain outcomes rather than risky ones even if the NPV of the former is lower.

If you are in the smaller group that still prefer playing the lottery because it has a larger NPV, consider the options you are given in the second game.

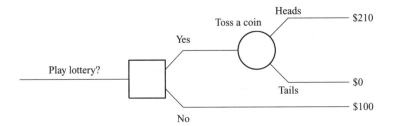

Figure 13.1
Decision tree for game 1 (the circle represents a decision made not by the decision maker but someone else; in this case mother nature—as the outcome of tossing a coin is random).

> **Exercise**
>
> ### Game #2 Including a Tricky Lottery
>
> Now you have to choose between these two alternatives: either obtaining $1 million (that is, one million US dollars) for sure now or playing a lottery, where a fair coin is tossed; if it is heads, you obtain $2.1 million now, if it is tails, you get nothing. Which alternative do you prefer?

Figure 13.2 shows the corresponding decision tree for the second game.

All we did was to add four zeros to all outcomes. However, we bet that, unless you are, say, Warren Buffet, you should strongly prefer the branch that gives 1 million for sure. Why is so? NPV may become useless as a selection criterion when one of the outcomes may have a tremendous undesired impact on your financials, such as not winning $1 million at once.

Consider a third game, which has to do with your salary.

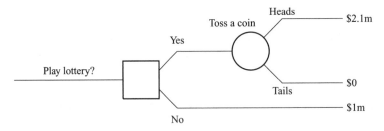

Figure 13.2
Decision tree for game 2.

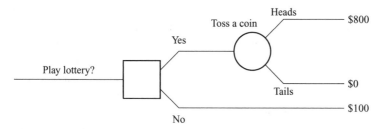

Figure 13.3
Decision tree for game 3.

 Exercise

Game #3 to Decide Your Salary every Month

Your boss (or boss to be) proposes you the following game. At the end of the month, you can choose between your current monthly salary, say $100, or playing a lottery, which consists of tossing a fair coin. If it is heads you receive $800, if it is tails, you get nothing that month. Which alternative do you prefer?

Figure 13.3 shows the corresponding decision tree. If you are rational, you will prefer the lottery, because (a) the net present value of the lottery is much higher—as $400 > 100$—and (b) it is ok to work during roughly half of the months for free as long as in the remaining months your salary is eight times larger.

Consider finally the fourth and last game, which a variation of the previous one.

 Exercise

Game #4 to Decide Your Salary on Day 1

On your first day at the company, your boss tells you that the salary policy of your new company is peculiar. You must choose between a fixed monthly salary at $100, or playing a lottery, which consists of tossing a fair coin. if it is heads, your salary is $800 *forever*; if it is tails, you have to work for free *all your life*. Which alternative do you prefer?

The outcomes do not change, but now the coin will be tossed only once: if you are rational, a little twist in the game leads to a dramatic change in your preferences. By virtue of eliminating repetition, again one of the outcomes has a tremendous undesired impact on your financials, thus NPV is useless as a decision tool in this case.

Coming back to the business sphere, things are not very different, as firms are managed by humans. NPV is not the right criterion to use when some of the outcomes may drag the firm into bankruptcy. Likewise, repetition plays a major role. NPV is suitable for repetitive decisions but may not be appropriate for single decisions. For instance, Zara can make use of NPV when deciding about opening a new store because they open dozens, if not hundreds, every year. However, for a small retailer with only two stores, opening a third one may be make or break for her business, thus a different approach is needed, such as minimizing the probability of having a big loss.

 On the use of NPV

NPV is *not* a suitable tool when the decision under consideration is not repetitive or when some of the outcomes may drag the firm into bankruptcy.

13.4   NPV Distributions

One way to get around of one of the drawbacks of NPV (the possibility of inadvertently ending up in very bad scenarios) is to use Monte Carlo simulation. To run a simulation, inputs can be defined as random variables (e.g., normal distributions) rather than point-wise estimations. Coming up with a net present value for each set of realizations of the random variables will naturally define an NPV distribution, a true random variable. The information conveyed by this NPV distribution will be much more than the sheer NPV value.

Monte Carlo simulation can be done in standard Ms Excel. Also, there is dedicated software to do so, such as Oracle's Crystal Ball, which works as an add-in on Ms. Excel.[1] We will illustrate the power of simulation for computing an NPV distribution by means of the next example.

 Exercise

Clean Energy Ltd.

Clean Energy Ltd. plans to invest $100 million in a new plant to treat industrial waste. The firm's management expects to obtain annual cash flows that may be assumed to follow a normal distribution with mean $25 million and standard deviation $5 million during the first three years. During the following two years, the mean is expected to remain constant but uncertainty will increase so that standard

---

1. As of May 2019, it is only available for Windows and is not free.

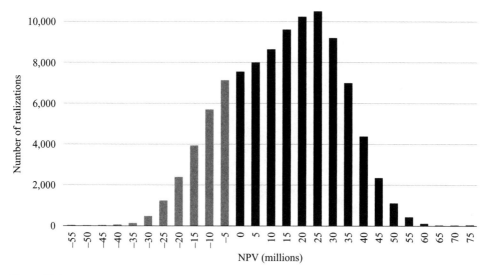

Figure 13.4
NPV distribution obtained by Monte Carlo simulation (100,000 iterations) in MS Excel.

deviation will double. Also, during next year, a $30 million subsidy for clean energies from the government may materialize with probability 60 percent. As for the discount rate, the management believes it can be 9 percent, 10 percent, or 11 percent, each with the same probability.

1. What is the NPV of the project?
2. What is the resulting NPV distribution of the project?
3. What is the probability that the investment will end up being profitable?
4. What are the key factors of the investment that have the most impact on NPV?

As said, Crystal Ball, or any other software that can perform Monte Carlo simulation, can be used to answer these questions. The first question can be computed in MS Excel by means of the expression: `=NPV(0.1, A1:A5) - 100`, where the range A1:A5 contains expected cash flows: $43 million in year 1 $(25 + 0.6 \cdot 30)$ and $25 million in years 2 to 5, and the average discount rate is used (10 percent). The resulting NPV is a promising $11.1 million.

If we now introduce uncertainty by changing expected values of inputs (i.e., cash flows, discount rate) by distributions, we will obtain an NPV distribution (figure 13.4).[2] The mean

2. The file Clean-Energy.xlsx, located at http://mitpress.edu/practical-finance, contains the details of the simulation.

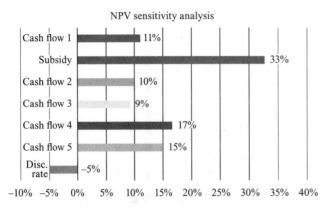

Figure 13.5
NPV sensitivity analysis as measured by the coefficient of correlation of each variable with the outcome. Figures are normalized such that they add up to the unity in absolute value. The figure has been done in standard MS Excel—no Crystal Ball required.

of the NPV distribution cincides with the NPV ($11.1 million), but additional information reveals that the probability that a realization of the NPV distribution is positive is around 71 percent. Why is so? Well, if the subsidy in year 1 is not granted, something that happens with probability 40 percent, then NPV is -$5.23 million. Also, as cash flows are now uncertain, some of them may now be lower than $25 million, possibly leading to a negative NPV realization. The combined effect of all seven sources of variability leads to a negative NPV realization in 29 percent of the cases. Losses can be as high as -$55 million.

Figure 13.5 shows a sensitivity analysis of the NPV distribution with respect to each parameter. The sensitivity analysis specifies the relative importance of changes in each variable to explain changes in the NPV distribution as measured by the relative value of the coefficient of correlation of each variable with the outcome. Note that the value of the discount rate is negative (-5 percent). That means that the mean of the NPV distribution decreases as discount rate increases. The figure reveals that the variable with the most importance by far is whether the government grants the subsidy to the firm. Also, cash flows 4 and 5 have higher impact on changes in NPV, as they are subject to significantly larger uncertainty. Also, other things equal, the values of the NPV distribution are less sensitive to cash flows that are further in the time horizon, as they are reduced more when discounted. For instance, the impact of cash flow 1 is larger than the impact of cash flow 2, which in turn is larger than the impact of cash flow 3. Finally, the impact of the discount rate is the least important and is negative. That tells that the mean of the NPV distribution decreases when the discount rate increases. Given the sensitivity chart, management focus should be on the potential subsidy, possibly refining the assumptions or paying attention to any change in the economy that might signal a change in the government environmental policy.

Still, it may make sense to invest in the project despite the relatively large probability of losing money if (a) this kind of decision is repetitive for the firm; and (b) eventual losses are admissible, in the sense that they will not put the continuity of the firm in danger. In any case, it should be noted that using NPV (based on expected cash flows) may not be appropriate to make sound decisions, especially when uncertainty is large.

13.5   Real Options

A major limitation of traditional methods for valuing investments, such as NPV analysis, is that they do not consider managerial flexibility—that is, management's ability to adapt decisions as new information is learned—available in many investment decisions. While this might not be a critical issue for projects that take place within low-volatility settings, ignoring managerial flexibility can lead to serious understatement of the value of investments made in today's complex, ever-changing environment.

Real options refer to actions a firm's management can take to adjust its investment plans based on changing economic, technological, or market conditions. For example, investing in a new manufacturing facility overseas with the purpose of reducing the production costs may also provide a company with the real option of introducing its products to the local market when the local economic conditions allow. We refer to these options as real because they relate to business choices associated with real investments on tangible assets, as opposed to financial instruments. Similarly though to financial options, the real options offer the right but not the obligation to make a business decision. Whatever the case, considering the potential benefits provided by real options may have a substantial impact on the valuation of an investment opportunity.

 Real options

> **Real options** are opportunities made available to the managers of a firm to alter an investment in response to changing circumstances.

Real options can be classified into different groups with most common the following:

Option to delay This is the option of deferring a business decision to the future. For instance, an oil company may participate in the bidding for a natural gas field but delay exploitation until prices are high.

Option to abandon The option to terminate a project if conditions are not favorable. For instance, a multinational may decide to leave a particular country and sell its assets—thus, avoid the losses from continuing operations—if the political situation is expected to create a hostile market environment in the long run.

Option to expand The option to make follow-on investments if the initial project is successful is the option to expand. For instance, a firm may increase the production capacity for a new product following its successful launch.

Real options are quite common in the investment valuation process for many R&D projects, particularly in industries with low success rate—such as the pharmaceutical industry, where the standard NPV analysis would probably hinder such projects. Also, the real options logic is reflected to the common practice followed by most companies to start with a small project when they consider introducing a new technology or business process and then scale up once some of the uncertainty has been resolved. Finally, a real options approach is not uncommon when it comes to construction of large-scale projects. Figure 13.6 shows an air photo of Athens international airport—Eleftherios Venizelos. Starting operations in March 2001, the airport was delivered with an option to expand embedded in its configuration. That is, a real estate investment was done keeping in mind the possibility of doubling the current terminal area (notice the empty area at the left of the photo). Due to its design, any future expansion can be done without disrupting the current operations—obviously at a lower cost than what would be the case if the option to expand was not embedded in the initial investment.

Figure 13.6
Athens international airport with the option to expand embedded in the design.
Source: Wikimedia Commons: https://en.wikipedia.org/wiki/Athens_International_Airport.

There are several challenges associated with real options analysis. First, the sources and potential resolution process of uncertainty associated with a particular investment need to be clearly identified, along with potential managerial options in response to uncertain outputs. Second, an estimation of the options' value shall be quantified not only for the purpose of evaluating the overall investment but also for deciding on potential actions to be taken today in order to have the option available in the future. For example, the Athens international airport authorities would not have invested for having the option to expand embedded in the design, if the future expected benefit from potential exercise of this option had not been greater than the option's cost.

Regarding the mapping and identification of a project's uncertainty and options available, the use of decision trees can provide some valuable insight. Regarding quantification of the value of real options, this can be quite difficult to establish or estimate. Real options function in ways similar to financial options in the sense that they capture the right, but not the obligation, to make a certain decision. Hence, methods used for pricing of financial options can also be applied to price real options. However, these methods often employ advanced modeling techniques the presentation of which is beyond the scope of this book. Instead, in the examples that follow we will use decision trees as a supplementary tool to classical NPV analysis to demonstrate how the consideration of real options can affect investment valuation. The idea is to recognize the value of flexibility through the availability of alternative courses of action in a project, despite the fact that our valuation approach is subject to several limitations (which are discussed later).

13.5.1   Option to Delay

We will discuss the option to delay by analyzing the investment decision of a chemical manufacturing company.

 Exercise

AgroChem

AgroChem is a chemicals manufacturer of products targeted at the agricultural industry. The firm investigates the opportunity to invest in a production facility for AgroTreat, one of its established products. The plant will be located next to a new extraction site of a specific mineral which is the key ingredient of AgroTreat. The mining company that will supply the mineral to AgroChem is planning to keep the mine open for five years. The cost of building a facility—with annual production capacity of 1 million product units—is $100 million. The market selling price per unit of product is quite stable and equal to $100. The unit cost, however, depends on the price of its key ingredient. In particular, while the current unit cost is equal to

$65, one year from now the cost can go up or down by $15 with equal probability,[a] and then remain fixed for the duration of the investment. Figure 13.7 illustrates the possible scenarios for the unit production cost of AgroTreat at time 0. Assume that due to its modular design, it takes less than a month to build the production facility for AgroTreat. Also, assume that the tax rate for income generated from this type of products is zero. If the discount rate used by AgroChem for evaluating investment in this type of projects is 20 percent, is this a profitable investment?

a. Cost uncertainty is not uncommon in this industry. Chemical plants are often built close to the source of raw materials—namely, ore deposits from which the value ingredient can be extracted—mainly due to high transportation costs associated with shipping ores from overseas. However, when a new ore deposit is discovered and extraction of the mineral begins, there are several uncertainties that are not resolved immediately, such as concentration of value ingredient, its quality, and overall exploitable size of the ore.

To answer this question, we will need to consider two cases. In the low-cost (LC) scenario (upper branch in figure 13.7), the production cost per unit of AgroTreat will be equal to $50 for the four years up to the retirement of the production plant. Under this scenario and assuming that AgroChem will be able to sell the entire production of 1 million units, the annual net income for the company will be equal to 1 million · ($100 − $65), or $35 million, for the first year of operation and 1 million · ($100 − $50), or $50 million, for the remaining four years. Then, the NPV that corresponds to the favorable cost scenario is calculated as follows:

$$\text{NPV}_{\text{LC}} = -100 + \frac{35}{1+0.2} + \sum_{n=2}^{5} \frac{50}{(1+0.2)^n} = \$37.03 \text{ million}$$

In the high-cost (HC) scenario (lower branch in figure 13.7,) the production cost per unit of AgroTreat will be equal to $80 resulting to a net income of 1 million · ($100 − $80), or $20 million, for the last four years of the investment. Similarly, the NPV that corresponds to the unfavorable cost scenario is calculated as follows:

$$\text{NPV}_{\text{HC}} = -100 + \frac{35}{1+0.2} + \sum_{n=2}^{5} \frac{20}{(1+0.2)^n} = -\$27.69 \text{ million}$$

As high- and low-cost scenarios can materialize with equal probability, the NPV of the project is calculated as follows:

$$\text{NPV} = \frac{1}{2} \cdot 37.03 + \frac{1}{2} \cdot (-27.69) = \$4.67 \text{ million}$$

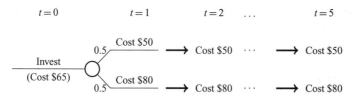

Figure 13.7
Decision tree for AgroTreat production facility.

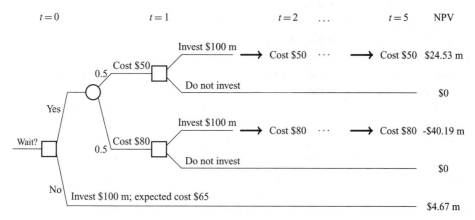

Figure 13.8
Decision tree for the AgroTreat plant investment with an option to delay.

Hence, the classical NPV approach to evaluating this investment opportunity at time zero would suggest that the production plant shall be built—as the NPV from the investment is positive. However, notice that if the investment is undertaken at time 0, there is still 50 percent probability that the investment will be highly unprofitable, which is the case if the unfavorable cost scenario materializes.

Based on this observation, interesting questions are raised. Are there any alternatives associated with this investment that could make it more attractive to AgroChem? What would be the value of the investment for AgroChem if the company can delay its decision for one year until all uncertainty has been resolved? The decision tree for this case is shown in figure 13.8.

From the decision tree analysis in figure 13.8 it becomes clear that the best decision for the company would be to hold the investment for one year until all costs are revealed. Then AgroChem will build the production plant only if the favorable cost scenario occurs. By doing so, the company can avoid being held up in the unfavorable cost scenario, under which the investment would not be profitable. Hence, if AgroChem delays its investment decision by one year, the investment's NPV would be equal to the NPV associated with the favorable cost scenario (upper branch in the decision tree) times the probability that this scenario will materialize. That is:

$$\text{NPV} = \frac{1}{2}\left(\frac{-100}{1+0.2} + \sum_{n=2}^{5}\frac{50}{(1+0.2)^n}\right) = \frac{1}{2} \cdot 24.53 = \$12.27 \text{ million}$$

The above analysis shows that by delaying its decision by one year, AgroChem can increase the value from this investment by $7.60 million (the difference between $12.27 and $4.67). This amount represents an estimate of the value of the option to delay for the company. Having a figure of the option's value can be quite useful for AgroChem in making decisions today that would maximize its expected return from this investment. For example, AgroChem could get into negotiations with the mining company that would involve making some down payment today in exchange of getting priority to the extracted mineral reserves if the favorable cost scenario materializes.

It must be noted here that the value for AgroChem of the option to delay as derived through decision tree analysis is only an approximation to the value that would be obtained if a formal real options valuation method was applied. As we have already mentioned, real options valuation involves advanced valuation techniques—based on the theory of financial option pricing—that are beyond the scope of this book. Nevertheless, decision tree analysis helps management visualize the contingent nature of investment decisions while providing the basic map for calculating NPVs associated with alternative decisions pertaining to an investment.

The analysis of real options on the basis of decision trees is also subject to several limitations. First, the assumption that different sources of uncertainty in an investment are resolved all at once in particular points in time might not be representative of reality. Second, uncertainty in decision trees analysis is modeled through discrete outcomes (e.g., high-cost versus low-cost scenario in our example), while usually in real life there is a continuum of potential outcomes. Third, the use of a single discount rate throughout the analysis is a weakness of decision trees. Shareholders' required rate of return is sensitive to the estimate of risk (i.e., volatility) in an investment. Consequently, as volatility changes within different branches of the tree—depending on uncertainty resolution and options exercised—so does the applicable (risk-adjusted) discount rate. For example, it would be reasonable to assume that if the favorable cost scenario materializes, the risk for AgroChem's investors—consequently, the applicable discount rate—should be lower than the existing risk at time zero. Finally, most investments have several options that may interact in some way. As the value of one option can potentially be affected by the value of another option, valuation of compound real options might be complex to handle (not only with decision trees but also with formal valuation methods). We will return to this point in our discussion of the option to abandon that follows next.

13.5.2 Option to Abandon

Let's revisit the AgroChem's case excluding for the moment the possibility that the firm can delay its investment decision by one year.

 Exercise

AgroChem (revisited)

Assume that AgroChem has a single window of selling the plant equipment for $50 million at the end of the second year of operations. In other words, the company has the option to abandon the investment at the end of year two. This might be the case if the equipment is acquired through a leasing contract with early termination clauses.[a] Considering the option to abandon, what would be the investment's NPV?

a. In this case, the acquisition cost of $100 million can be considered as the NPV of all AgroChem payments to the lessor during the entire lease period. Similarly, the salvage value of $50 million correspond to the NPV (measured at the end of year two) of the payments that will not be made minus some termination fee.

The decision tree for this case is shown in figure 13.9. Note that the best decision for AgroChem would be to continue with the investment until the end if the favorable cost scenario materialize and abandon the project at the end of year 2 otherwise. The NPVs that correspond to these two cases are calculated as follows:

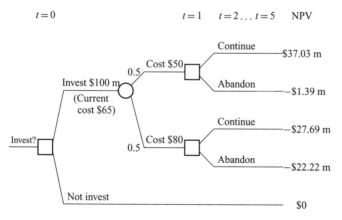

Figure 13.9
Decision tree for the AgroTreat plant investment with an option to abandon.

$$\text{NPV}_{\text{LC}} = -100 + \frac{35}{1+0.2} + \sum_{n=2}^{5} \frac{50}{(1+0.2)^n} = \$37.03 \text{ million}$$

$$\text{NPV}_{\text{HC}} = -100 + \frac{35}{1+0.2} + \frac{20+50}{(1+0.2)^2} = -\$22.22 \text{ million}$$

As the two scenarios can materialize with equal probability, the NPV of the investment is given by:

$$\text{NPV} = \frac{1}{2} \cdot 37.03 + \frac{1}{2} \cdot (-22.22) = \$7.40 \text{ million}$$

The above analysis shows that considering the option to abandon increases the value of the investment for AgroChem by $2.73 million (the difference between $7.40 and $4.67). That is, the classical NPV approach would underrate the value of the investment by $2.73 million exactly because of its inability to capture the dynamic nature of most investments. More important, while this increase might appear small, in some occasions it could make the difference for a negative NPV investment to become positive. Having an estimate of an option's value can have further practical implications for a company. In our example, AgroChem can use this analysis to determine how much it would be willing to pay as termination fee and structure the lease contact accordingly. Also, notice that if AgroChem has both the option to abandon and the option to delay available, then the valuation of the former has an impact on the valuation of the latter, which now becomes equal to $4.87 million (the difference between $12.27 and $7.40).

Figure 13.10 illustrates the decision tree for AgroChem's investment when both options are available. We can understand that the tree becomes difficult to manage as the number of chance and decision nodes, along with the chance outcomes and decision alternatives increase.

13.5.3   Option to Expand

To discuss the option to expand, we will address an investment problem faced by a high-tech firm.

 Exercise

SoundPro

SoundPro is a technology company specializing in high-fidelity sound systems. The company has recently developed and is ready to commercialize its STBT-2 wireless speaker series, which incorporates several innovative features. According to the firm's projections, there is 70 percent (30 percent) probability that demand for the new product will be high (low), something that will be known by the end of year 2. The following table shows the predicted net cash flows for these two scenarios (in millions).

Year						
	1	2	3	4	5	6
High demand	25	50	100	100	100	75
Low demand	25	50	50	50	50	25

Based on this information, SoundPro needs to make a decision about how much capacity to build and when. The investment in production capacity has two components. There is a fixed cost of $80 million which corresponds to the cost of leasing land and building a production facility. There is also a variable cost component associated with the production capacity installed and is equal to $0.7 million for each $1 million of net cash flows. Currently, the company is considering two options:

1. Bet on the high-demand scenario and invest from the beginning in a production facility with sufficient capacity to meet the maximum demand (i.e., $100 million of net cash flow). In this case the investment cost will be equal to $80 + 0.7 \cdot 100$, or $150 million, all incurred at the beginning of the project.

2. Start with a low-capacity facility for meeting the low-demand scenario (i.e., $50 million of net cash flow) and then expand this facility on the third year if the high-demand scenario materializes. In this case the initial investment cost will be equal to $80 + 0.7 \cdot 50$, or $115 million, followed up by a second investment of equal size in year 3 incurred only in the case the high-demand scenario materializes.

If the discount rate for this type of investment is 20 percent, which of the two options for capacity investment would be the most profitable on average for SoundPro?

The cash flows for the two demand scenarios and the two capacity investment options are shown in table 13.1.

It follows that option 1 (i.e., invest in high capacity at time 0) would be the most profitable option for SoundPro according to the following calculations:

$$\text{NPV}_{(1)} = 0.7 \cdot 77.0 + 0.3 \cdot (-12.9) = \$50.0 \text{ million}$$

$$\text{NPV}_{(2)} = 0.7 \cdot 45.4 + 0.3 \cdot 22.1 = \$38.4 \text{ million}$$

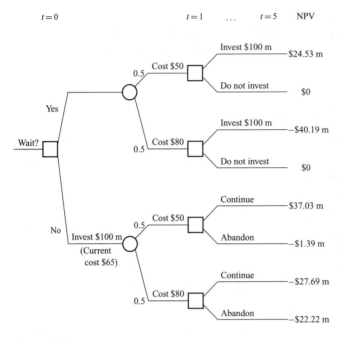

Figure 13.10
Decision tree for the AgroTreat plant investment with options to both abandon and delay.

Table 13.1
Predicted cash flows (in US$M) for high / low demand scenarios for STBT-2.

Year									
	Demand	Present value	0	1	2	3	4	5	6
Option	High	$77.0	−150	25	50	100	100	100	75
(1)	Low	−$12.9	−150	25	50	50	50	50	25
Option	High	$45.4	−115	25	50	−15	100	100	75
(2)	Low	$22.1	−115	25	50	50	50	50	25

Figure 13.11 illustrates the resulting decision tree for SoundPro's options.

There are several interesting observations from the above analysis. First, note that the resulting NPVs for the two options depend on the probability assigned to each demand scenario. For example, if the high- and low-demand scenarios were equally likely to materialize, then option 2 (i.e., option to expand) would be preferable. This confirms the general notion of positive relationship between volatility and the value of an option. Second, notice that the *spread* in NPVs corresponding to the two demand scenarios is much larger for

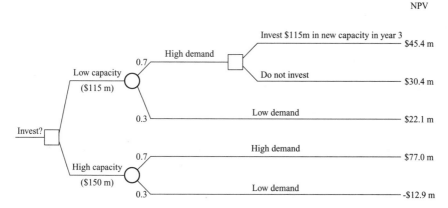

Figure 13.11
Decision tree for SoundPro's investment with the available options for low- and high-capacity investments.

option 1 compared to option 2. That is, maintaining the option to expand—instead of betting from the beginning to the more likely scenario—can protect the company from the negative consequences of the low-demand occasion. This observation gives rise to the third point, which again relates to the application of the same discount rate in all cash flows irrespective of the uncertainty present at the time of their occurrence. But how reasonable is to assume that the same discount rate of 20 percent is still representative of the investment's risk even after demand uncertainty has been resolved? Obviously, the risk associated with a binding investment decision taken at time 0 cannot be the same with the risk from investing in capacity expansion knowing that the product is successful. We leave it as an exercise to show that if SoundPro uses a 10 percent discount rate for any investment decision after year 2 (i.e., assuming that the high demand scenario materializes), then option 2 becomes more profitable.

At this point, we will briefly discuss a third option that may be available to SoundPro. Consider the case that the company can invest in some type of expandable capacity, say by leasing a larger place and/or building a facility configured to accommodate a second production line in the future. Assume that the fixed cost component for an expandable facility is equal to $100 million (i.e., 25 percent higher than in the previous cases), while the variable cost component is still equal to $0.7 million for each $1 million of net cash flows. Under this option, the firm will make an initial investment of $100 + 0.7 \cdot 50$, or $135 million, followed up by a second investment of $35 million in year 3 only if the high demand scenario materializes. The decision tree for this case is the same as in figure 13.11 with the only difference on the calculated NPVs which in this occasion correspond to the following cash flows:

Table 13.2
Present value calculations (in millions) for production option 3 for STBT-2.

			Year						
	Demand	Present value	0	1	2	3	4	5	6
Option	High	$71.7	−135	25	50	65	100	100	75
(3)	Low	$2.1	−135	25	50	50	50	50	25

It follows that option 3 (i.e., invest in expandable capacity at time 0) would now become the most profitable option for SoundPro, as shown below:

$$\text{NPV}_{(3)} = 0.7 \cdot 71.7 + 0.3 \cdot 2.1 = \$50.8 \text{ million}$$

Similar to our previous discussion, the value of this option increases with the volatility in the two demand scenarios (i.e., as the difference in the probabilities for the two scenarios becomes closer to zero) but also if a lower discount rate is used for the less uncertain cash flows later in the project (i.e., after year 3).

13.5.4 Flexible Capacity Option

The concept of flexibility is central in real options with several applications in the fields of operations and supply chain management. In this section we briefly discuss the concept of flexibility in the context of production capacity choice. The idea here is to present flexibility-related options which can affect the outcome of a firm's investments but without getting into any detailed NPV calculations.

To introduce the concept of production capacity flexibility, consider a manufacturer of two products, A and B. There are three demand possibilities for each product [50, 100, 150], equally likely and independent. That is, there are in total nine demand scenarios for the pair (A, B), each with probability $\frac{1}{9}$ to materialize: (50, 50), (50, 100), (50, 150), (100, 50), (100, 100), (100, 150), (150, 50), (150, 100), (150, 150). Due to high cost of capacity investment, the company has decided to install capacity equal to the total expected demand (i.e., 200 units), considering two options:

(1) Install *dedicated* capacity—for instance, capacity configured to produce only one product—of 100 units for each product.

(2) Install *flexible* capacity—namely, capacity configured to produce both products—of 200 units in total split among two production lines (one for product A and one for product B).

Multiproduct firms often use flexible capacity to cope with demand uncertainty, as this capacity choice provides the ability to reallocate production in response to demand realizations. Use of flexible resources is prevalent in many industries for which the cost of

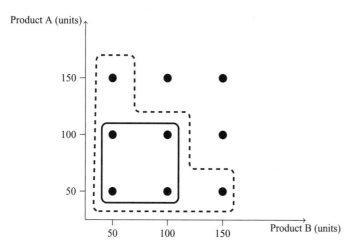

Figure 13.12
Demand captured by dedicated capacity (solid) versus flexible capacity choice (dashed).

capacity investment is very high (e.g., automotive, pharmaceutical, beverages, aerospace, etc.). However, as the investment in flexible capacity is often quite more costly than in dedicated capacity, a careful study is required for calculating the value of operational flexibility that the former provides.

Going back to our example, figure 13.12 illustrates how having flexible capacity in place can help the company hedge against demand uncertainty. For instance, compared to the dedicated capacity choice, the flexible capacity can fulfill the production requirements for two additional demand realizations—that is, when demand for product A is high while at the same time demand for product B is low, and vice versa. Moreover, it can be shown that with dedicated capacity, expected sales equal 167 units for capacity utilization of 83 percent, while with flexible capacity the same measures are 178 units and 89 percent, respectively (see exercise 6).

It must be noted that in real life, quantifying the benefits of capacity flexibility is not straightforward and depends largely on the demand characteristics of the products that share flexible resources. For instance, when the demands of the pooled products are negatively correlated, the value of capacity flexibility is high, while it diminishes as the demands become more positively correlated. There is also another challenge in estimating the value of capacity flexibility. In principle, operational flexibility has an impact on a firm's demand risk, which subsequently has an impact on the applicable discount rate (i.e., shareholders' required rate of return). Due to these complications, evaluating an investment in flexible capacity using the classical NPV approach might favor investment in dedicated resources. Hence, real options valuation methods might be more appropriate when it comes to evaluation of any operational flexibility opportunities.

13.6 NPV Is Not a Panacea: Deciding beyond the Numbers

Even when you feel strongly confident about the cash flow and discount rate assumptions made, NPV will only give you an economic answer to the question of whether to go ahead with an investment. However, there may be other relevant factors to take into consideration that cannot be calculated or estimated.

Some of the important questions to answer include:

Is this decision aligned with the strategy of the company? This is a key question that should always be formulated when facing an important investment decision. Obviously, if the answer is in the negative, the investment should be halted. Conversely, if the investment is aligned with the strategy, the investment should be approved even if the numbers tell you otherwise.[3]

Does the firm need the investment to survive in the medium term? A good example of this may be changing the ERP system in a firm. Benefits are usually very difficult to estimate, but sometimes implementing a new ERP is a matter of survival.

What is the impact of the investment on society? That includes environmental, political, and social aspects.

How is the investment going to be perceived by stakeholders? Say that an investment entails eliminating a supplier with whom you have had a long-term relationship. How is the supplier going to react and what will the consequences be? Even more important, how are other similar suppliers going to react? (Also consider customers, governments, etc.).

Specifically, how will people in the organization react? That includes both white- and blue-collar workers, and of course workers' representatives.

In short, a spreadsheet will help you with the decision, but it is not going to decide for you. The course of action to make a decision may be as follows: first, do the NPV analysis and get a sense of the risks and benefits involved; second, try to answer the qualitative questions described above; third, carefully ponder the quantitative and nonquantitative available information and make your decision. And remember that the decision will almost always be based on partial information, which means that you have to learn to live with uncertainty. As you cannot just ignore it, you will have to learn to handle it.

 On making investment decisions
A spreadsheet will help you decide, but it will not decide for you.

---

3. Someone told us once that, when it comes to approve investments, the words *strategic* and *unprofitable* are synonyms.

13.7 Roche: The Investment Decision Dilemma

In this section we present the case of Roche,[4] the Swiss pharma company whose operations management team had to make a decision regarding production batch size. Three methods were discussed, and none of them seemed to make any sense. The solution to the case is intentionally not given.

Case study

Roche: The Investment Decision Dilemma

Paul de Wit, head of supply performance in the pharmaceuticals division at Roche, read the three reports again and still remained perplexed. If the question was the same, how could the three answers be different? He knew that the final decision that he had to make about how best to determine the appropriate size of the campaign batches would have a big impact on the company's production costs, so he wanted to make sure that he knew what was going on before making the final proposal to the supply planning committee.

Background As of 2016, F. Hoffmann-La Roche Ltd.,[a] based in Basel, Switzerland, was one of the five largest pharmaceutical corporations in the world (Wikipedia 2019), with sales of more than 50 billion Swiss francs[b] in 180 countries and more than 80,000 employees worldwide. The company was created in 1896 in Switzerland and, since then, had enjoyed more than a century of continued expansion, internationalization, and diversification. Popular products in its portfolio included Tamiflu, used to prevent and treat influenza, and MabThera, Avastin, and Herceptin, leading oncology drugs. These shared its portfolio with less well-known products, such as the hepatitis drug Pegasys and the macular degeneration therapy Lucentis, some of which had annual sales in 2015 of more than 1 billion francs each. Between 2000 and 2015, Roche divested some noncore operations, such as its vitamin and fine chemical businesses, to focus on two main segments: pharmaceuticals and diagnostics. The pharmaceutical business unit, which produced biologic and small-molecule products, provided 80 percent of sales, with oncology drugs making the largest sales contributions. In order to expand its pharmaceutical product offerings and fight against patent expirations and other increasing competitive pressures, the company conducted widespread research and development programs, and it had more than one hundred drugs in the pipeline. The diagnostics division offered advanced DNA tests, diabetes monitoring supplies, and point-of-care diagnostics used in a variety of health-care settings. In both pharmaceuticals and

---

4. Case originally published by IESE Business School: Serrano and Kraiselburd (2019).

diagnostics, Roche focused on innovative products and personalized health care, targeting unmet medical needs and keeping the patient at the core of everything the company did. As with other leading companies in the industry, only a small percentage of Roche's enormous investment in R&D was converted into commercial products. Such investments had to be recouped with large gross margins and returns for its shareholders (see tables A1 and A2). Production costs were high because of the rigorous quality-compliance requirements. In fact, a quality problem in production could lead to an investigation (which could temporarily stop production), to a recall of a marketed product, or to a patient stock-out. Given that the company depended on a small number of highly profitable products, such quality-assurance issues could affect productivity significantly. This was one of the main reasons why Roche owned its key production facilities, together with the need to be flexible in a rapidly changing industry, the advantage of having development facilities next to factories, and the use of unique technologies. Manufacturing a specific drug was a complex task. Two main available methods were available to obtain the drug substance: synthesis and biotechnology. The goal of synthesis was to convert simpler components into the desired drug through a series of chemical reactions, whereas biotechnology involved the use of living organisms to produce a specific drug, sometimes using advanced techniques such as gene splicing or recombinant DNA technology.[c]

The pharmaceutical production process   The production process required several well-differentiated stages and usually started several months or even years before the drug would arrive at the distribution centers.

The production process could be split into three main stages (see chapter appendix 2). During the first stage, the drug substance was created. This process was, by far, the most expensive and sophisticated. It typically consisted of multiple steps, was very capital-intensive, and needed to comply with strict quality specifications and environmental safety regulations. The ability to use the drug substance in subsequent production phases critically depended on the successful execution of this stage.

The second stage took the active substance as a raw material and formulated it into the different dosage forms by adding the excipients—that is, the inactive substance of the tablet or the inactive liquid in which the active substance was suspended.

The third and final stage consisted of customizing the drug according to the market requirements: presentation (such as bottles and pills), prospect language, size, and so on. After this customization process, the number of stock keeping units (SKUs) increased dramatically from a few dozen to several hundred. Managing so many SKUs represented a major challenge, given the near-100 percent level of customer service required and the shelf-life constraints of the drugs, which was typically two or three years.

A critical decision in the manufacturing process was deciding on the campaign or batch size for the first stage at each facility since the setup costs could be considerable (the cost of a complete setup could be as high as 1 million Swiss francs in some cases). This was mostly due to the fact that setups often implied the complete shutdown of production facilities for a period of days or weeks (which would imply an enormous opportunity cost), along with expensive cleaning and maintenance operations to ensure the noncontamination of the process for the next campaign. Because of this, campaigns were typically of a size that meant a specific drug substance would be produced once a year or even every other year. The drug substance was kept in stock under quality-compliance conditions so that shorter campaigns could be run later for the subsequent steps.

The improvement program In the period between 2000 and 2015, the leading pharmaceutical companies were under increasing pressure to reduce costs to maintain their profitability.[d] The reasons included: (1) the increasingly demanding government regulations to have a new drug approved, which increased the cost and time to introduce a new drug in the market; (2) governments' need to reduce healthcare costs; (3) the pressure of the industry's followers, who did not usually invest in R&D but waited for patents to expire so they could sell generics at a significantly lower price; and (4) the increasing pressure from the international community for pharmaceutical companies to reduce the cost of drugs in developing countries (e.g., HIV/AIDS treatments).

In late 2015, Roche launched a renewed improvement program to reduce the cost of its products at several levels of the organization, with a special focus on production. Production costs represented roughly 40 percent of the total cost. A key driver of cost in the production phase was the size of the production campaigns during the first stage of the production process. Decreasing the total amount of batches was desirable for many reasons, the most important being that smaller batches lead to a decrease in inventory and operating working capital (OWC) along with improved flexibility and customer service. However, the huge setup costs had prevented this batch reduction from occurring for many years. In 2016, the production managers at Roche considered that it was time to assess whether such infrequent changes still made sense.

The Mainclas team De Wit was assigned the task of finding out the appropriate approach to determine the products' campaign size. Two other people were allocated to his team: Pierre Martin, a senior manager from the finance department, and Andreu Torregrosa, a graduate of a prestigious supply-chain program in southern Europe. De Wit's idea was to answer this question for a simple, relatively-easy-to-study product and then scale up the solution, once the value drivers had been identified. For the initial assessment, he picked Mainclas,[e] a product with fairly stable demand and sales and a long-enough history of production costs. Current coverage for this product was 1.28 years.[f] Another characteristic that made Mainclas suitable for the initial assessment was that this product was manufactured in only one facility that had plenty of capacity, so the team did not have to worry about potential production bottlenecks or other capacity constraints. Chapter appendix 3 provides data about this product in more detail.

During the kick-off meeting, after some discussion about the different alternatives, de Wit proposed that Martin and Torregrosa each work individually to come up with an answer, and they would all meet again a week later and compare results. Then they could decide the next steps. To avoid discrepancies, the team members decided to make some common assumptions, such as taxes being zero, the cost of capital being 12 percent, and using the selected data shown in chapter appendix 3. Later on, they could refine these assumptions if necessary. Martin and Torregrosa agreed and started working individually.

The consensus meeting   One week later, the three team members gathered again to share their answers. De Wit asked Martin, from the finance department, to go first. Martin explained: "As I see it, all our decisions in the company have to aim to increase value for the shareholders. Therefore, we should choose the campaign size that maximizes the value of the company for them. As is customary for us in the finance department, I performed an EVA analysis[g] to calculate the optimal campaign size. Here are my numbers" (see chapter appendix 6).

After Martin's detailed explanation, Torregrosa said: "Well, I took a different angle for solving the problem. From the historical data, I realized that the demand for Mainclas is very stable and so the problem almost exactly replicates the EOQ model that I learned in inventory theory during my master's program. According to this model, the objective should be minimizing the cost of the process rather than maximizing the value for the firm, and I believe that is why the results I obtained are different from Pierre's" (see chapter appendix 4).

At this point, de Wit was really surprised that the two approaches differed from his. "I have to admit that I expected differences in some of the results but not in the methods themselves," he said. "Let me explain what I did. Since changing the campaign size will impact the firm's cash flows, then making a decision on the batch size is equivalent to undertaking an investment. Therefore, I followed a standard NPV for investment valuation, estimating the expected incremental cash flows—which depend on the batch size chosen—and discounting them at the company's cost of capital. And I am astonished to have found a third, different result" (see chapter appendix 5).

Were the calculations in some of the reports incorrect? If the calculations were correct, then which approach was the right one? Were the other approaches inappropriate? If so, what assumptions invalidated those approaches? Alternatively, were some of the approaches just rough approximations? These questions came up one after the other in de Wit's head as he realized that an immediate answer was needed before the end of the following week, when the strategic production meeting for 2016 would take place.

a. Roche (2016).

b. In December 2015, one Swiss franc (CHF) was equivalent to $1.01.

c. For a good introduction to some of the technical challenges and changes involved in this industry, see Peters, "What is biotechnology?" and Pisano, Oestreich, and Ceruti (2002).

d. Wells and Raabe (2005).

e. Some names and figures have been changed to protect confidentiality.

f. Coverage is defined here as the number of years of demand that can be satisfied, on average, from one batch of production.

g. Some good references for EVA (economic value added) analysis are G. Bennett Stewart III, *The quest for value: The EVA management guide* (New York: Harper Business, 1991); and Mihir A. Desai, Fabrizio Ferri, and Steve Treadwell, "Understanding economic value added," Harvard Business School background note no. 206-016 (Boston: Harvard Business Publishing, July 1, 2006).

Chapter Appendix 1: Roche's Financial Statements

Table A.1
Group consolidated income statement (in millions of Swiss francs).

	2015	2014
Sales	48,145	47,462
Royalties and other operating income	2,258	2,404
Cost of sales	−15,460	−13,381
Marketing and distribution	−8,814	−8,657
Research and development	−9,581	−9,895
General and administration	−2,727	−3,843
Operating profit	13,821	14,090
Associates	–	1
Financing costs	−1,574	−1,821
Other financial income (expenses)	−260	246
Profit before taxes	11,987	12,515
Income taxes	−2,931	−2,980
Net income	9,056	9,535

Table A.2
Group consolidated balance sheet (in millions of Swiss francs).

	Dec. 31, 2015	Dec. 31, 2014	Dec. 31, 2013
Property, plant, and equipment	18,473	17,195	15,760
Goodwill	11,082	9,930	7,145
Intangible assets	13,861	12,799	3,944
Deferred tax assets	2,564	2,829	4,707
Defined-benefit plan assets	642	691	636
Other noncurrent assets	959	982	811
Inventories	7,648	7,743	5,906
Accounts receivable	8,329	9,003	8,808
Current income-tax assets	239	244	218
Other current assets	2,795	2,421	2,297
Marketable securities	5,440	7,961	7,935
Cash and cash equivalents	3,731	3,742	4,000
Total assets	**75,763**	**75,540**	**62,167**
Long-term debt	17,100	19,347	16,423
Deferred tax liabilities	545	504	1,282
Defined-benefit plan liabilities	8,341	8,994	6,062
Provisions	2,204	1,778	1,097
Other noncurrent liabilities	505	251	302
Short-term debt	6,151	6,367	2,220
Current income-tax liabilities	2,781	2,616	1,805
Provisions	2,432	2,465	2,148
Accounts payable	3,207	2,883	2,162
Other current liabilities	9,197	8,777	7,425
Capital and reserves attributable to Roche shareholders	20,979	19,586	19,294
Equity attributable to noncontrolling interests	2,321	1,972	1,947
Total liabilities and equity	**75,763**	**75,540**	**62,167**

Chapter Appendix 2: Production Process for a Standard Drug

Roughly speaking, the production process at Roche can be divided into three major phases:

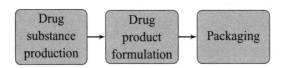

Some of the features of these phases are presented next.

Drug substance production Characterized by complex, sophisticated process, drug substance production is a mix of dedicated (biotechnology) and multipurpose facilities (chemical synthesis) using capital intensive equipment; large production campaigns (1 to 2 year demand); long manufacturing lead-times (two to ten months); and long setup times (weeks).

Drug product formulation Drug product formulation is characterized by multipurpose facilities; average production campaigns (one- to four-month demand); average manufacturing lead-times (weeks); and average setup times (days).

Packaging This is characterized by customization (country, market makeups); shared equipment with other products; several company sites and even contractors performing these operations for the same products; short production campaigns (two to ten weeks, depending on market demand); short manufacturing lead-times (hours); and short setup times (hours).

Chapter Appendix 3: Selected Data for Mainclas

Historic demand

Year	2010	2011	2012	2013	2014	2015	2016	2017	2018	2019
Kg	2,378	2,256	2,352	2,306	2,451	2,259	2,361	2,384	2,398	2,305

Unit cost breakdown

	$/Kg
Main raw material 1	1,171
Overhead	712
Main raw material 2	298
Others (solvents, packing, etc.)	73
Total	**2,254**

Setup cost breakdown

	$/batch
Facilities depreciation	689,523
Cleaning raw materials	65,826
Setup raw materials	21,086
Total	**776,435**

Inventory holding cost for this product was estimated to be 17 percent.

Chapter Appendix 4: Economic Order Quantity (EOQ) Calculations, According to Andrew

"I know that the EOQ depends on four parameters: demand, setup cost, unit cost, and inventory holding cost. Setup cost, unit cost, and inventory holding cost are already shown in exhibit 5 (respectively $776,435 per batch, $2,254 per kg, and 17 percent), so this part should be easy. On the other hand, demand has been very stable, so I guess that assuming that the demand is constant and that future demand will look like historic demand is a plausible approach. So, I can calculate the demand from the data in chapter appendix 3."

$$\frac{2{,}378 + 2{,}256 + \cdots + 2{,}305}{10} = 2{,}345 \text{ kg/year}$$

"Therefore, the economic order quantity should be:

$$EOQ = \sqrt{\frac{2kd}{ch}} = \sqrt{\frac{2 \cdot \$776{,}435 \cdot 2{,}345 \text{ kg/year}}{\$2{,}254/\text{kg} \cdot 0.17}} = 3{,}083 \text{ kg}$$

which is, interestingly, very close to the current campaign size.

  Just for curiosity, I can also calculate the optimal annual cost, adding ordering and inventory holding cost when the EOQ is chosen."

$$C(EOQ) = \frac{kd}{EOQ} + \frac{c}{2} \cdot EOQ \cdot h$$

$$= \frac{\$776{,}435 \cdot 2{,}345\text{kg/year}}{3{,}083\text{kg}} + \frac{1}{2} \cdot \$2{,}254/\text{kg} \cdot EOQ \cdot 0.17$$

$$= \$590{,}574 + \$590{,}574 = \$1{,}181{,}148 \text{ per year}$$

Recommendation: The campaign batch size should not be changed, as it is roughly the same as the current one.

Chapter Appendix 5: Cash Flow Discounting, or Net Present Value (NPV) Method Calculations, According to Paul

"The first step to calculate the NPV of the cash flows should be finding such cash flows. A key point that I have to remember is that only incremental cash flows are relevant, so I only have to consider those that change with the campaign batch size, namely the ordering cost and the inventory holding cost. In addition to this, average inventory will be higher (lower) every year if the proposed batch is larger (smaller) than the current one. So, I also have to consider that in my cash flow calculations, since changing inventory implies changing OWC.

But let us start simple. Using the data in chapter appendix 3, for the current batch size, I can calculate the average number of orders per year, and the ordering and holding costs for the current scenario. I will use averages to simplify my calculations; otherwise the cash flows will jump from one year to another as the batch size changes, and that would complicate calculations unnecessarily."

- Orders per year = annual demand/batch size = 2,345 / 3,000 = 0.782 batches per year
- Ordering cost per year = ordering cost · orders per year = $86,912 · 0.782 = $67,936 per year
- Holding cost per year = 0.5 · batch size · unit cost · inventory holding cost = 0.5 · 3,000 · 1,542 · 0.17 = $393,210 per year

"It is good that I remembered removing the fixed costs when calculating the ordering and unit costs, since those are not incremental.

Now, to calculate the corresponding costs for the proposed batch size, I can perform the very same cost calculations for *any* batch size in Excel, and then use Solver in a subsequent step to find the batch size that maximizes the net present value. This Solver tool comes really in handy.

Using the data above, I can prepare the following table."

		Orders (#/year)	Ordering cost ($/year)	Holding cost ($/year)
Current batch	3,000 kg	0.782	67,936	393,210
Proposed batch	453 kg	5.180	450,229	59,332
Difference			−382,293	333,878

"Because the proposed batch size in this example table was calculated using the Solver to maximize the NPV as explained below, this is the optimal. Of course, the same table would apply to any number. I have to remember to explain this in next week's meeting.

The cost difference between the two scenarios will be incremental cash flows, so I will use those as relevant cash flows in my calculations. As for inventory changes, I observe that inventory is *lower* at each period by

$$0,5 \cdot \text{unit cost} \cdot \Delta \text{batch size} = 0,5 \cdot 1,542 \cdot (3,000 - 453) = \$1,971,448$$

Therefore, I have to consider an identical *positive* cash flow at each period.

Alright! I think I am ready to perform the NPV calculations."

Relevant cash flows	2010	2011	2012	2013	...
Ordering cost		−382,293	−382,293	−382,293	...
Holding cost		333,878	333,878	333,878	...
Incremental inventory	1,963,985	1,963,985	1,963,985	1,963,985	...
Total	1,963,985	1,915,570	1,915,570	1,915,570	...

"Cash flows from 2011 on are always the same, so they define a perpetuity. Therefore, to calculate the NPV I can use a trick I learned for perpetuities:

$$\sum_{t=1}^{\infty} \frac{a}{(1+r)^t} = \frac{a}{r}$$

where r is the interest rate, a is any number, and t is the period number.

Finally, the discount rate should be the cost of capital, 12 percent, and so, at the optimal, according to the Solver:

$$NPV = 1,963,985 + \frac{1,915,570}{0,12} = \$17,927,071$$

which is the largest possible for any batch size."

Recommendation: The batch size should be should be reduced from 3,000 kg to 453 kg.

Chapter Appendix 6: Economic Value Added (EVA) Calculations, According to Pierre

"I know that MVA (see section 12.5.2) is a special case of NPV, where the cash flows to discount are EVAs. Then, my calculations should be similar to Paul's in the sense that the EVAs should be incremental. Given the definition of EVA:

$$EVA_t = NOPAT_t - (E_{t-1}^b + D_{t-1}^b)WACC$$

I should only consider incremental NOPAT and incremental net assets $(E + D) \cdot$ NOPAT, given that taxes are assumed zero, is just operating profit, so only the incremental ordering cost and holding cost are relevant, and these can be calculated exactly as Paul did (see chapter appendix 5). Likewise, incremental net assets only consist of incremental inventory (calculated as in chapter appendix 5).

I can use the following table to calculate incremental NOPAT:

		Orders per year	Ordering cost ($/year)	Holding cost ($/year)
Current batch size	3,000 Kg	0.782	67,936	393,210
Proposed batch size	955 Kg	2.455	213,412	125,172
Incremental NOPAT			**−145,476**	**268,038**

and, knowing that the WACC is the cost of capital, which is 12 percent, also incremental net assets as:

increasing inventory $\cdot$ WACC $= -1{,}576{,}695 \cdot 12\% = -\$189{,}203$.

Now I am ready to calculate EVAs as follows.

Relevant cash flows	2010	2011	2012	2013	...
Incremental inventory	−1,576,695	−1,576,695	−1,576,695	−1,576,695	...
...times WACC	−189,203	−189,203	−189,203	−189,203	...
Ordering cost		−145,476	−145,476	−145,476	...
Holding cost		268,038	268,038	268,038	...
EVA		**311,766**	**311,766**	**311,766**	...

The cash flows define a perpetuity, and then the market value added (MVA) is easy to derive."

$$MVA = \frac{311{,}766}{0{,}12} = \$2{,}598{,}050$$

Recommendation: The batch size should be should be reduced from 3,000 kg to 955 kg.

13.8 Summary

This chapter has discussed some additional topics regarding the use of net present value as a decision tool. Some of the key questions discussed include: when is expected NPV a valid criterion and what to do when it is not? The section on real options enriches the discussion of NPV showing the value of flexibility when firms have the option to delay, abandon, or expand potential investments. The case study at the end of the chapter challenges the general wisdom that decisions should be made either in the operations or the finance realms by presenting a dilemma that seems to be in the interface of the two worlds.

13.9 Suggested Reading

• Chod, Jiri N., and Jan A. Van Mieghem. 2010. "Operational flexibility and financial hedging: Complements or substitutes?" *Management Science* 56 (6): 1030–1045.

• Fine, Charles H., and Robert M. Freund. 1990. "Optimal investment in product-flexible manufacturing capacity." *Management Science* 36 (4): 449–466.

• Higgings, Robert. 2019. *Analysis for financial management*, 12th ed. New York: Mc-Graw Hill.

• Jordan, William C., and Stephen C. Graves. 1995. "Principles on the benefits of manufacturing process flexibility." *Management Science* 41 (4): 577–594.

• Northcott, Deryl. 1992. "Capital investment decision-making." London: Thomson.

• Serrano, Alejandro, Rogelio Oliva, and Santiago Kraiselburd. 2017. "On the cost of capital of inventory models with deterministic demand." *Int. J. Production Economics* 183: 14–20.

• Trigeorgis, Lenos. 1996. *Real options: Managerial flexibility and strategy in resource allocation*. Cambridge, MA: MIT Press.

Exercises

1. Repeat the Clean Energy Ltd. exercise when the discount rate is subject to variability, assuming that it comes from a triangular distribution, with parameter values: 0.08 (minimum), 1.00 (most likely), 1.20 (maximum).

   In problems 2 to 5, please use the logic of options through decision trees and classical discounted cash flows techniques—rather than a formal real options valuation approach—to approximate the value of options available to the corresponding investments.

2. A company is considering investing in a factory that will have the explicit right to produce a particular product forever. Under current prices, the cash flows generated from product sales are $100,000. Next year the cash flows from sales will be either $120,000, if market moves favorably, or decline to $80,000, otherwise, and then remain fixed. The cost of the factory is $600,000 and can be constructed in two weeks. Assume that the cost of capital for this investment is 16 percent.

   a. What is the investment's NPV if the company invests now? Should the company invest in the project?

   b. Suppose that the company can wait one year before deciding on this investment. What would be the investment's NPV in that case? What is the value of being able to wait?

   c. What is the maximum investment cost that the company would be willing to accept for having the opportunity to wait rather than investing now or never?

3. In the AgroChem example in section 13.5.1 we have assumed that a discount rate of 20 percent is applicable throughout the investment's duration. Now, assume that if the company delays its decision by one year (i.e., when all cost uncertainty has been resolved), then the applicable discount

rate if the low cost scenario materializes is 10 percent. What would be in this case the value of AgroChem's option to delay its investment decision by one year?

4. A company is considering investing $100 million in a new production facility for launching one of its established products in a new market. Historically, within one year the company knows with certainty whether the product introduction to a new market is successful or not, with the probability for the former being 40 percent. The present value of the future discounted expected cash flows from the product net sales is either $200 million if the market is favorable one year from now, or $60 million otherwise. The required rate of return for this investment is 20 percent.

a. Determine the NPV of this investment at time zero. Should the company invest in this project?

b. Next, assume that if the market is unfavorable one year from now, the company can abandon the investment and redeploy the relevant assets to other sites. By doing so, it can recover 70 percent of the value of its original capital investment. Should the company now invest in this project?

c. Now assume that if the market is favorable one year from now, the company could double the plant's capacity, making an additional capital expenditure of $85 million. In this case, the present value of the future discounted expected cash flows from the product net sales would increase by 50 percent. How should the company proceed now with this investment? What is the investment's NPV with the inherent flexibility?

5. Revisiting the SoundPro example in section 13.5.3:

a. Show that the value of the option to expand increases in the volatility of future cash flows. To do so, consider the cases that the high demand scenario may materialize with probabilities 60 percent and 50 percent.

b. Assume that a discount rate of 10 percent applies to any investment made in year 3 (given that the high demand scenario materializes), due to lower risk for the firm's investors. What would be the value of the options 2 and 3 in this case?

6. Referring to the example in section 13.5.4, calculate the expected sales and capacity utilization for the cases of (a) dedicated capacity investment and (b) flexible capacity investment.

7. Four project cash flows result in four NPV distributions whose mean and standard deviations are given.

Project	Mean	Std. deviation
1	20	15
2	5	7
3	15	12
4	17	16

Which of the four projects should be selected in order to:

a. Maximize the mean of the NPV distribution.

b. Minimize the probability of a loss.

References

Brealey, Richard A., Stewart C. Myers, and Franklin Allen. 2011. *Principles of corporate finance*, 10th ed. New York: McGraw-Hill.

Pisano, Gary P., Stephanie Oestreich, and Clarissa Ceruti. 2002. "The life sciences revolution: a technical primer." HBS case study no. 602118. Boston: Harvard Business Publishing.

Roche. 2016. "Finance report: 2015." Accessed May 14, 2019. https://www.roche.com/dam/jcr:2722d88c-601f -4451-a2ec-dfd428d4a464/en/fb15e.pdf.

Serrano, Alejandro, and Santiago Kraiselburd. 2019. *Roche: The investment decision dilemma* (P 1171 E). Reproduced with permission.

Wells, John R., and Elizabeth A. Raabe. 2005. "The pharmaceutical industry in 2005." HBR case study no. 706423. Boston: Harvard Business Publishing.

Wikipedia. 2019. "List of largest pharmaceutical companies by revenue." Last modified May 10, 2019. https://en.wikipedia.org/wiki/List_of_largest_pharmaceutical_companies_by_revenue.

14 Managing Operating Working Capital

Warehouses are cemeteries of working capital.
—Anonymous

This chapter presents the levers firms usually use to manage operating working capital. After the introduction, the first four sections are devoted to the constituent elements of OWC, namely inventory, payables, receivables, and cash. The last section reflects on the existence of optimal values for OWC.

14.1 Why Managing OWC Is Important

The main elements of OWC, namely accounts payable, accounts receivable, and inventory, are a significant portion of firms' balance sheets. (The fourth element of OWC, minimum cash, may be relevant, but it is usually smaller and harder to quantify as an outsider.) According to estimates done by GMT, an accounting research firm,[1] for the thirty largest global industry classification standard (GICS) industries worldwide, accounts payable stood at approximately 12 percent of assets in the period 2010–2015. The corresponding figures for accounts receivable and inventory are 16 percent and 15 percent. These figures vary heavily across industries: for instance, inventory at retailers makes up roughly 21 percent of assets, 40 percent higher than the average, although for most service companies (e.g., hotels, IT), inventory is barely significant.

This means that OWC is a significant portion of firms' balance sheets. One way to look at how large OWC is and how it has evolved over time is to look at the cash conversion cycle. Figure 14.1 shows the evolution of an average cash conversion cycle between 2006 and 2015 for S&P companies in the main GICS sectors (except financials). As the figure shows, the average cash conversion cycle is quite large, in the range of 70–80 days, but there are large differences across industries. For instance, the cash conversion cycle for health care industry is around 150 days, while for telecommunication services it is only 10 days. A key fact that explains part of this large variability is the amount of inventory that each industry holds.

---

1. See their website: https://www.gmtresearch.com/.

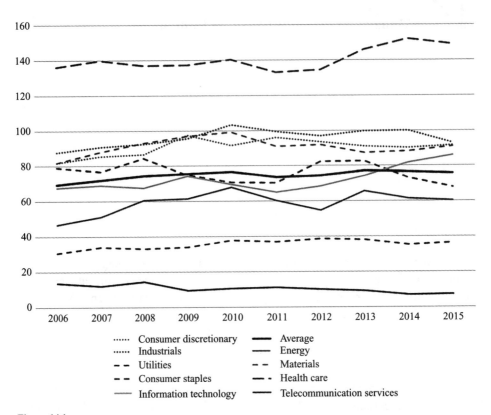

Figure 14.1
Evolution of average cash conversion cycle in days in the period 2006–2015 for S&P firms (except financial firms).
Source: Authors' elaboration based on GMT data.

If firms belonging to the S&P 500 index are representative of all firms, the data in the graph suggests that companies still have a long way to go to reduce their OWC. In fact, in ten years, the average cash conversion cycle has actually increased!

As described in chapter 5, *other things being equal*, decreasing OWC is a good way of creating value for a company. The tricky part is how to do it without jeopardizing essential parts of the business. For instance, a firm may decide to eliminate half of their SKUs to reduce OWC, but this may come at the cost of reducing their customer service level. Another firm may want to reduce accounts receivable by offering deep discounts to customers that pay early. But again, this comes at the cost of eroding the net sales of the firm and may not be a good idea.

Nevertheless, appropriately managing OWC is a powerful way to create value for companies. Firms such as Inditex or Dell Computer became prominent players in their industries because they made the connection between OWC and value the cornerstone of their

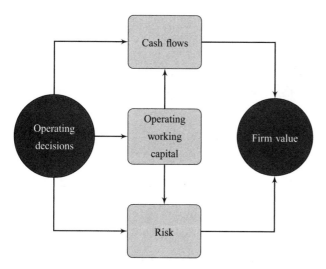

Figure 14.2
Impact of operating decisions on a firm's value.

competitive strategies. To understand why this connection is so powerful, let's have a look at how operating decisions by managers are linked to the value of a firm. Managers' decisions may impact future cash flows directly: for instance, shutting down an inefficient plant leads to medium- and long-term savings that lead to higher cash flows in the future. Also, decisions may have a direct impact on risk: for instance, a domestic company may decide to expand overseas by opening new plants in an unexplored country. This represents an opportunity but also a major risk, increasing the overall risk of the firm.

Managers' decisions also impact OWC, whose connection to the firm's value is not direct, as shown in figure 14.2. The most salient aspect in the figure is that there is no direct connection between OWC and firm value, although both are related through cash flows and risk. Indeed, the value of a firm depends on its ability to generate cash flows in the future. In fact, a firm can be valued by discounting those future cash flows at a rate, which increases with the risk of the company, as explained in chapter 12. But both cash flows and discount rate can be largely influenced by the level of OWC the company holds.

For instance, a firm may decide to increase inventory at its stores to raise customer service level. As sales boost, cash flows increase. But also, as inventory increases, inventory holding cost, both financial and nonfinancial, will increase, leading to a decrease of future cash flows. The overall impact will depend on the relative size of both effects.

As for the discount rate, let us share with you what happened to one of our colleagues while working as a consultant for a large company dealing with spare parts in the airline industry. As you can imagine, spare parts for that company were a large portion of total assets, since there are hundreds of thousands of parts to be kept in inventory and because

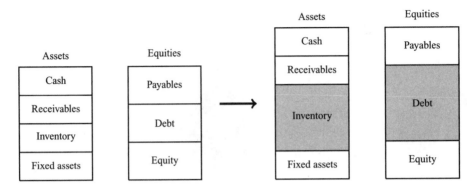

Figure 14.3
Change in the balance sheet structure when lot size is increased.

service levels are very high to guarantee prompt intervention at airports when needed. Our friend was checking to see if the lot sizes the firm was using to replenish spare parts from suppliers was appropriate. He found that overall that was not the case, and that lot sizes had to be increased significantly; that is, spare parts had to be replenished in larger amounts. So he went ahead and increased the values of the lot size parameter in the enterprise resource planning (ERP) of the firm. For a couple of months nothing happened, but then our friend got a call from the CFO of the company who told him: "Would you please stop changing the WACC of my company?" Our friend was astonished, in fact he thought at first that the CFO had misread the number. But since she kept insisting, he realized what had happened: heavily increasing lot sizes in the computer had led to suppliers sending not units, but whole boxes; or not boxes, but whole pallets. The overall effect of this change is that the inventory cycle increased. As a result, assets in the balance sheet suddenly increased. But we know that assets and equities are identical at any time. That means that some account on the equities side should have also increased. Not shareholders' equity, not accounts payable, but ... debt! Debt is the short-term adjustment lever so that the accounting equation holds. Figure 14.3 shows the incremental impact of increasing lot sizes in the balance sheet. Now, as debt increased, financial leverage of the firm also increased, effectively changing the risk (and the WACC!) of the entire company.

This anecdote should make you realize how important proper management of OWC is and how involved the connection of the operational and financial realms of a firm can be: again, the fact that there is no direct connection between OWC and firm value makes it difficult to grasp what the consequences of your operational decisions are on the financial side and the value of the company.

Having illustrated the power of managing OWC, let's have a look at how firms handle OWC in practice.

14.2   Reducing Inventory

Most of today's manufacturers and retailers want to be lean. Many times, they use this term as a synonym of "inventory-free." There are several ways of achieving this goal. The obvious methods to reduce inventory should include those prescribed by the inventory management discipline, such as improving forecasting techniques, reducing SKUs (for instance, through standardization of parts), centralizing inventory, defining sound safety inventory levels, reducing manufacturing batches, or postponing production. In addition to these standard techniques, there are other mechanisms firms resort to in order to reduce their inventories, either physically, in the books, or both. We will next present a few of the levers firms have to reduce inventory.

14.2.1   Passing Inventory to Suppliers and Customers

Powerful players in the supply chain may push suppliers, and sometimes customers, to hold inventory for them. This may not hold benefits for the entire supply chain, as the following two examples illustrate.

(1) A car manufacturer's COO brags about how little inventory he has in his manufacturing plants. However, he has reduced inventory by forcing suppliers and dealers to hold extra inventory for him. This is sometimes referred to as the toothpaste effect, because inventory accumulates at the beginning or at the end of the supply chain but not in the middle, where car manufacturers are positioned. Overall inventory is not reduced, and the costs of dealing with the extra inventory may actually increase the total cost of producing one unit of product if we consider the supply chain end-to-end.

(2) The head of purchasing of a large, powerful firm forces her supplier to hold an additional two weeks worth of inventory for her. After passing the inventory to the supplier, the buyer is happy because her balance sheet is leaner, as inventory has disappeared from her firm's books. That also means that she will pay for inventory two weeks later. As assets decrease with inventory, debt will also decrease so that assets = equities at any time, and therefore, the buyer's firm will save the holding cost of two weeks of inventory. In particular, it will save the financial portion of that inventory holding cost. In turn, the supplier will be worse off because it has to hold two extra weeks of inventory and take care of the corresponding inventory holding cost, including the financial portion. In this case there is an asymmetry that makes the situation noteworthy: The cost of debt will most likely be significantly lower for the powerful firm than for the relatively weaker supplier, say 6 percent for the buyer and 10 percent for the supplier. If that is the case, the buyer will save only 60 percent of the extra financial cost incurred by the supplier. Therefore, the supplier will be worse off by a larger amount that the powerful firm is better off. As a result, the total cost of the product will be larger.

A clear lesson from these examples is that powerful firms should not just reduce their inventory, but do it bearing in mind (a) the total cost of the supply chain, not only their suppliers' prices; and (b) the fact that in modern economies, it is not only firms who compete with each other but instead supply chains.

14.2.2 Consignment

A variation of passing inventory to suppliers is using consignment. Under consignment, inventory is held physically by the buyer, but it is in the books of the supplier, who has ownership of the inventory.

For instance, car manufacturers sometimes ask suppliers to consign subassemblies to them, but the ownership of the inventory stays with the supplier until the car is assembled by the manufacturer. Consignment may go upstream in the supply chain. For example, Ford may tell a tier-2 supplier such as Sony to consign the car audio equipment to Visteon, a tier-1 supplier for cockpits. Visteon will assemble the audio equipment from Sony in the cockpit and consign the assembly to Ford. When a car in the Ford plant passes through a control point in the assembly line, a signal is triggered for Ford to acquire the cockpit and all its elements, including the audio equipment from Sony. A noteworthy point is the fact that Visteon neither buys nor sells the audio equipment from Sony, although it physically holds it for a number of days.

Likewise, powerful retailers may ask their suppliers to consign their products. A case in point is Amazon's business model: under a fulfillment by Amazon agreement, suppliers physically send their products to Amazon while keeping the ownership of the products until they are sold; when orders come in, Amazon fills the orders, ships the products to the customer, and pays the supplier for the items while keeping its commission for the sale. Remarkably, not only does Amazon not own the products at its warehouse, but it will charge the supplier a storage fee for physically keeping the products at their fulfillment centers.[2]

14.2.3 Vendor-Managed Inventory

Another increasingly popular scheme is vendor-managed inventory (VMI), also known as supplier-managed inventory (SMI). Under VMI, the buyer of a product provides her supplier (vendor) with information and the supplier takes responsibility for maintaining an agreed inventory of the material at the buyer's premises. The owner of the product may be the buyer or the supplier (in the latter case VMI may be seen as a special case of consignment). The key point under VMI is that the buyer does not send orders to the supplier but instead periodic sales and current levels of inventory.

In contrast to some of the contracts presented before, VMI may well benefit both supplier and buyer. Suppliers typically benefit by gaining visibility of final demand—especially

---

2. Amazon's fulfillment and storage fees are available at: https://services.amazon.com/fulfillment-by-amazon/pricing.htmref=asus_fba_snav_p (May 2019).

in avoiding order spikes from the buyer, which leads to more efficient operations, lower inventories, and higher customer service levels. In turn, buyers benefit from lower complexity, lower inventories, and better service from suppliers. VMI has been successfully implemented by retailers such as Walmart and Home Depot.

 Exercise

Linner Inc.

The COO of Linner Inc. has proposed a VMI contract to its main raw material supplier. Under the VMI contract, set to go into effect at the beginning of next year, 60 percent of Linner's current raw materials—which account for 50 percent of total inventory—will become the property of the supplier.
The current balance sheet is as follows: (data as percentage of assets, which is $10 million).

Assets Cash 5 percent; receivables 20 percent; inventory 35 percent; fixed assets 45 percent.
Equities Payables 30 percent; debt 25 percent; equity 45 percent.

Linner's marginal cost of debt is 10 percent; the supplier's is 15 percent. For convenience, assume that interests are only paid at the end of the year and that there are no taxes.

1. Assess the impact of adopting VMI on next year's financial balance sheet for both Linner and its supplier.
2. Will these changes only impact this year's statements or also the following years'?

Let's first prepare Linner's current balance sheet. We multiply total assets by the percentages provided to obtain the balance sheet in table 14.1.

Fifty percent of inventory, or $1,750,000, is raw materials; and 60 percent of that, or $1,050,000, will change hands from Linner to its supplier. Therefore, this amount will

Table 14.1
Linner's current balance sheet ($).

Cash	500,000	Acc. payable	3,000,000
Acc. receivable	2,000,000	Debt	2,500,000
Inventory	3,500,000	Equity	4,500,000
Fixed assets	4,500,000		
Assets	10,000,000	Equities	10,000,000

Table 14.2
Linner's new balance sheet ($).

Cash	500,000	Acc. payable	3,000,000
Acc. receivable	2,000,000	Debt	1,450,000
Inventory	2,450,000	Equity	4,500,000
Fixed assets	4,500,000		
Assets	8,950,000	Equities	8,950,000

disappear from Linner's balance sheet. How will this occur? Say the supplier will buy back (and pay for) that inventory, so that $1,050,000 will enter Linner's cash account. That money will naturally be used to reduce the current debt. Linner's new balance sheet will be as shown in table 14.2. Note that Linner's balance sheet is now leaner, as total assets have been reduced by a bit more than 10 percent.

We could stop the analysis here, as we have quantified the immediate primary impact of the new contract, but there are additional indirect consequences. As Linner's debt decreases, annual interest will also decrease by 10 percent $\cdot$ $1,050,000 = $105,000. This is cash that Linner doesn't have to pay its bank in one year. Again, that saved money will be used to reduce the line of credit (and increase equity!), so that debt will further decrease by $105,000. But again, that leads to reduced interest payments (10% $\cdot$ $105,000 = $10,500) in two years, and so on and so forth. The long-term reduction of Linner's debt is $1,050,000 \cdot (1 + 0.1 + 0.1^2 + \ldots) \approx $1,166,667$.

As for the supplier, the analysis is identical at the qualitative level: inventory and debt will increase by $1,050,000 when inventory changes hands. Additional debt entails paying additional interest in one year, as much as 15 percent $\cdot$ $1,050,000 \approx $157,500. In order to pay for these interest expenses, debt will increase by $157,500 at the cost of additional expenses at $23,625 in two years, and so on and so forth. The long-term increase of the supplier's debt is $1,050,000 \cdot (1 + 0.15 + 0.15^2 + \ldots) \approx $1,235,280$.

Of course, if the payments schedule changes, the calculations will be a bit more involved, but the recursive mechanism is still the same. Also, if the tax rate is not zero, Linner's final situation won't be as good, as it will have to pay more taxes. However, its supplier's final situation won't be that bad, as they will have to pay fewer taxes. Exercise 6 asks you to perform these calculations.

Finally, be aware of the fact that Linner is better off by $1,166,667 (that is, it now has that much less debt than before), but its supplier is worse off by more than that ($1,235,280). Overall, the supply chain is apparently worse off by the difference, or $68,613. However, the referred VMI advantages for the supplier (visibility of final demand, avoidance of order spikes) will lead to a significant reduction of safety inventory, which will more than compensate for the initially-assumed inventory extra costs. (For instance, when a VMI program was first introduced by Barilla and its distribution channel, a 50 percent reduction in inventory was reported, while dramatically reducing stock-outs.[3])

14.3   Reducing Accounts Receivable

The second lever available to obtain a leaner balance sheet is to reduce the size of accounts receivable. Converting white papers into green papers, or receivables into cash, would certainly decrease the total of OWC. Best practices for reducing accounts receivable include sending early reminders to customers about next due dates and exerting tight control over customers whose invoices go beyond the due date. On top of that, an obvious way of reducing receivables is to negotiate with customers so they agree to pay earlier. Easier said than done: trade credit agreements are difficult to change once they are in place, as they have been defined based on the respective negotiating powers of buyer and supplier. And negotiating power doesn't usually change overnight. It is not a coincidence that retailers collect cash from final users at the time of delivery (even before, in the case of e-retailers), but they pay their suppliers in thirty or more days. In a business to business (B2B) environment, payment terms mainly depend on the industry practice and the relative size of firms. Therefore, companies usually resort to subtler ways to persuade customers to settle their invoices earlier, such as through sales discounts.

14.3.1   Sales Discount

Sales discount (sometimes referred to as cash discount) is the cash offered by a supplier to his buyer for early payment of an invoice. In essence, the supplier is telling the buyer: "if you pay me earlier, you will pay less." The buyer then decides whether or not to benefit from the discount. Say the credit terms of a sale are 2/10, net/45. This means that the due date is in forty-five days, but if the buyer pays in ten days or less she will get a 2 percent discount. However, the discount is not granted if the payment occurs after ten days, even if it is made in less than forty-five days. Therefore, the only two rational choices for the buyer are either pay 100 percent on day forty-five or 98 percent on day ten. The option the buyer chooses will largely depend on the liquidity status of the buyer. For instance, if the buyer is subject to cash tensions, she will choose not to pay early, even though it may be more profitable to do so. The choice will also depend on the cost of getting cash through other means. In fact, the buyer can reverse the way she sees the sales discount: "If I pay you later, I will pay more, but I will benefit from holding cash longer." In other words, for the buyer, sales discount converts the supplier into a sort of bank. Let's delve further into this parallelism through one example.

3. See Hammond (1994).

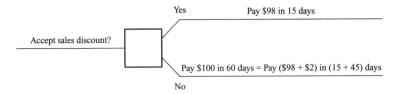

Figure 14.4
A decision tree representing the two rational options available to the buyer.

 Exercise

Shortofcash Inc.

Shortofcash Inc. has been offered credit terms at 2/15, net/60 by her main supplier. Currently she has a line of credit (unsecured short-term debt) with a local bank, whose marginal cost is 12 percent.

In order to maximize profitability, should the firm pay the supplier in fifteen or sixty days?

Without loss of generality, we can assume that the amount to pay at the due date is $100. Using a decision tree, we can plot the two rational decisions available to the buyer (figure 14.4).

By looking at the figure, it should be clear that the only difference between the two branches is that in the lower branch, Shortofcash pays the supplier an additional two dollars, forty-five days later. Think about it: this is equivalent to Shortofcash getting a loan of $98 from the supplier for a period of forty-five days at a cost of $2. To know whether or not this is a good idea, we can compare the equivalent annual cost of this loan with marginal cost paid to the bank.

Roughly speaking, the annual cost of the supplier's loan is:

$$\text{annual cost} = \frac{2}{98} \cdot \frac{365}{45} \cdot 100 \approx 16.6\%$$

The first term is the interest paid over the capital, that is, the cost of the loan over the forty-five-day period. To annualize it, we can multiply the first term by $\frac{365}{45}$, the number of times that the thirty-five-day period is contained in a year.

A more accurate calculation—using compound interest— would give:

$$\text{annual cost} = \left(1 + \frac{2}{98}\right)^{\frac{365}{45}} - 1 \approx 17.8\%$$

In any case, the annual cost of the loan granted by the supplier is larger than the marginal cost of the loan given by the bank, which is 13 percent. Therefore, in terms of profitability, it is better not to get the loan from the supplier, and Shortofcash should pay in fifteen days and benefit from the 2 percent discount.

When this approach to sales discounting is not available or has been used already, and companies are still in need of cash, they may resort to alternative or additional methods such as the ones described next, which do not involve their customers but banks.

14.3.2 Receivables Discounting and Factoring

Receivables (or bills) discounting and factoring are similar methods for companies to convert white papers into green papers before the due date on the invoice. When discounting or factoring are used, the firm's receivables decrease.[4]

Receivables or bill discounting Also known as recourse factoring, it is a mechanism for companies to get fresh money before the due date of an invoice. It involves a company and a bank or an alternative financial institution. The company presents an outstanding invoice (i.e., an invoice to be paid by its customer) to the bank. Then the bank pays the firm the money that appears in the invoice and charges a fee (made of interest rate plus various commissions) for doing so, keeping the accounts receivable as collateral. The fee is subtracted from the face value of the invoice so that the firm receives less money that the face value. Receivables are then sold at a discount—hence their name. At due date, the bank receives the money directly from the customer. If the customer doesn't pay, the firm should pay the face value to the bank and it is his responsibility, not the bank's, to collect the money.

Nonrecourse factoring Also known as simply factoring, it is a less common variation of accounts receivable discounting, in which the bank (called the factor) actually buys the receivable, so the bank bears the risk for collecting the money at the due date. In contrast to recourse factoring, the involved receivables disappear from the firm's books when the money is received. Also, fees are naturally larger in this case. Not all invoices are accepted by banks: banks may refuse to advance the money if the invoice comes from a nonreliable customer if there is a significant risk that the customer won't pay at the due date.

See Martínez Abascal (2012, section 4.3) for a description of these and other short-term bank finance products.

14.4 Increasing Accounts Payable

A third lever to reduce OWC is to increase accounts payable. Next we will describe two ways of doing so: trade credit and reverse factoring.

---

4. Strictly speaking, in the case of bill discounting, receivables do not decrease until the payment is made at due date.

14.4.1 Trade Credit

Firms may want to pay their suppliers later to improve OWC. In contrast to decreasing receivables, total assets do not shrink but grow larger when payables increase. Nevertheless, other things equal, paying late allows the buyer to enjoy loans from her suppliers for free. In this context, "for free" means that there is no explicit cost for the loan that the supplier grants. However, it may be the case that the supplier recovers part or the full cost of the loan through other means, for instance via a higher price.

On the other hand, paying suppliers too late compromises both the profitability and the liquidity of the supplier. In fact, weak suppliers may end up going bankrupt when they fail to collect due invoices from an important customer. That is why some governments try to protect small players by passing laws that oblige buyers to pay suppliers within a reasonable time frame. However, these laws are not always easy to enforce in practice.

Under some circumstances, trade credit may be beneficial for both buyer and supplier. For instance, a cash-constrained retailer may buy less inventory than is optimal in advance of the selling season because of a lack of cash. However, if she is allowed to pay their major suppliers later, she may get closer or even reach the optimal purchasing quantity. If that is the case, on average more demand will be satisfied and sales for both buyer and supplier will increase, making them both better off.

14.4.2 Reverse Factoring

Reverse factoring is a variation of the factoring scheme described in section 14.3.2, as the agreement is proposed not by the supplier but the buyer, hence the name. Under a reverse factoring agreement, three parties are involved: a buyer, a supplier, and a financial institution, usually a bank, which is referred to as the factor. To initiate a reverse factoring program, the buyer should have a solvent financial situation, while suppliers may be weaker and in need of cash. To start with, the buyer proposes that the supplier (usually, many of them) participate in a reverse factoring program. Once the supplier accepts, the supplier may decide, for each individual invoice issued to the buyer, to make use of the reverse factoring program to collect the money before the due date. If that is the case, the factor advances the money to the supplier, who benefits from having fresh cash earlier. The factor does charge the supplier a risk premium but does so based not on the supplier's risk but on the buyer's risk, which is usually significantly lower than the supplier's. Therefore, the supplier gets access to cash at a lower cost than otherwise. On the due date, the buyer pays the factor the amount of the invoice and the invoice is settled. The buyer is better-off because payment terms are usually extended under a reverse factoring agreement. If the buyer doesn't pay, the factor goes against the buyer, not the supplier.

Of course, for reverse factoring to work, all players, but especially the supplier, should be better off, despite the fact that he will get the money later than otherwise. For instance, if the buyer doubles the payment days, say from forty-five to ninety days, the supplier should get a price for the loan which is less than half what he can get outside of the reverse factoring agreement, say from 10 percent to less than 5 percent.

Reverse factoring is usually presented in the literature as a win-win-win solution, as the three parties involved benefit from the agreement: the supplier gets the money earlier, and at a significant lower cost; the factor charges a price for the service rendered and gains access to a wide span of suppliers, which may lead to ample cross-selling; finally, the buyer usually benefits from extending the number of days allowed to pay the supplier. In fact, reverse factoring gained momentum after the economic downturn that started in 2008 as a need arose for companies to free up cash. Currently, there are many multinationals from all industries (such as Procter & Gamble, Unilever, ABInBev, Kimberly-Clark, Scania, Caterpillar, and others), which have in place reverse factoring programs with their suppliers. However, there is an inherent risk attached to this contract, as it is based on the ability of the buyer to settle invoices on the due date. For example, if a buyer gets into financial problems, the factors reserve the right to withhold the reverse factoring agreements with the buyer's wide array of suppliers, some of which may go bankrupt due to lack of cash. Therefore, an insolvent powerful buyer may drag her tier-1 (and with them her tier-2 and so on) suppliers into bankruptcy. That is why buyers that set reverse factoring programs should be financially strong.

14.5   Managing Cash

So far, we have focused on managing receivables or payables in isolation. A manager wants to reduce accounts receivable or increase accounts payable because, other things equal, that is good for business profitability. However, so far we have been oblivious to the fact that managing receivables and payables may have a major impact on cash dynamics and thus on the level of liquidity of the company over time. Although cash management is not under the purview of the COO, it is important to be aware of the impact that the operational features and decisions may have on the cash level over time. This is especially important for companies subject to seasonality: cash fluctuations over time may compromise the liquidity of the firm at some periods in the year. Being aware of when cash tensions occur allows for sound planning of agreements with customers and suppliers in order to mitigate that tension. That is precisely the goal of cash profiling.

14.5.1   Improving the Cash Profile

Consider a company subject to seasonality, so that sales are 40 percent higher from March to June (table 14.3). The company collects from customers and pays to suppliers in sixty days. Raw materials (RM) account for 50 percent of sales and are bought three months before the corresponding sales are realized. Costs other than raw materials are considered fixed and are paid at a constant rate throughout the year. If cash is $30 million at the end of the previous year, the cash position at the end of the month is as shown in the last line

Table 14.3
Evolution of sales, collections, payments, and cash over the year (millions).

	Jan	Feb	Mar	Apr	May	Jun	Jul	Aug	Sep	Oct	Nov	Dec
Sales	100	100	140	140	140	140	100	100	100	100	100	100
Collections	100	100	100	100	140	140	140	140	100	100	100	100
Payments (RM)	50	70	70	70	70	50	50	50	50	50	50	50
Payments (other)	50	50	50	50	50	50	50	50	50	50	50	50
Increasing cash	0	−20	−20	−20	20	40	40	40	0	0	0	0
Cash position	30	10	−10	−30	−10	30	70	110	110	110	110	110

Table 14.4
Evolution of sales, collections, payments, and cash over the year (millions).

	Jan	Feb	Mar	Apr	May	Jun	Jul	Aug	Sep	Oct	Nov	Dec
Sales	100	100	140	140	140	140	100	100	100	100	100	100
Collections	100	100	100	100	175	140	105	140	100	100	100	100
Payments (raw materials)	50	70	35	70	105	50	50	50	50	50	50	50
Payments (other)	50	50	50	50	50	50	50	50	50	50	50	50
Increasing cash	0	−20	15	−20	20	40	5	40	0	0	0	0
Cash position	30	10	25	5	25	65	70	110	110	110	110	110

of table 14.3. It can be seen that cash decreases by $60 million from January to April due to seasonality. That creates cash tensions in March, April, and May. To alleviate situations such as this one, companies may resort to a line of credit (a short-term loan) from a bank that is automatically triggered when the cash position becomes negative.

As an alternative, the company could work with suppliers and customers as follows:

• Grant discounts to some customers for prompt payment from April to July so that money is received earlier, say, in thirty days.

• Negotiate payment extensions with some suppliers in January and February. For instance, an agreement can be reached to pay some suppliers in ninety days in January and February and, in return, pay earlier (say in thirty days) in some of the months where there is plenty of cash (e.g., August to December). This might suit some suppliers' needs for cash given that the seasonality cycles of the firm and those of their suppliers may not be coincidental.

In our example, say that the firm delays half of the payments to suppliers in March and April and collects one-fourth of the receivables due in June and July thirty days earlier. The impact of these actions on the treasury of the firm is shown in table 14.4.

As the last line reveals, cash position is now expected to be always positive. The main advantage of this approach is that it may be cheaper than resorting to a line of credit. Of course, both solutions can be combined. The overall effect of this cash flattening can be quantified, for instance, by calculating the coefficient of variation of the cash position. In

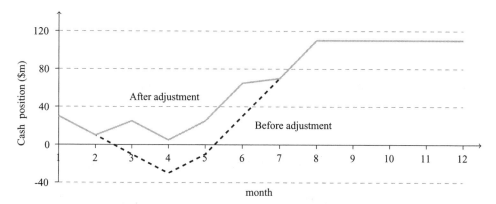

Figure 14.5
Cash position over time before and after modifying agreements with customers and suppliers.

this case, it decreases from 1.00 to 0.65. Plotting both cash positions in a graph may also be useful (figure 14.5).

14.5.2   Coming Up with the Minimum Cash Level

Minimum cash is the amount of cash a firm needs to run daily operations. It has to be sufficient to cope with both daily cash fluctuations and industry disruptions.

Daily cash fluctuations Cash is constantly changing due to the discrete nature of payments made or received. Also, payments are subject to cycles—payroll payments occur at the end of the month, tax payments on two or more specific months of the year, and so on—and seasonality—if 80 percent of a firm's sales occur in winter, then collection from customers and, possibly, payments to suppliers will be mainly concentrated in a single quarter. That means that the treasurer of a firm has to forecast future cash needs in order to not run out of cash and get reasonable yields from excess cash. In addition to that, and given that forecasts are almost always wrong, a certain amount of safety cash must be kept to deal with these fluctuations. Safety cash can be substituted by a line of credit allowances; that is, the firm should have a line of credit open but not used. Only when the need for cash is larger than the forecast, the unused portion of a line of credit should be used temporarily.

Industry disruptions By definition, sales in risky industries are much more volatile than in others. This is true either if sales are measured in units (demand may change dramatically very quickly, supply may be suddenly compromised because of a supply chain disruption) or dollars (e.g., due to price or exchange rate fluctuations) or both. In such industries, treasurers should keep a portion of the firm's cash as strategic cash to be used only in case there is a disruption.

To prevent a firm from running out of cash—and eventually going bankrupt—firms resort to a number of strategies, such as limiting the amount of sales from a single customer, keeping insolvency insurance, or hedging against commodity price fluctuations by buying futures or other derivatives. Irrespective of whether or not these measures are taken, a key underlying question is how much cash (or credit allowance) is needed to guarantee that the firm doesn't run out of cash? Although we may not have an accurate answer for this question, we can shed some light by proposing two techniques that are commonly used in operations and supply chain management. To begin with, safety and strategic cash should be addressed differently.

Safety cash To calculate the right amount of safety cash, managers can use the newsvendor logic used in inventory models. Indeed, often the three conditions provided in appendix C.2 concur:

(1) There is a source of variability, as some future cash flows are subject to uncertainty. To measure this variability, the standard deviation of historical forecasting errors can be used (exercise 12 asks you to calculate this).

(2) The option to obtain cash from other sources may not exist. Once a line of credit has been exhausted, a firm may encounter difficulties in obtaining additional funds quickly from other sources.

(3) There is an underage and an overage cost. The underage cost is the cost of running out of cash, which may have mild consequences (the firm has to pay a premium to get a more expensive credit) or severe (the firm may even go bankrupt). The overage cost is the cost of having too much idle cash. The unit cost is typically the marginal cost of short-term debt. Admittedly, underage costs are much larger than overage costs and are harder, if not impossible, to quantify. To get around this difficulty, managers may impose a small probability of going bankrupt, which plays the same role as the customer service level (CSL) in the newsvendor model. For instance, a service level of 99.9 percent means that the firm is expected to run out of cash only once in one thousand times (exercise 12 elaborates on this).

Strategic cash To estimate the amount of strategic cash, managers can use the same logic as in calculating strategic or risk mitigation inventory, as explained in Simchi-Levi, Schmidt, and Wei (2014). The main idea is that strategic inventory should be able to cover expected demand during recovery time from a disruption. Likewise, strategic or risk mitigation cash should be able to cover for cash disruptions during the time to recovery from the moment a disruption occurs.

14.6 Is There an Optimal Level for OWC?

We have presented several methods that firms use to reduce OWC. A valid question at this point is: Is there is a limit beyond which reducing OWC further may be counter productive? This question is related to the fact that some finance books recommend that current assets

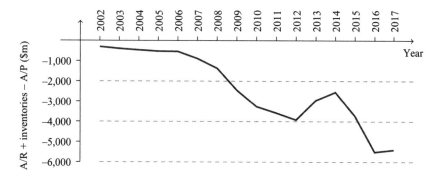

Figure 14.6
Evolution of OWC (receivables + inventory − payables) for Amazon between 2002 and 2017 (minimal cash is assumed zero).
Source: Amazon (2019).

should be larger than current liabilities or the firm may face liquidity tensions that may drag it into bankruptcy.

First let's see why the two subjects are related. Given a seven-item balance sheet, the condition current assets > current liabilities can be written as:

cash + receivables + inventory > payables + short-term debt ⇒

excess cash + (required cash + receivables + inventory − payables) > short-term debt ⇒

OWC > short-term debt − excess cash

Therefore, if OWC is smaller than short-term debt less excess cash, then current assets will be smaller than current liabilities or, equivalently, current ratio will be smaller than one. But, as we discussed in section 9.2.4.2, this is not necessarily a bad thing. Consequently, having negative OWC is not necessarily a bad thing either. Furthermore, designing a business based on holding negative OWC may actually be a great idea if the defined strategy is sustainable over time.

A case in point is that of Amazon, which collects relatively fast, pays relatively late, and holds a moderate amount of inventory, so that OWC is negative. Figure 14.6 shows the evolution of OWC for Amazon for the period 2002–2017. OWC was not only negative for sixteen years in a row but decreased in all but two years. That means that the more Amazon's sales grow, the more excess cash the business generates to invest in additional distribution centers, inventories, and technology. Accordingly, Amazon's cash conversion cycle has been negative since the company began operations.

That generated cash was not given to shareholders but was kept in the company to protect it from demand fluctuations and to undertake new investments. As figure 14.7 shows, the amount of cash relative to sales decreases over time as demand becomes less volatile (the secondary axis in the graph shows the five-year moving average of the coefficient of

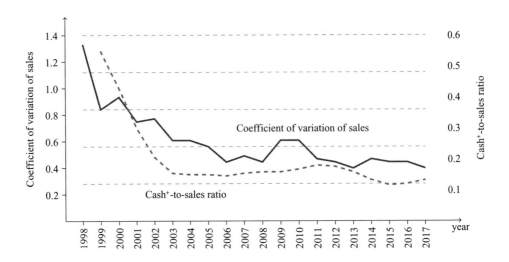

Figure 14.7
Evolution of cash$^+$ (cash + cash equivalents + marketable securities) / sales and the coefficient of variation of sales (five-year moving average) for Amazon between 1998 and 2017.
Source: Amazon (2019).

variation of sales). At the qualitative level, this makes sense: as market risk decreases, less cash is needed to buffer against market uncertainty. At the quantitative level, it is certainly notable that the ratio cash$^+$-to-sales closely follows the variability of sales.

In 1997, when the company went public, Amazon's net profit was -18.7 percent. Subsequent years brought even worse news. (Net profit was -20.4 percent in 1998, -43.9 percent in 1999, and -51.1 percent in 2000!) Despite this fact, shareholders understood that their funds and (mainly) suppliers' were supporting Amazon's growth, and they were patient enough to wait for better times. After eight consecutive years of losses, Amazon's net profit turned black for the first time in 2003. As of 2018, Amazon is the most valuable retailer in the world in terms of market capitalization. This stunning success would not have been possible if OWC had been positive, which illustrates how important it is to focus on OWC, even at the design phase of a business.

14.7   Summary

This chapter has presented the levers firms usually have available to manage their operating working capital. By definition, the options are reducing cash, receivables, and inventory or increasing payables. Although reducing operating working capital may be easy, the actual challenge is how to do it without going against the strategy of the firm or putting in danger the continuity of the firm due to lack of cash. Likewise, a firm's actions to reduce OWC may go against its suppliers or customers. Ideally, firms should improve OWC by taking win-win approaches that make the whole supply chain better off.

Exercises

1. Define operating working capital.

2. Other things being equal, is it better that OWC is large or small?

3. Discuss the pros and cons of paying suppliers late.

4. Firm A operates in a B2B industry. Firm B operates in a business to consumer (B2C) industry. Which firm is likely to have lower accounts receivable as a percentage of its sales?

5. Firm A operates in a make-to-order operations environment. Firm B operates in a make-to-stock operations environment. Which firm is likely to have lower inventory as a percentage of its COGS?

6. Firm A operates as a brick-and-mortar retailer. Firm B is a e-commerce retailer. Which firm is likely to have lower operating working capital?

7. Firm A faces more demand uncertainty than Firm B. As far as demand uncertainty is concerned, which firm is likely to have a higher average level of cash during the year?

8. Calculate the annual rate equivalent to the sales discount given by the terms 1/10, 30/net.

9. What might be an issue with having small or even negative OWC?

10. Repeat the VMI example in section 14.2.3 assuming this time that the tax rate to be paid by Linner and the supplier is not zero, but 20 percent.

11. A firm buys a key manufacturing part from a supplier. Lot size is one hundred units, worth one week of (steady) production on average. In order to save transportation costs, the firm is considering increasing the lot size to eight hundred units. The cost of the part is $400 and the firm pays its supplier in thirty days.

    a. Explain why average inventory will increase by $140,000 in the long term.

    b. What is the impact of increasing the lot size on the assets of the firm upon the reception of the first larger batch?

    c. What is the impact of increasing the lot size on the assets of the firm upon the payment of the first larger batch?

    d. Will accounts payable increase in the long term? Explain why or why not.

12. Given the following historic levels of cash (actual and forecast) of a firm:

	Jan	Feb	Mar	Apr	May	Jun	Jul	Aug	Sep	Oct	Nov	Dec
Actual	220	210	180	240	235	220	200	190	170	200	220	205
Forecast	190	170	200	220	205	220	210	180	240	235	220	200

    a. Calculate the standard deviation of the forecasting errors.

b. Calculate the safety cash needed to cope with cash flows fluctuations if the treasurer of the firm wants the probability of running out of cash to be below 0.1 percent.

13. If the marginal cost of debt is 15 percent, what payment extension terms of a trade credit offer would make use of trade credit preferable over a 2 percent / ten-day payment discount?

References

Amazon. 2019. "Annual report 2019." Accessed July 18, 2019. https://ir.aboutamazon.com/annual-reports.

Hammond, Janice H. May 1994. "Barilla SpA (A)." *HBS* 694-046 (Revised March 2008).

Martínez Abascal, Eduardo. 2012. *Finance for managers*. Berkshire, UK: McGraw Hill.

Simchi-Levi, David, William Schmidt, and Yehua Wei. 2014. "From superstorms to factory fires: Managing unpredictable supply-chain disruptions." *Harvard Business Review*, January–February.

15   Solving Operations and Supply Chain Trade-Offs

There are no solutions, there are only trade-offs.
—Thomas Sowell, economist

The previous chapter was devoted to understanding and managing OWC. Attaining the correct amount of OWC, although extremely important for a firm, cannot be done without regard for other aspects of the business. Improving OWC may be at the expense of other—equally important—parts of the value proposition. For instance, reducing inventory improves OWC, but, other things equal, worsens customer service level. This perfectly illustrates the need for a broader view when making decisions in the operations management realm. These decisions, more often than not, imply solving a trade-off between two opposing goals that cannot be achieved simultaneously.

This chapter is aimed at shedding some light on how to address some of the most important decisions involving trade-offs that arise in operations and supply chain management. For some decisions, a short case study is presented, and pros and cons are analyzed when addressing the case. Particular emphasis is made on studying the impact of each decision on the three most important financial statements—namely the balance sheet, income statement, and cash flow statement—as well as on risk, and, ultimately, value creation for stakeholders.

15.1   Offshoring versus Local Sourcing

In today's globalized economy, confronted by rising costs and fierce competition, firms perceive offshoring as a decision of strategic significance.[1] The original idea behind offshoring was that Western firms with high labor costs could make huge savings by

---

1. *Offshoring* and *outsourcing* are often used interchangeably in news articles. Outsourcing is defined in the popular press as "obtaining certain services or products from a third party company, essentially sourcing something like accounting services or manufacturing of a certain input to another company" (Glen 2019). Offshoring refers to "obtaining services or products from another country, [...] it can also refer to simply re-locating certain aspects of a business to another country" (Glen 2019). From these definitions it becomes clear that offshoring does not necessarily preclude outsourcing and vice versa. In this section, we use offshoring to refer to sourcing from a location abroad, whether a third party or own facility.

relocating business processes to low-wage locations. For many years this strategy has worked fairly well in many industries. However, as labor costs in some Asian countries have steadily increased over the last decades, companies with primary markets based in Western countries have begun reassessing their offshoring strategies. Recently, *reshoring*—the practice of reintroducing domestic manufacturing to a country—has been gaining momentum and considerable attention in the popular press.

The question underlying offshoring is therefore: What is the fundamental trade-off from a financial point of view for a company that may decide to offshore part of its business? As mentioned, the obvious advantage of offshoring is labor savings, at least in the short- and medium-term. The less obvious drawback of offshoring is that typically lead times grow dramatically. Longer lead times entail not only higher complexity but also a number of other undesired effects, such as higher pipeline inventory or extra difficulty in forecasting demand, which in turn implies increasing safety inventory for the same level of service and increasing leftovers due to obsolescence or mismatches with the market preferences. Roughly speaking, and put in financial terms, there is a primary trade-off between the income statement (reducing labor cost) and the balance sheet (reducing inventory). Quantifying both effects in a comparable way is key to making sound decisions regarding offshoring.

The case of Hy-Lite Blocks, outlined below, serves to shed some light on these issues that many firms are faced with when they offshore their manufacturing to countries located far away from their product markets.

🔍 Case study

Hy-Lite, a U.S. Block Windows Company

Hy-Lite Blocks, a division of U.S. Block Windows since March 2009, molds acrylic architectural blocks for use in privacy windows, indoor radius walls, and partitions. Its acrylic product line, ranging from picture windows to interior systems that make up walls and doors, is sold mainly to residential home builders throughout the United States but also to retail stores such as Home Depot and Lowe's. A key process in the company's production system is the molding of the acrylic cubes that are linked together like Legos to create Hy-Lite's products. Seeking cost savings in this labor-intensive process, the company moved its window block manufacturing segment to China to save on labor costs. However, after reassessing the financial pros and cons of outsourcing to China, in 2010 Hy-Lite decided to reshore its molding operation back to its company headquarters and manufacturing facility in Pensacola, Florida.

As Roger Murphy, Hy-Lite's president, says, "five years ago, the molds used to make the blocks were moved to China … to save costs. [This involved] a long, complex supply chain, and complicated inventory planning and forecasting, and as oil got more expensive, so did shipping costs, effectively eradicating any cost savings that we were realizing. We found that the hidden costs and complexities of sourcing in China included carrying excess inventory, which we were able to reduce by over $500,000 and bring down warehouse space requirements by 35,000 square feet" (Goldsberry 2010). In addition, the longer and more uncertain lead time associated with offshoring had an adverse impact not only on the inventory carried by the company but also on the service level. "With the manufacturing in China, you had to forecast out lead time that with transportation could mean 12 to 14 weeks to delivery," said Murphy. "So you were always carrying more inventory than you needed and you also were at risk of being out of something if demand spiked" (Johnson 2015).

Reshoring the acrylic molding jobs back to Pensacola, Hy-Lite has reduced its typical lead time on filling orders to four days, being able to quickly fill customer orders in the volatile American building market. Finally, other hidden costs associated with manufacturing in China included higher employee turnover, lower productivity, threat of intellectual property theft, and the cost of quality. "Defective blocks in China were usually thrown away," whereas "by making them in-house, we can regrind that block, so our scrap cost basically goes to nothing," said Murphy (Johnson 2015). At the same time, if a quality problem is discovered in parts reaching customers in the United States, there are likely quality problems throughout the entire supply chain, stretching all the way back to China. That makes the true cost of manufacturing offshore in places such as China a whole lot more than the quoted price of the parts on the RFQ.

Sources: Goldsberry (2010); Johnson (2015).

As the Hy-Lite case suggests, one mistake companies often make is focusing on the cost savings from cheaper labor instead of considering the total cost of sourcing from offshore suppliers. As a result, they may underestimate the tactical costs of manufacturing overseas. In the following paragraphs, we provide an outline of these costs sorted into three broader categories: quality costs, hidden logistics costs, and lead time.

Quality costs Maintaining product quality and integrity is often a critical issue for firms offshoring their manufacturing operations. Quality issues are often tied to difficulties in establishing an effective quality culture; to language, time-zone, and local culture differences that make communication difficult and can cause misunderstandings; but also to high employee turnover that reduces the benefit of training. Quality costs may also rise because of a lack of visibility into offshore manufacturing operations that reduce a firm's ability

Figure 15.1
A Hy-Lite window.
Source: https://www.hy-lite.com/Hy-lite-US-Block-Windows-Gallery.cfm?galleryID=79#group-9.

to rapidly identify and resolve quality issues before it is too late. A case in point is that of Mattel, the multinational toy manufacturer. In August and September 2007, the company made a series of product recalls, involving more than 20 million toys manufactured in China, due to lead contamination and magnets that could become loose.[2] Hefty mitigation costs aside, the accompanying bad press caused severe reputation damage, with the knock-on effect of a plunge in sales, forcing inevitable price drops.

Hidden logistics costs Transportation and logistics are key considerations for companies that go offshore. Remote manufacturing will incur more shipping costs than manufacturing closer to customers and suppliers. In addition to the cost paid directly for the transportation of goods, there are also costs associated with insurance, fees, permits, duties, tariffs, and compliance with import/export restrictions that must be taken into account when compiling a business case for offshore manufacturing. There are also several risks that need to be considered, such as potential disruption caused by natural disasters or macroeconomic changes, volatility in fuel prices, exchange rates, and so on. Incorporating these risks into the total cost calculations of producing overseas is crucial, as hidden logistics costs may offset much of the expected cost savings from cheaper labor. Section 15.2 presents in more detail the financial considerations in global supply chains.

2. See Barboza and Story (2007).

Lead time When a company offshores its production, it will have to deal with longer and more uncertain lead times. Long, trans-continental supply chains are usually prone to delays associated with longer shipping times, unexpected weather, batched shipments, slower production, labor inefficiency, quality problems, customs inspections, and so forth. In addition to these delays, producing overseas limits a firm's ability to respond quickly to fluctuating customer demand. While effective forecasting can deal with this challenge, even the most accurate forecasting methods will not remain accurate when they must project customer demand up to several months in advance of production. A direct consequence of the longer, more uncertain lead times and the subsequent forecasting inefficiency is the buildup of inventory in order for firms to meet short-term demand surges and protect themselves from delayed or defective deliveries.

To evaluate the total cost of sourcing from offshore suppliers, companies are increasingly interested in putting a monetary value on the above cost elements. This is generally done by introducing certain assumptions and projections in pro forma financial statements. For example, to account for quality costs, firms will need to incorporate extra expenses for training, oversight, and even inventory write-offs into their projections. Similarly, they may need to project extra logistics costs for expediting the delivery of inventory in case of demand surges or shipping disruptions. They may also consider the cost of hedging for some of the risks associated with transcontinental logistics, such as weather, fuel price, or currency exchange volatility.

ⓘ **On the cost of offshoring**
When evaluating offshore opportunities, firms need to also consider inconspicuous costs associated to quality, logistics, and lead time.

Valuing lead time is more challenging—though, the implications of longer lead time on the tactical costs of producing overseas may be quite significant. When the length of time between placing and receiving an order is long, firms need to carry more inventory to properly address unexpected contingencies. This drives up not only the cost of acquiring the larger inventory of goods but also the cost of carrying more inventory. The latter includes both direct expenses associated with storing, managing, and maintaining the goods (such as warehouse space, administrative costs, cost of obsolescence and deterioration, and insurance) but also the opportunity cost associated with capital tied up in goods that are not utilized or sold in a timely manner. Inventory management requires trading off the costs against the benefits of having more goods available on demand. In the following case, we use conventional inventory management models to demonstrate the impact of lead time on a firm's finances.

Exercise

Kitchef: Closeby, TX or Faraway, China?

Kate Mansfield has just finished her master's in supply chain management and works as an intern for Kitchef, a U.S. company that produces high-quality innovative cookware appliances and utensils for the contemporary home kitchen. The company is considering offshoring the production of one of its top selling products to Asia. Before presenting the idea to the executive board, Bill Gliatis, the company's COO, has asked Kate to evaluate the implication of such a decision on the firm's finances.

The Breadmaker Plus 100, a stainless-steel, special-purpose oven with a comprehensive selection of preprogrammed recipes for homemade bread cooking, is one of the company's top selling products in the US market. The product is available through a network of selected retail stores to which Kitchef sells the product at a wholesale price of $95. Weekly demand at the company's Dallas, TX warehouse is i.i.d. normally distributed with a mean of 1,000 units and a standard deviation of 400 units. The warehouse aims for a customer service level of 97 percent. For the production of Breadmaker Plus 100, the company is currently using a contractor manufacturer located in the city Closeby, TX. Kitchef places its orders with the contractor manufacturer weekly. The variable cost per manufactured item is $50 (including transportation costs) and the lead time is two weeks. In an effort to improve the product margins, the company's procurement manager recently explored the possibility of producing the Breadmaker Plus 100 overseas. After evaluating several Asian manufacturers, he identified a high-quality contract manufacturer located in the city of Faraway in China.

Based on the offer by this manufacturer, each unit will cost $30 to Kitchef under free-on-board port terms. According to the logistics manager of Kitchef, the transportation cost for shipping a product unit from China to Texas will be $10. Moreover, using historical data, he estimates that the transportation lead time from offshoring production to China will be normally distributed with a mean of twelve weeks and a standard deviation of two weeks. Finally, due to economies of scale (full 20-foot container load) in transportation, each order to the new manufacturer must be a multiple of 4,000 units. Faced with these numbers, Bill is quite confident that offshoring production of Breadmaker Plus 100 presents a great opportunity for the company. Even when considering the high transportation cost of shipping the product from China, the Faraway option's variable cost would still be 80 percent of the current one. However, knowing that the firm's cash reserves are limited and the company's CFO is concerned about the firm's ability to continue financing its working capital at good terms (at the moment, the annual cost of short-term financing is 10 percent), Bill has asked Kate to double-check the numbers and provide her estimates on the overall changes that offshoring will have in Kitchef's finances.

To help Kate with this exercise, we will have to resort to relevant material from basic courses on inventory management (see appendix C for a brief introduction to inventory models). In particular, we need to start by computing total inventory for each scenario, which consists of safety inventory (to protect against demand and lead time randomness), cycle inventory (half of expected replenishment quantity), and pipeline inventory (i.e., inventory in transit).

Current scenario As Kitchef places its orders with the local manufacturer on a weekly basis, it makes sense to assume that the company follows a base-stock policy. That is, at the beginning of each week, the company reviews the inventory position of Breadmaker Plus 100 and places an order that raises its inventory position up to a predetermined quantity, commonly known as base-stock level. For a base-stock policy with review period of R weeks, deterministic lead time of L weeks, normally distributed weekly demand with mean D and standard deviation σ_D, and desired service level CSL, we can apply the following formulas to calculate the different types of inventory (see section C.3.2):

- safety inventory $= \Phi^{-1}(\text{CSL}) \cdot \sigma_D \cdot \sqrt{L+R} = 1.88 \cdot 400 \cdot \sqrt{2+1} = 1{,}303$
- cycle inventory $= \frac{D \cdot R}{2} = \frac{1{,}000 \cdot 1}{2} = 500$
- pipeline inventory $= D \cdot L = 1{,}000 \cdot 2 = 2{,}000$

Alternative scenario In the case of offshore manufacturing, the order quantity (Q) is fixed. Therefore, it makes sense for the company to follow a continuous review policy and place its orders whenever its inventory position *hits* an appropriately selected reorder point that will consider the uncertainty in both weekly demand and supply lead time. For normally distributed lead time with mean L and standard deviation σ_L, the applicable formulas are the following (see the Random Lead-Time exercise in section B.5.2):

- safety inventory $= \Phi^{-1}(\text{CSL}) \cdot \sqrt{L\sigma_D^2 + D^2\sigma_L^2} = 1.88 \cdot 400 \cdot \sqrt{12 \cdot 400^2 + 1{,}000^2 \cdot 2^2} = 4{,}576$
- cycle inventory $= \frac{Q}{2} = \frac{4{,}000}{2} = 2{,}000$
- pipeline inventory $= D \cdot L = 1{,}000 \cdot 12 = 12{,}000$

Table 15.1 summarizes the inventory results for each scenario.

A direct consequence of the long lead time associated with moving its production overseas will be that Kitchef needs to carry about five times as much inventory as it currently holds. Notice that an important portion of the extra inventory represents products in transit, which, while part of the firm's overall inventory, may be easily overlooked because it is not sitting in a warehouse.

Table 15.1
Average inventory.

Source	Cycle	Safety	Pipeline	Total
Closeby, TX	500	1,303	2,000	3,803
Faraway, China	2,000	4,576	12,000	18,576

How does the increase in inventory directly affect the firm's finances? To answer this question, we will need to consider the effects on each of the three financial statements, namely the balance sheet, income statement, and statement of cash flows. (Indirect effects as described in section 14.2.3 are ignored.)

Balance sheet In terms of dollar value, the total inventory with offshoring is equal to $743,040 $(18,576 \cdot 40)$ versus $190,150 $(3,803 \cdot 50)$ for domestic production.[3] That is, the capital that is tied up in inventory with offshoring is about four times the amount with local production. The increase in inventory by $552,890 in the firm's balance sheet translates into a direct increase of OWC by the same amount. Assuming that Kitchef doesn't hold excess cash (that is, the firm only holds the necessary cash for running the as-is business), it will have to resort to external funds for financing its increased working capital position. In other words, the firm will be required to renegotiate its credit lines or take up long-term debt for sustaining its operational needs. Therefore, we expect that the debt on Kitchef's balance sheet will increase by $552,890.

Cash flow statement The increase in working capital has a similar impact on the statement of cash flows. The cash outflows for operating activities, associated with the increase in inventory, must be counterbalanced by either a decrease in initial cash (if the firm holds excess cash reserves) or an increase in debt (which is what we have assumed in our example). Whatever the firm's choice, by the time it transfers its production overseas, it will need to secure $552,890 to uphold this decision.

Income statement The impact on the income statement is somewhat trickier. First, debt comes at a cost. As a general rule, the greater the amount of debt a firm holds, the higher the risk for the debt holders. Interest rates are linked to the size of the loan; therefore, larger loans imply higher interest payments. Consequently, the debt holders would require greater interest payments in order to be compensated for the higher risk they have undertaken. Assuming that Kitchef can extend its credit line at no additional cost, the annual interest for the extra $552,890 in debt the firm will have to hold for offshoring its production amounts to $55,289. Second, in addition to the cost of debt (interest), the firm's income statement will also incorporate the transportation cost of $10 per unit, which will appear as

3. Notice that the value of inventory incorporates the transportation cost (from China to Texas), which is necessary for getting the product in place and ready for use.

part of the cost of goods sold. Finally, the inventory holding costs requires careful attention. Note that in our calculations, other than the interest expenses, we have not considered any inventory holding costs, such as warehouse space, handling and administration, obsolescence and deterioration, insurance, and cost of equity. Depending on a firm's accounting practices, these costs may appear in different entries in the income statement. Practitioners often estimate inventory carrying costs as a fixed percentage of the total inventory value, which may range well into the double digits. In our example, we avoid applying a proportional inventory holding cost, recognizing that there may be economies of scale for some of the elements of carrying cost (e.g., warehouse space, handling and administrative costs, etc.). Nonetheless, a key takeaway is that the total cost of inventory, which includes both capital and carrying costs, should be considered when evaluating the impact of higher inventory on the income statement.

Summarizing the above points, Kate can provide the following feedback to her boss about the implications on the firm's finances of producing overseas.

• The working capital will increase by approximately $552,890 as a result of higher inventory needed to support its operations.

• The firm will need to increase its debt by $552,890 to fund its decision to produce overseas.

• The interest expenses will increase by $55,289 if the firm's current interest terms do not change as a result of the increase in debt.

• The annual EBIT must incorporate the extra costs associated with carrying 18,576 versus 3,803 units of inventory. These may include handling and administrative costs, cost of obsolescence and deterioration, and insurance.

• New investment in warehouse space may also be needed. Such investment will require additional external funds that may deteriorate the firm's borrowing capacity but also will further decrease earnings through depreciation.

• Depending on the total costs and the resulting margins from producing overseas, some key performance metrics, such as the ROA and GMROI, may eventually become worse.

The Kitchef case illustrates that while companies may be enticed by the cost savings from moving production to low-wage locations, they need to do extensive research and consider the total landed cost to make sure that the benefits actually do outweigh the drawbacks. Total landed cost includes purchasing, transportation, port charges, duties, taxes, and insurance but also the cost of human resources for planning and control. Equally important is the cost of lead time. In addition to constraints on a firm's ability to respond quickly to changing demand, long lead times result to stockpiling of inventory and extra costs for storing, handling, and financing that inventory. The impact of offshoring on a firm's OWC and the subsequent cost in capital are important considerations that are often overlooked.

15.2 Financial Considerations in Global Supply Chain Design

The previous section focused on offshoring; namely, the practice followed by companies to serve their domestic market by moving their production overseas mainly to take advantage of the low labor costs in the selected factory location. This is the simplest version of international supply chains. However, the present economy operates with a large number of multinational companies competing all over the globe that have to deal with an important challenge that is part of the growth at international level: complex manufacturing and distribution networks. As companies' operations expand around the world, many businesses established for years in developed countries are locating manufacturing plants and distribution in developing countries—actually, globalization and the rising incomes in these countries make them extremely desirable as markets, not just manufacturing hubs. The focus of this section is on the financial considerations of global supply chains, where products are supplied, manufactured, and distributed from variable facilities located throughout the world.

Over the last decades, world trade patterns have been changing, and this has driven subsequent transformations in supply chains. Based on U.S. census data, the share of products imported to the United States from related corporate entities constitutes nearly half of all U.S. imports in 2013 (Hersh and Gurwitz 2014). It is readily apparent that global operations are becoming increasingly significant, as many supply-chain activities such as sourcing, manufacturing, and logistics are now widely dispersed around the world. While this expansion brings a lot of complexity in terms of logistics and supply chain design, at the same time an important number of opportunities are brought up.

In this global competitive environment, many governments are willing to provide incentives to attract business—via tax breaks or trade agreements—in order to support the economic development of their countries. Other governments use tariffs and trade restrictions as a form of protection mechanism to safeguard domestic production output. These political and economic forces have a profound impact on the cost of doing international business, eventually influencing the companies' choices regarding supply chain design.

Next, we briefly outline the most important factors that affect global trade and we discuss their implications on supply chain activities.

Sales tax Also known as VAT, sales tax is a consumption tax imposed by the government on the sale of goods and services. In a business-to-consumer context, VAT is collected at the point of sale and passed on to the government. In business-to-business context, VAT is charged by the seller to the buyer in each stage of a production process; then, it is usually recovered at each stage except the last (i.e., final consumer).

Corporate income tax This is the income tax imposed by the government to firms that have created a taxable presence in a country. As the taxation rules among countries are different, this often creates incentives for companies to locate their sales organizations—thus, shift their profit—to low-tax countries. Such practices, however, might give rise to tax-avoidance issues, especially if the majority of a company's sales take place in higher-tax countries.

Tariffs or customs duties These are taxes levied upon goods as they cross national boundaries. Tariffs may be further classified into three groups—transit duties, export duties, and import duties. **Transit duties** are levied by a country through which the goods pass on their transportation from the originating to the destination country. **Export duties** are levied by the originating country of goods and are usually applicable to raw material export sectors—such as coffee, rubber, palm oil, and various forest and mineral products—rather than advanced industrial products. **Import duties** are the most common types of custom duties, levied by the destination country of goods. The applicable rates, usually known as a tariff schedule, depend on the country of origin and type of good—on the basis of existing trade agreements and the importing country's policies.

Duty drawbacks Border tax adjustments, whereby the duties or taxes levied on imported goods are refunded—in whole or in part—when the goods are re-exported or used in the manufacture of exported goods are called duty drawbacks. Duty drawbacks may depend on the country where the components are coming from but not on the final destination of the finished product.

Local content requirement A requirement that some specific fraction of a good must be produced with domestic supply. This may be imposed by a government to companies as a prerequisite for installing a production facility in the country but also in conjunction with duty drawbacks to assure a certain percentage of local content in the final product that goes out of the country.

Quotas These are trade restrictions imposed by a government to set a physical limit on the quantity of a good that a country can import or export during a particular period. Countries use quotas in international trade as a means for regulating the volume of trade between them and other countries.

Regional trade agreements Reciprocal trade agreements between two or more partners, which include free trade and import duty harmonization, are regional trade agreements. In January 2019, there were 291 regional trade agreements in force, corresponding to 467 notifications from members of the World Trade Organization (World Trade Organization n.d.).

Preferential trade arrangements Preferential trade arrangements are unilateral trade preferences, under which developed countries grant preferential tariffs to imports from developing countries.

Exchange rate The rate at which a nation's currency will be exchanged for another is the exchange rate. Exchange rates can be floating—when their value is determined by the foreign-exchange market—or fixed when domestic currencies are fixed to a widely accepted currency like the US dollar. Furthermore, they can be categorized as the spot rate—which is the current rate at the spot market—or a forward rate, which is the rate at which market participants can lock in by purchasing and selling future contracts.

From the above list, it becomes clear that global supply chains are inextricably linked with these factors. On one hand, there are regional trade agreements that create opportunities for companies to expand their operations to new markets. On the other hand, there are trade protection mechanisms that put serious constraints in the firms' global supply chain design choices. For instance, tariffs, quotas, and local content requirements may encourage manufacturers to establish plants inside the countries they want to enter commercially to benefit from tariff and trade concessions. Given that duties can easily account for 15 to 20 percent of total supply chain costs, the consideration and effective management of indirect taxes and incentives should be important considerations in global supply chain network design.

 Politico-economic forces and global supply chains

> Changing global supply chains have an impact on the firms' indirect tax burden, risk, and competitiveness. But also changing economic and political forces (such as tariffs, trade agreements, protectionism, quotas, and exchange rates) create challenges for global supply chain design.

There are also some recent developments that will most likely affect the shaping of global supply chains in the near future. First, several countries are providing tax incentives and grants aimed at stimulating job creation in high-technology and nonpolluting industries. These are accompanied by new *green* taxes—on the basis of a product's environmental footprint—to influence consumer behavior and protect the environment. Second, closer attention is placed by tax authorities and international economic organizations on intracompany transactions—among entities located around the globe—in response to corporate tax avoidance. Third, political turmoil under different forms—such as the British exit from the European Union, the trade war initiated by the Trump administration in the United States, or the rise of populist parties around the world—might give rise to protectionist policies, often against any economic logic (hence, difficult to plan for). Finally, the economic growth in developing countries—and the huge amounts of resources needed to support this growth—does not only contribute to volatility in commodity prices, exchange rates, and labor costs but also might influence the appetite of developed countries to take measures for protecting their local economies.

The case of Volvo, outlined below, may help shed some light on the issues companies face with their global supply chain due to changes in the regulatory environment and the duties' status quo.

🔍 **Case study**

Volvo Cars

Over the last few years, Volvo Cars, the Swedish auto manufacturer, has realized a remarkable growth—reaching record sales in 2018—following its acquisition by the Zhejiang Geely Holding Group (a Chinese holding company) in 2010. Apart from Europe—Volvo's traditional market—the company has a strong presence in China and the United States where it realized double digit sales growth in 2018 (14.1 percent and 20.6 percent, respectively) (Volvo Car Group 2019). Currently, Volvo operates assembly plants in Europe, China, Malaysia, and the United States, where various models are produced and distributed around the world. For example, Volvo's midsize SUV model XC60—voted as World Car of the Year 2018 and the company's top-selling model accounting for 30 percent of total sales—is produced in Sweden and China, with the U.S. market being served only by the latter since March 2018 (Shepardson 2018). Also, Volvo has started production of the latest generation of S60 sedan in the United States' first Volvo factory in Ridgeville, South Carolina—planning to have the United States as the sole global source for this model (Priddle 2017).

Things would be dreamlike for the company if it weren't for the trade war by President Trump's administration—which escalated in 2018—in an effort to decrease the country's trade deficit and protect domestic production. As part of this trade war, the United States imposed a 25 percent tariff on Chinese cars, on top of the 2.5 percent already in place. In retaliation, China imposed an additional 25 percent tariff on U.S. vehicle imports, on top of the original 15 percent in place (Kiley 2018). Obviously, these extra charges in import duties will have a direct impact on Volvo's ability to market its models in the two countries, potentially causing severe economic harm. Currently, the company—along with other automotive manufacturers—is trying to get exemption from the new levies, which are unlikely to happen. As a consequence, Volvo is currently halting its plans for capacity expansion of its U.S. facility, while it may need to eventually reconfigure its assembly lines and trade routes if the trade war continues (Kiley 2018).

Sources: Priddle (2017); Shepardson (2018); Kiley (2018); Volvo Car Group (2019).

The above situation has not only affected Volvo and other automotive manufacturers but also many businesses in several industries. Of course, in addition to changes in the regulatory environment, firms with global supply chains are faced with other types of risk presented in this section. This gives rise to an interesting question: What actions can companies—and operations, in particular—take to protect against the risks outlined in this section?

One thing that companies can do is utilize financial hedging—a type of insurance policy—to protect against exchange rate risk or volatility in the prices of commodities. For example, industries that have the majority of their costs realized in one currency but a large portion of their revenue collected in another may wish to protect against the risk of devaluation of the latter by investing in some currency forwards or options contract—a legal agreement to buy or sell a specific currency at a predetermined price within a pre-set time frame. Similarly, companies whose operating costs rely heavily on the prices of some commodities—as, for example, the airline industry on the price of fuel—can invest in options contracts to hedge against rising commodity prices by buying the right to purchase the commodity in the future at a predetermined price. Actually, fuel hedging has been a strategic component for Southwest—the world's third largest airline by passengers carried—since a long time ago, helping the company achieve forty-five consecutive years of profitability—an exceptional performance in this industry (Bailey 2007). Other low-cost carriers, such as Primera Air, Monarch, and Cobalt, which were not vigilant in taking similar measures, were not so lucky, eventually going bankrupt due to a combination of currency and fuel price risk (Topham 2018).

While companies can effectively hedge against currency or commodity price risk, can they also use financial hedging to protect against unfavourable future political changes? Most likely, this would be quite difficult—though, this is exactly where operations may help by treating supply chains themselves as dynamic hedges against uncertainty. A firm's manufacturing network can be designed in such a way that it can be easily reconfigured to adapt to changing economic and political conditions. For example, BMW Group's production network includes thirty sites in fourteen countries on four continents, while complete automobiles are manufactured in the company's factories in Germany, the United States, Mexico, South Africa, and China (BMW Worldwide 2019). Global supply chains can also be designed with multiple suppliers and sufficient manufacturing capacity in different countries, so that production can be relocated as economic conditions (i.e., exchange rates, labor costs, tariffs, etc.) change. Adidas and Nike, for example, both pioneers in emerging-market production, are now producing most of their footwear in Vietnam, gradually shifting their production out of China, their main producer for many years (Bain 2018).

 Global supply chains as risk hedging mechanisms

By carefully designing their global supply chain network so that assets can be reconfigured according to changing economic and political conditions, firms can achieve resilience and superior financial performance.

However, to be able to take advantage of their global supply chain networks as a protection mechanism against uncertainties in the external environment, firms should actively evaluate their supply chain footprint with an eye towards economic conditions several years ahead. First, they need to have a system in place for monitoring the indirect cost—such as tariffs and incentives—of the current supply chain configuration. Second, they need to optimize their supply chains by taking into consideration the current indirect cost scheme. Third, they should identify and quantify areas of future risk and opportunity associated with changing economic conditions. It is critical for organizations to ask questions such as: Will our global supply chain network make sense if, for example, China's currency appreciates by 15 percent, oil costs $80 a barrel, and shipping lanes have 10 percent excess capacity? By doing so, firms can make sure that their supply chain *portfolio* is resilient and well-suited to deal with changing circumstances in an uncertain world.

15.3   Broad versus Narrow Product Assortment

Product assortment refers to the number and type of products that a business makes or a retailer offers for sale. The two main components of a company's product assortment are the breadth or number of product types/lines and the depth or number of product varieties within a product line. An automobile manufacturer, for example, may have three product lines (coupés, sedans, and SUVs) with three versions (basic, standard, and luxury) in each product line. A firm's assortment decisions are based on several parameters, such as historical demand, buying trends, expected choices made by customers, but also the firm's competitive strategy in the market.

In today's business environment, where customers demand a wider variety of products, the number of SKUs held by most firms has increased, as companies are matching products to more particular customer preferences. SKU proliferation is the phenomenon that occurs when a product is segmented and transformed into niche products in order to offer people more choices and drive up sales. Variations, like a low-fat version of a food product, contribute to SKU proliferation but so do shorter development cycles, advances in production technologies, marketing campaigns, seasonality, and expansion to new markets (i.e., to different customer preferences and legal requirements). Also, companies that undergo periods of active merger and acquisition cycles will often inherit both added distribution channels as well as associated SKUs.

There are more SKUs in the retail sector today than ever. One report states that grocery stores, for example, carried 7,000 SKUs in the 1990s, a figure that escalated to more than 40,000 by 2017 (Malito 2017). In manufacturing companies, it is very common for each product offering to have fifty to one hundred different SKUs, namely, variations that allow for selling the product in different markets and market segments. In a traditional business sense, SKU proliferation is not a bad thing, as it is always good to have many products for customers to choose from. However, while SKU proliferation might have tangible and measurable effects on sales, it creates big challenges in supply chain management.

On product assortment

When evaluating its product assortment, a company should also consider the impact of the additional complexity associated with SKU proliferation on the firm's financials.

When the number of SKUs offered by a firm is left to increase unchecked, this can have negative effects on the supply chain's ability to operate efficiently. Managing product variety is costly as forecasts are less accurate, more administration is required, and supplier, production, distribution, and warehouse management become more complex. In addition, because of customers' changing expectations towards delivery speed, firms are forced to hold more items in stock to meet targets for quick order fulfillment. As demand for some SKUs may not be large enough to quickly clear inventory, maintaining a large number of SKUs can lead to an increased cost of holding inventory. Since SKU proliferation may impact operations, customer service, and, ultimately, the bottom line, firms do occasionally need to reconsider their SKU basis. To motivate our discussion further, let's take a look at the following example.

Case study

Adidas AG

Adidas AG is a multinational corporation, founded and headquartered in Herzogenaurach, Germany, that designs and manufactures shoes, clothing, and accessories. It is the largest sportswear manufacturer in Europe and the second largest in the world, after Nike. In April 2012, Mr. Herbert Hainer, then-CEO of Adidas, announced a reduction of 25 percent of the company's 46,897 SKUs. An argument used by Mr. Hainer to justify their decision is that 20 percent of the current assortment generates 80 percent of sales.

Source: Köhn (2012).

If this roughly is the case—which should not be surprising, according to Pareto's law—it means that 80 percent of the assortment accounts for 20 percent of sales. And most likely, within the remaining 80 percent SKUs, Pareto's law still holds; that is, 80 percent of that 80 percent account for 20 percent of the remaining 20 percent of sales, and so on and so

Table 15.2
How much SKUs with the least sales sell according to Pareto's law.

Number of SKUs	% of total SKUs	% of sales
46,897	100	100
37,518	80	20
30,014	64	4
24,011	51	0.8
19,209	41	0.16
15,367	33	0.032
12,294	26	0.006

forth. Working in this fashion we can prepare table 15.2 to estimate how much the SKUs with the least sales sell.

As the last row suggests, cutting the number of SKUs by 25 percent means removing those items that contribute to 0.006 percent of sales, or $1.2 million, since Adidas sells roughly $18 billion (2012 figures). Remarkably, those 12,294 items only sell $83 each (roughly 1 or 2 units) on average worldwide! Most likely, the sales generated by these SKUs will not cover the operational cost of maintaining these SKUs in the portfolio. Therefore, it seems to make sense to remove them from the assortment. The natural question to ask at this point is why prune only 25 percent of the items and not more. Should Adidas also remove the second-to-last row items (15,367 SKUs!), which sell $400 each on average worldwide? What about the third-to-last row?

These questions nicely illustrate the usual trade-off between marketing and supply chain departments in the retailing industry. A typical marketing-driven organization, like Adidas, would argue that adding an SKU to the assortment increases sales. The more variety offered, the higher the chances that the customer likes whatever is on the shelf; hence, the probability of making one additional sale. The penalty to pay is in the form of, mainly, inventory holding and distribution cost and overhead. In good times (Adidas increased sales by 14 percent in 2016) this penalty tends to be underestimated.

Indeed, there is no clear answer to the questions posed above, but we can take a look at other industries to shed some light on the issue. In the consumer electronics industry, Apple has been a leader in controlling the number of SKUs offered in the market. iPhone 4, Apple's flagship mobile for several years, was introduced in June 2010 in only two colors (black and white), whilst during the same period, Nokia was selling at least one model in each market segment (for instance, there were thirty-seven different models in Germany alone).

In 2014, the leading consumer goods company Procter & Gamble embarked on an ambitious portfolio restructuring program. Under the program, the company reduced their number of brands from 170 to 65 and the number of product categories from sixteen to ten. While these brands represented 6 to 8 percent of profit, SKU rationalization eventually had a positive overall impact on the firm's financials. In the period 2012–2017, the company achieved cost savings (in COGS, marketing, and manufacturing overhead) of more than $10 billion, while the days inventory outstanding (DIO) decreased from seventy to fifty-eight days. Finally, other successful companies, such as Lidl in Germany or Mercadona in Spain have based their overall strategy on the variety versus cost trade-off. By displaying only 8,000 SKUs (a typical U.S. grocery store sells 30,000 SKUs or more), the latter has enjoyed several years of growth, reaching an impressive 24.6 percent market share (leading position) in Spain in 2018.

From the above discussion, it becomes clear that in their product assortment decision making, firms should carefully consider the impact of wide assortment selection on their financial performance. In the following short case, we use conventional inventory management models to illustrate the impact of increasing assortment on a firm's inventory and OWC performance.

 Exercise

Nicole Jones

Nicole Jones is the inventory planner for a small local soft drinks producer in Ohio, United States. The top selling soda product, O-Cola, is currently offered in two variants, regular and light. A recent study from the marketing department has shown that increasing the product portfolio by offering the current products in flavored versions would boost the company's sales. In particular, the study suggests that offering four variants (flavors) for each of the current colas would increase sales of that category by 20 percent. John Papas, the firm's owner and CEO, has asked Nicole to evaluate the implications of such decision on the firm's inventory performance before the next directors' meeting where the idea will be discussed.

Daily demand for each of the two current variants is normally distributed with a mean of 1 million cans and a standard deviation of 300,000 cans. The variable cost of producing one unit of each of the current variants is 30 cents, while the selling price for both products is 95 cents. Due to intense competition in this market, the company aims for a customer service level (in-stock probability) of 95 percent. Inventory position for both products is reviewed daily, and the lead time for replenishing inventory for each product is currently three days. As the company's sales have been quite stable over the last few years, John believes that an increase of 20 percent in revenue from the firm's top-selling products would be a great opportunity. Being small in size makes the firm's access to long-term debt financing very costly, and therefore internally generated funds would be an important source for financing the firm's plans to expand its distribution network to neighboring states. At the same time, John is aware that the firm's OWC should be maintained at a low level due to unavailability of equity financing and to limitations in the firm's credit line ($1 million roof at 10 percent annual interest rate). Having presented the entire situation to Nicole, John is eagerly waiting for her assessment of this great opportunity.

Because the demand functions of the two current products are identical, it is sufficient for Nicole to evaluate the implications of increasing the assortment of only the regular O-Cola.

First, she needs to estimate the new demand parameters for the four-variant assortment. This is not straightforward, so some assumptions are necessary. Nicole recalls from her course on probabilities that when a normally distributed random variable is multiplied by a positive number k, the resulting distribution is still normal with mean and variance equal to the original values multiplied by k. By applying this rule to the original demand for regular O-Cola, she finds that the aggregate daily demand for the four variants will be normally distributed with mean 1.2 million and standard deviation $\sqrt{1.2 \cdot 300,000} = 328,634$.

Then, she needs to estimate the demand parameters for each of the four variants. Without any additional information, she can assume that the demands for each of the four variants will be independent and identically normally distributed, so that their sum will have the same parameters as the aggregate demand (calculated above). By following the rules for adding normally distributed random variables (see appendix B), Nicole can calculate the daily demand for each of the variants, which will be normal with mean 300,000 and standard deviation 164,317. To confirm this, note that if we add four normally distributed random variables with these parameters, we get a normal distribution with mean $4 \cdot 300,000 = 1,200,000$ and standard deviation $\sqrt{4} \cdot 164,317 = 328,634$.

As the company applies a base-stock policy to replenish inventory, Nicole will use the relevant formulas for computing the safety inventory and cycle inventory. Knowing that the lead time is actually due to production scheduling (the factory has a single production line for all products), she thinks it is a reasonable assumption to ignore pipeline inventory.[4] Her only concern is whether increasing the number of SKUs would have implications in production planning that would eventually increase the lead time. However, she decides to evaluate this possibility later. For a base-stock policy with review period of R days, deterministic lead time of L days, normally distributed daily demand with mean D and standard deviation σ_D, and desired service level CSL, the following formulas can be applied to calculate the different types of inventory (see appendix C).

- safety inventory = $\Phi^{-1}(CSL) \cdot \sigma_D \cdot \sqrt{L+R}$
- cycle inventory = $\frac{D \cdot R}{2}$

---

4. Of course, things would be different in the case of a retailer, where pipeline inventory would be relevant depending on whether the retailer has ownership of inventory while in transit.

Table 15.3
Average inventory for one versus four product variants (units).

# of variants	Cycle inventory	Safety inventory	Total
1	500,000	986,912	1,486,912
4	600,000	2,162,216	2,762,216

By using the information in the case, we can compute the total inventory for each scenario as shown in table 15.3.

As table 15.3 reveals, increasing the number of variants from one to four will require an increase in inventory of 86 percent to support such strategy. Nicole is aware that carrying more inventory will have an impact on the firm's financial performance. She summarizes the implications per product (regular, light) as follows. (Indirect effects as described in section 14.2.3 are ignored.)

Balance sheet In terms of dollar value, the total inventory with four variants is equal to $828,665 versus $446,074 for one variant. That is, the OWC will increase by the same amount, which must be financed by either debt or equity (assuming that the firm does not hold any excess cash reserves).

Cash flow statement At the moment that the firm starts implementing the wider assortment, a cash outflow of $382,591 will occur, which should be counterbalanced by additional debt. That is, the firm cannot move on with this decision without first securing $382,591 of external financing.

Income statement Assuming that the firm can secure access to extra debt to support the implementation of the wide-assortment plan, then the additional annual interest that will appear in the income statement will be equal to $38,259. This cost is based on the assumption that the company can negotiate an extension in its credit line at the same cost (10 percent annual interest rate). On the revenue side, offering a wider assortment will generate additional expected gross profit of $130,000 (20 percent $\cdot$ $1,000,000 \cdot (0.95 - 0.30)$), which makes the overall idea of widening the product assortment profitable—if sales really increase by 20 percent.

Financial ratios With a wider assortment, sales will hopefully increase by 20 percent. However, to achieve this result the firm must increase its inventory by 86 percent. As the increase in inventory is much higher than the increase in sales, all inventory-related ratios, namely IT, DIO, and GMROI will deteriorate. Consequently, ROA is also expected to decline.

The above analysis shows that increasing variants from one to four can be profitable for the business as long as the necessary financing can be secured. The company will trade off some of its inventory and assets performance for higher profit. We have made, however, some key assumptions which might seriously affect the attractiveness of the idea if they do not hold. Specifically:

Demand In our analysis, we assumed that the total variability in the demand for the four variants is equal to the variability in the aggregated demand. This might not be a valid assumption, particularly given the very short inventory and production planning horizon. Hence, the actual increase in inventory due to the wide assortment might be greater than 86 percent. In real life, a product assortment may consist of fast-moving and slow-moving, as well as high- and low-variability variants. As demand variability is the main driver of safety inventory, a thorough analysis of demand variability is a key input to assortment planning.

Lead time While the lead time of three days was due to production scheduling needs, we assumed that the addition of three more variants per product (i.e., additional six variants in total) would have no impact on lead time. Obviously, this may not be a valid assumption as the complexity in production sequencing increases considerably with the number of SKUs that are produced by a single production line. Assuming that the lead time increases by two days with the introduction of the new SKUs, then the resulting increase in inventory would be 118 percent (and the annual interest cost would be $52,838 instead of $38,259).

Inventory-related costs In our calculations, we have considered that interest expenses are the only cost incurred due to the increase in inventory. In practice, a portion of the inventory carrying cost is associated with holding or storing inventory for sale, namely, warehouse space, handling and administration, obsolescence and deterioration, insurance, and cost of equity. As the average inventory held by the firm almost doubles, housing more items requires a larger space (which increases land cost or rent), while holding more SKUs might lower worker efficiency by making the picking/packing process more convoluted. Also, the firm may have to deal with larger number of suppliers, as well as with higher machine setup times (i.e., lower productivity), which might both increase overhead expenses.

The bottom line is that if we take into account all the costs associated with the wider product assortment (including, also, some additional marketing expenses), it might not be such a good idea for the firm to move on with this opportunity. Depending on several factors (such as current storage capacity, machine utilization, availability of affordable external financing, etc.), the 20 percent increase in gross profit might be outweighed by the extra cost of carrying more inventory.

15.3.1 SKU Rationalization

Given the two examples provided, there is little doubt that SKU proliferation can drive up complexity and supply chain inventory and distribution costs. The quest for higher market share can induce a company to increase the number of products it offers, which results in a suboptimal product portfolio. As the complexity of the supply chain increases, so does the overall cost per unit delivered. SKU rationalization is a process used by companies to determine the benefit of adding, retaining, or eliminating products, so that a firm can reduce inventory costs and cut down on complexities in procurement, production, and distribution processes. The idea is not to prevent SKU proliferation from happening but to regulate it so that when SKUs do increase, they are adding value and not damaging the firm's ability to effectively conduct business. While rationalization is most commonly used among manufacturers and retailers with tens of thousands of brands, products, and variations in their inventory (e.g., Adidas, Procter & Gamble, Unilever, etc.), it is becoming a trend across companies in all sectors and of all sizes.

Our discussion above shows that SKU rationalization calls for an integrated approach across the organization involving cross-functional collaboration among several departments including sales, marketing, distribution, operations, procurement, finance, and accounting. The goal is to weigh the benefit of selling against the cost of producing and stocking each product, so that companies can increase the share of profits earned with SKUs that add value while reducing the impact of SKUs that increase costs. As there are several approaches that managers follow for SKU rationalization, discussing the topic in detail is outside the context of this section (see Fisher and Raman [2010] for a thorough presentation of the application of product assortment in retailing). Next, we will only briefly discuss how basic concepts from the present book might be useful to that end.

SKU rationalization is essentially the output of a segmentation process. Once a product family has been selected as a candidate for rationalization (possibly due to SKU proliferation issues), an initial Pareto analysis (see the Adidas case for an application of the Pareto's law) of the sales per SKU can help identify the 60 to 80 percent of SKUs with the smallest contribution to the sales of the entire product family. For those SKUs, further analysis is required to select the SKUs that are cost drivers and do not add value to the product family. Such analysis can include several financial metrics (e.g., inventory turns, gross margin, GMROI, allocated overhead), but also operational metrics (e.g., forecast accuracy, demand trend, product returns, setup and processing time, defects, supplier lead-time, storage requirements). Then, the low-performing SKUs should be traced back to their raw materials, related finished goods, and overhead. The application of the contribution logic (see chapter 11) at the product family level is key here, particularly in identifying the portion of the overhead (i.e., manufacturing, distribution, warehousing, marketing, etc.) that can be eliminated. With all of this information, managers can have a more accurate estimate of the impact of eliminating some SKUs. For example, while eliminating an SKU may come at a loss (e.g., sacrificing sales or writing off of inventory), at the same time it may have a substantial positive impact on other areas of the business (say, by reducing storage space requirements and improving handling efficiency).

Summarizing, the product-assortment issue is a good illustration of how the lack of a holistic view of the supply chain can worsen a company's working capital level. Often, the marketing department believes that introducing more SKUs delivers more buying opportunities and hence boosts sales. While the advantages of SKU proliferation cannot be ignored, marketers may fail to consider how the wider product selection both decentralizes and increases inventory and has an adverse effect on the company's balance sheet and on the efficiency of the supply chain organization. The cost of providing a product to the end customer increases with SKU proliferation, which might eventually diminish the sales boost obtained from product diversification. SKU rationalization can help determine which SKUs a firm can do without and release cash flow and resources for the benefit of products that work best.

15.4   Other Operational Risk Pooling Strategies

Risk pooling refers to practices used by firms to reduce or hedge uncertainty in their operations. It usually involves the redesign of the supply chain, the production process, or the product so that a firm is in a better position to deal with the consequences of demand uncertainty in its markets. Reducing the breadth or depth of product varieties—often referred to as *product pooling*—is just one of a firm's available risk pooling strategies. In the product assortment section we have discussed how reducing the assortment of SKUs can help a company protect against the demand uncertainty associated with using a wide variety of the same product type to serve the market (see demand calculations in the O-Cola case study). Some other commonly used inventory risk pooling strategies (see Cachon and Terwiesch [2013] for a detailed discussion) include:

Consolidated distribution   This refers to the pooling benefits of consolidating distribution from several demand locations. Consider the case of a decentralized distribution network where a number of stores (or regional warehouses) have their inventory replenished directly from the suppliers (or own production sites) to meet local demand. By pooling these demand streams into a single location—for instance, by adding a central distribution center (DC) to the existing network—a firm can reduce the demand uncertainty of the pooled location as the random fluctuations of different demand streams will be partially canceled out. Consequently, the redesigned distribution network will carry less safety inventory than the decentralized one, while economies of scale in transportation can also be achieved. On the other hand, the capital investment and operating cost of the DC, along with transportation cost from the DC to stores (or regional warehouses), are important considerations to a firm's decision to centralize its distribution. In general, consolidating distribution can lead to large savings if the inventory replenishment lead time is long and the demand is highly volatile. Procter & Gamble, for example, anticipates five-year savings (starting 2015) in excess of $1 billion from the consolidation of its US distribution network into fewer, larger centers, strategically located near major demand clusters, so that 80 percent of destinations are within a one-day distance (Trefis 2015).

Delayed differentiation or postponement   An alternative to product pooling, postponement is the ability of a supply chain to delay differentiation or customization of a product until the latest possible stage in the supply network. Delayed differentiation makes sense when customers demand variety, and this variety can be created late in the production or distribution process easily and inexpensively. Hewlett Packard and Benetton have been pioneers in applying this strategy in their respective industries. In the early 1990s, Hewlett Packard redesigned its distribution network to be able to implement a build-to-order approach—that is, assembling the final product (integrating circuit board, chassis, power supply and software) in locations close to customers in response to their orders (Feitzinger and Lee 1997). Similarly, Benetton redesigned its sweater manufacturing processes so that dyeing of preknitted, uncolored sweaters was taking place later in the selling season, once the company had a more accurate idea of the trending colors. By postponing the point of product differentiation, both firms were able to save millions of dollars through significant reduction of obsolete inventory.

Capacity pooling Capacity pooling typically refers to using manufacturing flexibility as a hedging mechanism against uncertain future product demand. We have presented the concept in section 13.5 where we discussed the flexible capacity real option. The basic idea is that firms can reduce their investment in expensive fixed assets by pooling the uncertain demand of different products into flexibly configured production sites. Studies have shown that it takes only a limited amount of flexibility (e.g., assuring that each product in a firm's portfolio can be manufactured at two sites) to effectively hedge demand uncertainty in a system with multiple products and production sites (Jordan and Graves 1995). This type of risk pooling is particularly popular in industries characterized by costly capacity investment, such as the automotive and pharmaceutical industries.

The basic idea behind demand risk pooling is that statistical economies of scale can be achieved by pooling individual demand streams at the product level (universal design), production process level (point of differentiation), distribution level (central DC), or fixed asset level (flexible capacity). As the uncertainty of the pooled demand is reduced, this has further implications for the firm's investment in finished goods inventory (product pooling and consolidated distribution), work-in-progress inventory (delayed differentiation), or fixed assets (capacity pooling). The general case of evaluating the impact on OWC investment from consolidating distribution is presented in appendix C. The analysis there can be extended, though, to all pooling strategies.

Next we discuss the case of location pooling through an example inspired by Procter & Gamble's decision to consolidate its US-based distribution network.

 Exercise
Consolidating LogiCom's Distribution Network in the United States

LogiCom is a US-based computer technology company that develops, sells, repairs, and supports computers and related products and services. The company uses two channels to sell its products in the US market: direct online store and through consumer electronics retail partners. LogiCom manufacturing is located in Asia, where the company purchases components and materials from various suppliers, then gets them shipped to its assembling plant in China. All finished products are shipped to the company's two regional warehouses located in San Jose, California and Huston, Texas. From there, goods are shipped by parcel to online customers and by truck to the retailers.

The company's new management team believes that when it comes to technology, such as laptops and desktops, inventory depreciates very quickly, losing 1 to 2 percent of value each week. In the words of the new CEO to the firm's shareholders, "inventory is fundamentally evil," continuing by saying, "reducing operating working capital will be one of our top priorities." Faced with this mandate, the company's chief supply chain officer (CSCO) is wondering whether consolidating the two central distribution centers into one would lead to a significant reduction in the company's inventory investment.

To evaluate the impact of such move, the CSCO decided to base her analysis on historical data for a typical LogiCom product (basic laptop configuration for home use), which is usually manufactured and sold over a horizon of twelve months, before being phased out and replaced by a new model. The regional distribution centers usually place their replenishment orders for such products on a weekly basis, while it takes about eight weeks for each replenishment order to be delivered from China. Weekly demands for the latest model at the warehouse level have been i.i.d. normally distributed with mean and standard deviation (μ, σ) of (1,020; 408) in California and (1,215; 472) in Texas. The average unit (assumed variable) cost for this model has been \$290 and the firm has a target service level (CSL) of 95 percent (in-stock probability).

To assess the impact on inventory investment from consolidating distribution, we will calculate first the safety inventory for the decentralized case. Note that consolidating the warehouses into one location will only affect the safety inventory that is required for achieving the desired service level but not the cycle and pipeline inventories.

As the firm applies a periodic inventory replenishment model with lead time (L) of eight weeks and review period of one week, the safety inventory in each location (California and Texas) is given by the following formula (see appendix C for the details):

safety inventory $= \Phi^{-1}(\mathrm{CSL}) \cdot \sqrt{L+1} \cdot \sigma$

Given the demand parameters for the particular product at the LogiCom case, it follows that the safety inventory (in product units) in the current decentralized system is equal to $2,013 \, (= 1.64 \cdot \sqrt{8+1} \cdot 408)$ in California and $2,329 \, (= 1.64 \cdot \sqrt{8+1} \cdot 472)$ in Texas. This corresponds to inventory investment of \$1,259,300 for the particular product in LogiCom's balance sheet.

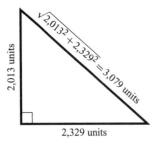

Figure 15.2
Illustration of safety inventory reduction at LogiCom. Given same lead time and service level at all locations, when demands in two regions are independent and normally distributed, the lengths of the sides of the squared triangle are proportional to the levels of optimal safety inventory.

In a centralized distribution system the pooled (or aggregate) demand will also be normally distributed with mean 2,235 ($=1{,}020+1{,}215$) and standard deviation 624 ($=\sqrt{408^2+472^2}$). By applying the same formula for safety inventory at the aggregate level, it follows that the safety inventory in the centralized system would be equal to 3,079 ($=1.64\cdot\sqrt{8+1}\cdot624$) units or \$892,811, which translates into almost 30 percent reduction in the firm's investment in safety inventory.

Given same lead-time and service level at all locations, and assuming that demands at both regions are independent and normally distributed, we could have come up with the same answer pictorially, as shown in figure 15.2. Given a squared triangle whose leg lengths are the safety inventory levels at the two regions, the aggregate safety inventory at the pooled location will be the length of the hypotenuse. This length can easily be computed using the Pythagorean theorem, as the figure illustrates.

The LogiCom case illustrates that the operational benefit from consolidating distribution is realized in terms of reduction in safety inventory. This is true for most risk pooling strategies (except from the capacity pooling case, where the benefit has the form of lower fixed assets investment). In financial terms, this translates into a reduction in OWC investment, the benefit from which is not trivial. In the short run, cash tied up in operations—equal to the OWC reduction—will become available for other usages by the firm. In the LogiCom case, the freed-up cash from inventory reduction after consolidating the distribution of the particular product under study (and only) will be equal to \$366,489. The benefit can be even greater for products whose demand is more volatile. In the long run, the OWC reduction will result to further savings for the company in terms of lower financing costs for funding its OWC.

🛈 Risk pooling and OWC
Firms can reduce their OWC investment by exploiting operational risk hedging opportunities through product, process, or supply chain network redesign.

However, as with most decisions discussed in this chapter, there are trade-offs that need to be considered. For example, in the consolidated distribution case, a firm needs to balance the benefit from inventory reduction with the cost associated with building (or expanding) and operating a central distribution center, as well as the extra cost for shipping the goods from the distribution center to the demand points. In the delayed differentiation case, the firm will need to consider the cost of product or process redesign but also potential deterioration of customer service due to delays in the postponement stage. Last but not least, in the capacity pooling case, the cost of flexibility (i.e., equipment investment, coordinating effort, etc.) might be higher than the cost of installing dedicated capacity. Further discussion on how these trade-offs shall be evaluated in a unifying framework can be found in section 15.7.

15.5   Push versus Pull

In chapter 1 we discussed Inditex—the clothing and footwear retailer—and its unique business model that has helped the company become a leader in the so-called fast-fashion market. Due to the inherent trade-offs in the company's operational strategy, in this section we will present this strategy in more detail and how this reflects on the firm's financial results.

During the last decades, a common practice in the apparel industry has been for businesses to locate their production in low-wage countries—mainly in Asia—with a focus on reducing production costs to compete more successfully. At first glance, this strategy makes sense due to the labor-intensive nature of the production processes in the apparel industry, the relatively low-quality requirements, the small volume of items that leads to very low transportation cost, and the availability of thousands of manufacturing contractors around the world with the capability to produce quality goods at low cost. At the end of the day, companies in this industry compete in design and retailing—not manufacturing—and the vast majority of them (such as Gap, Nike, H&M, and many more) have adopted this strategy.

Inditex, however, has been a notable exception to this rule. The ability to change collections rapidly to adapt to consumer tastes is probably the primary challenge in competing in the fast-fashion industry, where companies that are able to identify, design, manufacture, distribute, and retail the latest fashion trends at the right time gain an edge over competition. In this environment, Inditex literally embodies the idea of fast fashion by taking about three weeks from designing an item on the drawing board to placing the item on the shelf (Inditex n.d.). This astonishing speed-to-market allows Inditex to capture in real time the new styles and trends—whether these appear on the catwalks of famous designers' shows, on the streets, or at large social events. For example, when Madonna wore a certain blouse at the beginning of her 2005 concert tour in Spain, thanks to Zara—the flagship Inditex brand—teenage girls in massive numbers were able to wear the same outfit at her last performance (Sheffi 2012). As a result, the group's brands are able to launch several collections per year and achieve high SKU rotation. Zara, for instance, sells more than 11,000 distinct items per year as opposed to its competitors that carry 2,000 to 4,000 (Gorrepati 2016).

Inditex's responsive retailing model would not be possible without having a well-orchestrated production and distribution system in place. Achieving this level of responsiveness might not have been an issue in the first decades of the firm's operations when almost the entire production was taking place in-house in Spain (including a network of local workshops). However, as the company kept growing so did its production network, which now consists of 1,824 suppliers in forty-seven countries, organized into eleven production clusters (Inditex 2017). Actually, Inditex currently owns only 2 to 3 percent of its production capacity, which is mainly concentrated on value-adding activities that require skilled labor, such as fabric cutting (Butler 2013). It follows that Inditex is not much different from its peers in its outsourcing profile. What really distinguishes the firm from its competitors is how it organizes and manages its supply chain network to serve its unique operational strategy. A brief outline of the most salient aspects of this strategy follows.

Proximity of operations A key enabler to the firm's high speed-to-market performance is the proximity of its production sites and distribution centers. Currently, 57 percent of the factories manufacturing products for the group's brands are in close proximity to the company's headquarters, mainly in Spain (where the company also operates eleven of its own factories), Portugal, Turkey, and Morocco. Inditex also operates a network of ten centralized logistics centers—all located in Spain—where all manufactured items from the entire production network are first gathered before being distributed directly to group stores and online worldwide (Inditex 2017).

Production flexibility In addition to proximity of manufacturing sites, production flexibility is also an important component of the firm's capability to respond quickly to market trends. Flexibility is achieved by reserving a large percentage of manufacturing capacity for in-season adjustments with regard to amount, production frequency, and variety of new products. At Zara, for instance, only 15 to 25 percent of a line is designed ahead of the selling season, while over 50 percent of items are designed and manufactured in the middle of a season based on popular trends (Gorrepati 2016). Production flexibility also allows experimentation in terms of testing the market's response to new designs without facing the risk of being left with unsold inventory (Hanbury 2018). This is in direct contrast to most other retailers, who commit almost 100 percent of their designs ahead of a season, resorting then to heavy discounting for getting rid of excess inventory.

Information management Proximity of operations and production flexibility would not be sufficient to support Inditex's quick response strategy without the right information systems in place. Information management starts at the individual store level, where customer feedback is systematically collected regarding preferences or desires. This information is transmitted in real time—by means of automated information systems—to data processing centers at the headquarters, where designers, marketers, and buyers work together to make sure that the desired items will be manufactured and made available for sale as soon as possible. The company also uses technology and software designed by in-house expert teams to manage the distribution of goods in the most efficient, precise, and speedy manner (Inditex 2017). Actually, according to some analysts, the firm's remarkable growth would not have been possible without large investments in IT—such as a billion Euro investment in RFID technology in 2016—that gave the company a lead over its competitors in managing information in the end-to-end supply chain (García Aller 2017).

Global—rather than local—optimization of production and distribution Instead of taking advantage of economies of scale, the company's optimization approach is focused on improving efficiency given flexibility and responsiveness objectives. This is reflected in two aspects: (a) production of small batches and (b) frequent deliveries—often through air shipments—directly from one of the ten central warehouses to stores. At Zara, for instance, production does not exceed a limited number of pieces (around 8,000) for any particular design; however, if an item sells well, similar designs are quickly manufactured and delivered to capture the demand potential (García Aller 2017). This is supported by the firm's distribution policy of refreshing the physical and online store collections twice a week, with small shipments per product (usually three to four pieces) reaching European stores in twenty-four to thirty-six hours and those in the rest of the world within forty-eight hours (Inditex 2017). This optimization approach has a dual benefit for the group's brands. First, the combination of centralized distribution and frequent deliveries can help the company locate the inventory in the best possible way to tap into the actual demand per store. Second, this approach leads to very little leftover stock, reducing the need for markdowns. Furthermore, while the inevitable stock-outs created by this system might appear undesirable, these actually serve as a valuable source of information for driving design choices, and are aligned with the firm's marketing strategy to promote frequent customer visits, in anticipation of new variants of the popular designs that were out of stock.

Based on our presentation of the key components in Inditex's operations strategy, we can almost safely conclude that the firm's manufacturing and distribution systems have been designed on the principles of a pull supply chain model. This is quite surprising—given the firm's massive number of SKUs and unit sales volume—and would not have been possible without the integration and flexibility that characterize all phases of the company's value chain: design, production, distribution, stores, and clients. This is also a paradigm shift in a traditionally push type of industry, for which any responsiveness is usually limited to only a second (midseason) replenishment option.

However, foregoing economies of scale in production and distribution and keeping production in close proximity to its central warehouses should come at a cost premium. A natural question then follows: What is the impact of the firm's operational strategy on its financial performance? Table 15.4 shows Inditex's basic financial ratios for the period 2015–2017, along with those of H&M—its closest and most similar rival—which also has

Table 15.4
Inditex and H&M financial ratios for the period 2015–2017 based on the firms' annual reports (Inditex 2017; H&M 2017). Return ratios and turnover ratios are calculated using average values. OWC values for Inditex and H&M are respectively reported in million euros and SEK (average exchange rate for the three-year period is 1 EUR = 9.5 SEK).

	Inditex			H&M		
	2017	2016	2015	2017	2016	2015
Growth ratios						
Sales growth	8.7%	11.5%	15.4%	4.0%	6.3%	19.4%
Number of stores growth	2.5%	4.0%	4.9%	8.9%	10.9%	11.8%
Return ratios						
Return on equity	25.7%	26.2%	26.4%	26.8%	31.2%	38.1%
Return on assets (EBIT / assets)	21.7%	21.7%	22.5%	20.1%	25.8%	33.4%
Return on net assets	25.5%	25.8%	25.9%	26.3%	30.9%	37.7%
Margin ratios						
Net margin	13.3%	13.6%	13.8%	8.1%	9.7%	11.6%
Gross margin	56.3%	57.0%	57.8%	54.0%	55.2%	57.0%
Net operational margin (EBIT/Sales)	17.0%	17.2%	17.6%	10.3%	12.4%	14.9%
GMROI (gross profit to avg. inventory)	5.5	5.6	6.0	3.3	3.7	4.7
Turnover ratios						
Asset turnover	1.3	1.3	1.3	1.9	2.1	2.2
Inventory turns	4.2	4.2	4.3	2.8	3	3.5
Property, plant, equipment turnover	1.5	1.4	1.4	2.3	2.4	2.6
OWC ratios						
Days receivable	6	7	5	9	8	8
Days inventory	86	86	84	130	120	104
Days payable (evaluated at COGS)	36	36	35	29	28	27
OWC (A/R + Inventory – A/P)	−114	47	−42	36,043	31,884	24,702
OWC ÷ Sales	−0.5%	0.2%	−0.2%	18.0%	16.6%	13.7%

a great reputation for its operational performance and practices. H&M employs a blend of traditional and fast-fashion business models, offering two main collections each year and several subcollections that allow H&M to continually refresh its inventory. The primary collections are basic long lead-time items, while the subcollections are trendier items with three to six week lead-times. H&M's entire production is outsourced to about 800 manufacturers, mainly located in Asia (about 70 percent of the group's sourcing) and Europe. Also, the firm maintains some flexible capacity that allows 20 percent of its items to be produced in-season based on market trends (Hiiemaa 2016).

We can first observe in table 15.4 that sales growth for both firms has been slowing down over the last three years. We leave it to the industry experts to figure out whether this is due to market saturation or to competition from regional firms and online retailers. What is remarkable, though, is the consistency in all Inditex ratios (including the sales to store number growth) despite the decelerating sales. Actually, the same stability in Inditex's ratios can be traced back for several years. This is not the case, however, with H&M's ratios, which seem to have been seriously deteriorated as a result of the drop in sales growth.

Considering that both firms operate in an environment characterized by rapid changes in customer preferences and intense competition between rivals, one might reasonably infer that the behavior of H&M's ratios—particularly the return ratios—is a more accurate reflection of the impact of slowing sales on the industry's financial performance. In the end, even the best managed firms need time to respond to changes in the external environment before bringing their profitability and other ratios back to normal. However, this is not the case for Inditex, which can rely on its responsive and flexible operations to hedge against variability in external market conditions—including demand shifts, supply disruptions, or even currency fluctuations. In that sense, if financial hedging is used by firms to reduce the impact of variability in a firm's assets, Inditex's operational flexibility can be considered a substitute to financial hedging.

 On the benefit of a pull supply chain strategy
Firms operating a pull supply chain model can better hedge their financial results against volatility and slow-downs in market conditions.

A second point from table 15.4 is Inditex's performance in the margin ratios. Given the premiums the firm pays as a result of its production and logistics practices, one would expect lower margins compared to the closest rival. However, to evaluate the two firms' performance in this aspect, we also need to consider the impact of markdowns. According to some estimates, Zara sells 85 percent of its products at full price, while unsold items account for less than 10 percent of the total stock, against industry averages of 60 to 70 percent and 17 to 20 percent, respectively (Berfield and Baigorri 2013). For instance, in the first quarter of 2018, H&M had been left with $4 billion worth of unsold inventory. Therefore, it appears that the revenue gains from matching demand with supply compensate for the extra labor and shipping costs needed to accommodate Inditex's responsive strategy. However, to support this strategy, the company also needs more assets in place—that is, company-owned warehouses and production plants—which result in lower turnover ratios for total and fixed assets.

The final point relates to inventory performance, where Inditex is the indisputable market champion. The group is able to consistently achieve at least an extra turn of its inventory and gain a higher return on inventory investment compared to H&M, a firm also distinguished for its sound inventory management practices—all this despite its considerably wider product assortment. Actually, even in good years for H&M, such as 2015, when the firm largely outperformed Inditex in all return ratios, it still lagged behind when it comes to ratios associated with inventory management (including margin ratios).

Inditex's sound inventory management has further implications all the way down to the funds required for financing operations. While on average, H&M needs funds—either cash or debt—well above 15 percent of sales to support its operations, Inditex's operations are self-financed—in the sense that suppliers' credit is sufficient to fund the firm's investment in accounts receivable and inventory. Note that the calculations shown in table 15.4 consider only the notes payable to suppliers as accounts payable and not the sum of noninterest-bearing current liabilities (i.e., AP^+). If the latter holds, then operating working capital becomes a source of cash for Inditex (on average equal to 7 percent of sales), while H&M's operating capital still ties up cash in excess of 5 percent of the company's sales.

The two models presented in this section have respective trade-offs. H&M and most of its peers in the fashion industry are focused on lowering production cost at the expense of increased lead times. On the other hand, Inditex enjoys the marketing benefits of a highly responsive supply chain at the expense of increased investment in production and distribution. To maintain the ability to adapt the firm's internal and supplier production to changing customer needs, Inditex had to become much more vertically integrated than its peers in terms of the control it exerts on the end-to-end supply chain. Finally, by focusing its strategy on inventory optimization rather than production cost minimization—in other words, by shifting attention from the income statement to the balance sheet—Inditex has been able to achieve not only superior but also highly robust financial results.

15.6   Chasing versus Leveling

Different firms use different strategies to plan and schedule their manufacturing production to fulfill downstream demand. Depending on the product and market characteristics, some companies produce goods in response to customer orders—a *make-to-order* strategy—some produce goods to meet forecast demand so that customers can place their purchase orders at their discretion—a *make-to-stock* strategy—while others apply a hybrid approach—an *assemble-to-order* strategy. In practice, however, it is not common for companies to follow a pure strategy for their entire product and customer portfolio. Take Dell, for example, the multinational computer technology company. In an effort to reduce costs and improve responsiveness, the company has decided to tailor its overall supply chain to its product and customer segments. As a result, Dell follows a make-to-order approach for its corporate clients; a make-to-stock approach for its retail and online popular configuration channels; while an assemble-to-order strategy is followed for the firm's online low-volume configurations (Simchi-Levi, Clayton, and Raven 2013).

Regardless of which strategies they follow to fulfill their customers' orders, companies need to plan to have the right resources in place for supporting these strategies. To that end, *aggregate production planning* is the process of developing an approximate schedule of an organization's operations so that demand and capacity are matched. Basic inputs to this planning process include sales forecasts, current and desired inventory levels, nominal machine hours, number of workers, amount of raw materials, and so on. The term *aggregate* is used because planning at this level considers both product demand and capacity resources at the aggregate; namely, at the product line or family level. For example, in the automotive industry, aggregate planning may consider the total number of cars planned for production but not individual models, colors, or features. When the output units consume different levels of production resources, then equivalent units are often determined. Aggregate plans are usually intermediate-term activities, covering a period of three to eighteen months, and they set the basis for short-term planning activities such as production scheduling and sequencing. The basic idea is to balance capacity with demand in the longer run so that costs are minimized and disruptions from severe short-term changes are avoided.

Obviously, the characteristics of customer demand play a central role in aggregate production planning. If demand for a company's products is stable over time, then aggregate planning is trivial. In this case, demand forecasts are converted into resource requirements, which, once in place, are utilized to meet demand in the most efficient way. Then any small demand variability is handled with minor adjustments in capacity (e.g., through overtime or undertime). Aggregate production planning becomes a challenge, though, when there is seasonality in sales over the planning horizon. In this case, there are two pure planning strategies available—a *level* strategy and a *chase* strategy—an outline of each follows.

Level strategy Manufacturers that use a level production strategy set their production at a steady rate—usually equal to average demand for the planning horizon—while they use inventory as a means for hedging against seasonal variations in demand. That is, during the low sales season, overproduction is stored as inventory which is then used to meet demand during the high sales season. Steady employment environment and high capacity utilization throughout the year are the main advantages of the level strategy, while its main disadvantage is related to the cost of holding inventory, including the cash tied up for that purpose.

Chase strategy Companies that use the chase strategy match the production plan to the demand pattern and absorb fluctuations in demand by adjustments in capacity. Such adjustments may consist of: hiring, firing, or using part-time workers; increasing or decreasing working hours; and subcontracting work to other firms. The major advantages of a chase strategy include higher flexibility on the firm's part to adapt to market changes, as well as the cash and cost benefits associated with maintaining a low level of inventory. On the other hand, disadvantages include the cost of adjusting manpower (i.e., hiring and firing costs, paying overtime premiums, etc.), low utilization of plant and equipment during low sales season, and quality and lead time issues when subcontracting is used.

One aggregate production planning strategy in isolation is not always preferable to another. Actually, most firms utilize a combination of the level and chase strategies (also referred to as a hybrid or mixed strategy) in order to minimize their production costs while meeting their business goals and policies. In addition to demand characteristics, the most effective strategy (or strategy mix) depends on various parameters such as the cost structure of the product family, inventory holding costs, nominal and maximum capacity available, cost of capital investment, inventory targets (e.g., desired safety inventory and inventory levels), workforce policies (including overtime), subcontracting and supplier options, back-order policies, and potentially other less explicit elements (such as the possibility of loss of customer goodwill). Apart from the difficulty in quantifying several of these factors, an additional source of complexity in the aggregate planning problem is the interrelationships among several parameters. For example, the cost structure of a product family will differ for different options (i.e., subcontracting versus producing in-house, using overtime, etc.). Nevertheless, there are several quantitative techniques for aggregate planning—the most advanced of which are based on linear programming applications—which can deal with the above complexities to derive aggregate plans that efficiently balance capacity and demand.

While a presentation of these techniques is beyond the scope of this book, it should be mentioned that they are overly focused on cost minimization, which would be fine if a firm were assumed to have ample financial resources. In real life, though, there are limitations to the available funding for operations, and these cannot be relaxed under some conditions. Therefore, even if these techniques incorporate financial constraints, they cannot completely capture the impact of production planning on a firm's financial burden or the overall performance and interrelationships among them. Next, we will capture these dynamics by discussing the case of a company that is faced with the dilemma of selecting between chase and level strategies for its production planning.

15.6.1   Financial Planning at BeerCo

BeerCo is a beverage producer serving the local market in a midwestern state of the United States. The market environment in this area has been quite stable over the last few years, while the company's revenues have been slowly growing at an annual rate of about 4 percent (in alignment with overall industry growth). One key characteristic in this industry is high seasonality, with 70 percent of annual dollar volume being reached between May and September. Despite seasonality, sales volume forecasts for BeerCo have proved quite reliable in the past. Table 15.5 shows monthly sales data for the year 2017 and the firm's forecast for 2018.

Traditionally, BeerCo's production schedules have been seasonal, reflecting the seasonality in sales. The firm's policy is to produce and ship each order within three days of order placement. While following a chase production strategy has helped the company to maintain low levels of inventory in the past, it also has some implications on equipment utilization and production costs. In particular, during the low season, only 40 percent of nominal one-shift manufacturing capacity is actually used on average. On the other hand, the increased demand of the high season is met with seasonal work force (for staffing two shifts instead of one) and overtime. As a result, in 2017 alone, the firm's overtime premiums amounted to $500,000.

455453434545545544545555455

Table 15.5
BeerCo's 2017 monthly sales data and 2018 forecast ($'000).

	2017	2018
January	900	922
February	880	900
March	1,006	1,037
April	1,426	1,494
May	2,664	2,710
June	4,171	4,350
July	4,391	4,590
August	4,464	4,670
September	3,886	4,040
October	1,918	2,030
November	1,070	1,107
December	1,188	1,235
Total	**27,965**	**29,086**
Annual growth		4.01%

Due to the seasonality in sales, BeerCo pays special attention when preparing its financial forecasts in order to make sure that the necessary funding will be in place and readily available. This is very important, as the company's monthly financial needs during the high sales season can escalate very quickly. Table 15.6 presents BeerCo's actual income statement and balance sheet for the year 2017, along with its monthly pro forma statements for the year 2018. To develop these statements, the firm has followed the process outlined in chapter 10 using some information and assumptions summarized below:

• The cost of goods sold has averaged 71 percent of sales in 2017 and is expected to remain at the same proportion throughout 2018.

• Operating expenses are expected to grow at the same rate as sales and are likely to be incurred evenly throughout each month of 2018.

• Interest is calculated on the basis of the company's monthly balance for a credit line of $2 million that it has with its banking partner. This line of credit is secured by BeerCo's accounts receivable and incurs an interest rate of 0.83 percent monthly—which roughly corresponds to a 10 percent annual rate—applicable on the amount of credit used each month. In addition, the firm pays $10,000 interest on its long-term debt at the beginning of June (until its final retirement). The long-term debt is retired at an annual rate of $100,000, payable in October each year.

• BeerCo's tax rate is 40 percent and tax payments are made on three dates. In October and November, the firm makes two payments each corresponding to 33 percent of the estimated end-of-year tax, while the payment of the clearing amount for the year takes place in January. The clearing amount for year 2017 is $170,000, payable January 15th, 2018.

Table 15.6
BeerCo's year 2017 (actual) and year 2018 (monthly pro forma) income statement and balance sheet assuming a chase production strategy.

Income statement ($'000)	2017 Dec 31	2018 pro forma Jan	Feb	Mar	Apr	May	Jun	Jul	Aug	Sep	Oct	Nov	Dec	Total
Net sales	$27,965	922	900	1,037	1,494	2,710	4,350	4,590	4,670	4,040	2,030	1,107	1,235	$29,086
Cost of goods sold	19,855	655	639	736	1,061	1,924	3,089	3,259	3,316	2,868	1,441	786	877	20,651
Gross profit	8,110	267	261	301	433	786	1,262	1,331	1,354	1,172	589	321	358	8,435
Operating expenses	6,711	582	582	582	582	582	582	582	582	582	582	582	582	6,984
Interest	72	0	1	5	8	14	24	6	0	0	10	0	0	68
Earnings before tax	1,326	−315	−322	−286	−157	190	655	743	772	590	−3	−261	−224	1,383
Taxes	530	−126	−129	−114	−63	76	262	297	309	236	−1	−104	−89	553
Net profit	$796	−189	−193	−172	−94	114	393	446	463	354	−2	−157	−134	$830

Balance sheet ($'000)	2017 Dec 31	2018 pro forma Jan	Feb	Mar	Apr	May	Jun	Jul	Aug	Sep	Oct	Nov	Dec
Assets													
Cash	$1,420	1,156	930	930	930	930	930	930	985	2,027	3,076	2,610	1,569
Accounts receivable	1,188	922	900	1,037	1,494	2,710	4,350	4,590	4,670	4,040	2,030	1,107	1,235
Inventory	475	475	475	475	475	800	800	800	800	800	475	475	475
Current assets	3,083	2,553	2,305	2,442	2,899	4,440	6,080	6,320	6,455	6,867	5,581	4,192	3,279
Plant & equipment, net	4,052	4,052	4,052	4,052	4,052	4,052	4,052	4,052	4,052	4,052	4,052	4,052	4,052
Total assets	$7,135	6,605	6,357	6,494	6,951	8,492	10,132	10,372	10,507	10,919	9,633	8,244	$7,331
Equities													
Accounts payable	$723	677	587	624	815	1,502	2,422	2,880	2,983	2,806	1,808	863	$755
Notes payable, bank	0	0	164	550	972	1,637	1,702	741	0	0	0	0	0
Accrued taxes	170	−126	−255	−369	−432	−356	−94	204	512	748	562	274	185
LT debt, current portion	100	100	100	100	100	100	100	100	100	100	100	100	100
Current liabilities	993	651	596	905	1,456	2,883	4,130	3,924	3,595	3,654	2,470	1,237	1,039
Long-term (LT) debt	1,600	1,600	1,600	1,600	1,600	1,600	1,600	1,600	1,600	1,600	1,500	1,500	1,500
Shareholders' equity	4,543	4,354	4,161	3,989	3,895	4,009	4,402	4,848	5,311	5,665	5,663	5,507	4,792
Total equities	$7,135	6,605	6,357	6,494	6,951	8,492	10,132	10,372	10,507	10,919	9,633	8,244	$7,331

- The minimum amount of cash necessary for running the business is calculated to be $930,000.

- Based on historical data, the end-of-month inventory during the low season is $475,000 on average, while this amount increases to $800,000 during high-season months.

- BeerCo offers quoted terms of net thirty days to its customers—mainly wholesalers and grocery chains—without facing any invoice collection problems so far.

- Purchases of net sixty days are made from the company's suppliers in amounts proportional to estimated monthly production. Total purchases in 2018 are estimated to $9.37 million (compared to $9.01 million in 2017), corresponding to the firm's projected annual growth.

- Following a large initial investment in plant and equipment, capital expenditures have been held equal to depreciation; so no change is considered in the firm's net fixed assets.

- BeerCo has a standard policy of distributing dividends to the firm's owners of 70 percent of its net profit, paid at year end.

The pro forma statements suggest that BeerCo's current credit line of $2 million will be sufficient to finance the company's operations. However, the firm's management wonders if following a chase production strategy is still the best approach. In addition to the large overtime premiums paid throughout the years, there were occasions where the firm faced problems in the recruitment of temporary workers—beyond the cost associated with their training. These issues were more serious in periods of economic growth, during which the demand for skilled labor can be quite high. Also, following a chase strategy has been detrimental to equipment utilization due to switching from idle to heavy use, while scheduling was gradually becoming more difficult due to frequent setup changes during the high season. Finally, under a chase production strategy, the firm will soon need to invest in fixed assets, as it is already approaching its maximum capacity utilization in the high-season months of 2018.

Bearing these issues in mind, BeerCo's management would like to consider whether shifting to a level production strategy could be beneficial to the company. Based on some initial calculations, the management believes that with a level production strategy, the company might need to slightly increase its full-time workforce and eliminate completely the need for temporary labor for the benefit of cost performance. Specifically, it has been estimated that if the firm produces at a constant rate of $1.84 million per month—measured in terms of value of products manufactured—there would be a 2 percent improvement in the cost of goods sold; that is, the cost would drop to 69 percent of sales dollar volume. On the flip side, they are aware that the total inventory in the system would increase—particularly during the low sales season—resulting to higher inventory storage and handling costs. Their biggest concern, however, is the impact that this strategy might have on the firm's ability to finance its operations, given the current arrangements with its bank partner.

15.6.2   Switching from Chase to Level Production at BeerCo

To estimate the impact on BeerCo's financials of switching from a chase to a level production strategy, first we need to construct pro forma statements that capture the changes in the firm's operational environment, given the new strategy. Based on the information provided in the case, the pro forma statements for a level strategy are presented in table 15.7.

Comparing the results of the pro forma statements for a level production strategy with those in table 15.6 we can draw several interesting observations:

• Projected earnings before taxes are $425,000 (or 31 percent) greater, despite the much higher interest charges associated with the level strategy. At the bottom line, net margin improved by 0.9 percentage points, which can be considered significant given the thin margins in the industry.

• The average level inventory is four times larger than the chase inventory ($2.34 million versus $600,000) and the same holds for end-of-year inventory. With the current plan of producing at a monthly rate of $1.85 million in order to meet peak demand in 2018, inventory coverage is over one year. This is not the case with the chase strategy, where the total production exactly matches the total projected demand (i.e., cost of goods sold). However, in subsequent periods, the company can use the ending inventory to lower its production rate so that total production to be equal to total demand.

• The average short-term debt required to fund level production is 4.2 times larger compared to the chase case ($1.89 million versus $444,000). More importantly, the bank credit needed not only exceeds the current ceiling of $2 million for several consecutive months (March to July), but it also cannot for the most part be secured by accounts receivable.

Based on our observations above, switching into a level strategy would not be possible for BeerCo without first renegotiating the credit line it has in place with its bank. As the projected accounts receivable would not be sufficient to secure its short-term debt, other assets—such as inventory—would also be used for that purpose. Still, the bank might not be willing to accept the higher risk associated with tripling the current credit line. Alternatively, BeerCo could consider raising long-term debt to support its financing needs until it accumulates the cash reserves necessary to support the level strategy. Whatever the case, increasing the firm's leverage might have implications on the cost of debt, something that has not been considered in our analysis.

The management might think that the escalated funding requirements will be temporary, and that the actual funds needed would be less when the company operates in steady state. This view relates to our second observation. As already mentioned in chapter 10, one of the key advantages of pro forma statement analysis is testing of what-if scenarios. Hence, to test the steady-state scenario, the firm can assume that starting inventory (i.e., on December 31, 2017) is higher so that total demand can be met with a lower production rate. By assuming

Table 15.7
BeerCo's year 2017 (actual) and year 2018 (monthly pro forma) income statement and balance sheet assuming a level production strategy.

Income statem. ($'000)	2017 Dec 31	2018 pro forma Jan	Feb	Mar	Apr	May	Jun	Jul	Aug	Sep	Oct	Nov	Dec	Total
Net sales	$27,965	922	900	1,037	1,494	2,710	4,350	4,590	4,670	4,040	2,030	1,107	1,235	$29,086
Cost of goods sold	19,855	636	621	715	1,031	1,870	3,002	3,167	3,222	2,788	1,401	764	852	20,069
Gross profit	8,110	286	279	321	463	840	1,349	1,423	1,448	1,252	629	343	383	9,017
Operating expenses	6,711	582	582	582	582	582	582	582	582	582	582	582	582	6,984
Interest	72	3	12	25	37	45	53	27	9	0	10	0	3	224
Earnings before tax	1,326	−300	−315	−285	−156	213	713	814	856	670	37	−239	−202	1,808
Taxes	530	−120	−126	−114	−62	85	285	325	343	268	15	−96	−81	723
Net profit	$796	−180	−189	−171	−93	128	428	488	514	402	22	−143	−121	$1,085

Balance sheet ($'000)	2017 Dec 31	2018 pro forma Jan	Feb	Mar	Apr	May	Jun	Jul	Aug	Sep	Oct	Nov	Dec
Assets													
Cash	$1,420	930	930	930	930	930	930	930	930	2,057	3,320	2,681	$930
Accounts receivable	1,188	922	900	1,037	1,494	2,710	4,350	4,590	4,670	4,040	2,030	1,107	1,235
Inventory	475	1,684	2,908	4,037	4,851	4,826	3,670	2,348	970	28	472	1,553	2,546
Current assets	3,083	3,536	4,738	6,004	7,276	8,466	8,950	7,868	6,570	6,125	5,822	5,341	4,711
Plant & equipment, net	4,052	4,052	4,052	4,052	4,052	4,052	4,052	4,052	4,052	4,052	4,052	4,052	4,052
Total assets	$7,135	7,588	8,790	10,056	11,328	12,518	13,002	11,920	10,622	10,177	9,874	9,393	$8,763
Equities													
Accounts payable	$723	1,242	1,723	1,723	1,723	1,723	1,723	1,723	1,723	1,723	1,723	1,723	$1,723
Notes payable, bank	0	403	1,439	2,991	4,418	5,395	5,166	3,270	1,116	0	0	0	331
Accrued taxes	170	−120	−246	−360	−422	−337	−52	274	616	885	659	322	241
LT debt, current portion	100	100	100	100	100	100	100	100	100	100	100	100	100
Current liabilities	993	1,625	3,016	4,454	5,818	6,881	6,937	5,366	3,555	2,707	2,482	2,145	2,395
Long-term (LT) debt	1,600	1,600	1,600	1,600	1,600	1,600	1,600	1,600	1,600	1,600	1,500	1,500	1,500
Shareholders' equity	4,543	4,363	4,174	4,003	3,909	4,037	4,465	4,954	5,467	5,870	5,892	5,749	4,868
Total equities	$7,135	7,588	8,790	10,056	11,328	12,518	13,002	11,920	10,622	10,177	9,874	9,393	$8,763

beginning inventory value of $2.55 million (instead of $475,000) and a monthly production rate of $1.67 million (measured as cost of goods produced), one can show that the average debt used by the firm would be around $1.5 million with its peak at well above $4.5 million in May. The verification of this result is left as an exercise.

There are several aspects not considered in our analysis so far. First, in addition to the financial debt cost of holding more inventory under a level strategy, there might be extra charges associated with storage and handling of that inventory as well as the cost of equity. In the BeerCo case, the financial component of inventory holding cost is theoretically equal to 10 percent—that is, equal to the cost of external financing—which is very close to the figure we get by dividing total interest expenses by average inventory for both strategies. Assuming that the physical component of the inventory holding cost is around 4 to 5 percent in annual terms (as it might usually be the case), a level strategy would still be considerably more profitable.

The second point relates to inventory risk. Holding large amounts of inventory might expose firms to several risks, such as shrinkage (i.e., inventory that is damaged, lost, or expired), surplus (i.e., when there is a mismatch between supply and demand), value loss (i.e., due to obsolescence), and so on. In the BeerCo case, these risks might be manageable and would not influence the firm's decision about switching from a chase to a level production strategy. This might not be the case for manufacturers of fashionable products that are usually faced with high product and price competition. In these occasions, inventory risk would be an important component that somehow must be identified, measured, and accounted for in the analysis.

The final point has to do with capacity considerations, particularly with plant machinery and equipment throughput. Under a level strategy, we have shown that the required production capacity is a function of the average demand rate. However, this is not the case with a chase production strategy, where the required production capacity is a function of the peak demand—assuming that subcontracting is not an option. Consequently, choosing a production strategy will have an impact on a firm's investment in fixed assets. In the BeerCo case, it is mentioned that the company is about to reach the maximum capacity utilization of its production equipment. Eventually, the firm might need to consider a mixed production strategy to avoid unnecessary investments in production equipment. Nevertheless, pro forma statements can be a valuable tool to execute a cost-benefit analysis associated with the different options.

From our discussion so far, there is a clear trade-off between the two production strategies regarding their impact on a firm's financials. A level strategy might have a positive impact on profitability (due to production efficiencies) at the cost of higher inventory in the system and consequently higher financing needs. A chase strategy, on the other hand, creates lower inventory in the system but might require a greater investment in fixed assets. Notice that the whole picture can be adequately captured by RONA, the indicator that provides an accurate picture of a firm's operational performance:

$$RONA = \frac{EBIT(1-t)}{OWC + FA}$$

Evaluating projected RONA in the BeerCo case—by using average annual values for the denominator to capture the impact of seasonality—it can be shown that a level strategy would result in a RONA value of 14.6 percent, which is greater than the 12.8 percent result of the chase strategy, despite the fact that fixed assets remain constant. Therefore, from a financial point of view, BeerCo should adopt a level production as long as it can secure the necessary funding to support this strategy.

It must be noted here that the same recommendation would probably result from the application of a typical technique for aggregate planning. The latter might also provide better guidance—assuming that costs can be captured correctly—on how much the company should produce in each month and exactly how to utilize the operating resources in the best possible way. However, as we have already mentioned, these techniques often do not consider funding limitations—or, if they do, they treat them as hard constraints. What these techniques definitely do not capture is all this rich discussion about the impact of production planning strategies on a firm's financial results. Therefore, linking aggregate planning with financial planning can be quite beneficial, particularly for firms operating in unstable business environments.

15.6.3   Cash Budgeting

We finish this section with a brief discussion of cash budgets. To motivate our discussion, first note the high fluctuation in almost all components of the pro forma income statements and balance sheets for either of the two strategies considered in the BeerCo case. As these changes indicate cash tied up or released from the different accounts, the firm would probably like to have in place a short-term cash forecasting tool to manage its cash reserves appropriately and avoid the unpleasant situation of not having the right amount of funds to support its operations.

While the cash and short-term debt accounts can provide information about the firm's monthly cash surplus or shortage, they do not provide insights on the causes of these changes—these pro forma statements have been developed by using accrual accounting. Cash budgets resolve this issue by providing an itemization of cash sources and uses in a future period. To that end, cash budgeting adjusts for all time lags associated with actual receipt or payment of credit sales, credit purchases, taxes, interest, and so on to provide an accurate picture of the actual balance between sources and uses. Due to the importance of cash budgets for ascertaining a firm's solvency, cash budgeting often takes place on a more frequent basis (e.g., weekly or even daily) for short-term cash management purposes.

To illustrate the mechanics of cash budgeting, tables 15.8 and 15.9 present BeerCo's monthly cash budgets under the two production strategies discussed.

Table 15.8
BeerCo's monthly cash budgets for year 2018 under chase production strategy ($'000).

Cash budget (chase)	Jan	Feb	Mar	Apr	May	Jun	Jul	Aug	Sep	Oct	Nov	Dec
Cash inflows												
Collection of sales	1,188	922	900	1,037	1,494	2,710	4,350	4,590	4,670	4,040	2,030	1,107
Cash outflows												
Payment of materials (accounts payable)	342	380	297	290	334	481	1,020	1,401	1,479	1,504	1,301	507
Tax payments	170	0	0	0	0	0	0	0	0	184	184	0
Principal payment on long-term loan	0	0	0	0	0	0	0	0	0	100	0	0
Operating expenses	582	582	582	582	582	582	582	582	582	582	582	582
Wages of production workforce	358	349	402	580	1,229	1,687	1,780	1,811	1,567	610	429	479
Interest payments	0	1	5	8	14	24	6	0	0	10	0	0
Dividends	0	0	0	0	0	0	0	0	0	0	0	581
Total	1,452	1,313	1,286	1,460	2,158	2,775	3,389	3,795	3,628	2,990	2,497	2,149
Cash balancing												
Net cash gain (loss) during month	−264	−391	−386	−423	−664	−65	961	795	1,042	1,050	−467	−1,041
Beginning cash	1,420	1,156	930	930	930	930	930	930	985	2,027	3,077	2,610
Ending cash if no financing	1,156	765	544	507	266	865	1,891	1,725	2,027	3,077	2,610	1,569
Desired minimum cash balance	930	930	930	930	930	930	930	930	930	930	930	930
Cumulative cash surplus (or shortage)	226	−165	−386	−423	−664	−65	961	795	1,097	2,147	1,680	639
Cumulative short-term debt at end of month	0	165	550	973	1,637	1,702	741	0	0	0	0	0
Cash ending of month	1,156	930	930	930	930	930	930	985	2,027	3,077	2,610	1,569

Table 15.9
BeerCo's monthly cash budgets for year 2018 under level production strategy ($'000).

Cash budget (level)	Jan	Feb	Mar	Apr	May	Jun	Jul	Aug	Sep	Oct	Nov	Dec
Cash inflows												
Collection of sales	1,188	922	900	1,037	1,494	2,710	4,350	4,590	4,670	4,040	2,030	1,107
Cash outflows												
Payment of materials (accounts payable)	342	380	861	861	861	861	861	861	861	861	861	861
Tax payments	170	0	0	0	0	0	0	0	0	241	241	0
Principal payment on long-term loan	0	0	0	0	0	0	0	0	0	100	0	0
Operating expenses	582	582	582	582	582	582	582	582	582	582	582	582
Wages of production workforce	984	984	984	984	984	984	984	984	984	984	984	984
Interest payments	3	12	25	37	45	53	27	9	0	10	0	3
Dividends	0	0	0	0	0	0	0	0	0	0	0	759
Total	2,081	1,958	2,452	2,464	2,472	2,480	2,454	2,436	2,427	2,778	2,668	3,189
Cash balancing												
Net cash gain (loss) during month	−893	−1,036	−1,552	−1,427	−978	230	1,896	2,154	2,243	1,262	−638	−2,082
Beginning cash	1,420	930	930	930	930	930	930	930	930	2,057	3,319	2,682
Ending cash if no financing	527	−106	−622	−497	−48	1,160	2,826	3,084	3,173	3,319	2,682	599
Desired minimum cash balance	930	930	930	930	930	930	930	930	930	930	930	930
Cumulative cash surplus (or shortage)	−403	−1,036	−1,552	−1,427	−978	230	1,896	2,154	2,243	2,389	1,752	−331
Cumulative short-term debt at end of month	403	1,439	2,991	4,417	5,395	5,165	3,269	1,116	0	0	0	331
Cash ending of month	930	930	930	930	930	930	930	930	2,057	3,319	2,682	930

As suggested in tables 15.8 and 15.9, cash budgets are usually organized in three parts. The top part lists all cash collections associated with the firm's operations. In the BeerCo case this only includes collections from customers; however, other items can also be considered here, such as projected cash from sales of capital assets, income from financial assets, and so forth. Notice that the cash budget adjusts sales to match the projected cash collection by taking into account the one-month credit period offered by the firm to its customers. In real life, a firm might need to make more elaborate estimates to consider cash sales, sales on discount, late payments, and other issues associated with the business's capability to collect from its customers.

The second part of the cash budget lists the company's projected payments to suppliers, banks, tax authorities, employees, shareholders, and so on. Similar to the previous group, these flows have been adjusted to reflect the actual timing of payments according to the information provided in the case. For example, payments to suppliers refer to two-month-old purchases, while tax payments take place on three particular months. Also, note that production costs are separated into material and production workforce cash payments—these will eventually become the cost of goods sold and the cost of inventory by the application of accrual accounting. The reason is that all planned expenditures included in the cash budget typically come from different budgets (i.e., direct materials, direct labor, manufacturing overhead, and selling and administrative expenses).

Finally, the bottom part provides an estimate of the cash surplus or deficit by comparing the period's ending cash—that is, the resulting balance after the period's net cash gain (loss) has been added to (subtracted from) the beginning cash—with the minimum cash required to run the business. Then, if there are any large surpluses projected for some period and no short-term debt outstanding, the finance department can consider these balances for making suitable investments. On the other hand, if there are any negative balances, the cash budget indicates the timing and amount of debt that is needed to be raised to offset these balances. Particularly in the BeerCo case, the surplus is used to pay back short-term debt (or is added to the cash account if debt is zero), leading to the last two lines being nearly identical (apart from a couple of rounding differences) to the cash and notes payable accounts in the balance sheet—as should be the case.

15.7   The Supply Chain Trade-Off Triangle

In previous sections, our discussion was mainly focused on a firm's tactical decisions to improve its income statement performance—that is, revenue versus expenses—often at the cost of higher investment in OWC. For example, we have shown how manufacturing offshoring, adopting a level production strategy, or offering a broad product assortment can help boost gross profits—either through cost reduction (offshoring and leveling) or an increase in revenue (broad assortment). However, this needs to be balanced with the required investment in OWC and associated costs in order to maximize business efficiency.

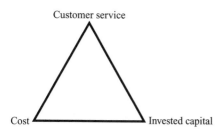

Figure 15.3
A supply chain trade-off triangle.

In this section, we will extend our discussion in two ways. First, we introduce a third dimension—that of customer service—to construct a more holistic model which effectively captures the various relationships between supply chain and finance. Second, we reflect on how different product/market strategies are associated with different trade-offs in the triangle. Figure 15.3 shows a supply chain trade-off triangle.

Customer service This refers to a firm's product/service offering and it includes product-specific elements, such as product functionality, quality, and range but also order fulfillment elements, such as lead times, service levels (i.e., in-stock probability and fill rate), and credit terms. Customer service is directly related to the firm's capability to charge premium prices and generate revenues.

Cost Cost indicates how much it costs the firm to generate its revenues. Hence, cost incorporates several elements, such as: manufacturing, purchasing, and logistics costs; expenses for research and development; depreciation of fixed assets; and selling, general, and administrative expenses.

Invested capital Invested capital specifies how much capital is employed by the firm's investors (i.e., debtors and equity holders). As shown in chapter 5, the invested capital can be represented by the sum of OWC and fixed assets.

Ideally, any company would wish to maximize its performance throughout the triangle—that is, be able to generate high sales at premium prices while keeping its costs and invested capital as low as possible. However, this is not feasible, as each corner in the triangle is associated with the other two through several trade-offs. Next, we will discuss these trade-offs through some particular examples.

Consider first a firm that wishes to decrease its costs by taking advantage of production efficiencies associated with switching from a chase to a level production strategy. This was the topic presented in section 15.6 where we showed that a level strategy often results in significant investment in OWC—mainly inventory. But this is only one side of the story. To capture the whole picture, it is necessary to consider the impact of level production on customer service. As production under a level approach may become less responsive to sudden changes in demand patterns, the number of backorders might grow, occasionally leading to lower service levels. Eventually, the firm might have to offer price discounts on backorders or even see some orders lost to competition, both of which would have an impact on its revenues.

Next, let's consider the example of a company that wishes to improve its customer service as a vehicle for increasing its prices and revenues. This might take the form of offering its customers higher service levels—namely, target fill rates, lower lead times, product customization, or even better credit terms. Any of these actions, however, would require some investment in OWC either in the form of inventory or accounts receivable, while further investment in fixed assets—say, for adding responsive capacity—might also be necessary. In addition to the impact on invested capital, the firm might also be faced with cost increases due to the added complexity in its production planning, customer service, and logistics processes.

The two examples discussed above show that a firm contemplating improving its position in any of the three corners in the supply chain triangle will need to consider the impact on the other two corners and manage the associated trade-offs efficiently.

The discussion so far has been focused on supply chain choices at the tactical or operational level. This framework, however, is equally applicable when it comes into the evaluation of a firm's product/market strategy. At that level, companies are usually positioned somewhere on the spectrum between product leadership versus cost leadership.

Product leaders are mainly focused on bringing innovative products to the market, which they usually sell at a high premium to niche markets or high-end segments. To be able to develop, produce, and distribute their innovative products, product leaders are faced with high costs—mainly due to significant research and development (R&D) and marketing efforts but also because they usually source from premium and innovative suppliers. Product leaders also have higher capital investment, as they have in place more specialized and costly equipment. Moreover, they are faced with high demand uncertainty and production complexities (at least until production reaches maturity on the learning curve), all of which drive investment in OWC.

Companies adopting a cost leadership strategy, on the other hand, are mainly focused on achieving operational efficiencies, through which they are able to compete in the market by offering the lowest prices. Cost leaders are last in implementing innovative features into their products/services—usually, they do so after the technology and production processes are quite mature. Instead, they continuously seek opportunities to reduce their cost of doing business, usually in sourcing, production, distribution, or order fulfillment. By cutting down on the services they provide to their customers, cost leaders cannot charge any price premiums but they perform better in the cost and invested capital dimensions.

It should be clear by now that different companies within an industry are positioned differently in the triangle depending on how they choose to compete in the market. We have already provided an example in section 9.3.2 of four retailers operating in the consumer electronics market whose distinct marketing approaches have placed them in different regions on the trade-off between inventory turns and gross margin.

A question that follows is: How can we evaluate a firm's performance given its position in the triangle? If there is a ratio that can effectively capture the impact of different supply chain strategies in the triangle, it must be RONA—which shows the rate of return earned on the total capital invested in the business, regardless of its origin as debt or equity. In other words, by neutralizing the impact of a firm's financial strategy (i.e., its capital structure), RONA is a purely operational ratio showing how effectively and efficiently the company is using its assets to generate earnings—and this is most likely the investors' main concern.

Having a unified ratio that can capture the various dynamics in the triangle is useful for several purposes. First, it can provide a business with valuable insights in evaluating alternative strategies. Take for example a company that considers offshoring as an option to reduce its cost. In addition to the direct positive impact in EBIT, the firm should estimate the changes in invested capital (i.e., higher investment in inventory) and also try to quantify potential deterioration in service (i.e., revenue loss due to lower responsiveness). It follows that offshoring might be a good option only if the projected RONA is greater than the one achieved under the current sourcing strategy. This exercise is applicable to almost all topics discussed in this chapter. In general, a firm contemplating changes in its supply chain practices would first need to carefully balance the trade-offs in the triangle to make sure that the desired financial results will be achieved.

Second, the use of a single ratio might be useful for benchmarking. For example, comparing a product leader to a cost leader (operating in the same industry) on the basis of ratios such as operating margin or inventory turns would not be representative of their overall performance, as the two firms follow fundamentally different strategies. This became obvious in section 15.5 where we benchmark Inditex against H&M—the two leaders in the fast fashion industry. While Inditex's responsive operations model has helped the company outperform its rival in both operating margin and inventory turns metrics, H&M is still able to generate relatively higher returns on invested capital—mainly due to Inditex's large fixed assets investment—justifying its reputation as being one of the top supply chain actors across all industries. A thorough and practical view of benchmarking on the triangle can be found in DeSmet (2018).

Summarizing this section, a company's positioning on the triangle is directly related to its product/market and supply chain strategies—and this must be taken into account when benchmarking against its peers. A firm's competence at balancing the trade-offs between customer service, cost, and invested capital is more important to achieving superior financial performance—as measured by RONA—than individually excelling in any of these elements of the supply chain triangle.

15.8   Summary

This chapter has presented several topics from the operations and supply chains realms, which—when seen under a financial prism—bring up some notable trade-offs that require special attention by management, as they are reflected in a firm's financial statements and performance. We have shown how overly focus on the income statement performance might induce firms offshore their production just to end up with tons of idle inventory, eventually hurting their overall financial performance. Similar trade-offs are relevant when a firm contemplates its product assortment strategy. We have also used the Inditex example to show how firms with sound management of their operational levers, such as in determining their push-pull frontier, can achieve superior and (equally important) robust financial results, outperforming their competition. We have discussed the importance of coordination between the production planning and financial planning processes within a company in order to identify plans that exploit the levers from both spheres and can help firms improve their overall performance. Finally, we have summarized a firm's trade-offs in a conceptual triangular relationship—between cost, service level, and invested capital—and proposed RONA as a metric that can be used for both evaluating those trade-offs and benchmarking.

15.9   Suggested Reading

- DeSmet, Bram 2017. *Supply chain strategy and financial metrics*. London: Kogan Page.
- Fisher, M., and A. Raman. 2010. *The new science of retailing: How analytics are transforming the supply chain and improving performance*. Cambridge, MA: Harvard Business Press.
- Xiang Wan, Philip T. Evers, and Martin E. Dresner. 2012. "Too much of a good thing: The impact of product variety on operations and sales performance." *Journal of Operations Management* 30: 316–324.

Exercises

1. A firm is considering outsourcing its domestic production from the United States to a third-party manufacturer located in Asia. What is the impact of offshoring on the firm's provisions (including inventory reserves) in the balance sheet? Which financial ratios will most likely be affected by such move and how? Please explain briefly.

2. HydroPure manufactures several models of water purifiers in its company-owned factory in the state of Tennessee in the United States. Due to plant capacity limitations, the company considers outsourcing the production of one of its top selling models to China. The product's wholesale price is $70 with a variable manufacturing cost of $40 per unit. The weekly demand for this model at the company's central distribution center in Tennessee is normally distributed with mean 300 and standard deviation 100. Currently, the warehouse places inventory replenishment orders on a weekly basis and it takes one week for the orders to be delivered. HydroPure has found a potential

subcontractor in China from which it can source the product for $30 per unit (including transportation costs); however, a minimum order quantity of 600 units will be required. Also, if the production is outsourced to the Chinese manufacturer, the lead time for order replenishments will be normally distributed with mean six weeks and standard deviation two weeks.

a. What will be the impact on HydroPure's financial statements if the firm finally decides to offshore its production? Assume that HydroPure can finance any increase in current assets by using a credit line bearing 10 percent interest rate.

b. Please outline the major risks (not addressed in the problem description) associated with the firm's decision to outsource its production to China. Which of the financial statements might be affected by these risks?

3. In early March 2018, US President Trump announced a 25 percent tariff on all steel imports, and 10 percent on aluminum. How will this move affect the supply chains of US companies—such as from the automotive or defense industry—that use these commodities? Please explain briefly.

4. Suppose that due to global pressure, there is a possibility that China will appreciate its currency by 10 percent by 2020. What implications will this move have on global trade? Do you think that ocean transportation costs will be affected? How could global supply chains be reconfigured to address this risk? Please explain briefly.

5. A boutique cosmetics manufacturer is considering reducing the assortment in one of its product families to decrease complexity in its operations. The following table shows the mean and standard deviation of weekly demand for each of the ten different products comprising this product family.

Product	Mean weekly demand	Standard deviation
A	26,348	5,006
B	22,692	4,992
C	18,941	4,356
D	5,320	1,543
E	4,702	1,458
F	3,116	1,091
G	2,250	855
H	1,004	412
I	865	424
J	762	404

Suppose that the company intends to remove products H, I, and J from its portfolio. To answer the following questions, assume that for all products the unit wholesale price is $50, the standard cost per product unit is $22 (assume all variable), and annual inventory holding cost is 20 percent.

a. If inventory orders for each product are placed weekly, and it takes two weeks for each order to be fulfilled (i.e., a periodic review inventory system), what will be the impact of removing these products on the firm's three financial statements? Please show your calculations.

b. Which ratios will most likely be affected and how? Please explain briefly.

6. Returning to problem 5, now assume that the products to be removed are strategic—in the sense that they drive sales from some key customers—and also that their wholesale price is $70 (instead of $50). After reviewing its production processes, the company has realized that these three

products share some key ingredients, which makes possible the application of postponement. That is, the firm can maintain inventory of a generic intermediate product, which then can be differentiated to each of the H, I, or J products within one week of each inventory replenishment order. The other parameters in problem 5 remain unchanged. If the company is planning to replace this product family in two years, what is the maximum investment cost it would be willing to accept for implementing this capability? Please use the NPV approach to base your answer to this problem.

7. Please follow the logic of section 15.5 (push versus pull) to compare GM with Toyota. What do their financial ratios say about the two firms' operational strategies?

8. Table 15.7 shows BeerCo's pro forma income statement and balance sheet if the firm adopts a level production strategy (by incorporating the assumptions associated with this strategy). Assuming that BeerCo's inventory at the end of 2017 is $2.55 million (instead of $475,000), what should be the monthly production rate (in terms of cost of goods produced), so that projected sales are met? What would be the projected average and maximum short-term debt for 2018 in this case? To answer the questions, it is required to reconstruct table 15.7 by considering the new information.

9. In the BeerCo case discussed in section 15.6, the company's pro forma statements that correspond to the current chase production strategy are compared to the level strategy ones. Now assume that BeerCo considers the possibility of following a mixed production strategy (i.e., a combination of chase and level). Construct the pro forma statements that correspond to a mixed strategy, where the level monthly production rate is equal to $1.2 million (in terms of cost of goods produced), while any additional production requirements are fulfilled by a chase system. In your calculations, please note that the cost of goods produced—as percentage of sales dollar volume—is estimated differently under the two strategies.

    a. What would be the average and maximum short-term debt requirements under the mixed strategy?

    b. What is the projected RONA under a mixed strategy? How does it compare with the projected RONA of a pure level or chase strategy?

    c. Optional: Which is the optimal production strategy that maximizes RONA? To answer this question, please test different values for the level monthly production rate component of the mixed strategy.

10. Benchmark the performance of Inditex, H&M, and Gap on the supply chain trade-off triangle for the years 2015–2018. To do so, you may construct three two-dimensional plots on the following metrics: "EBIT (as percent sales) versus inventory turns," "EBIT (as percent sales) versus cash conversion cycle," and "SGA (as percent sales) versus inventory turns" (DeSmet 2018). On each of these plots, show how the three firms' performance on the suggested metrics change through years 2015–2018. Based on the resulting graphs, what can be inferred for the companies' performance on the triangle?

References

Bailey, Jeff. 2007. "Southwest Airlines gains advantage by hedging on long-term oil contracts." *New York Times*, November 28. https://www.nytimes.com/2007/11/28/business/worldbusiness/28iht-hedge.4.8517580.html.

Bain, Marc. 2018. "To see how Asia's manufacturing map is being redrawn, look at Nike and Adidas." *Quartz*, May 10. https://qz.com/1274044/nike-and-adidas-are-steadily-ditching-china-for-vietnam-to-make-their-sneakers/.

Barboza, David, and Louise Story. 2007. "Matel issues new recall of toys made in China." *New York Times*, August 14. https://www.nytimes.com/2007/08/14/business/15toys-web.html?%5C_r=0.

Berfield, Susan, and Manuel Baigorri. 2013. "Zara's fast-fashion edge." Bloomberg, November 14. https://www.bloomberg.com/news/articles/2013-11-14/2014-outlook-zaras-fashion-supply-chain-edge.

BMW Worldwide. 2019. "BMW worldwide production." BMW Worldwide (website). https://www.bmwusfactory.com/manufacturing/bmw-worldwide/.

Butler, Sarah. 2013. "Inditex: Spain's fashion powerhouse you've probably never heard of." *The Guardian*, December 14. https://www.theguardian.com/fashion/2013/dec/15/inditex-spain-global-fashion-powerhouse.

Cachon, Gérard, and Christian Terwiesch. 2013. *Matching supply with demand: An introduction to operations management*, 3rd ed. New York: McGraw Hill.

DeSmet, Bram. 2018. *Supply chain strategy and financial metrics*, 1st ed. London: Kogan Page.

Feitzinger, Edward, and Hau. L. Lee. 1997. "Mass customization at Hewlett-Packard: The power of postponement." *Harvard Business Review*, January–February.

Fisher, Marshall, and Ananth Raman. 2010. *The new science of retailing: How analytics are transforming the supply chain and improving performance*. Boston: Harvard Business Press.

García Aller, Marta. 2017. "Zara: Technology and user experience as drivers of business." *IE Insights*, December 15. https://www.ie.edu/insights/articles/zara-technology-and-user-experience-as-drivers-of-business/.

Glen, Jeffrey. 2019. "Offshoring vs. outsourcing." BusinessDictionary. Accessed May 15, 2019. http://www.businessdictionary.com/article/1090/%20offshoring-vs-outsourcing-d1412/.

Goldsberry, Clare. 2010. "Bringing manufacturing back to the United States." *Area Development*, December–/January. https://www.areadevelopment.com/siteSelection/dec09/united-states-manufacturing-insouring-costs1102.shtml.

Gorrepati, Kris. 2016. "Zara's agile supply chain is the source of its competitive advantage." *Digitalist*, March 30. https://www.digitalistmag.com/digital-supply-networks/2016/03/30/zaras-agile-supply-chain-is-source-of-competitive-advantage-04083335.

H&M. 2017. "Annual report 2017." Accessed June 2, 2019. https://about.hm.com/content/dam/hmgroup/groupsite/documents/en/Digital%20Annual%20Report/2017/Annual%20Report%202017.pdf.

Hanbury, Mary. 2018. "H&M is making a drastic change to keep its rivals and get rid of its mountain of clothes." *Business Insider*, May 8. https://www.businessinsider.es/hm-stores-will-be-different-by-location-2018-5?r=US&IR=T.

Hersh, Adam, and Ethan Gurwitz. 2014. "Offshoring work is taking a toll on the U.S. economy." Center for American Progress, July 30. https://www.americanprogress.org/issues/economy/news/2014/07/30/94864/offshoring-work-is-taking-a-toll-on-the-u-s-economy/.

Hiiemaa, Kris. 2016. "In the success stories of H&M, Zara, Ikea and Walmart, luck is not a key factor." *ERPLY*, March. https://erply.com/in-the-success-stories-of-hm-zara-ikeaand-walmart-luck-is-not-a-key-factor/.

Inditex. 2017. "Annual report 2017." Accessed June 2, 2019. https://www.inditex.com/documents/10279/563475/Annual+Accounts%2C+management+report+and+audit+report+of+Inditex+Group+2017/77a7def2-b502-ac22-003e-d1e7c900233c.

Inditex. n.d. "Design." Inditex (website). Accessed May 16, 2019. https://www.inditex.com/how-we-do-business/our-model/design.

Johnson, Rob. 2015. "'Reshoring' brings jobs back to U.S., including Pensacola." *Pensacola News Journal*, January 17. https://www.pnj.com/story/news/2015/01/17/reshoring-brings-jobs-back-us-including-pensacola/21929659/.

Jordan, C. William, and Stephen C. Graves. 1995. "Principles on the benefits of manufacturing process flexibility." *Management Science* 41 (4): 577–594.

Köhn, Rüdiger. 2012. "Wir müssen unseren WM-Ball überall verkaufen." *Frankfurter Allgemeine Zeitung*, April 7. http://www.faz.net/aktuell/wirtschaft/unternehmen/adidas-chef-hainer-wir-muessen-unseren-wm-ball-ueberall-verkaufen-11709766.html.

Kiley, David. 2018. "Volvo is revitalized in U.S. by Chinese ownership, but faces headwinds from Trump Tariffs." *Forbes*, October 16. https://www.forbes.com/sites/davidkiley5/2018/10/16/volvo-is-revitalized-in-u-s-by-chinese-ownership-but-faces-headwinds-from-trump-tariffs/#31e7b42660bc.

Malito, Alessandra. 2017. "Grocery stores carry 40,000 more items than they did in the 1990s." *MarketWatch*, June 17. https://www.marketwatch.com/story/grocery-stores-carry-40000-more-items-than-they-did-in-the-1990s-2017-06-07.

Priddle, Alisa. 2017. "Volvo to build next-gen XC90 in U.S. in 2021." *Motortrend*, September 25. https://www.motortrend.com/news/volvo-to-build-next-gen-xc90-in-u-s-in-2021/.

Sheffi, Yossi. 2012. *Logistics clusters: Delivering value and driving growth*. Cambridge, MA: MIT Press.

Shepardson, David. 2018. "Volvo cars seeks U.S. tariff exemption for Chinese-made SUV." Reuters, September 14. https://www.reuters.com/article/us-volvo-tariffs/volvocars-seeks-u-s-tariff-exemption-for-chinese-made-suv-idUSKCN1LU2OI.

Simchi-Levi, David, Annette Clayton, and Bruce Raven. 2013. "When one size does not fit all." *Sloan Management Review* 54 (2): 15–17.

Topham, Gwyn. 2018. "After Cobalt, will any more European airlines go bust?" *The Guardian*, October 18. https://www.theguardian.com/business/2018/oct/18/cobalt-cyprus-european-airlines-explainer.

Trefis. 2015. "With brand divestments almost over, here's how P&G plans to cut costs next year." Forbes, May 7. https://www.forbes.com/sites/greatspeculations/2015/05/07/with-brand-divestments-almost-over-heres-how-pg-plans-to-cut-costs-next/#2455ef3e32e2.

Volvo Car Group. 2019. "Volvo cars sets new global sales record in 2018; breaks 600,000 sales milestone." News release, January 4. https://www.media.volvocars.com/global/en-gb/media/pressreleases/247393/volvo-cars-sets-new-global-salesrecord-in-2018-breaks-600000-sales-milestone.

World Trade Organization. n.d. "Regional trade agreements." World Trade Organization (website). https://www.wto.org/english/tratop_e/region_e/region_e.htm.

Appendix A: The Triple-Seven Financial Statements

Operations and supply chain managers do not need to understand every single detail of financial statements. Most of the time, understanding the basics is enough for them to obtain the big picture of the firm. Aware of this fact, we have simplified the three main financial statements (balance sheet, income statement, statement of cash flows) and have come up with the 777-financial statements—each one composed of exactly seven items—which are shown next.

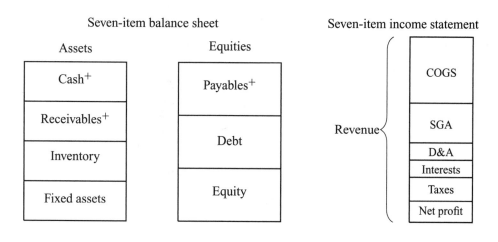

Appendix B: Probability Review

This quick review of probability topics assumes some basic previous knowledge of probability and calculus. It is meant to be a quick refresher of relevant topics rather than a rigorous presentation of concepts. If you are not familiar with the field of probability, you may want to have a look at some introductory books on the topic instead, such as Ross (2010) or Bertsekas and Tsitsiklis (2008).

B.1   The Concept of Random Variable and Its Characterization

We will first introduce the idea of a random variable and how to characterize it.

B.1.1   Random Variable

A random variable is a numerical variable whose values are realizations of a random event. For instance, the number of points obtained when rolling a standard dice is a random variable. The random event is rolling the dice, and the possible realizations are the integer numbers from one to six.

Random variables can be discrete or continuous. If the number of outcomes is countable (read: finite) the random variable is discrete, otherwise it is continuous. For instance, the number of points obtained when rolling a dice is a discrete variable; the time until a light bulb fails is continuous, as time itself is a continuous variable.

Random variables, also known as probability distributions, are usually denoted by a capital letter, such as X, and are completely characterized by their probability mass (density) function—denoted pmf (pdf) if the variable is discrete (continuous)—or their cumulative distribution function—CDF, presented next.

B.1.2   The Probability Mass Function (pmf) and Probability Density Function (pdf)

A pmf is a map from $\mathbb{R}$ to $[0,1]$ that assigns a probability to each value of $\mathbb{R}$. For instance, when rolling a fair standard dice, the pmf assigns $\frac{1}{6}$ to each possible outcome—as the probability of obtaining any number between one and six, say five, is exactly one over

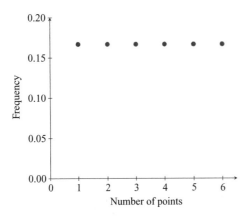

Figure B.1
Graphical representation of the pmf of the random variable rolling a fair dice.

six—and zero otherwise. It should be clear that the values assigned by a pmf function are always nonnegative and that they add up to one. For instance, in the case of a fair dice, $\frac{1}{6} + \frac{1}{6} + \frac{1}{6} + \frac{1}{6} + \frac{1}{6} + \frac{1}{6} = 1$.

A pmf characterizes a random variable, that is, it unequivocally defines all its properties. It is usually represented by a small letter, such as f. For instance, the pmf of the random variable X, rolling a fair dice, can be written as:

$$f(x) = \begin{cases} \frac{1}{6} & \text{if } x \in \{1, 2, 3, 4, 5, 6\} \\ 0 & \text{otherwise} \end{cases}$$

A pmf can be represented graphically (figure B.1).

A pdf is the counterpart of the pmf for the continuous case. It gives the *relative* likelihood of each outcome; in the continuous case, the absolute likelihood of each outcome is always zero. For instance, consider the following pdf:

$$f(x) = \begin{cases} \frac{x}{2} & \text{if } x \in [0, 2] \\ 0 & \text{otherwise} \end{cases}$$

Figure B.2 shows its graphical representation. By observing the graph, it should be clear that obtaining 2 is twice as likely as obtaining 1, but the probability of obtaining either 1 or 2 are zero. Think of it: there are infinite numbers between zero and two. Therefore, the probability of obtaining any of them is zero. That is the reason why it is only of interest to calculate the probability of intervals in the continuous case. For instance, the probability of obtaining a number between 0 and 1 is:

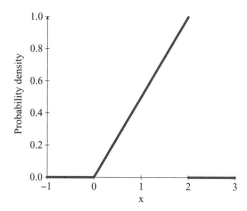

Figure B.2
Graphical representation of the pdf given by $f(x) = \frac{x}{2}$ if $x \in [0, 2]$ and 0 otherwise.

$$\int_0^1 \frac{x}{2} dx = \frac{1^2}{4} = 0.25$$

Here we use an integral to sum all relative likelihoods through the interval $[0, 1]$. The probability can also be calculated as the area of the figure under the pdf curve. In this case, the figure under the curve between $x = 0$ and $x = 1$ is a triangle, whose area is:

$$A = \frac{1}{2} \cdot (1 - 0) \cdot 0.5 = 0.25$$

As in the discrete case, the sum of all probabilities should be the unity:

$$\int_{-\infty}^{\infty} \frac{x}{2} dx = \int_0^2 \frac{x}{2} dx = \frac{x^2}{4} \Big|_0^2 = \frac{2^2}{4} - 0 = 1$$

which reveals that $f(x)$ is a well-defined pdf.

B.1.3   The Cumulative Distribution Function (CDF)

A CDF is just the cumulative function of a pmf or a pdf. As such, when evaluated at x, the CDF returns the probability that the random variable takes a value less than or equal to x. The representations of the CDFs of the two pdfs already presented follow.

Note that the range of the CDF always goes from zero to one, as it represents a probability. Also, in the case of continuous random variables, the CDF coincides with the area under the curve to the left of x in the pdf. For instance, in the right panel of figure B.3, see that $CDF(1) = 0.25$, the same value we found in the previous subsection.

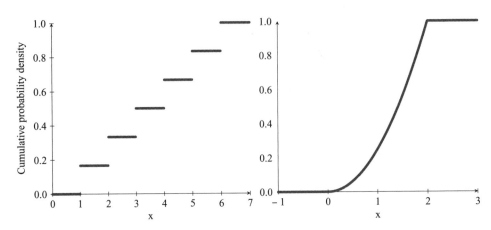

Figure B.3
Examples of cumulative distribution functions: discrete (left) and continuous (right). The corresponding pmf/pdf are shown in figures B.1 and B.2, respectively.

B.2   The Normal Distribution

The normal distribution is the most important distribution, as it is very prevalent in practice. Its ubiquity stems from the fact that this distribution results from the aggregation of many other common distributions.

B.2.1   Characterization of the Normal Distribution

A random variable that follows a normal distribution, $X \sim \mathcal{N}(\mu, \sigma^2)$, is characterized by its pdf, which is:

$$f(x) = \frac{1}{\sigma\sqrt{2\pi}} e^{-\frac{(x-\mu)^2}{2\sigma^2}} \tag{B.1}$$

The pdf depends on two parameters, μ (the mean) and σ (the standard deviation). Therefore, each pair of μ and σ results in a particular normal distribution. The mean measures the location of the values, while the standard deviation measures the dispersion of values around the mean. Figure B.4 shows a number of examples of normal distributions for various parameter values. Note that the pdf representation is flatter as σ grows.

Other useful properties of the normal pdf is that it is symmetric with respect to the vertical axis that passes through the mean and that its mean and median—the value that leaves half of the area under the pdf to each side of it—coincide.

The CDF of a normal distribution cannot be represented analytically, as the integral of its pdf cannot be calculated analytically. To get around this difficulty, the MS Excel function NORMALDIST is used, which returns the CDF of a normal distribution, a great substitute for old-fashioned numerical tables.

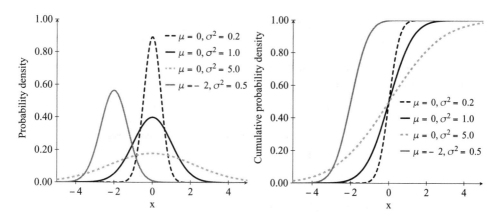

Figure B.4
Examples of pdf (left) and CDF (right) of normal distributions for various parameter values.

 Exercise

Weighing Pallets

The weight of a pallet is a random variable W, normally distributed with mean 200 kg and standard deviation 20 kg: $W \sim N\left(\mu, \sigma^2\right) = N\left(200, 20^2\right)$.

1. What is the probability that a pallet weighs exactly 200 kg?
2. What is the probability that a pallet weighs more than 240 kg?
3. What is the probability that the weight of a pallet is between 200 and 220 kg?

❓ Question 1

What is the probability that a pallet weighs exactly 200 kg?

Well, the probability that a pallet weighs exactly 200 kg is zero, as the distribution is continuous. (Note that "exactly 200" means 200.0000...00...)

❓ Question 2

What is the probability that a pallet weighs more than 240 kg?

We could try calculating the integral (P(·) denotes probability):

$$P(W > 240) = \int_{240}^{\infty} \frac{1}{20\sqrt{2\pi}} e^{-\frac{(x-200)^2}{800}} \, dx$$

But, as mentioned, this integral has no analytical solution. Thus, we should resort to using the MS Excel function NORM.DIST, which requires the following parameters:

$$F(\mu, \sigma, x) = P\,(X_{\mu,\sigma} < x) = \texttt{NORM.DIST(x,mu,sigma,TRUE)}$$

where TRUE means that the function is a normal CDF (FALSE would return a normal pdf). The probability that a pallet weighs more than 240 kg is then:

$$P(W > 240) = 1 - P(W \le 240) = 1 - \texttt{NORM.DIST(240,200,20,TRUE)}$$

$$\approx 1 - 0.977 = 0.023 = 2.3\%$$

Question 3

What is the probability that the weight of a pallet is between 200 and 220 kg?

Much like we did for the last question:

$$P(200 \le W \le 220) = P(W \le 220) - P(W \le 200)$$

$$= \texttt{NORM.DIST(220,200,20,TRUE)} - 0.5 \approx 0.84 = 84\%$$

We made use of the fact that $P(W \le 200) = 0.5$ because $w = 200$ is the mean (hence the median) of this normal distribution.

Exercise

Linking Inventory Level and Service Level

Suppose that daily demand for widgets is a random variable D, which is known to be normally distributed with $\mu = 100$ and $\sigma = 30$. How many widgets do you need to keep in stock so that customer service level is 98 percent?

We want to find the threshold value, S, that is higher than random demand, D, 98 percent of the times; that is, we want to solve:

$$P(D \le S) = 0.98$$

The value of S can be found using the *inverse* normal distribution function, which is also available in MS Excel:

$$S = F_{100,30}^{-1}(0.98) = \texttt{NORM.INV(0.98,100,30)} \approx 162$$

Therefore, in order to achieve a 98 percent service level we need to have 162 widgets in stock.

B.2.2   The Standard Normal Distribution and the z-Score

A special type of normal distribution is the *standard* normal, which is a normal distribution with zero mean ($\mu = 0$) and unit variance ($\sigma^2 = 1$). Its pdf is usually denoted as φ, and its CDF as Φ. By substituting $\mu = 0$ and $\sigma = 1$ back in expression B.1, the pdf of a standard normal results:

$$\varphi(x) = \frac{1}{\sqrt{2\pi}} e^{-\frac{x^2}{2}}$$

The standard normal has useful properties, and is intimately related to the concept of z-score, presented next.

Given a normal random variable $X \sim \mathcal{N}(\mu, \sigma^2)$, we can define a new random variable Z as

$$Z = \frac{X - \mu}{\sigma} \tag{B.2}$$

This random variable Z can be shown to follow a standard normal distribution: $Z \sim \mathcal{N}(0,1)$.

Indeed, solving for x in expression B.2 gives $x = \mu + z\sigma$. Substituting x with z in eq B.1, we obtain

$$f(z) = \frac{1}{\sigma\sqrt{2\pi}} e^{-\frac{z^2}{2}} \tag{B.3}$$

which is a pdf only if $\int_{-\infty}^{\infty} f(z) = 1$, which implies that $\sigma = 1$. The resulting pdf is identical to $\varphi(x)$, therefore Z is a standard normal distribution.

Note that the transformation given in B.2 is a bijection, which means that there is a one-to-one correspondence between the variables X and Z (figure B.5). For every value x of the original random variable, we can find its *unique* corresponding z value, called z-score, and vice versa. This means we can move from the x-domain to the z-domain, work more conveniently in the z-domain, and come back to the x-domain once the work is done.

Note that when moving to the z-domain, we are simply recentering and stretching the original pdf so that the new pdf has null mean and unit standard deviation.

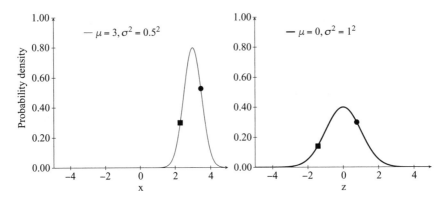

Figure B.5
pdf of the original random variable X (left) and the transformed random variable Z (right). Each point x has its correspondent z, called the z-score.

Exercise

Weighing Pallets Revisited

Again, suppose the weight of a pallet is normally distributed, $W \sim \mathcal{N}(200, 20^2)$. If a pallet weighs 220 kg, what is the corresponding z-score?

We can calculate the z-score for $w = 220$ as:

$$z = \frac{220 - 200}{20} = 1$$

It is not a coincidence that we get the unity: the weight of the pallet is exactly one sigma away from the mean weight. The z-score tells how many sigmas away a particular realization is from the mean of the distribution.

Exercise

One Sigma Away

Let X follow a normal distribution, $X \sim \mathcal{N}(\mu, \sigma^2)$. What is the probability that any value x drawn from X is within one standard deviation of the mean?

For any random normal variable X, we can move to the z-domain:

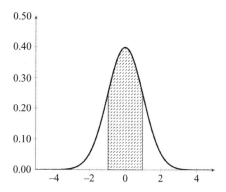

Figure B.6
The shaded area represents the probability that the random variable is within one standard deviation from the mean.

$$P(\mu - \sigma \leq x \leq \mu + \sigma) = P(-\sigma \leq x - \mu \leq \sigma) = P\left(-1 \leq \frac{x - \mu}{\sigma} \leq 1\right) = P(-1 \leq z \leq 1)$$

$$\text{(B.4)}$$

$$P(-1 \leq z \leq 1) = 1 - 2 \cdot P(z \geq 1) = 1 - 2 \cdot [1 - P(z \leq 1)]$$
$$= 1 - 2 \cdot [1 - \texttt{NORM.S.DIST(1,TRUE)}] \approx 68.3\%$$

This probability can be expressed in terms of the pdf of the standard normal distribution (figure B.6):

We can conclude that about 68.3 percent of values drawn from *any* normal distribution are within one sigma of the mean. Likewise, it can be shown that about 95.5 percent of the values lie within two standard deviations, and about 99.7 percent are within three standard deviations.

Returning to the pallet example, we can assert that about 68.7 percent of the pallets' weights are expected to be in the interval $(200 - 20, 200 + 20) = (180, 220)$.

B.3 Central Limit Theorem

B.3.1 An Insightful Experiment

To intuit the consequences of the central limit theorem, we can start by doing an experiment.

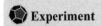 **Experiment**

Rolling Dice

1. Roll a dice 10,000 times (we advise you to use a computer, not a real dice) and keep track of the resulting (10,000) outcomes.

2. Roll two dice and calculate the *mean*. For instance, if you get 3 and 4, the mean is 3.5. Repeat 10,000 times and keep track of the resulting means.

3. Repeat the previous step using ten dice instead of two.

4. Finally, repeat the previous step using thirty dice.

In the first case, the histogram of the 10,000 outcomes (figure B.7a) will resemble the pdf of a distribution where all six outcomes have equal probabilities, which is known to be the distribution when rolling a fair dice.

In the second case (two dice), the histogram (figure B.7b) shows that the underlying pdf is not flat anymore—it is actually triangular! Indeed, the sum of two uniform distributions is known to be a triangular distribution.

As we increase the number of dice thrown (figures B.7c and B.7d), the histogram gets narrower and adopts a more and more normal shape, while remaining centered at around 3.5.

B.3.2   The Central Limit Theorem (CLT)

Let $X_1, \ldots, X_n$ be a random sample of n independent variables, with an expected value μ and standard deviation σ. As n gets larger, the sample average $\bar{X} = \frac{X_1 + \ldots + X_n}{n}$ approximates a normal distribution with mean μ and standard deviation $\frac{\sigma}{\sqrt{n}}$.

$$X \text{ any random variable with } (\mu, \sigma^2) \xrightarrow{\text{large n}} \bar{X} \sim N\left(\mu, \frac{\sigma^2}{n}\right)$$

Some remarks are in order:

• For n large enough (say around thirty), the sample average $\bar{X}$ approximates a normal distribution no matter what the distribution of X is. If the original distributions are well-behaved (for instance, symmetric and with relatively more density in the center, not in the tails), the value of n for which this is true decreases. (For instance, the sum of only two normal distributions is normal as well.)

• The standard deviation of $\bar{X}$ decreases with n.

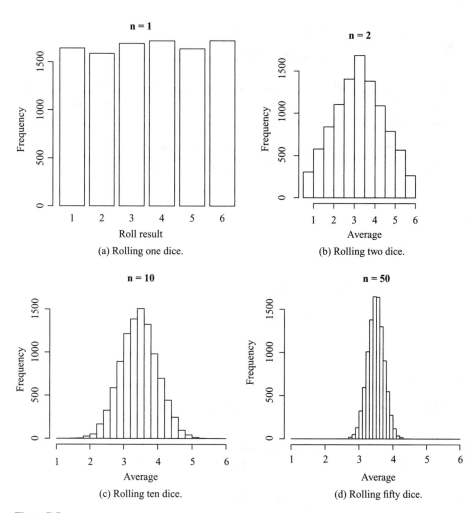

Figure B.7
Experiment results for 10,000 repetitions.

Exercise

How Many Pallets on a Truck?

The weight of a pallet is a random variable W, normally distributed with mean 600 kg and standard deviation 30 kg. A truck fits thirty-three pallets and the maximum weight it can carry is $20T$.

1. What is the probability that a pallet weighs more than 606 kg?
2. What is the probability that the total weight W_T exceeds $20T$?

? Question 1

What is the probability that a pallet weighs more than 606 kg?

Much like we did in a previous exercise:

$$P(W \geq 606) = 1 - P(W \leq 606) = 1 - \text{NORM.DIST}(606,600,30,\text{TRUE})$$

$$\approx 1 - 0.58 = 0.42 = 42\%$$

? Question 2

What is the probability that the total weight W_T exceeds $20T$?

The probability that the total weight exceeds $20,000\,kg$. is the same as saying that, on average, the weight of each pallet is greater than $20,000/33 = 606$ kg:

$$P(W \geq 20T) = P\left(\bar{W} \geq \frac{20,000}{33}\right) = P(\bar{X} \geq 606)$$

The central limit theorem tells us that the average weight $\bar{W}$ follows a normal distribution:

$$P(\bar{W} \geq 606) = 1 - P(\bar{W} \leq 606)$$

$$= 1 - \text{NORM.DIST}(606,600,30/\text{SQRT}(33),\text{TRUE}) \approx 12.5\%$$

This is truly remarkable: even if a single pallet exceeds 606 kg 42 percent of times, the average pallet exceeds 606 kg only 12 percent of the time. This makes sense because, just as some pallets in the sample will exceed 606 kg, others will be lighter, and therefore it is much less likely that the average amounts to 606 kg or more.

This is an example of how the CLT not only concerns the mean but can also be used to deal with sums. This is because the sum is the same as the mean up to a constant.

B.4 Measures of Location and Variability for Continuous Random Variables

We next present three important definitions that deal with random variables, namely the expectation, the variance, and the covariance.

B.4.1 Expectation of a Continuous Random Variable

Let X be a continuous random variable with known pdf, $f(x)$. Its expectation or mean is defined as:

$$\mathbf{E}[X] = \mu = \int_{-\infty}^{+\infty} x f(x) \mathrm{d}x \tag{B.5}$$

For instance, the expectation of the random variable defined at the end of section B.1.2 is

$$\mathbf{E}[X] = \mu = \int_{-\infty}^{+\infty} x f(x) \mathrm{d}x = \int_{0}^{2} x \frac{x}{2} \, \mathrm{d}x = \frac{4}{3}$$

Likewise, the expectation of a function of the random variable, $g(X)$ is defined as

$$\mathbf{E}[g(X)] = \int_{-\infty}^{+\infty} g(x) f(x) \mathrm{d}x$$

Some properties of the expectation follow:

- $\mathbf{E}[X + Y] = \mathbf{E}[X] + \mathbf{E}[Y]$ for any random variables X and Y.
- $\mathbf{E}[aX] = a\mathbf{E}[X]$, where a is a real number.

B.4.2 Covariance of Two Continuous Random Variables

The covariance of two random variables X and Y is defined as

$$\mathbf{Cov}[X, Y] = \mathbf{E}[(X - \mathbf{E}[X])(Y - \mathbf{E}[Y])]$$

The covariance reveals how two random variables move together. The covariance will be in different intervals given how X and Y move together:

- If X and Y have nothing to do with each other (for instance, the results of rolling two dice) the covariance is zero and the variables are said to be uncorrelated.

- If they move up and down together (for instance, the number of cars bought in a year in a country and the gross domestic product (GDP) of the country) the covariance is between 0 and 1 and the variables are said to be positively correlated.

- If one goes up when the other goes down, and vice versa, the covariance is between -1 and 0 and the variables are said to be negatively correlated. For instance, life expectancy and infant mortality rate in a country are negatively correlated.

- If the covariance is 1 or -1 the variables are said to be perfectly correlated. For instance, if $Y = -X$, $\mathbf{Cov}[X, Y] = -1$.

Some properties of covariance include:

- $\mathbf{Cov}[X, Y] = 0$ if X and Y are independent. For instance, the results obtained by rolling two dice are independent. The number of cars bought in a year in a country and the GDP of the country are not independent, and thus not uncorrelated.

- $\mathbf{Cov}[aX, bY] = ab\,\mathbf{Cov}[X, Y]$, where a and b are real numbers.

- $\mathbf{Cov}[X, Y + Z] = \mathbf{Cov}[X, Y] + \mathbf{Cov}[XZ]$.

B.4.3 Variance and Standard Deviation of a Continuous Random Variable

The variance of a random variable X is defined as the expected value of the squared deviation from the mean.

$$\mathbf{V}[X] = \mathbf{E}[(X - \mu)^2] = \sigma_X^2$$

where σ_X (or $\sigma[X]$) is the standard deviation, defined as the square root of the variance.

$$\sigma[X] = \sqrt{\mathbf{V}[X]}$$

Given the definitions, it should be clear that variance and standard deviation measure dispersion around the mean.

Some properties of variance and standard deviation include:

- $\mathbf{V}[X] = \mathbf{E}(X^2) - (\mathbf{E}[X])^2$, which can be used to compute the variance more easily.

- $\mathbf{V}[X] = \mathbf{Cov}[X, X]$, which gives an alternative definition of covariance.

- $\mathbf{V}[X + Y] = \mathbf{V}[X] + \mathbf{V}[Y]$, if X and Y are uncorrelated.

- $\mathbf{V}[aX] = a^2\mathbf{V}[X]$, where a is a real number. Do not forget to square the a^2 in the right-hand side, a common mistake.

- Equivalently and more intuitively: $\sigma[aX] = a\sigma[X]$

- $\mathbf{V}[X \pm Y] = \mathbf{V}[X] + \mathbf{V}[Y] \pm 2\mathbf{Cov}[X, Y]$.

The last property is of particular interest to us. From this property, we can derive several very useful properties of independent variables:

- $\mathbf{V}[X + Y] = \mathbf{V}[X] + \mathbf{V}[Y]$.

- $\mathbf{V}[X_1 + X_2 + \ldots + X_n] = \mathbf{V}[X_1] + \mathbf{V}[X_2] + \ldots + \mathbf{V}[X_n]$.

Furthermore, if n variables are i.i.d. (independent and identically distributed), then

$$\mathbf{V}[X_1 + X_2 + \ldots + X_n] = n\mathbf{V}[X_i] \text{ for any } i. \tag{B.6}$$

B.4.4 Coefficient of Variation of a Random Variable

The coefficient of variation of a random variable is defined as the ratio of standard deviation to mean.

$$\mathbf{CV} = \frac{\sigma}{\mu}$$

It measures dispersion not in absolute terms but in relative terms, as sigma is divided over the mean. As such, the coefficient of variation is dimensionless, which is advantageous when comparing the variability of distribution with different means. The flatness of a pdf graph depends only on the coefficient of variation of the corresponding distribution.

B.5 The Concept of Conditional Probability: Two Useful Theorems

B.5.1 The Concept of Conditional Probability

Conditional probability is a measure of the probability of a random event, given that another event has already occurred. The latter event may come from a random variable—in which case we talk about conditioning one random variable on another—or not.

For instance, if a dice may or may not be loaded, the probability of getting a six when rolling the dice given that the dice isn't loaded is an example of conditional probability. The definition of conditional probability will be useful in the next section.

B.5.2 Theorems of Total Expectation and Total Variance

We will make use of conditional probability (conditioning one random variable on another) to state two useful theorems, namely the law of total expectation and the law of total variance.

Let X and Y be random variables. The theorem of total expectation reads:

$$\mathbf{E}[X] = \mathbf{E}[\mathbf{E}[X|Y]]$$

and the theorem of total variance:

$$\mathbf{V}[X] = \mathbf{E}[\mathbf{V}[X|Y]] + \mathbf{V}[\mathbf{E}[X|Y]]$$

where $\mathbf{E}[X|Y]$ is the expectation of X given Y, and $\mathbf{V}[X|Y]$ the variance of X given Y.

These theorems are useful in calculating expectation and variance when there are *two* sources of variability. For instance, when computing safety stock when demand is random, it is useful to characterize demand during lead-time. This is relatively easy when lead-time is constant, but what if lead-time is also random?

Exercise

Computing Safety Inventory when Both Demand and Lead-Time Are Random

A firm faces daily positive i.i.d. continuous demand, characterized by its mean and standard deviation, $D(\mu_D, \sigma_D)$. Likewise, the supplier's discrete lead time measured in days is also random, $L(\mu_L, \sigma_L)$. Let $X(\mu_X, \sigma_X)$ be demand during lead-time.

- What is the expected demand during lead time, $\mathbf{E}[X]$?
- What is the variance of demand during lead time, $\mathbf{V}[X]$?

? Question 1

What is the expected demand during lead time, $\mathbf{E}[X]$?

As both daily demand and lead time are random, we have two sources of variability and the two theorems just presented come in handy.

Let's start with the mean. The expected demand during lead-time is:

$$\mathbf{E}[X] = \mathbf{E}[\mathbf{E}[X|L]] \tag{B.7}$$

We first calculate $\mathbf{E}[X|L=l]$, where l represents a realization of random variable L. Denoting D_i the demand during day i, we can write:

$$\mathbf{E}[X|L=l] = \mathbf{E}[D_1] + \mathbf{E}[D_2] + \ldots + \mathbf{E}[D_l] = l\mu_D$$

Therefore $\mathbf{E}[X|L] = L\mu_D$, and we have: $\mathbf{E}[\mathbf{E}[X|L]] = \mathbf{E}[L\mu_D]$. We can take out μ_D, which *is* a constant, to get:

$$\mathbf{E}[X] = \mu_D \mathbf{E}[L] = \mu_D \mu_L$$

which is an intuitive result.

? Question 2

What is the variance of demand during lead time, $\mathbf{V}[X]$?

Now for the variance. According to the law of total variance, the variance during lead-time is:

$$\mathbf{V}[X] = \mathbf{E}[\mathbf{V}[X|L]] + \mathbf{V}[\mathbf{E}[X|L]]$$

Let's first compute the term $\mathbf{V}[X|L=l]$. As daily demands are i.i.d, and $X|L=l=D_1 + D_2 + ... + D_l$ it follows that:

$$\mathbf{V}[X|L=l] = \mathbf{V}[D_1 + D_2 + ... + D_l] = \mathbf{V}[D_1] + \mathbf{V}[D_2] + ... + \mathbf{V}[D_l] = \mathbf{V}D = l\sigma_D^2$$

and then $\mathbf{V}[X|L] = L\sigma_D^2$. Using this result now we have:

$$\mathbf{E}[\mathbf{V}[X|L]] = \mathbf{E}[L\sigma_D^2] = \sigma_D^2\mathbf{E}[L] = \sigma_D^2\mu_L$$

and given that we found that $\mathbf{E}[X|L] = L\mu_D$ it follows that:

$$\mathbf{V}[\mathbf{E}[X|L]] = \mathbf{V}[L\mu_D] = \mu_D^2\mathbf{V}[L] = \mu_D^2\sigma_L^2$$

Finally,

$$\mathbf{V}[X] = \sigma_D^2\mu_L + \mu_D^2\sigma_L^2$$

Note that this is *not* an intuitive result.

References

Bertsekas, Dimitri P., and John N. Tsitsiklis. 2008. *Introduction to probability*, 2nd ed. Belmont, MA: Athena Scientific.

Ross, Sheldon M. 2010. *A first course in probability*, 10th ed. Upper Saddle River, NJ: Pearson.

Appendix C: Inventory Management Review

This quick review of inventory management theory presents some topics that are used in this book: a few models for inventory optimization and the pooling effect. First, the economic order quantity formula and the newsvendor model are developed. Then, the optimal safety stock levels for (r, Q) and (R, S) replenishment models are derived. Finally, the concept of pooling effect is introduced. The derivation of most expressions requires a shallow understanding of probability (refer to appendix B if needed).

C.1   The Economic Order Quantity Formula

The economic order quantity (EOQ) formula, also known as the Wilson formula, gives the optimal purchasing or production batch size in order to minimize total cost. The formula was first presented more than a century ago by Harris (1913).

Consider a cost-minimizing firm that buys or manufactures a single product at *variable cost c*, faces a constant demand rate per period *d*, and incurs an ordering cost or setup cost *k* when an order is placed and a cost *h per dollar* per period for holding inventory. This inventory holding cost includes nonfinancial costs, such as handling, obsolescence, and insurance; and a financial cost, which is a mix of interest expenses and shareholders' opportunity cost—given that tying resources in inventory prevents shareholders from investing their money somewhere else.

In its standard version, the firm minimizes the total relevant cost over a period of time (say, a year) by choosing the appropriate order quantity, *q*. Formally, the problem can be formulated as:

$$\min_{q \geq 0} C(q) = \frac{kd}{q} + \frac{q}{2}ch$$

where the first term is the annual cost of ordering or setups, and the second term is the cost of holding inventory during the same period, which is proportional to average inventory.

The first-order condition, $C'(q) = 0$, gives:

$$\frac{-kd}{q^2} + \frac{1}{2}ch = 0$$

which yields:

$$q^* = \text{EOQ} = \sqrt{\frac{2kd}{ch}} > 0$$

The second-order condition reveals that this solution is a minimum, as the second derivative is positive at the optimal point.

The optimal quantity grows with ordering cost and demand, and decreases with the cost of the item and the inventory holding cost. There are other costs related to inventory, but they are not relevant to the EOQ. For example, the fixed portion of the cost of the item or the fixed portion of transportation cost do not depend on the quantity ordered and are therefore not relevant. (In fact, they disappear when taking the first derivative.)

The EOQ model solves the trade-off between ordering or setup cost and inventory holding cost. A difficulty of the model is to find accurate enough figures for some of the parameter values, such as ordering cost and inventory holding cost. The model is sometimes criticized for making too-simple assumptions, such as deterministic demand. Despite that, the model can be used to figure out the order of magnitude of the appropriate lot size when placing orders, either from a supplier or the manufacturing shop.

 Exercise

Coming up with an Optimal Order Quantity

A European firm that buys an item from a supplier in Asia wants to know how much to order every time an order is placed. Demand rate is 100 units per month, unit variable cost is $40, ordering cost is $300 (this includes the fixed fee per shipment to be paid to the forwarder for instance), and holding cost is 10 percent per dollar per year,

What is the economic order quantity that minimizes total anual cost?

The EOQ is simply:

$$q^* = \text{EOQ} = \sqrt{\frac{2kd}{ch}} = \sqrt{\frac{2 \cdot 300 \cdot (12 \cdot 100)}{40 \cdot 0.1}} \approx 424 \text{ units.}$$

That means that items should be purchased in batches of approximately 424 units. Of course, this number will need to be adjusted depending on other variables, such as how many

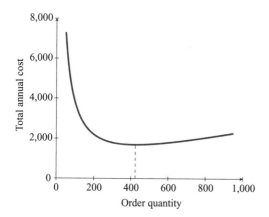

Figure C.1
Total annual cost as a function of the ordering quantity. The vertical line marks the optimum.

units fit in a shipping container, but will give a valid indication of whether you should order one box, one pallet, or one forty-foot container every time you order. Even if you depart from the optimum a significant percentage (say 20 percent), the total cost won't change much, as the function $C(q)$ is quite flat around the mean, as figure C.1 shows.

C.2   Newsvendor Model

The newsvendor model, the politically correct version of what was formerly known as the newsboy's model, is the cornerstone of most inventory models subject to random demand. It gives the optimal ordering quantity for a given time period in the presence of random demand.

Consider a newsvendor that sells newspapers every day. The newsvendor buys newspapers early in the morning at *variable* cost c and sells them at unit price p. Both c and p are determined by the market conditions. Newspapers can neither be replenished nor returned during the day. At the end of the day unsold newspapers are useless. Daily demand, ξ, follows a distribution with mean μ and standard deviation σ. The newsvendor wants to know how many newspapers, S, to stock in the morning every day in order to maximize his expected profit, $\mathbf{E}\pi$.

The problem can be formulated as:

$$\max_{S \geq 0} \pi(S) = \mathbf{E}\left[p\min(S,\xi) - cS\right]$$

where the first term accounts for sales in dollars and the second term takes care of cost. We will assume that p is large enough that expected profit is positive for some values of S (that is, the solution is economically feasible). The objective function can be worked out as:

$$\pi(S) = p\mathbf{E}\left[\min(S, \xi)\right] - cS = p\int_{-\infty}^{\infty} \min(S, \xi)f(\xi)d\xi - cS$$

$$= p\int_{-\infty}^{S} \xi f(\xi)d\xi + p\int_{S}^{\infty} Sf(\xi)d\xi - cS$$

The first-order condition is:

$$p\frac{d}{dS}\int_{-\infty}^{S} \xi f(\xi)d\xi + p\frac{d}{dS}\int_{S}^{\infty} Sf(\xi)d\xi - c = 0$$

We make use of Leibniz's rule for differentiation of integrals so that the condition becomes:

$$pSf(S) + p\int_{S}^{\infty} f(\xi)d\xi - pSf(S) - c = 0 \Rightarrow p\left(1 - \int_{-\infty}^{S} f(\xi)d\xi\right) = c \Rightarrow$$

$$1 - F(S) = \frac{c}{p} \Rightarrow S^* = F^{-1}\left(\frac{p-c}{p}\right) \tag{C.1}$$

To better understand the solution, let's further assume that demand is normally distributed. Then, if $S^* = F^{-1}\left(\frac{p-c}{p}\right)$:

$$\frac{S^* - \mu}{\sigma} = \Phi^{-1}\left(\frac{p-c}{p}\right)$$

where Φ is the CDF of a standard normal distribution (see appendix B). Finally, we solve for the optimal stocking quantity:

$$S^* = \mu + \sigma\Phi^{-1}\left(1 - \frac{c}{p}\right)$$

The calculations can easily be performed in MS Excel by means of the formula:

```
= mu + sigma * NORMSINV(1-c/p)
```

The second term is called safety inventory, as it partially protects the business from demand fluctuations. The argument of Φ^{-1} is usually called the critical fractile.

The optimal stocking quantity increases with the mean of the demand, μ, and the margin in percentage, $\frac{c}{p}$. The impact of σ is a bit more involved, as $\Phi^{-1}\left(1 - \frac{c}{p}\right)$ may be positive or negative. If $\frac{c}{p} > \frac{1}{2}$, then $\Phi^{-1}\left(1 - \frac{c}{p}\right)$ is positive, then the stocking quantity increases with σ. But the stocking quantity will decrease with σ if $\frac{c}{p} < \frac{1}{2}$. Therefore, if the margin is lower than 0.5, the optimal quantity will be below the mean.

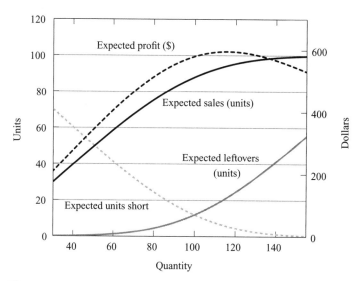

Figure C.2
Expected sales, leftovers, units short, and profit in the newsvendor model.

For instance, if $p = 10$, $c = 6$, $\mu = 100$, $\sigma = 30$, the optimal inventory is:

$$S^* = \mu + \sigma\, \Phi^{-1}\left(\frac{p-c}{p}\right) = 100 + 30\Phi^{-1}\left(\frac{4}{10}\right) \approx 92 \text{ units} < 100.$$

However, if $p = 10$, $c = 3$, $\mu = 100$, $\sigma = 30$, the optimal inventory is

$$S^* = \mu + \sigma\, \Phi^{-1}\left(\frac{p-c}{p}\right) = 100 + 30\Phi^{-1}\left(\frac{7}{10}\right) \approx 116 \text{ units} > 100.$$

For the latter parameter values, figure C.2 shows the expected units of sales, leftovers, and units short; as well as expected profit in dollars. The optimal inventory can be observed to be around 116 units.

Finally, as $S^* = F^{-1}\left(1 - \frac{c}{p}\right)$ (equation C.1), note that $1 - \frac{c}{p}$ coincides with the service level perceived by the customer (figure C.3). For instance, if $1 - \frac{c}{p} = 1 - \frac{3}{10} = 0.7$, the area to the left in the pdf of figure C.3 is exactly 0.7. That means that demand will be lower than S^* 70 percent of times. Therefore, 70 percent of times the firm will be able to fully satisfy demand.

The newsvendor model can accommodate more complex situations, such as adding a salvage value or endogenizing the price. There are literally hundreds of papers in the literature dealing with extensions of this model. Also, it can be extrapolated to other scenarios, even if there is no inventory involved. Three conditions are needed to obtain the same model pattern:

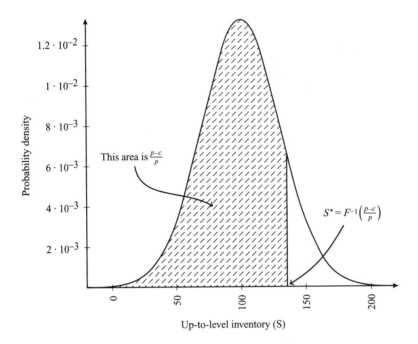

Figure C.3
Relationship between the critical fractile and customer service level.

(1) A source of uncertainty: demand, in the examples we have seen, but can also be cost or exchange rate, among other things.

(2) No opportunity for replenishment or returns.

(3) A unit cost for acquiring too much or too little. For instance, in the basic model, the cost of buying one more paper and not selling it (called overage cost) is $C_o = c$, whereas the cost of not buying one more paper and selling out by one unit (called underage cost) is $C_u = p - c$, the unit margin in dollars.

The newsvendor model is sometimes criticized because it is not easy—sometimes impossible—to quantify some of the *unit* costs involved. The trickiest to quantify may be the cost of a customer angry because she cannot buy due to sell outs.

> **The newsvendor pattern is more frequent than you think**
> The logic of the newsvendor model can be applied if these conditions hold:
>
> 1. There is a source of uncertainty.
>
> 2. There is no opportunity for replenishment or returns.
>
> 3. There exists a *unit* cost of acquiring too much and too little.

C.3 Safety Inventory in Multi-Period Replenishment Settings

We will now present two common inventory replenishment policies—(r, Q) and (R, S)—and focus on how to calculate the required safety inventory in the presence of random demand. These policies are applicable to products with long life cycle, whose inventory is replenished several times over the product's life cycle. To simplify the exposition, we will assume that lead time—the response time from supplier—is relatively short—that is, there are never simultaneous outstanding orders (see Chopra and Meindl 2016, for details). However, the results we'll show also hold even when there is more than a single order outstanding (as is usually the case with overseas supply), under the assumption that orders arrive in the same sequence placed (i.e., no order crossover). Also, we assume that any customer order that cannot be fulfilled from inventory on-hand, will become backorder (and will be fulfilled when inventory becomes available).

As at any point in time there may be both replenishment orders outstanding and back-orders, we need to keep track of these orders when determining the replenishment order quantity. To that end, we define inventory position as the sum of inventory on hand plus outstanding orders minus backorders.

C.3.1 The Continuous (r, Q) Policy

Under an (r, Q) policy, a replenishment order of Q units will be released as soon as inventory reaches level r or less. The order will arrive L periods later. For instance, under a $(60, 40)$ policy, an order of forty units will be placed every time inventory position goes below sixty units. Obviously, this policy entails that inventory should be checked continuously, or it cannot be exactly followed. The dynamics of this policy are shown in figure C.4.

Under an (r, Q) policy, parameter r determines the level of safety inventory. Assume that demand during *constant* lead-time is $X(\mu_X, \sigma_X)$ and that desired service level is CSL.

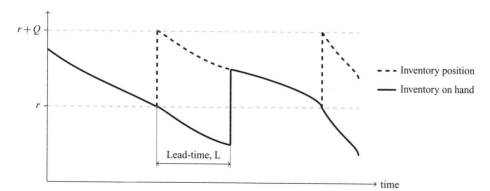

Figure C.4
Inventory dynamics under an (r, Q) policy.

From the moment the order is placed until it arrives we have an equivalent situation to the one faced by the newsvendor. Demand is random and there is no opportunity to replenish inventory during that period. Inventory r should be enough to cope with demand during the vulnerability period L. Therefore, in order to achieve service level CSL we should set r as:

$$r = \mu_X + \sigma_X \cdot \Phi^{-1}(\text{CSL})$$

where safety inventory is:

$$\text{SS} = \sigma_X \cdot \Phi^{-1}(\text{CSL})$$

C.3.2   The Periodic (R, S) Policy

Under an (R, S) policy, a replenishment order of size S less current inventory position is placed every R periods. For instance, under a $(7,100)$ policy, if inventory position on day seven in the (R, S) policy inventory is thirty units, an order of seventy $(100 - 30)$ units will be placed on day seven. In contrast to the (r, Q) policy, inventory has to be checked only once every R periods. The dynamics of this policy is shown in figure C.5.

Parameter $S(R)$ determines the level of safety inventory. Assume that demand during the review period (R) plus *constant* lead time (L) is $X(\mu_X, \sigma_X)$ and that desired service level is CSL. From the moment an order is placed, again we have an equivalent situation to the newsvendor. However, the vulnerability period in this case is $R + L$. To see this, consider that at the beginning of any given period, we review the inventory position and we place an order that brings inventory position up to S. As any orders placed after that moment will not arrive before $R + L$ periods from now, the order-up-to level S will be the only inventory available to deal with random demand during the vulnerability period $R + L$.

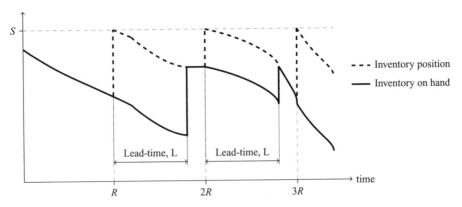

Figure C.5
Inventory dynamics under an (R, S) policy.

Therefore, in order to achieve service level CSL we should set $S(R)$ as:

$$S = \mu_X + \sigma_X \cdot \Phi^{-1}(\text{CSL})$$

and safety inventory is:

$$\text{SS} = \sigma_X \cdot \Phi^{-1}(\text{CSL})$$

C.4   Risk Pooling

Risk pooling is a statistical concept that suggests that demand variability is reduced if a firm can aggregate demand across locations, across products, or across time. The application of risk pooling usually requires the redesign of the supply chain, the production process, or the product so that a firm is in a better position to deal with the consequences of demand uncertainty in its markets. Some commonly used risk pooling strategies addressed in the context of inventory management include product pooling, capacity pooling, delayed differentiation (or postponement), location pooling, and consolidated distribution. Next we discuss risk pooling only in the context of consolidated distribution for illustrative purposes. Our analysis can be extended to all pooling strategies.

Consider a firm with its manufacturing facilities located in a low-cost country that sells its products in n regions in the United States. Demand in each region is normally distributed with the following characteristics:

- D_i: mean weekly demand in region i, $i = 1, 2, \ldots n$.
- σ_i: standard deviation of weekly demand in region i, $i = 1, 2, \ldots n$.
- $\rho_{i,j}$: Correlation of weekly demand in regions i, j, with $i, j = 1, 2, \ldots n$ and $i \neq j$.

The firm has two options for distributing its products: (a) decentralized distribution (i.e., shipping inventory from the manufacturing site directly to n regional warehouses); (b) centralized distribution (i.e., replenishing its regional inventory through a central DC conveniently located in the United States). Assume that inventory for both cases is reviewed weekly and the lead time from the manufacturing site to the United States is deterministic and equal to L weeks for all sites. Next, let's evaluate the safety inventory for each network design, assuming a target service level (in-stock probability) of CSL.

Decentralized distribution   The total safety inventory in this case (denoted as SI^d) is equal to the sum of the safety inventorys in each individual location:

$$\text{SI}^d = \sum_{i=1}^{n} \text{SS}_i = \Phi^{-1}(\text{CSL}) \cdot \sqrt{L+1} \cdot \sum_{i=1}^{n} \sigma_i$$

Centralized distribution To calculate the safety inventory in this case, we first need to compute the parameters for the pooled demand distribution. The aggregate demand is normally distributed with a mean of D^c and standard deviation of σ^c, where:

$$D^c = \sum_{i=1}^{n} D_i$$

$$\sigma^c = \sqrt{\sum_{i=1}^{n} \sigma_i^2 + \sum_{\{(i,j)\,|\,i \neq j\}} \rho_{i,j}\sigma_i\sigma_j}$$

It follows that the total safety inventory for the centralized case (denoted as SI^c) is given by:

$$\text{SI}^c = \Phi^{-1}(\text{CSL}) \cdot \sqrt{L+1} \cdot \sigma^c$$

In calculating SI^c we have ignored the regional safety inventory, which is a reasonable assumption if the lead time from the central DC to the regional warehouses is very small (compared to the lead time from the production site to the DC). To get a better idea of the inventory reduction potential, let's assume that the regional demands are independent (i.e., $\rho_{i,j} = 0$) and identically distributed with mean D and standard deviation σ. Then, it can be shown that:

$$\frac{\text{SI}^c}{\text{SI}^d} = \frac{1}{\sqrt{n}}$$

This relationship is often referred to as the *square root law* of inventory pooling, according to which, if we serve n independent demand streams from a single stock of inventory, the expected level of safety inventory will be reduced by the square root of n. For instance, if we centralize the distribution for four locations, the total safety inventory in the system—compared to the decentralized case—will be reduced to half for the same customer service level!

From the above analysis, it becomes clear that the pooling benefits—in terms of reduction in safety inventory—largely depend on demand characteristics, as the square root law holds only in the case of independent demand streams that follow a normal-type distribution. However, if demands are positively correlated (which is usually the case), the reduction in the uncertainty of the aggregate demand—consequently, the pooling benefit—is not so large (see calculation of σ^c above). Furthermore, recent studies have shown that if the demand streams follow a heavy-tailed distribution—as is often the case for trendy items such as movies, books, music, and so on—the pooling benefits can also be significantly lower than the square root of n (Bimpikis and Markakis 2016). Therefore, a careful study of the demand characteristics is an important step before a company moves ahead with the implementation of any risk pooling strategies.

References

Bimpikis, Kostas, and Mihalis G. Markakis. 2016. "Inventory pooling under heavy-tailed demand." *Management Science* 62 (6): 1800–1813.

Chopra, Sunil, and Peter Meindl. 2016. *Supply chain management: Strategy, planning, and operation.* 6th ed. Harlow, Essex, UK: Pearson Education Limited.

Harris, Ford W. 1913. "An econometric analysis of inventory turnover in retail services." *Factory: The Magazine of Management* 10 (2): 135–136.

Glossary

absorption costing   A method of calculating the cost of a product by taking into account indirect expenses (overheads) in addition to direct costs. Other name: *full costing*.

accelerated depreciation   Depreciation that occurs at a nonconstant rate. Under accelerated depreciation, annual depreciation of a given asset decreases over the years.

account   Record used in accounting to keep track of the balances of assets, equities, revenues, and expenses.

accounting cash flow   See *funds from operations*.

accounting criterion   The criterion according to which shareholders are happy when equity at book value increases and sad when equity at book value decreases.

accounting equation   See *accounting identity*.

accounting identity   Assets = equities. Other name: *accounting equation*.

accounting period   The period covered by a dynamic financial statement. Usual accounting periods are years, quarters, and months.

accounting policies   See *accounting principles*.

accounting principles   Set of rules, conventions, and guidelines that govern the way financial statements are prepared. Other names: *accounting standards*, *accounting policies*.

accounting standards   See *accounting principles*.

accounts payable   The amount of money owed to a supplier by a firm for products or services bought on credit. Other names: *payables*, *A/P*.

accounts receivable   The amount of money owed to a firm by a customer for products or services sold on credit. Other names: *receivables*, *A/R*.

accrual basis   Accounting principle that states that revenues should be recorded when earned and expenses when incurred, irrelevant of when collection of payment occurs. For instance, sales are recorded when the products are sent to the customer, not when the customer actually pays for the products. Other name: *accrual principle*.

accrual principle   See *accrual basis*.

accumulated depreciation   The amount of depreciation accumulated since the corresponding fixed asset was acquired.

activity-based costing   A costing methodology that identifies activities in a firm and assigns the cost of each activity to the products according to their consumption. Other name: *ABC*. See *activity-based costing*.

adverse selection A situation where a party in a negotiation makes a bad decision due to having less information than the other party.

amortization Depreciation of intangible assets.

A/P Acronym for accounts payable.

A/R Acronym for accounts receivable.

assets The left hand side of the accounting equation. It represents what the firm owns.

average cost flow method An inventory valuation method in which the cost of each item is calculated on the basis of the average cost of all similar goods in inventory.

balance sheet Financial report showing what a firm owns and owes at a given point in time. Other name: *statement of financial position*.

bankruptcy The legal situation of a firm that cannot pay to creditors (e.g., suppliers). It may lead to a debt restructuring so that the firm may continue doing business (e.g., chapter 11 bankruptcy in the United States) or the liquidation of the firm (e.g., chapter 7).

bill See *invoice*.

board See *board of directors*.

board of directors A group of people who represent shareholders, establish policies, makes major decisions, and oversees a firm's activities. Other names: *BOD*, *the board*.

BOD Acronym for board of directors.

book value The value of assets and equities of a firm as shown in the balance sheet. See also: *market value*.

bottom line See *net profit*.

break-even See *break-even point*.

break-even point The amount of sales (measured either in units of dollars) a firm requires during a period to exactly cover total costs in that period. Other name: *break-even*.

business entity See *entity*.

CAPEX Acronym for capital expenses.

capital expenses Investments in fixed assets. Oddly enough, despite its name, capital expenses are *not* period's expenses, but investments. Other name: *CAPEX*.

capital structure The composition of noncurrent equities (i.e., the various types of debt and equity) of a firm.

cash budget An estimation of the cash inflows and outflows for a business over a specific period of time.

cash discount An incentive offered by some suppliers that reduce the amount owed by a percentage of the total invoice if the payment is made before the due date.

cash earnings See *funds from operations*.

cash equivalent Assets that can be converted to cash very easily, such as a one-month certificate of deposit.

cash flow statement See *statement of cash flows*.

cash generated from operations The difference between cash flow from operations and increasing operating working capital. It may larger or smaller than CFO depending on whether ΔOWC is negative or positive. Other names: *CGO*.

CEO   Acronym for chief executive officer.

certificate of deposit   A financial product that pays the holder a fixed interest rate and has a fixed maturity term, typically ranging from one month to ten years. The interest rate weakly increases with the maturity term and is defined by the bank that pays the interests. If the deposited money is withdrawn before maturity date, large penalties apply.

CFO   Acronym for chief financial officer.

CGO   Acronym for cash generated from operations.

chase strategy   When production is varied as demand varies.

chief executive officer   The highest person in a firm, reporting to the board of directors, and ultimately responsible for making managerial decisions. Other names: *CEO, managing director.*

chief financial officer   The person with primary responsibility in the firm's finances reporting to the CEO. Other name: *CFO.*

chief operating officer   The person with primary responsibility in the firm's operations, usually reporting to the CEO. Other names: *COO, chief operations officer.*

chief operations officer   See *chief operations officer.*

COGS   Acronym for cost of good sold.

collection period   See *days sales outstanding.*

common stock   The part of equity that is contributed by shareholders.

conservatism (concept)   Accounting principle that states that if a situation arises where there are two acceptable alternatives for reporting an event, the more conservative alternative should be chosen—that is, the one that leads to lower profits or assets. Other names: *prudence concept.*

consistency (concept)   Accounting principle that states that accountants have to apply accounting procedures uniformly over time. For instance, the criteria to determine when to recognize sales should be fixed over the periods; they cannot be changed for convenience.

contribution margin   The difference between an item's net price and its variable cost. Other name: *contribution.*

COO   Acronym for chief operating officer.

corporate income tax   A tax a firm should pay the country it belongs to (or other jurisdiction). It is a percentage of earning before taxes, although more complex rules abound.

cost accounting   The process of recording and organizing the costs incurred in a firm in a way that the resulting information can be used to improve the firm's management. Other name: *managerial accounting.*

cost driver   In activity-based costing, a factor that causes a change in the cost of an activity.

cost of capital   See *weighted average cost of capital.*

cost of goods sold   Expense made of all costs used to create a product. The expense is incurred at the time of selling. For manufacturers, it includes the sum of direct material, direct labor, and a fraction of factory overheads incurred in making the products. Other name: *COGS.*

cost of sales   Expense made of all costs used to create a product or a service. The expense is incurred at the time of selling. In a manufacturing context, cost of sales and cost of goods sold are equivalent terms. In a service context, the term cost of sales is more appropriate.

current assets   Portion of assets made of cash or other items expected to become cash within a year, such as accounts receivable or inventory. In a seven-item balance sheet, current assets is the sum of cash, accounts receivable, and inventory.

current liabilities   Portion of liabilities made of future monetary obligations due within a year, such as accounts payable or short-term debt.

current ratio   The ratio current assets to current liabilities.

customs duties   See *tariffs*.

days inventory outstanding   A measure of the average number of days that it takes a firm to turn its inventory into sales. Other names: *DIO, inventory flow period*.

days payables outstanding   A measure of the average number of days that it takes a firm to pay suppliers after purchases have been made. Other names: *DPO, payment period*.

days sales outstanding   A measure of the average number of days that it takes a firm to collect payments from customers after sales have been made. A more consistent name would be days *receivable outstanding*, or *DRO*, but that name is not used. Other names: *DSO, collection period*.

debt   Money borrowed by the firm from other entity, usually a bank.

decision tree   A decision mapping tool that uses a tree-like graph to model decisions and their possible consequences.

depreciation   A noncash expense that reduces the value of a tangible asset as a result of age or obsolescence. In this book, depreciation also includes amortization.

derivative   A contract whose value depends on the performance of a financial asset, such as a share market price.

DIO   Acronym for days inventory outstanding.

direct cost   A cost that can be directly attributed to a cost object, such as product, function, facility, and so on.

direct costing   A method of calculating the cost of a product by applying only direct material, direct labor, and the variable portion of manufacturing overhead costs. Other name: *variable costing*.

discount rate   When computing a present value, the rate at which expected cash flows are discounted.

discounted cash flow   See *net present value*.

discounting   The process of calculating the equivalent amount to a given quantity of money at a previous point in time.

dividends   Payments made by a firm to its shareholders.

DPO   Acronym for days payable outstanding.

DSO   Acronym for days sales outstanding.

duty drawbacks   Border tax adjustments, whereby the duties levied on imported goods are refunded when the goods are re-exported or used in the manufacture of exported goods.

earnings before interest and taxes   The difference between EBITDA and depreciation. Other name: *EBIT*.

earnings before interest, taxes, depreciation, and amortization   The difference between gross profit and SGA. Other names: *EBITDA, operating profit*.

earnings before tax   The difference between EBIT and interest expenses. Other names: *profit before tax, EBIT*.

earnings statement   See *income statement*.

EBIT   Acronym for earnings before interest and taxes.

EBITDA   Acronym for earnings before interest, taxes, depreciation and amortization.

EBT   Acronym for earnings before tax.

economic order quantity   The order quantity that minimizes the sum of relevant holding cost and ordering cost. Other name: *EOQ*.

entity   A firm or other organization with a similar structure that benefits from the practice of accounting, such as a nongovernment organization or an association. In this book, we use *firm* as a synonym of *entity*. Other name: *business entity*.

EOQ   Acronym for economic order quantity.

equities   The right hand side of the accounting equation. It represents what the firm owes, that is, monetary claims that may be made by a firm's creditors (suppliers and banks) and shareholders. In this book, equities is the sum of liabilities and shareholders' equity.

equity   See *shareholders' equity*.

excess cash   The difference between cash$^+$ and minimum cash, that is, the extra cash (and similar products, such as very short term investments) a firm holds that is not necessary to run the business.

exchange rate   The rate at which a country's currency will be exchanged for another.

extraordinary profit   Profit generated by nonrecurrent sources, such as property revaluations, the disinvestment of an asset (e.g., a subsidiary, a building), or exchange rate differences.

FFO   Acronym for funds from operations.

FIFO   Acronym for first-in, first-out.

financial forecasting   The process of estimating a firm's future financial outcomes on the basis of historical data and market assumptions.

financial leverage   A measure of the amount of debt a firm has at a point in time.

financial planning   The process of determining the financial resources needed to achieve the business goals.

financial risk   The risk of default borne by a firm due to the burden imposed by interest expenses.

financial statements   Specific financial reports prepared by firms at the end of the accounting period. The three most important are the balance sheet, the income statement, and the statement of cash flows.

finished good   Inventory that doesn't require further processing and is ready to be distributed or consumed.

first-in, first-out   A valuation method for inventory, where the oldest inventory is assumed to leave the firm first. Other name: *FIFO*.

fixed assets   Items not consumed or sold during the normal course of a business. Examples include land, buildings, equipment, and machinery. Other names: *noncurrent assets*.

fixed cost   A cost that does not increase with the level of activity, but stays constant in a considered range.

forward contracts   A legal agreement to buy or sell a currency or commodity at a predetermined price within a specified time window.

full costing   See *absorption costing*.

funds from operations   The sum of net profit, depreciation, and other noncash expenses. The amount of cash that operations would have generated during a period if operating working capital had not change, for instance if all payments were made in cash. Other names: *FFO, cash earnings, accounting cash flow*.

GAAP   Acronym for generally accepted accounting principles.

general ledger   A detailed record of economic transactions over the life of the firm.

generally accepted accounting principles   The set of accounting principles adopted by governments or other institutions. For example, IFRS are referred to as international GAAP.

going concern See *ongoing concern*.

goodwill When a firms buy another firm, the difference between the price paid and the book value of the firm acquired at the time of the sale. It becomes a fixed asset for the buying firm.

gross fixed assets The total price a firm has paid for its fixed assets. See also *net fixed assets*.

gross margin The ratio cost of goods sold to revenue, expressed as a percentage.

gross profit The difference between revenue and the cost of goods sold.

hedge An investment made to protect a firm's finances from a risky situation.

historical cost The cost of a good or service at the time of acquisition.

IFRS Acronym for International Financial Reporting Standards.

i.i.d. independent and identically distributed (referred to two or more random variables).

income statement Financial report containing a summary of the changes in shareholders' happiness during a period of time. Other names: *statement of profit or loss, statement of income, profit-and-loss statement, P&L, operating statement, earnings statement*.

indirect cost A cost that is not directly traceable to a cost object, such as product, function, or facility.

industry risk The risk of default borne by a firm due to uncertainty in demand or other factors external to the firm.

intangible asset An assets with no physical substance, such as patents or goodwill.

interest Fee charged by a lender to a borrower for the use of borrowed money, usually expressed as an annual percentage of the principal.

internal rate of return The discount rate that results in zero net present value. Other name: *IRR*.

International Financial Reporting Standards A set of accounting standards developed by the International Accounting Standards Board that is becoming the global standard for the preparation of financial statements. Other names: *IFRS*.

inventory Value of materials and goods held by a firm, typically to support production or for sale.

inventory cost flow assumptions The various methods available for moving the costs of a company's products from its inventory account to its cost of goods sold.

inventory flow period See *days inventory outstanding*.

inventory turnover The number of times per year that a firm's inventory turns over. Other name: *IT*.

inventory write-off Reduction in a firm's inventory account due to decrease of its market value.

invoice A document issued by a supplier specifying the amount owed by the firm for the goods provided or services rendered. Other name: *bill*.

IRR Acronym for internal rate of return.

IT Acronym for inventory turnover.

last-in, first-out A valuation method for inventory, where the newest inventory is assumed to leave the firm first. Other name: *LIFO*.

level strategy When production remains at a constant level in spite of demand variations.

liabilities Current monetary firm obligations with creditors (it doesn't include shareholders), such as suppliers, employees, banks, or governments.

LIFO   Acronym for last-in, first-out.

line of credit   An agreement between a bank and a firm that establishes the maximum amount of a loan that the firm can borrow. The firm can get funds from the line of credit at any time, as long as it does not exceed the maximum amount set in the agreement.

linear depreciation   See *straight-line depreciation*.

liquidity   An attribute of an asset that measures how close in time it is to cash. For instance, inventory is less liquid than accounts receivable.

local content requirement   A requirement set by a government to companies–as a prerequisite for installing a production facility–that some specific fraction of a good must be produced with domestic supply.

long-term debt   The portion of debt due in one year or more.

lower of cost or market value   An accounting principle which requires firms devaluate their inventory when its accounting value is less than its net realizable value. Other name: *lower of cost or net realizable value*.

managerial accounting   See *cost accounting*.

managing director   See *chief executive officer*.

manufacturing overhead   All indirect factory-related costs that are incurred when a product is manufactured.

market value   The price of the assets and equities of a firm if they were sold or bought in an actual market. See also: *book value*.

marketable securities   Financial instruments that can be easily converted to cash.

matching (concept)   Accounting principle that states that revenues and the corresponding costs (i.e., those needed to obtain the revenue, such as the cost of the item or its distribution cost) should be recognized in the same period.

materiality (concept)   Accounting principle that allows accounting to be inaccurate when reporting an event if the relative importance of the inaccuracy is not expected to have an impact on the decisions made by any stakeholders. For instance, an expenditure of ten cents on paper is immaterial. Other names: *relevance*.

minimum cash   The minimum level of cash that a firm need to conduct business.

moral hazard   The negative behavior that can arise from an individual being protected by some sort of insurance, knowing that their risk-taking is borne by others.

need of funds for operations   See *operating working capital*.

net assets   The difference between assets and accounts payable+.

net earnings   See *net profit*.

net fixed assets   The difference between gross fixed assets and accumulated depreciation.

net income   See *net profit*.

net margin   The ratio net profit to sales, expressed as a percentage. Other names: *ROA, return on sales*.

net operating profit after taxes   The net profit a firm would have had if debt had been zero. Other name: *NOPAT*.

net present value   The equivalent value at present time of a series of future cash flows evaluated at a given discount rate. Other names: *NPV, [discounted cash flow] present value*.

net profit   The difference between earnings before taxes and tax. Other names: *net income, net earnings, bottom line* (informal).

net realizable value An item's estimated selling price minus estimated costs to complete and sell the item.

net revenues Revenue net of discounts.

net worth See *shareholders' equity*.

newsboy model See *newsvendor model*.

newsvendor model A mathematical model used to determine optimal inventory levels when demand is uncertain. Other names: *newsboy model*.

noncompensation principle An accounting principle that states that the accounting information should show the full details of transactions and not seek to compensate (for instance, a revenue with an expense).

NOPAT Acronym for net operating profit after taxes.

NPV Acronym for net present value.

OEM Acronym for original equipment manufacturer.

off-shoring The relocation of a business process from one country to another.

ongoing concern (concept) Accounting principle that states that, when preparing the financial statements, a firm will continue to exist for a sufficiently long period of time and will not be liquidated in a foreseeable future.

operating expenses See *selling, general, and administrative expenses*.

operating profit See *earnings before interest, taxes, depreciation, and amortization*.

operating risk The risk of default borne by a firm due to the burden imposed by fixed operating costs.

operating statement See *income statement*.

operating working capital The amount of cost-bearing funds required to finance a firm's operations. It is calculated as minimum cash plus receivables$^+$ plus inventory less payables$^+$ Other names: *OWC, working capital requirements, need of funds for operations*.

OPEX Acronym for operating expenses.

option to abandon The option to terminate a project if conditions are not favorable.

option to delay The option of deferring a business investment decision to the future.

option to expand The option to make follow-on investments to a successful project.

options contract A legal agreement that gives the purchaser of the option the right to buy or sell a particular asset at a later date at an agreed upon price.

outsourcing An agreement in which a firm obtains certain services or products from another company.

OWC Acronym for operating working capital.

P&L Acronym for profit and loss (statement).

payables See *accounts payable*.

payback period A criterion to decide whether to make an investment.

payment period See *days payable outstanding*.

preferential trade arrangements Unilateral trade preferences, under which developed countries grant preferential tariffs to imports from developing countries.

prepaid expenses   Amounts paid in advance of the accounting period when expenses will be recognized.

present value   See *net present value*.

principal   An amount of money that a bank lends a firm in return for some payments (called interests).

principle   See *accounting principles*.

product assortment   The various types of products made by a manufacturer or offered by a retailer for sale.

profit and loss statement   See *income statement*.

profit before tax   See *earnings before tax*.

pro forma financial statements   Financial statements that are estimated in advanced.

provision   An amount set aside out of profits for a potential liability—whose specific amount is not know—or for the reduction in value of an asset.

prudence concept   See *conservatism*.

pull strategy   An operational strategy where production and distribution are demand-driven rather than to forecast.

push strategy   An operational strategy where production and distribution are driven by long-term projections of customer demand.

quota   A trade restriction on the quantity of goods imported to or exported from a country.

raw material   The basic material acquired from a supplier from which a product is made, such as a coil of steel to manufacture a car.

real option   An opportunity made available to the managers of a company to alter an investment in response to changing economic, technological, or market conditions.

receivables   See *accounts receivable*.

recognition   The act of recording a transaction in the firm books.

regional trade agreement   Reciprocal trade agreement made between two (or more) partners that include free trade and import duty harmonization.

relevance   See *materiality*.

residual value   The remaining market value of an asset after it has been fully depreciated. Other name: *salvage value*.

retained earnings   The difference between accumulated net profit and accumulated dividends since the inception of the firm.

return on assets   The ratio net profit to assets, expressed as a percentage. Sometimes, other measures of profit might be used instead of net profit, such as EBITDA or EBIT. Other name: *ROA*.

return on capital employed   The ratio EBIT to net assets, expressed as a percentage. Other name: *ROCE*.

return on equity   The ratio net profit to equity, expressed as a percentage. Other name: *ROE*.

return on invested capital   See *return on net assets*.

return on investment   The ratio net profit to net assets, expressed as a percentage. Other names: *ROI*.

return on net assets   The ratio net operating profit after taxes to net assets, expressed as a percentage. Other names: *ROIC, RONA*.

return on sales See *net margin*.

revenue The amount generated from selling goods or services, or any other use of capital or assets (e.g., cash interest, royalties). Other names: *top line* (informal).

revenue and expense account A temporary account that concludes all the changes in equity within a period.

risk pooling The various practices used by firms to reduce the negative impact of demand uncertainty in their operations.

risk premium The difference between the discount rate and the risk-free rate.

risk-free rate When computing a present value, the rate at which risk-less cash flows are discounted.

ROA Acronym for return on assets.

ROCE Acronym for return on capital employed.

ROE Acronym for return on equity.

ROI Acronym for return on investment.

ROIC Acronym for return on invested capital.

RONA Acronym for return on net assets.

ROS Acronym for return on sales.

sale Revenue recognition from the delivery of merchandise or from rendering a service.

sales tax A consumption tax imposed on the sale of goods or services. Other name: *VAT*.

salvage value See *residual value*.

selling, general, and administrative expenses (SGA) Expenses incurred to promote sales (e.g., sales force salaries and advertising) and manage the overall company (e.g., office rents, executives salaries). Other names: *SGA, OPEX, operating expenses*. (Although sometimes operating expenses are meant to include also manufacturing costs.)

semifixed cost A cost that, within a considered range, is fixed over subranges of activity, but cost levels are different within each subrange.

semivariable cost A cost made of the sum of a variable and a fixed cost.

seven-item balance sheet A simplified balance sheet that contains seven elements, namely cash$^+$, accounts receivable$^+$, inventory, fixed assets, accounts payable$^+$, debt, and equity.

seven-item income statement A simplified income statement that contains seven elements, namely revenue, cost of goods sold, SGA, depreciation, interest, tax, and net profit.

seven-item statement of cash flows A simplified statement of cash flows that contains seven elements, namely dividends, investments, increasing WCR, increasing excess cash, increasing debt, equity issued, and funds from operations.

SGA Acronym for selling, general, and administrative expenses.

share Each of the portions in which a firm's equity is divided. Other name: *stock*.

shareholder A person (or institution) that owns shares in a firm. Other name: *stockholder*.

shareholders' equity The difference between assets and liabilities. It represents the shareholders' claims on the assets of a firm. Other names: *equity*, *net worth*.

short-term debt   The portion of debt due in less than one year.

SKU   Acronym for stock keeping unit.

SME   Acronym for small and medium enterprise.

stakeholder   See *shareholder*.

standard costing method   Method that assigns predetermined costs to all inventory items produced during an accounting period.

statement of cash flows   Financial report showing the sources and uses of cash during a period.

statement of financial position   See *balance sheet*.

statement of income   See *income statement*.

statement of profit or loss   See *income statement*.

stock   See *share*.

straight-line depreciation   Depreciation that occurs at a constant rate over the accounting periods. Other name: *linear depreciation*.

sunk cost   A cost that has already been incurred and cannot be recovered by a future decision.

sustainable growth   The rate of growth a firm can maintain that is consistent with a defined financial policy.

T-account   A graphic representation of an account in the general ledger. The name of the account is placed above the T, with increase and decrease entries shown at both sides of the T.

tariffs   Taxes levied upon goods as they cross national boundaries. Other name: *customs duties*.

tax   Fee charged by the government based on the amount of profit generated by the firm.

tax shield   A reduction in taxes usually due to interest expenses.

temporary account   An account that is reset to zero at the end of the accounting period.

top line   See *revenue*.

trade credit   Money that a customer borrows from a supplier for free.

transaction   A firm's event that results in a change in assets or equities.

variable cost   A cost that increases with the level of activity.

variable costing   See *direct costing*.

VAT   Acronym for value-added tax. See *sales tax*.

WACC   Acronym for weighted-average cost of capital.

weighted-average cost of capital   A weighted average of the cost of debt after taxes and a required return from rational shareholders. Other names: *cost of capital*, *WACC*.

work in progress   The value of inventory which is being processed. It includes the cost of raw materials plus direct production costs plus a reasonable portion of indirect production costs.

working capital   The difference between current assets and current liabilities.

working capital requirements   See *operating working capital*.

Index